Lecture Notes in Computer Science 8967

Commenced Publication in 1973
Founding and Former Series Editors:
Gerhard Goos, Juris Hartmanis, and Jan van Leeuwen

More information about this series at http://www.springer.com/series/7407

James Brodman · Peng Tu (Eds.)

Languages and Compilers for Parallel Computing

27th International Workshop, LCPC 2014
Hillsboro, OR, USA, September 15–17, 2014
Revised Selected Papers

 Springer

Editors
James Brodman
Intel Corporation
Santa Clara, CA
USA

Peng Tu
Intel Corporation
Santa Clara, CA
USA

ISSN 0302-9743   ISSN 1611-3349 (electronic)
Lecture Notes in Computer Science
ISBN 978-3-319-17472-3   ISBN 978-3-319-17473-0 (eBook)
DOI 10.1007/978-3-319-17473-0

Library of Congress Control Number: 2015938086

LNCS Sublibrary: SL1 – Theoretical Computer Science and General Issues

Printed on acid-free paper

Springer International Publishing AG Switzerland is part of Springer Science+Business Media
(www.springer.com)

Preface

The 27th International Workshop on Languages and Compilers for Parallel Computing was held during September 15–17, 2014, at the campus of Intel Corporation in Hillsboro, Oregon, USA. The Sixth Annual Concurrent Collections Workshop was also colocated with LCPC 2014 and was held during September 18–19, 2014. Since 1988, LCPC has been a forum to present and discuss research on both theoretical and practical aspects of parallel computing. LCPC 2014 upheld that tradition with 39 submissions, of which 25 were selected by the Program Committee to appear at the workshop. This year's submissions spanned a wide range of topics including algorithms for parallelism, debugging and replay, new techniques for parallel compilers, programming models for accelerators, and vectorization. Approximately 60 researchers attended from all over the world.

Two speakers were invited to present keynote addresses this year. Xinmin Tian, Principal Engineer at Intel Corporation, gave the first talk, titled "Vanquishing SIMD Hurdles: Look Back and Look Forward." David Padua, Professor at the University of Illinois at Urbana–Champaign, gave the second keynote, titled "Compiler Research - Are We Done Yet?." Both talks were very well received and elicited good discussions.

We would like to thank Romain Cledat for all his work on the local arrangements. The workshop excursion this year was a lovely dinner cruise on the Willamette River. It was a very enjoyable evening full of great conversation and amazing views of the Portland skyline. We would also like to thank our sponsors Intel Corporation and the Parasol Laboratory at Texas A&M University without whom the workshop could not have happened. Finally, we would like to thank the authors, attendees, and members of the Program Committee who continue to make LCPC the great workshop that it is.

February 2015

James Brodman
Peng Tu

Organization

Program Committee

James Brodman	Intel Corporation, USA
Calin Cascaval	Qualcomm Research, USA
Romain Cledat	Intel Labs, USA
Hironori Kasahara	Waseda University, Japan
Keiji Kimura	Waseda University, Japan
Jaejin Lee	Seoul National University, Korea
Yuan Lin	Nvidia, USA
Pablo Montesinos	Qualcomm Research, USA
David Sehr	Google, USA
Xipeng Shen	North Carolina State University, USA
Peng Tu	Intel Corporation, USA
Peng Wu	Huawei America R&D Laboratory, USA

Steering Committee

Rudolf Eigenmann	Purdue University, USA
Alex Nicolau	University of California, Irvine, USA
David Padua	University of Illinois at Urbana–Champaign, USA
Lawrence Rauchwerger	Texas A&M University, USA

Additional Reviewers

Chakrabarti, Gautam
Chen, Guoyang
Dan, Umeda
Dao, Thanh Tuan
Ding, Yonghua
Ding, Yufei
Duchateau, Alexandre Xavier
Evans, G. Carl
Gupta, Vishakha
Hayashi, Akihiro
Holewinski, Justin
Ishizaka, Kazuhisa
Jo, Gangwon
Jung, Jaehoon

Jung, Wookeun
Kamiya, Sachio
Kenji, Kise
Kim, Junghyun
Konstantinidis, Athanasios
Larkin, Jeff
Lee, Seyong
Mamoru, Shimaoka
Marathe, Jaydeep
Mase, Masayoshi
Mikami, Hiroki
Mochiyama, Takashi
Nodomi, Akira
Park, Jungho

Shin, Jaeho
Shin, Seunghoon
Shirako, Jun
Tsumura, Tomoaki
Venkataraman, Vyas
Wada, Yasutaka
Wang, Weilin
Wu, Bo
Yamamoto, Hideo
Yazdani, Reza
Ye, Feng
Zhao, Zhijia
Zhou, Mingzhou
Zhou, Xing
Zhu, Qi

Contents

Vectorization

Accelerator Programming

Optimistic Parallelism on GPUs

Min Feng[1]([✉]), Rajiv Gupta[2], and Laxmi N. Bhuyan[2]

[1] NEC Laboratories America, Princeton, NJ, USA
mfeng@nec-labs.com
[2] University of California, Riverside, CA, USA

Abstract. We present speculative parallelization techniques that can exploit parallelism in loops even in the presence of dynamic irregularities that may give rise to cross-iteration dependences. The execution of a speculatively parallelized loop consists of five phases: scheduling, computation, misspeculation check, result committing, and misspeculation recovery. While the first two phases enable exploitation of data parallelism, the latter three phases represent overhead costs of using speculation. We perform misspeculation check on the GPU to minimize its cost. We perform result committing and misspeculation recovery on the CPU to reduce the result copying and recovery overhead. The scheduling policies are designed to reduce the misspeculation rate. Our programming model provides API for programmers to give hints about potential misspeculations to reduce their detection cost. Our experiments yielded speedups of 3.62x-13.76x on an nVidia Tesla C1060 hosted in an Intel(R) Xeon(R) E5540 machine.

1 Introduction

Many top-500 supercomputers today have adopted Graphics Processing Units (GPUs) for high performance computing. A number of research works [2,3,9] have explored loop-level data parallelism using GPUs, whose massive number of computing units are ideal for accelerating data-parallel computations. The presence of dynamic irregularities prevents existing techniques from parallelizing the loops for GPUs. Therefore optimizing performance in their presence has been widely studied [3,9,18,20]. In this work, we consider a new class of dynamic irregularities in loops that may cause cross-iteration dependences at runtime. In particular, we have identified two types of dynamic irregularities, illustrated in Fig. 1, that may dynamically cause cross-iteration dependences to arise preventing the loops from being parallelized by compilers for GPUs.

Dynamic irregular memory accesses refer to memory accesses whose memory access patterns are unknown at compile time. They may result in infrequent cross-iteration dependences at runtime. In Fig. 1(a) the memory access patterns of $A[P[i]]$ and $A[Q[i]]$ are determined by the runtime values of the elements in arrays P and Q. It is possible that an element in array A is read in one iteration and written in another causing a dynamic cross-iteration dependence.

This work is supported by NSF grants CNS-1157377 and CCF-0905509 to UCR.

J. Brodman and P. Tu (Eds.): LCPC 2014, LNCS 8967, pp. 3–18, 2015.
DOI: 10.1007/978-3-319-17473-0_1

```
for (i=0; i<n; i++) {
    ... = A[P[i]];
    A[Q[i]] = ...;
}
```

(a) Irregular memory access

```
for (i=0; i<n; i++) {
    ... = A[i];
    if (A[i]) A[i+1] = ...;
}
```

(b) Irregular control flow

Fig. 1. Examples of dynamic irregularities that cause cross-iteration dependences.

Irregular control flow is introduced by conditional statements, which may cause execution of paths that may give rise to cross-iteration dependences at runtime, as illustrated in Fig. 1(b), where each iteration of the loop usually only reads $A[i]$. In the loop, there is a conditional branch that guards a write to $A[i + 1]$, which is to be read in the next iteration. The true outcome of the branch condition gives rise to a cross-iteration dependence.

Software thread-level speculation (TLS) [5,7,13] has been used with success to parallelize loops that may contain cross-iteration dependences for execution on CPUs. However, developing similar speculative techniques for GPUs is challenging due to the architectural differences between CPUs and GPUs. This is due to the need for logically separate space to store results of thousands of threads and high overhead of complicated thread synchronizations [8].

This paper presents a speculative execution framework for GPU computing. It parallelizes loops that may contain cross-iteration dependences caused by above dynamic irregularities. The execution of a speculative parallel loop consists of five phases: scheduling, computation, misspeculation check, result committing, and misspeculation recovery. For efficiency, we develop a scheduling policy that is optimized for different types of cross-iteration dependences to reduce the misspeculation rate. We reduce the runtime overhead by performing misspeculation check on the GPU. We optimize the result committing procedure to reduce the size of data transferred between the CPU and GPU. Recovery is performed on the CPU for as few iterations as possible to minimize its runtime overhead. We present programming constructs for specifying speculatively parallel loops. Our implementation achieves 3.62x-13.76x speedups for speculatively parallelized loops on nVidia Tesla C1060 hosted in a Intel Xeon E5540 machine.

2   Execution Framework

Figure 2 gives the overview of executing a speculative parallel loop using GPUs. The procedure consists of five phases: *scheduling, computation, misspeculation check, result committing,* and *misspeculation recovery,* among which *computation* and *misspeculation check* are performed on the GPU. The five phases are repeated until the entire loop is finished.

Scheduling, performed on the CPU, determines the proper number of iterations to execute on the GPU – assigning too many iterations to the GPU can cause excessive misspeculations while assigning too few iterations limits performance by leaving the GPU underutilized. In the Computation phase the GPU

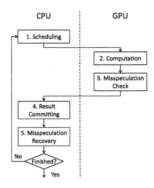

Fig. 2. Execution framework of a speculative parallel loop with GPUs.

executes the iterations in parallel by speculating on the absence of cross-iteration dependence while tracking the irregular memory accesses and control flow. Next the GPU performs the Misspeculation Check in two steps: detection and localization. Misspeculation detection is used to determine whether the iterations have been executed correctly. If misspeculation is detected, the localization step identifies the iterations that were executed incorrectly. In addition, we identify the correctly computed results so they can be copied back to the CPU memory. To make misspeculation checks efficient, they are performed in parallel on the GPU. Result committing phase copies the results from the GPU memory to the CPU memory. Finally, Misspeculation Recovery phase re-executes the iterations where misspeculation occured on the CPU or GPU depending on whether a few or a large number of iterations are to be executed. In the subsequent sections we first illustrate the GPU part of the execution model, i.e., the second and third phases. Then we will elaborate on the fourth and fifth phases, which are performed on the CPU. Finally, we will describe our scheduling policy.

3   Speculative Execution on GPUs

In this section, we describe how a loop is speculatively executed in parallel on GPUs. The infrequent cross-iteration dependences in a speculative parallel loop are usually caused by two types of dynamic irregularities – irregular memory accesses and irregular control flow. We elaborate the strategies for speculative execution for the types of irregularities separately.

3.1   Irregular Memory Accesses

Figure 3(a) shows the kernel of the loop example given in Fig. 1(a). The conversion from loops to GPU kernels has been studied in [2,9]. In this example, tid is the GPU thread ID and each GPU thread executes one iteration of the loop. Depending upon the runtime values of the elements in arrays P and Q, two iterations of the loop may read and write the same element of array A, causing cross-iteration dependence at runtime. Consider the runtime values of arrays P

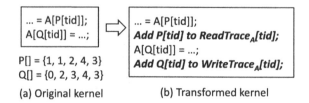

(a) Original kernel   (b) Transformed kernel

Fig. 3. Code transformation of a loop with irregular memory accesses.

and Q shown in Fig. 3(a). Because iteration 1 (starting from 0) writes $A[2]$ and iteration 2 reads $A[2]$, there exists a RAW cross-iteration dependence. Similarly, since both iteration 2 and 4 write to $A[3]$, there is a WAW dependence between them. Therefore, the results computed by iterations 2 and 4 will be incorrect following parallel execution. Our speculative execution of this kernel on GPUs consists of three phases: execution with memory access tracking, misspeculation detection, and misspeculation localization.

Memory access tracking – to detect cross-iteration dependences, we track which elements of the arrays with irregular access patterns are accessed in each iteration. This is done by inserting a tracking operation after each irregular memory access. For low tracking overhead, we use two static arrays of a predefined size for each iteration to store the indices of the read and written elements. We assume that we know the maximum number of elements that will be accessed in each iteration. This is often true, including for all benchmarks used in our experiments. Figure 3(b) shows the transformed kernel with a tracking operation after each irregular access to array A.

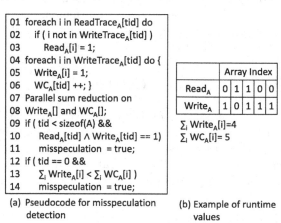

(a) Pseudocode for misspeculation   (b) Example of runtime
    detection   values

Fig. 4. Misspeculation detection.

Misspeculation detection checks whether a cross-iteration dependence was encountered during parallel execution. Unlike recent speculative parallelization techniques [7] for CPUs, which only need to detect RAW dependences, speculative parallelization on GPUs requires detecting RAW, WAR, and WAW. Speculative parallelization on CPUs resolves WAR and WAW dependences by committing the results of the iterations in a sequential order. However, these techniques cannot be efficiently implemented on GPUs because they require complicated synchronizations. Since all computations are performed simultaneously on GPUs, we need to detect all kinds of dependences. Additionally, in some cases, privatizing a shared array can solve WAR and WAW dependences on the array. However, privatization is not always possible. A shared array can be privatized only if the compiler can guarantee that every read access to an element is preceded by a write access to the same element within the same iteration. Since this is not always true in real applications, speculative parallelization on GPUs should be able to detect WAR and WAW dependences.

We simplify the traditional shadow memory-based misspeculation detection method [13] and adapt it for GPU computing. We perform the misspeculation detection on the GPU to exploit the data parallelism in the detection procedure. Our lightweight misspeculation detection method only detects the existence of cross-iteration dependences. Only if there is a dependence, we perform the misspeculation localization phase to determine in which iterations misspeculation has occurred. Figure 4(a) shows the pseudocode for misspeculation detection for the kernel example given in Fig. 3. In our implementation, all trace data are stored in the global memory. The detection procedure is as follows.

1. Compute $Read_A$ in parallel (line 1–3). $Read_A[i]$ is set when $A[i]$ is read but not written in an iteration. It records the elements of array A which are read-only in some iteration(s). It is safe to allow multiple blocks to simultaneously update $Read_A$ since each update is just setting an element to 1.
2. Compute $Write_A$ and WC_A in parallel (line 4–6). $Write_A[i]$ is set when $A[i]$ is written in an iteration. It records the elements of array A that have been written. WC_A stores the number of elements written in each iteration. We allow multiple blocks to simultaneously update $Write_A$.
3. Compute sums of $Write_A$ and WC_A in parallel (line 7–8). The sum of $Write_A$ is the number of elements that have been written, where multiple writes to the same element in an iteration count as 1. The sum of WC_A is the number of writes to array A.
4. Compute the intersection of $Read_A$ and $Write_A$ in parallel using threads $0 \ldots sizeof(A)$ (line 9–11). If $\exists i, Read_A[i] \land Write_A[i] = 1$, then $A[i]$ is read-only in some iteration(s) and written in some other iteration(s). In this case, misspeculation occurs due to a RAW or WAR dependence. In some cases, an element may be read and written in an iteration(s) and also written in another iteration(s). We treat such dependences as WAW dependences, which are detected in the next step.
5. Compare the sum of $Write_A$ and WC_A. If $\sum_i Write_A[i] < \sum_i WC_A[i]$, then there must exist multiple iterations that write the same element. This indicates the existence of WAW dependences.

Figure 4(b) shows the calculated values of array $Read_A$ and $Write_A$ for the P and Q given in Fig. 3(a). The values indicate that there exist both RAW/WAR and WAW dependences in the kernel execution. $Read_A[2]$ and $Write_A[2]$ are both equal to 1 since iteration 1 writes $A[2]$ and iteration 2 reads $A[2]$. $\sum Write_A[i] = 4$

```
01  for (i=BK_A[tid]; i<BK_A[tid+1]; i++)
02      RW_A[i]=ReadA[i] & WriteA[i];
03  if (tid < N)
04      for(i=BK_T[tid]; i<BK_T[tid+1]; i++)
05          foreach j in WriteTrace_A[i] do
06              WW_A[tid][j] ++;
07  Combine WW_A[1][] … WW_A[N][];
08  foreach i in ReadTrace_A[tid] do
09      if ( RW_A[i] == 1)
10          Misspec[tid] = 1;
11  foreach i in WriteTrace_A[tid] do
12      if (WW_A[i] > 1)
13          Misspec[tid] = 1;
14  if (Misspec[tid] == 1)
15      foreach i in WriteTrace_A[tid] do
16          Wrong_A[i] = 1;
17  Parallel reduction on Wrong_A[]
18  and Misspec[];
```

	Array Index				
RW_A	0	0	1	0	0
WW_A	1	0	1	2	1
$Wrong_A$	0	0	0	1	0
	Thread ID				
Misspec	0	0	1	0	1

$Wrong_{A\ reduced}[]=\{3\}$
$Misspec_{reduced}[]=\{2, 4\}$

(a) Pseudocode for misspeculation   (b) Example of runtime
    localization   values

Fig. 5. Misspeculation localization.

is smaller than $\sum WC_A[i] = 5$ since $A[3]$ is written in two iterations. The read and write of $A[3]$ happens in the same iteration. Thus, $A[3]$ is not recorded in $Read_A$. Therefore, there is no dependence detected on $A[3]$.

Misspeculation localization method identifies not only the misspeculated iterations but also the incorrect elements of arrays with irregular access patterns. With the information of incorrect elements, we can optimize the copying of results from the GPU to the CPU. The localization procedure is also parallelized for performance. Figure 5(a) shows the misspeculation localization for the kernel example. The details of the localization procedure are described below.

1. Compute RW_A in parallel (line 1–2) by intersecting $Read_A$ and $Write_A$, which indicate elements that are read and written in different iterations. To calculate RW_A in parallel, we divide array A into blocks. Block boundaries are stored in BK_A. Each thread calculates RW_A for one block of array A.
2. Compute WW_A in parallel (line 3–7). WW_A stores the number of iterations that write each element. $WW_A[i]$ is larger than 1 if $A[i]$ is written in multiple iterations. We use the first N threads to calculate WW_A in parallel. Each of the N threads calculates partial WW_A using arrays $WriteTrace_A$ from a block of threads. The block boundaries are stored in BK_T. A reduction merges the values of these subsets. The total size of WW_A is $N * sizeof(A)$.
3. Check RW_A in each thread (line 8–10). If $RW_A[i]$ is set and $A[i]$ is read in the current thread, then the iteration performed by the current thread reads an element that is written in another iteration. The iteration is misspeculated due to a RAW/WAR dependence. Array *Misspec* stores such iterations.
4. Check WW_A in each thread (line 11–13). If $WW_A[i]$ is larger than 1 and $A[i]$ is written in the current thread, then the iteration performed by the current

original   **transformed**

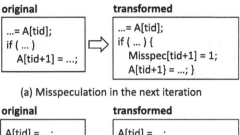

(a) Misspeculation in the next iteration

original   **transformed**

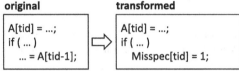

(b) Misspeculation in the current iteration

original   **transformed**

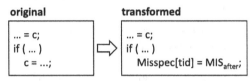

(c) Misspeculation in all subsequent iterations

Fig. 6. Loops with irregular control flow.

thread writes an element that is written in some other iteration(s). The iteration misspeculates due to a WAW dependence. $Misspec[tid]$ is set when the iteration calculated by the current thread is involved in a misspeculation.

5. Compute $Wrong_A$ in parallel (line 14–16), which indicates the incorrect elements of array A. An element is incorrect only when it is written by at least one misspeculated iteration.
6. Perform parallel reductions on $Wrong_A$ and $Misspec$ to store the incorrect elements and misspeculated iterations in lists. The CPU uses these to perform commit and recovery instead of having to inefficiently scan sparse arrays $Wrong_A$ and $Misspec$.

Figure 5(b) shows the values of RW_A, WW_A, $Wrong_A$, and $Misspec$ for the P and Q given in Fig. 3(a). Since iteration 2 reads $A[2]$ which is written by iteration 1, iteration 2 is involved in misspeculation. Since iteration 4 writes $A[3]$ which is written by multiple iterations, it is misspeculated. As $A[3]$ is written by misspeculated iterations 2 and 4, its value is incorrect.

3.2   Irregular Control Flow

Figure 6 shows three types of cross-iteration dependences that are caused by irregular control flow. In Fig. 6(a), the true branch condition causes a write to an element that is read in the next iteration and thus causing misspeculation in the next iteration. In Fig. 6(b), the true branch condition reads an element that is written in the previous iteration and thus causing misspeculation in the current iteration. In Fig. 6(c), the true branch condition writes a scalar variable that is read in all iterations and therefore makes them all wrong. We parallelize such loops by speculating the branch will not be executed. To verify the correctness of the parallel execution, we must monitor the execution of these branches. Once these branches are executed, we should be able to detect the misspeculation and identify the misspeculated iterations.

The cross-iteration dependences in the branches can be either marked by the programmer or detected by the static data race detection techniques. The static data race detection techniques identify dependences in a conservative way. Therefore, they may cause false misspeculations. Programmers can better identify the branches using their knowledge of the application. We propose a programming model that allows programmers to mark such branches (Sect. 6).

Once we have identified the cross-iteration dependences in the branches, we transform the branches for speculative execution in two steps.

1. In the branches that cause cross-iteration dependences, we insert an operation for recording the misspeculated iterations. We use the same array $Misspec$ to store the misspeculated iterations as shown previously.
2. We remove the statements in a branch from the GPU kernels if the branch execution will cause previous or current iterations to misspeculate.

We explain the rationale behind this transformation using examples. Figure 6 gives the transformed code for the branches. In Fig. 6(a), we insert an operation that marks the next iteration as misspeculated. The statements in the branch are kept since they will not pollute previous iterations. In Fig. 6(b), we insert an operation that marks the current iteration as misspeculated. Since the current iteration is misspeculated, executing the statements in the branch is meaningless. Therefore, we remove the statements from the branch. In Fig. 6(c), the operation inserted in the branch sets a special flag in $Misspec$. The flag indicates that all subsequent iterations including the current iteration are misspeculated. Since executing the statements in the branch also make previous iterations wrong, we remove the statements from the branch so that the results of previous iterations will be correct. In this branch, the current iteration is included in the misspeculated iterations because the statements in the branch need to be re-executed during recovery.

Having identified which iterations have misspeculated, we next identify the incorrect elements in the output array (i.e., incorrect results). Since the memory accesses are regular, we can use polyhedral tools to capture the mapping between the iterations and array elements. Once the mapping is known, the elements that are written in the misspeculated iterations can be easily found. These elements are incorrect and should be stored in array $Wrong$ as shown in the previous section. As in the previous section, we use GPU to perform parallel reductions on $Wrong_A$ and $Misspec$ to store the incorrect elements and misspeculated iterations in lists. This reduces the commit and recovery overhead on the CPU.

4   Scheduling

The synchronization granularity is critical to the GPU performance. Scheduling more iterations in one assignment may not give better performance because larger number of iterations in one assignment may cause excessive misspeculations. However, if we reduce the synchronization granularity to lower the misspeculation rate, we will also increase the kernel launching overhead. Thus, when scheduling iterations, we need to balance the above factors.

For *loops with irregular memory accesses* scheduling more iterations in one assignment will increase the chance of dependences between iterations. The optimal assignment size cannot be found since the cross-iteration dependences are unknown at compile time. Therefore we propose a runtime scheme.

In the first assignment, we schedule n/m iterations to the GPU, where m is the number of elements written in each iteration and n is the number of elements in the array. If we assign more than n/m iterations, there must exist two iterations that writes the same element. From the second assignment, we adjust the assignment size based on the observed misspeculation rate. If the misspeculation rate is higher than a predefined threshold, we halve the assignment size to reduce the misspeculation rate in the next round of scheduling. If the misspeculation rate stays zero for a number of consecutive iterations, we double the assignment size for better utilizing the large number of stream processors on the GPU. We do not increase the assignment size beyond n/m.

For *loops with irregular control flow*, in the first two cases in Fig. 6, we schedule as many iterations as possible in one assignment. This is because the number of misspeculated iterations are almost solely determined by the number of iterations that execute the branches. Therefore we can only change the misspeculation rate if we schedule the iterations that execute the branches as the first or last iteration in an assignment, which is very unlikely.

For the third example in Fig. 6, where all subsequent iterations are marked misspeculated if the branch is executed, we measure the average interval between two iterations that executes the branch at runtime and uses the interval as the assignment size when scheduling. This is because once an iteration executes the branch, all subsequent iterations are misspeculated. Therefore, we want the iterations that execute the branch to appear near the end of an assignment.

```
01 copyFromGPUToCPU(Misspec);
02 copyFromGPUToCPU(WrongA);
03 if ( sizeof(WrongA) == 0 )
04    copyFromGPUToCPU(A);
05 else {    // copy only correct part of array A
06    prepend(-1, WrongA);
07    append(size(A), WrongA);
08    for (i=0; i<size(WrongA); i++)
09       copyFromGPUToCPU(A[WrongA[i]+1 ... WrongA[i+1]-1]);
10 }
11 for (i=0; i<size(Misspec); i++)
12    reexecute(Misspec[i]);
```

Fig. 7. Commit and misspeculation recovery for the example given in Fig. 3.

5   Commit and Recovery

The commit and misspeculation recovery are performed on the CPU. Figure 7 shows the pseudocode of commit and misspeculation recovery for the example given in Fig. 3. The procedure is described next in detail.

1. We first copy the reduced arrays $Misspec$ and $Wrong$ from the GPU to CPU. These arrays are required for the commit and misspeculation recovery. This step has very low overhead since the arrays are usually very small.
2. We then commit the data back to the CPU. For an array, if all elements are correct, we directly copy the whole array from the GPU to the CPU and overwrite the original array on the CPU. If misspeculation is detected, we scan array $Wrong$ and only copy the correct elements between the wrong elements stored in array $Wrong$.
3. Finally, we perform the misspeculation recovery step that reexecutes the misspeculated iterations on the CPU. For loops with irregular memory accesses, we scan array $Misspec$ and redo every iteration inside. For the loops with irregular control flow, we perform recovery depending on the misspeculation type. For the first two cases in Fig. 6, where only one iteration is misspeculated with the execution of the branch, we redo every misspeculated iteration in array $Misspec$. For the third case in Fig. 6, where all subsequent iterations are misspeculated, we only reexecute the first iteration on the CPU. All remaining misspeculated iterations are assigned to the GPU in the next scheduling assignment.

Array $Wrong$ can also be used to reduce the copy-in (copy from the CPU to GPU) overhead. For loops with irregular memory accesses, we do not know the array elements that will be accessed in an assignment of iterations. Therefore, we keep the whole array in the GPU memory. After the recovery procedure, all elements that are re-calculated on the CPU are stored in array $Wrong$. In the next assignment, we only copy the elements stored in array $Wrong$ from the CPU to GPU. All other elements in the GPU memory are already up-to-date.

6   Programming Speculative Parallel Loops on GPUs

Our extensions to OpenMP basically tell the compiler which variables/branches to speculate on. Code offload and data transfer is handled by OpenMPC. To extend OpenMP for GPUs, previous works [2] have introduced the target clause, which can be applied to worksharing constructs:

```
#pragma omp for target(device)
```

This clause is also similar to the target device clause introduced in OpenMP 4.0. The intent of the target clause is to specify the device on which a given computation will be executed. The valid device specified by the target clause can be cuda, cell, and etc. We use target(cuda) for loop parallelization on GPUs.

6.1 Irregular Memory Accesses

To enable speculative parallelization of loops with irregular memory accesses, we introduce the `speculate` clause:

```
#pragma omp for speculate(array)
```

The `speculate` clause is designed to be used with worksharing constructs. Programmers can specify which arrays may cause cross-iteration dependences in the `speculate` clause. The memory accesses to these arrays will be monitored at runtime for misspeculation check. Although the compiler can identify the arrays that have irregular access patterns [18], not all of them will cause cross-iteration dependence at runtime. Programmers can better identify which arrays need to be monitored. This construct was useful in parallelizing a loop from the benchmark `ocean`, a Boussinesq fluid layer solver.

6.2 Irregular Control Flow

To enable speculative parallelization of loops with irregular control flow, we introduce the `branch` construct:

```
#pragma omp branch misspeculate(iterations)
```

The `branch` construct is designed to be inserted at the beginning of a branch that will cause cross-iteration dependences once its branch condition is true. The `misspeculate` clause is used to specify the misspeculated iterations if the branch is executed. A loop that is parallelized with worksharing constructs and contains the `branch` construct will be executed speculatively using the scheme described in Sect. 3.2.

The `iterations` expression in the `misspeculate` clause is designed to allow the following forms: absolute iterations, relative iterations, and iteration ranges. Absolute iterations can be expressed as (i), where i is the iteration index. For example, (10) denotes the 10th iteration. Relative iterations can be expressed as (+i/-i), where i is the relative iteration index. For example, (+1) denotes the next iteration. Iteration ranges can be expressed as (i:j), where i and j can be either absolute iteration index or relative iteration index. For example, (+0:+4) denotes the current iteration and next four iterations. Multiple iterations can be separated by comma in the expression. For example, (-1,+1) denotes the previous and next iterations. We found this construct useful in parallelizing a loop from benchmark `mdg`, which dynamically calculates water molecules in the liquid state at room temperature and pressure.

7 Evaluation

We implemented our framework whose core components consist of: a source-to-source translator and a runtime library. The translator is based on OpenMPC [9], which is an OpenMP-to-CUDA compiler. The programmers use pragmas to annotate the variables or control flow. The runtime library implements the core steps.

Table 1. Benchmark summary: benchmark name, type of irregularities, percentage of total execution time taken by the loop, and number of pragmas inserted.

Benchmark	Irregularities	% of time	# of pragmas
ocean	Irregular memory accesses	45 %	1
trfd	Irregular memory accesses	6 %	1
fftbench	Irregular memory accesses	20 %	1
mdg	Irregular control flow	94 %	2
strcat	Irregular control flow	99 %	2
gothic	Irregular control flow	99 %	2
alvinn	Irregular control flow	97 %	8

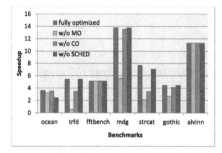

Fig. 8. Loop speedups for different optimization.

Fig. 9. A comparison with other approaches.

We used an nVidia Tesla C1060 as our platform which includes a single chip with 240 cores organized as 30 streaming multiprocessors. The device is connected to a host system consisting of Intel Xeon E5540 processors. The machine has CUDA 3.0 installed. The benchmarks are summarized in Table 1.

7.1 Performance Overview

Figure 8 shows the speedups for the loops considered. The baseline is the sequential execution time of the loops on the host system. Bars higher (lower) than 1 indicate speedup (slowdown).

For each benchmark there are four bars – the first bar shows the performance of our technique with all optimizations. The rest of the bars show the performance with different optimizations individually omitted (for discussion of optimization results see Sect. 7.2). The speedups for the fully optimized version are between 3.62x and 13.76x, with five (out of seven) benchmarks achieving over 5x. *The speedups demonstrate the effectiveness of our framework in using GPUs for irregular loops considered.*

Figure 9 compares the loop speedups achieved by our approach, speculative parallelization on a CPU, and non-speculative parallelization on a GPU.

Benchmark	Misspeculation Rate	
	w/o opts	w/ opts
ocean	0.53%	0.14%
trfd	100%	0.52%
fftbench	0.0%	0.0%
mdg	0.0018%	0.0018%
strcat	41.23%	2.10%
gothic	0.92%	0.67%
alvinn	0.0%	0.0%

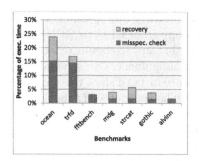

Fig. 10. Misspeculation rates   **Fig. 11.** Time overhead.

We implemented non-speculative GPU versions for two benchmarks – fftbench and alvinn since they do not have cross-iteration dependences at runtime. The other benchmarks cannot be parallelized in a non-speculative way without changing the algorithms. From the figure, we can see that our approach always outperforms speculation on the CPU. This is because we can run the benchmarks using more concurrent threads on the GPU and the transactional memory on the CPU has high time overhead.

7.2 Effectiveness of the Optimizations

Let us examine Fig. 8 to study the effectiveness of optimizations. The second bar ("w/o MO" in Fig. 8) gives the performance without misspeculation optimization (i.e., misspeculation detection without misspeculation localization and re-executing all iterations on the host system once misspeculation is detected). The third bar ("w/o CO" in Fig. 8) shows the performance without copy optimization (i.e., copying all data between CPU and GPU for every assignment of iterations). The last bar ("w/o SCHED" in Fig. 8) shows the performance without our scheduling policy (i.e., scheduling all iterations to the GPU in the first assignment). These three groups of bars are intended to show the importance of misspeculation localization, copy optimization, and our scheduling policy. Figure 10 shows the misspeculation rate (i.e., the number of iterations re-computed on the CPU divided by the total number of iterations) with and without the optimizations. We can see that our optimizations greatly reduces the misspeculation rate. The details of each benchmark will be described next.

For the ocean benchmark, our scheduling policy improves the performance by around 32 % over the one ("w/o SCHED") with minimum speedup. Our scheduling policy decreases the size of each assignment so that there is almost no misspeculation after the first few assignments. Misspeculation and copy optimizations do not improve the performance much since no misspeculation occurs in most assignments of iterations. Misspeculation optimization improves the performance of trfd greatly because there is always only one misspeculation in each execution of the loop. Without misspeculation optimization, we have to always re-execute all iterations on the CPU, which apparently will cause slowdown. Copy optimization improves its performance by 36 %. The copy-in (i.e., copy from CPU to GPU) overhead is greatly reduced as we only copy elements that are re-computed on the CPU (for recovery) to the GPU memory for every assignment. Our scheduling policy does not have much impact on the performance of trfd since there is only one misspeculation for each execution of the loop. The speedup of fftbench is partially offset by the number of memory access tracking. Since no cross-iteration dependences occur at runtime for the test input, misspeculation localization and recovery are never performed. There-fore, none of the optimizations has a performance impact. The speedup of mdg is high because the loop body has a lot of computation which can fully utilize the massively parallel architecture of the GPU. Also, only a few iterations execute the branch at runtime. Therefore, most computations are performed in parallel. With misspeculation optimization, we only re-execute the first misspeculated iteration on the CPU. The rest of the misspeculated iterations are assigned to the GPU in the next assignment of iterations. If we re-execute all misspecu-lated iterations on the CPU, the performance will be degraded by 60 %. The speedup for strcat is good since the misspeculation rate is very low due to the rapid growth of buffer size. Misspeculation optimization improves the perfor-mance by 72 % for the same reason as in mdg. Copy optimization is critical for performance of strcat. By avoiding copying the correct results back and forth between the CPU and GPU, we improve the performance by 55 %. In gothic, a misspeculation makes all subsequent iterations incorrect. Thus, misspeculation optimization greatly reduces iterations executed on the CPU and improves the performance. The speedup of alvinn is high because no misspeculation hap-pens in our experiments. The increment of the *weight* pointer does not change according to the input and thus the optimizations make no impact.

Figure 11 shows the time overhead (recovery and misspeculation check) as the percentage of the loop execution time. The time of computation and copy is a necessity for all GPU computations. The misspeculation check overhead for the ocean benchmark is the highest among all benchmarks because it requires memory access tracking, and its misspeculation check needs to detect both RAW/WAR and WAW dependences. The recovery overhead is high for ocean since the first few schedules of the loop cause many misspeculations. The mis-speculation check overhead for trfd is lower than ocean since its misspeculation check only needs to detect WAW dependences. In fftbench and alvinn, since no cross-iteration dependence occurs for the test input, misspeculation localization and recovery are never performed. The recovery overhead for mdg and gothic is low since we only re-execute the first misspeculated iteration on the CPU. In strcat, the overhead for misspeculation check is low since we only monitor the execution of the branch that reallocates the buffer.

8   Related Work

Speculative execution has been used to explore task-level parallelism on multi-GPU systems [6]. Usually, the runtime system must block the execution of a kernel until its predecessors in the control flow graph (CFG) have finished. On multi-GPU systems, the performance is limited by the runtime system's inability to execute more kernels in parallel. Diamos and Yalamanchili [6] alleviated this problem by speculating the control flow between kernels. Unlike their work, this paper explores thread-level speculative parallelism in a kernel. An exploratory study has been done for speculative execution on GPUs [10,11]. They explored the hardware implementation of speculative execution operations on GPU architectures to reduce the software performance overheads. The GPU-TLS system [19] adapted CPU speculative parallelization techniques for GPU use. Like previous speculative parallelization works for CPUs, it only checks RAW dependences at runtime and handles other types of dependences (i.e., WAW and WAR) by keeping the sequential order of iteration commits. Paragon [14] is the work closest to ours. It is a framework to speculatively run possible parallel loops on a GPU. However, unlike our framework, Paragon is not able to locate the misspeculated iterations. Therefore, on misspeculation, Paragon has to throw away any result on the GPU and re-execute the entire loop sequentially on the CPU.

Instead of causing cross-iteration dependences, irregularities may severely limit the efficiency of GPU computing due to the warp organization and SIMD execution model of GPUs. Zhang et al. [20] proposed runtime optimizations with the support of a CPU-GPU pipeline scheme to remove thread divergences. Baskaran et al. [3] use a polyhedral compiler model to optimize affine memory accesses in regular loops. Yang et al. [18] presented an optimizing compiler for memory bandwidth enhancement, data reuse, parallelism management, etc.

Several programming models have been proposed for GPU computing including OpenCL [15], CUDA [12], OpenACC [16], PGI Accelerator [17], OmpSs [2] which is based upon OpenMP standard [4], and Par4All [1]. *None of these programming models support speculative parallelization for GPU computing.*

9 Conclusion

We presented a framework for employing GPUs to speculatively parallelize loops that may have cross-iteration dependences at runtime due to irregularities. Several optimizations were proposed to improve the performance, including parallelizing misspeculation check on the GPU, optimizing the procedure of result committing and misspeculation recovery, and adaptive scheduling policy for different types of cross-iteration dependences. Our implementation achieves 3.62x-13.76x speedup for the seven parallelized loops.

References

1. Amini, M., Goubier, O., Guelton, S., Mcmahon, J.O., Pasquier, F.X., Pean, G., Villalon, P.: Par4All: from convex array regions to heterogeneous computing. In: IMPACT (2012)
2. Ayguadé, E., Badia, R.M., Igual, F.D., Labarta, J., Mayo, R., Quintana-Ortí, E.S.: An extension of the StarSs programming model for platforms with multiple GPUs. In: Sips, H., Epema, D., Lin, H.-X. (eds.) Euro-Par 2009. LNCS, vol. 5704, pp. 851–862. Springer, Heidelberg (2009)

3. Baskaran, M.M., Bondhugula, U., Krishnamoorthy, S., Ramanujam, J., Rountev, A., Sadayappan, P.: A compiler framework for optimization of affine loop nests for GPGPUs. In: ICS, pp. 225–234 (2008)
4. Dagum, L., Menon, R.: OpenMP: an industry-standard API for shared-memory programming. IEEE Comput. Sci. Eng. **5**(1), 46–55 (1998)
5. Dang, F.H., Yu, H., Rauchwerger, L.: The R-LRPD test: speculative parallelization of partially parallel loops. In: IPDPS (2002)
6. Diamos, G., Yalamanchili, S.: Speculative execution on multi-GPU systems. In: IPDPS, pp. 1–12 (2010)
7. Ding, C., Shen, X., Kelsey, K., Tice, C., Huang, R., Zhang, C.: Software behavior oriented parallelization. In: PLDI, pp. 223–234 (2007)
8. Feng, W., Xiao, S.: To GPU synchronize or not GPU synchronize? In: ISCAS, pp. 3801–3804 (2010)
9. Lee, S., Min, S.-J., Eigenmann, R.: OpenMP to GPGPU: a compiler framework for automatic translation and optimization. In: PPoPP, pp. 101–110 (2009)
10. Liu, S., Eisenbeis, C., Gaudiot, J.-L.: Speculative execution on GPU: an exploratory study. In: ICPP, pp. 453–461 (2010)
11. Liu, S., Eisenbeis, C., Gaudiot, J.-L.: Value prediction and speculative execution on GPU. Int. J. Parallel Program. **39**(5), 533–552 (2011)
12. Nickolls, J., Buck, I., Garland, M., Skadron, K.: Scalable parallel programming with CUDA. Queue **6**(2), 40–53 (2008)
13. Rauchwerger, L., Padua, D.: The LRPD test: speculative run-time parallelization of loops with privatization and reduction parallelization. In: PLDI, pp. 218–232 (1995)
14. Samadi, M., Hormati, A., Lee, J., Mahlke, S.: Paragon: collaborative speculative loop execution on GPU and CPU. In: GPGPU, pp. 64–73 (2012)
15. Stone, J.E., Gohara, D., Shi, G.: OpenCL: a parallel programming standard for heterogeneous computing systems. IEEE Des. Test **12**(3), 66–73 (2010)
16. Wienke, S., Springer, P., Terboven, C., an Mey, D.: OpenACC — first experiences with real-world applications. In: Kaklamanis, C., Papatheodorou, T., Spirakis, P.G. (eds.) Euro-Par 2012. LNCS, vol. 7484, pp. 859–870. Springer, Heidelberg (2012)
17. Wolfe, M.: Implementing the PGI accelerator model. In: GPGPU (2010)
18. Yang, Y., Xiang, P., Kong, J., Zhou, H.: A GPGPU compiler for memory optimization and parallelism management. In: PLDI, pp. 86–97 (2010)
19. Zhang, C., Han, G., Wang, C.-L.: GPU-TLS: an efficient runtime for speculative loop parallelization on GPUs. In: CCGrid, pp. 120–127 (2013)
20. Zhang, E.Z., Jiang, Y., Guo, Z., Shen, X.: Streamlining GPU applications on the fly: thread divergence elimination through runtime thread-data remapping. In: ICS, pp. 115–126 (2010)

Directive-Based Compilers for GPUs

Swapnil Ghike[1], Rubén Gran[2]([✉]), María J. Garzarán[1],
and David A. Padua[1]

[1] Department of Computer Science,
University of Illinois at Urbana-Champaign, Champaign, USA
{sghike2,garzaran,padua}@illinois.edu
[2] Departamento de Informática e Ingeniería de Sistemas,
Universidad de Zaragoza, Zaragoza, Spain
rgran@unizar.es

Abstract. General Purpose Graphics Computing Units can be effectively used for enhancing the performance of many contemporary scientific applications. However, programming GPUs using machine-specific notations like CUDA or OpenCL can be complex and time consuming. In addition, the resulting programs are typically fine-tuned for a particular target device. A promising alternative is to program in a conventional and machine-independent notation extended with directives and use compilers to generate GPU code automatically. These compilers enable portability and increase programmer productivity and, if effective, would not impose much penalty on performance.

This paper evaluates two such compilers, PGI and Cray. We first identify a collection of standard transformations that these compilers can apply. Then, we propose a sequence of manual transformations that programmers can apply to enable the generation of efficient GPU kernels. Lastly, using the Rodinia Benchmark suite, we compare the performance of the code generated by the PGI and Cray compilers with that of code written in CUDA. Our evaluation shows that the code produced by the PGI and Cray compilers can perform well. For 6 of the 15 benchmarks that we evaluated, the compiler generated code achieved over 85 % of the performance of a hand-tuned CUDA version.

Keywords: Directive-based compiler · OpenACC · GPGPU · Evaluation · Cray · PGI · Accelerator

1 Introduction

GPUs have started to play an important role in performance critical applications in computer graphics, scientific computing, gaming consoles and mobile devices, primarily because GPUs offer massive parallelism and computational power that is not available with the heavyweight multicore CPUs. GPUs have also shown better performance per watt in studies [15] conducted in the past using applications that represented varying domains and computational patterns. Many supercomputers including NCSA's Blue Waters supercomputer [31]

© Springer International Publishing Switzerland 2015
J. Brodman and P. Tu (Eds.): LCPC 2014, LNCS 8967, pp. 19–35, 2015.
DOI: 10.1007/978-3-319-17473-0_2

at the University of Illinois employ GPUs. With the introduction of NVIDIA Tegra processor in tablet devices [26, 27], the applicability of heterogeneous architectures, i.e., architectures that combine a traditional general purpose CPU and specialized co-processors like the GPU, seems evident in all forms of computing.

As parallelism increases, memory bandwidth becomes a bottleneck. GPUs try to hide memory latencies by maintaining a large pool of thread contexts and switching between these contexts at virtually no cost. Thus, GPUs perform best when its multiprocessors are kept busy with hundreds or even thousands of threads that execute in parallel. However, extracting the best performance out of GPUs using APIs that are closer to hardware and C-like programming languages such as CUDA [28] and OpenCL [19] is a time consuming process for programmers. Correctness issues like avoiding deadlocks and race conditions, and performance issues like making optimal use of device memory bandwidth, avoiding cyclic CPU-GPU data movement and pipelining of asynchronous data movement have to be dealt with explicit instructions or algorithms by the programmer. Thus, increased performance comes at the cost of programmer productivity. On top of the existing programmer productivity drains, manually writing code using CUDA and OpenCL often leads to programs that are fine-tuned to perform only on a particular device. Performance portability thus becomes another major problem.

Loops are the natural candidates for translating to GPU kernels. A programmer can use CUDA or OpenCL to manually translate loops into GPU kernels. However, today a new programming paradigm for heterogeneous systems is emerging. Programmers can now use compilers to translate conventional CPU programs to heterogeneous code that is fine-tuned to the resources of the GPU being used. These compilers may need the programmer to provide hints or instructions in the form of directives. Providing directives in an OpenMP-like manner usually takes less efforts than writing a CUDA or OpenCL program. The heterogeneous code can then offload loops to the GPU and take care of host-GPU data communication. This approach has the potential to obtain the best of both worlds - good performance, if not the best as that obtained with optimized CUDA or OpenCL programs, and increased programmer productivity and code portability.

The goal of this work is to evaluate the limitations of the PGI [30] and Cray [9] compilers to generate efficient accelerator codes when using compiler directives: PGI programming model's proprietary directives and OpenACC [5], respectively. For the version of PGI compiler that we used, the OpenACC directives were not available. More recent versions of the PGI compiler support the OpenACC directives, and it has been shown that heterogeneous programs using the PGI directives have the same performance as those using the PGI compiler with the OpenACC directives [22]. The paper makes the following contributions:

1. We first evaluate standard loop transformations developed for autoparallelization, such as distribution and privatization. Our experiments show that the compilers studied applied few of the studied transformations - loop alignment, distribution, interchange, privatization, reversal and skewing. Furthermore,

the compilers were able to generate optimized code for reduction, but not for prefix scan or histogram reduction loops.

2. We present a comprehensive set of the transformations that programmers should apply so that compilers can generate efficient code for accelerators. For this study we applied a sequence of manual transformations to 15 OpenMP programs from the Rodinia benchmark suite to convert them to a form that can be understood by the PGI and Cray compilers. Our results show that with the Cray compiler, fewer manual transformations were needed in the case of 8 out of 15 benchmarks. We also demonstrate the impact of each transformation on the performance of the heterogeneous programs.

3. We assess the performance obtained by these compilers. We compare the performance of the heterogeneous versions of Rodinia benchmarks compiled by the PGI and Cray compilers with that of the manually-optimized OpenMP and CUDA versions of those programs. Our results show that the code generated by the compilers achieves more than the 85 % of the performance of 6 out 15 manually optimized versions of Rodinia, and perform worse for other benchmarks depending on various factors such as data communication between the host and the device, non-coalesced device memory accesses, etc.

The rest of this paper is organized as follows: Sect. 2 briefly discusses related work; Sect. 3 describes experimental framework; Sect. 4 is an evaluation of the abilities of these compilers to analyze dependences and perform loop transformations; Sect. 5 presents the transformations required to convert OpenMP programs to their heterogeneous versions and the impact of each transformation on their performance; Sect. 6 evaluates the performance of Rodinia benchmarks when compiled with the PGI and Cray compilers and discusses the performance bottlenecks; and finally Sect. 7 concludes.

2 Related Work

GPUs are an attractive platform for scientific simulation and general purpose applications that can exploit the data parallelism they provide. However, programming and tuning for these devices is onerous [2,11]. Compilers such as CUDA [28] and OpenCL [19] aim at easing the low level programming of GPUs, but they expose the GPU architecture (including the different memory domains and the SPMD/SIMD architecture) to the programmer, which makes a program implementation hardware dependent. This also increases the learning and development phase, what makes the programming task more error-prone.

Cray [9], CAPS [4], and PGI [30] have recently introduced a high-level programming paradigm, similar to that of OpenMP [29], called OpenACC [5]. In this paradigm, the programmer uses pragmas or directives to annotate the sequential code and specify the loops and regions of code that can be offloaded from a host CPU to a GPU, as well as the data to be transferred. OpenMP4.0 [29] has also recently introduced extensions to support accelerators.

hiCUDA [12] sits between the two extremes described above. It relies on pragmas, but it does not ease the programmer task as much as the Cray, CAPS or PGI compilers. Other experimental compilation tools like CGCM [16] and PAR4ALL [1] aim at automating the process of CPU-GPU communication and the detection of the pieces of code that can run in parallel. The work by Lee and Eigenmann [20] proposes OpenMPC, an API to facilitate translation of OpenMP programs to CUDA, and a compilation system to support it.

Previous studies, like [8,10,13,14,17,22,24,32] also evaluate directive-based compilers that generate code for accelerators. The main difference is that this work covers more programs and includes a study of transformations. While some of the previous works have performed assessments similar to those presented in this paper, they typically focus on one or two applications or on benchmarks sets containing small and regular kernels, such as Polybench. In this paper we evaluate the Rodinia v2.0.1. benchmark suite [6,7], which contains regular and irregular applications from different domains. Also, this paper evaluates two of the three currently available commercial compilers (CAPS is the only other commercial compiler that we did not consider in this work).

While we perform our evaluation using the Rodinia benchmark suite, which contains applications from different domains, most previous works only experiment with 1 or 2 applications, except for the project discussed by Grauer et al. [10] and Lee and Vetter [22]. The work by Grauer et al. uses the PolyBench collection which contains regular kernels mostly from the linear algebra domain. We intend not to limit our results to a reduced type of applications and we show results for a larger variety of benchmarks, in an effort of covering the real world application spectrum, including irregular benchmarks like PathFinder for Dynamic Programming and Breadth First Search for Graph Traversal. The work by Lee and Vetter [22] is the most comprehensive with respect to the number of applications and compilers evaluated. Lee and Vetter evaluate 8 Rodinia benchmarks (out of the 15 we evaluate) and some scientific kernels, such as Jacobi or kernels from the NAS benchmarks. They also evaluate the PGI, CAPS, Open-MPC [20,21], and R-Stream [23] compilers. However, the main difference with this study, is that the work reported here also includes the transformations steps that programmers must follow to transform OpenMP programs into directive-based programs so that these compilers can generate efficient accelerator code.

In our work we also evaluate whether the studied compilers perform standard transformations, such as loop distribution or privatization to enable parallelism. We have not found a similar study on previous works. Only the work by Grauer et al. [10] evaluates the use of three of the CAPS-specific pragmas (permute, unroll, and tiling) intended to drive code transformations for code optimization. However, this work has a much more limited scope than ours.

3   Environmental Setup. Target Platform and Compilers

Our experiments were performed using a single Cray XK6 node. Table 1 presents characteristics of this experimental hardware platform, and Table 2 shows for each compiler, the compiler version and flags used in our experiments.

We evaluated two directive-based compilers for heterogeneous systems: PGI [30] and Cray [9] compilers. With the Cray compiler we used the OpenACC

Table 1. Hardware characteristics

Type	CPU	GPU
Name	AMD Opteron 6200	NVIDIA Tesla X2090
Cache	L2/L3 - 512 kB/12 MB	L2(shared) 42 Kb(Multiprocessor)
# cores	16 cores	512 CUDA cores
Peak Perf.	294.4 GFLOPS	1331 GFLOPS
Frequency	2.1 GHz	1.3 GHz

Table 2. Compilation flags for each compiler

Specification/flags	PGI	CRAY XK	NVCC/GCC
Version	11.10-0	CCE v 8.1.0.139	4.0.17a/4.3.4
		PrgEnv-cray v 4.0.46	
Baseline optimizations	-fast -fastsse -O3	-O3	-O3/-O3 -Ofast
Platform optimizations	-tp = bulldozer-64	-h cpu = interlagos	-arch = sm_20
			-march = bdver1
Sequential flags	None	-h noacc -h noomp	NA
		-h noomp_acc	NA
OpenMP flags	-mp = allcores	-h noacc -h noomp_acc	NA
Heterogenous flags	-ta = mnvidia,keepgpu	-h noomp_acc	NA
Compilation report	-Minfo	-hlist = m	NA

1.0 [5] directives, while with the PGI compiler we used the PGI programming model's proprietary directives [30]. For the version of PGI compiler that we used, the OpenACC directives were not available. More recent versions of the PGI compiler support the OpenACC directives, but it has been shown that heterogeneous programs using the PGI directives have the same performance as those using the PGI compiler with the OpenACC 1.0 directives [22]. The PGI and the OpenACC 1.0 directives are semantically equivalent (as they both enable the same functionality), but they differ syntactically.

3.1 Benchmarks

We used two benchmark suites. First, a micro-benchmark suite that we developed for this project and the other is the Rodinia benchmark suite 2.0.1 [6,7]. Our micro-benchmark suite consists of a set of loops to assess the ability of the compilers to perform standard loop transformations for exposing parallelism. These micro-benchmarks were designed to verify if the PGI and Cray compilers can perform loop transformations that remove loop carried dependences to expose parallelism.

In the experimental section, we used the Rodinia benchmark suite 2.0.1 [6,7]. Out of the 16 benchmarks available in the Rodinia benchmark suite, we have

Table 3. PGI and Cray: loop transformations to micro-kernels

Transformation	Improves GPU kernel	Speedup		Conclusions	
		PGI	Cray	PGI	Cray
Alignment	Yes	299.14	33.73	No	No
Distribution	Yes	212.22	15.59	No	No
Interchange	No, threads spawn once	1.00	1.00	Not needed	
Privatization	Yes	0.99	1.00	Yes	Yes
Reversal	Yes	13.59	30.42	No	No
Skewing	No, skewed iteration space	0.72	0.28	No	No

used 15. We did not include Mummer-GPU in our analysis because of the limitations of using unions in the compilers that we studied. These applications are provided with two different implementations, OpenMP and CUDA. The CUDA implementation exploit the different types of memories available in the GPU: global, shared, constant and texture memories.

3.2 Performance Measurement

Our time measurement excludes any setup and initial I/O performed by the program. In case of CUDA programs and heterogeneous programs, we also measure the time spent in three separate components of the program using the CUDA profiler [25]: time spent in the GPU kernels, time taken to transfer data between CPU and GPU, and the summation of the time spent in any sequential computation that is an integral part of the program and the overhead of launching GPU kernels and initiating data transfers.

4 Micro-Kernels

In this section, we report the results of our analysis that determines the effectiveness of the PGI and Cray compilers in automatically applying standard transformations that remove cross-iteration dependences that prevent a loop from being parallelized. For this analysis, we wrote a set of 9 loop nests. In 6 of the loop nests, application of a single transformation among alignment, distribution, interchange, privatization, reversal and skewing will allow iterations of that loop nest to run in parallel with each other using multiple threads [18]. The other 3 loop nests perform reduction, prefix scan, and histogram reduction operations, and can be parallelized on a GPU by changing the algorithm.

Table 3 shows the first 6 loops. The first column shows the name of the transformation; the second column states whether the transformation enables a loop nest to efficiently use the GPU.

We used the compiler reports to determine if the compiler applied the transformations automatically. However, since these reports were not always clear,

Table 4. PGI and Cray: automatically parallelizing computational patterns

Idiom	Conclusions	
	PGI	Cray
Reduction	Yes	Yes
Prefix scan	No	No
Histogram	No	No

for each case we executed both the original and the transformed loop nests and recorded their execution times. The original loop nest needs to be transformed to be parallelizable. If the compiler is not able to automatically apply the transformation, then the transformed version of the loops executes significantly faster than the original version. The third column of Table 3 shows the speedups of the transformed versions of the loop nests over the original loop nests. The last column of Table 3 shows our conclusions on whether the compilers were able to automatically perform the corresponding transformation.

Table 3 shows that out of all the transformations, the ones that enable a loop to make efficient use of GPU parallelism are alignment, distribution, privatization and reversal. Interchange and skewing are not helpful in improving performance on a GPU.

Loop interchange can improve performance when an outer loop executes sequentially with an inner parallelizable loop. If the inner loop is parallelized, each outer iteration spawns and joins the multiple threads executing the inner loop. In this case, the inner parallel loop can be interchanged with the sequential outer loop as long as no dependences are violated, thereby spawning threads only once. However, this transformation is not necessary to parallelize loops on a GPU while using the PGI and Cray compilers, because the PGI and Cray compilers split the inner parallel loop across multiple threads and execute all the iterations of the sequential outer loop in each thread (redundantly). The skewing transformation is not suitable for GPUs, because the code that results after applying the transformation executes in a skewed iteration space, that leads to warp divergence.

We also wrote 3 loop nests that perform reduction, prefix scan and histogram reduction. These computational patterns, in particular reduction, are used often among scientific applications and they can be parallelized only by a change of algorithm. However, compilers can potentially recognize these patterns and produce the parallelized algorithms automatically. When the compilers do not recognize the computation patterns, the generated code results in a naive GPU implementation that executes serially and obtains low performance. As there is no equivalent parallelizable sequential loop nests for these patterns, these computational patterns can only be parallelized in a programming language like CUDA or OpenCL that gives the programmer a fine grained control of the code executed by each thread and memory barriers. The first column of Table 4 shows the transformation; the second column shows whether the compilers were able to automatically parallelize the computational patterns. Table 4 shows that none of the compilers was able to parallelize prefix scan and histogram reduction automatically. In such cases, providing a finer control over parallelism would benefit programmers when the automatic recognition/parallelization of computational patterns does not succeed.

In the second part of this work, we study 15 benchmarks from the Rodinia suite. We observed that in these benchmarks loop distribution, privatization, reduction, and prefix-scan optimization transformations were necessary. The other loop transformations were not applicable, but might be useful for a different set of applications.

5   Transformation Steps

We have used the Rodinia benchmarks to assess the transformations that were necessary to convert the OpenMP programs to a format that the PGI and Cray directive-based compilers can understand and compile to produce device kernel code. Section 5.1 describes the transformations steps that we had to follow to transform programs. Section 5.2 describes why each transformation was needed and the performance impact of each transformation.

5.1   Transformations

While most previous works discuss the individual transformations applied to each benchmark, in this Section we have tried to synthesize the overall strategy that we followed to transform all the OpenMP Rodinia benchmarks. Next, we describe the transformations in the order in which were applied:

T1: Convert the program to C99 from C++, if using the PGI compiler. The version of PGI compiler used did not allow C++ code in the parallel regions.

T2: Insert *parallel regions*, in order to delimit parallel loops.

T3: *restrict* attribute, PGI explicitly requires removing array aliasing.

T4: Convert a multi-dimensional array to an array stored in contiguous memory. When GPU kernels work with sub-dimencions of a multi-dim array, host-device communication must be conscious of multi-dim array memory mapping. Flattening these arrays improves these communication tasks.

T5: Remove pointers to arrays in structures and stop the use of unions. T5 is applied because the compiler cannot de-reference the pointers to the arrays in the structure to perform the data transfer between CPU and GPU. Similarly, the compilers could not correctly allocate space on the GPU when unions were used inside the parallel regions[1].

---

[1] In the PGI version of CFD Solver, we also had to separate the individual float values included in a structure, but this was most probably due to a bug.

Table 5. Summary of directives and transformations applied in 15 Rodinia benchmarks

Directives and Transformations			Total		Others
			PGI	Cray	
Directives. Programmer applied		Parallel Regions (T2)	15	15	0
		Data Clausues (T7)	13	14	0
		Independent (T8)	11	10	0
		T8.a	1	1	0
		T8.b	1	1	0
		T8.c	9	1	0
		T8.d	0	7	0
		Data Regions (T9)	14	14	0
		Collapse (T11)	0	6	0
Transformations	Compiler Applied	Privatization	15	15	0
		Reduction	5	5	6
	Programmer Applied	C++ to C99 (T1)	5	0	0
		restrict (T3)	15	0	0
		multi to single (T4)	3	3	0
		remove pointers (T5)	6	5	0
		inline (T6)	9	1	0
		distribution (T10)	11	11	0
		T10.a	2	2	0
		T10.b	3	3	0
		T10.c	3	3	0
		T10.d	3	3	0
		alignment	0	0	0
		reversal	0	0	0
		skewing	0	0	0
		prefix-scan	0	0	1
		histogram	0	0	0

T6: Inline procedures. The PGI compiler required all the procedures inside a parallel region to be manually inlined. The Cray compiler could inline procedures with primitive data type arguments.

T7: Add *data clauses* to *parallel regions*. Both compilers were able to automatically generate a CPU-GPU memory copy command to transfer data between CPU-GPU when the array size is known at compilation time. Otherwise, the programmer has to manually specify the array size in data clauses.

T8: Use the independent clause. The programmer can enable compiler parallelization using the independent clause to inform the compiler that the following loop does not carry dependences across iterations. This is done for the following reasons:

a. The loop iterations have an output dependence, but parallelizing the loop results in a benign data race in which threads write the same value to a given memory location (BFS).

b. The compiler detects false dependences between iterations due to array index calculations that involve runtime variables, whose values are unknown to the compiler. Programmers can assert that there are no data dependences (NW).

c. Compilers could not analyze the array index calculations.(PGI: KM, BP, HS, LUD, CFD, LC, PF, HW; Both: SRAD).

d. The Cray compiler generated incorrect GPU code due to a bug. As a work around we used the independent clause. This bug will likely go away in the coming compiler releases.(KM, BP, LUD, SC, LC, PF, HW).

T9: Insert *data regions*. They help to avoid cyclic data movement between the CPU and GPU. The programmer can specify the variables or arrays to be copied into the GPU memory at the entry point of the data region and the variables or arrays to be copied out at the exit point of the data region.

T10: Change the size and/or number of parallel regions with respect to the OpenMP code. Exploiting parallelism in tightly nested loops is crucial to obtaining high performance. Also, expanding the parallel regions, changing the loops that are parallelized etc. can help in obtaining higher performance. Our results show that this is an important step that requires manual effort and manual tuning from the programmer. This is done for the following reasons:

a. Distribute a parallel loop over an inner loop if the inner loop is parallel and contains sufficient amount of computation. The resulting loop is a good candidate for GPU computation. For some applications distribution has to be applied after procedure inlining.

b. Remove the reduction from an accelerator region to facilitate compiler optimization of the remaining code. The reduction can be performed in a separate parallel region or on the CPU depending on the amount of computation and the amount of CPU-GPU data communication involved.

c. Change the boundaries and/or number of the parallel regions. Depending on the availability of statements that can execute in parallel, we can expand the parallel regions to include more computation in them and/or generate new parallel regions. On the contrary, we should not run in GPU a loop that has a small amount of computation and requires a large amount of CPU-GPU transfer.

d. Change loops that are parallelized while maintaining the same number of parallel regions. This is achieved by interchanging loops or by merely changing the position of parallel directive if the loops are loosely nested and interchanging those loops is not possible without substantial manual effort.

T11: Use collapse clause, for CRAY only (PGI does automatically). Using a collapse clause leads to an increase in multiprocessor occupancy which is a ratio of the number of threads executing on the GPU at a given time to the maximum number of threads that could execute on that GPU. This may increase the utilization of the GPU parallelism and reduce the execution time.

Table 5 classifies these transformations as insertion of compiler directives and other transformations. Compiler directives must always be inserted by the programmer, the other program transformation can be classified based on whether they are applied by the compiler or the programmer. The Column Total shows for how many benchmarks each directive or transformation was applied when using the PGI and the Cray compilers. Column Others shows the number of times a transformation could have been applied, but was not applied for reasons that will be explained next.

With respect to transformations, privatization and reduction are the only two transformations that were automatically applied by the compilers. Privatization was needed in all the benchmarks and both compilers applied it successfully. Both compilers applied reduction to 5 benchmarks (BP, BFS, LMD, PF, SC), but both failed to take advantage of it for 6 benchmarks. When the reduction

Table 6. Relative slow-ness after each step with the PGI and Cray compilers.

PGI	PFDR	KM	BFS	BP	HS	LUD	NN	NW	SRAD	SC	CFD	LC	PF	HW	LMD
T10	1.0	1.0	1.0	1.0	1.0	1.0	1.0	1.0	1.0	1.0	1.0	1.0	1.0	1.0	1.0
T9	1.0	100.5	2.5	1.0	1.0	1.0	1.0	1.0	2.7	∞	1.0	∞	1.0	∞	∞
T8	5.3	102.4	6.7	5.0	13.7	537.1	1.0	∞	10.6	∞	14.2	∞	3.3	∞	∞
T7	5.3	∞	128.3	59.4	∞	5859.7	1.0	∞	858.6	∞	14.2	∞	3.6	∞	∞
Cray	PFDR	KM	BFS	BP	HS	LUD	NN	NW	SRAD	SC	CFD	LC	PF	HW	LMD
T11	1.0	1.0	1.0	1.0	1.0	1.0	1.0	1.0	1.0	1.0	1.0	CF	CF	CF	CF
T10	1.0	1.0	1.0	1.0	4.5	1.0	1.0	1.0	4.7	1.0	1.0	CF	CF	CF	CF
T9	1.0	∞	2.7	1.5	4.5	1.0	1.0	1.0	6.7	CF	1.0	CF	CF	CF	CF
T8	350.8	∞	7.5	4.3	34.1	20.4	1.0	∞	19.2	CF	50.6	CF	CF	CF	CF
T7	350.4	∞	170.2	11.2	34.1	21.1	1.0	∞	26.3	CF	50.6	CF	CF	CF	CF

appears alone in a single loop both compilers can recognize it. However, when several reductions appear in a single loop or the reduction is intermixed with other computations in the same loop, the compilers usually fail to recognize it. This occurred in 6 benchmarks (CFD, HW, KM, LUD, SRAD, SC), as shown in the column Others. When we manually distributed the loops to isolate the reduction in a single loop the compiler recognized it.

For the PGI compiler, the use of the restrict keyword and procedure inline was needed for 15 and 9 benchmarks, respectively. With the Cray compiler we did not have to use the restrict keyword and inlining is necessary only for one benchmark. PGI also required to transform the codes from C++ to C99. With respect to the other directives and transformations, both compilers perform very similar. Therefore, we conclude that Cray requires less effort than PGI.

The transformations alignment, reversal, skewing, and histogram were not needed for these benchmarks although they could be helpful for other benchmarks. Prefix scan was present in HW, it was not recognized (Sect. 4).

5.2 Impact of Each Transformation on Performance

Table 6 shows the performance impact of the previous transformation steps on the Rodinia benchmarks for the PGI and Cray compilers. Each row in the table specifies the last transformation that has been applied and the slow-ness in performance with respect to the performance obtained after applying all transformations in Sect. 5.1 (step T10 for PGI and T11 for Cray). In the same column, the same slow-ness means that the transformation was either not needed or it had no effect. We show results only after applying T7, because heterogeneous compute regions can execute in the GPU in most cases only after T7 has been applied. To assess the impact on performance of a transformation we need to compare two consecutive rows. Thus, to asses the impact of T8 we need to compare the data in row T7 with the data in row T8. Notice that the Cray compiler was still under development and some benchmarks (PF, LC, HW, LMD and

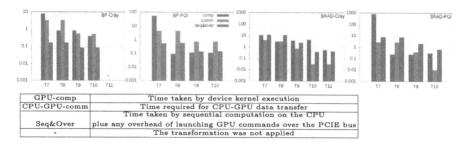

GPU-comp	Time taken by device kernel execution
CPU-GPU-comm	Time required for CPU-GPU data transfer
Seq&Over	Time taken by sequential computation on the CPU plus any overhead of launching GPU commands over the PCIE bus
-	The transformation was not applied

Fig. 1. Distribution of time after the application of transformations.

SC) could not be compiled correctly (shown as CF in Table 6) due to internal compiler bugs. In some cases, executing a program version took so long, that we decided to stop the execution and label it as ∞.

In Fig. 1, we show results for BP and SRAD (the rest are not shown due to space limitations) with both compilers. Each chart shows for each transformation step, the breakdown of the program execution time into its three components - device kernel execution time in the GPU, time of CPU-GPU data communication, and the time of sequential computation and any overhead of launching the device commands over the PCIE bus. The bars for the three components of each program are plotted such that the sum of these three components (which equals the overall program time) represents the slow-ness with respect to the performance obtained after applying all transformations in Sect. 5.1. Thus, the three components of transformations T10, in case of PGI, and T11, in case of Cray, sum up 1 (note the logarithmic scale).

In the charts, label - states that the transformation was not applied/needed. As expected, performance improves as more transformations are applied to each benchmark. From Fig. 1 and Table 6, we can observe that there is not a single transformation responsible of the whole performance improvement. For each benchmark, each transformation step has a varying degree of impact on the performance.

The impact of each transformation on the individual components (kernel, communication and seq. and overhead time) of the overall program time can be seen in Fig. 1. The application of T8 reduces the time spent in device kernel execution. The application of T9 reduces the time spent in CPU-GPU data communication. The application of T10 has an effect on all three components. The magnitude of these components can increase or decrease depending on which combination among T10.a, T10.b, T10.c and T10.d is applied and how effective each of these transformation is for that program. Finally, the application of T11 reduces the time spent in device kernel execution.

6   Performance of Rodinia Benchmarks

In this section, we evaluate the performance of five versions of the Rodinia benchmark suite: OpenMP, sequential, CUDA and two heterogeneous versions

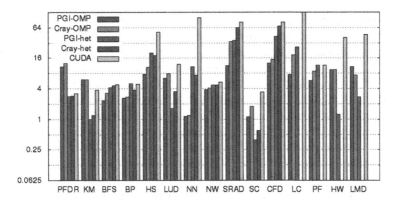

Fig. 2. Speedups over sequential programs compiled with PGI. Notice that for LC, the speedup of the CUDA code is 2100.

(following the steps in Sect. 5). For each benchmark, the suite provides two versions - an OpenMP version and an optimized CUDA version [6,7]. One heterogeneous version uses OpenACC 1.0 directives (Cray compiler), while the other uses the PGI programming model directives (PGI compiler).

Figure 2 shows speedup of the OpenMP, heterogeneous, and CUDA versions against the performance of the sequential version compiled with the PGI compiler. Since PF, LC, HW, and LMD could not be correctly compiled by the Cray compiler, the corresponding spaces in the figure have been left blank. The comparison of heterogeneous versions and the CUDA counterparts will help us to identify the performance bottlenecks and understand the effectiveness of the PGI and Cray compilers in exploiting the GPU resources.

For a total of 6 benchmarks (PFDR, BFS, BP, NW, CFD, PF) at least one of the heterogeneous versions managed to reach a performance over the 85 % of the CUDA performance. In fact, three benchmarks were able to achieve close to 100 % of the CUDA performance (BFS, BP, and PF). Even more, in some cases the heterogeneous version performs slightly better than the CUDA version. This is due to T10 (Sect. 5) transformation which parallelizes portions of code that were not formerly running in parallel. However, 8 benchmarks (KM, HS, LUD, NN, SC, LC, HW, LMD) obtain less than 50 % of the CUDA performance. The poor performance of the heterogeneous programs is due to issues such as poor computation to data communication ratio, excessive device global memory accesses, non-coalesced memory accesses and inefficient use of shared memory etc. We briefly explain the reasons behind the poor performance achieved by individual heterogeneous programs as compared to their CUDA versions.

The heterogeneous versions of KM suffer from both high amount of data transfer and non-coalesced memory accesses in the GPU kernels, hence they produce slow performance. In the case of HS, the heterogeneous versions perform a data copy within the GPU as part of the stencil computation, whereas CUDA achieves the same effect by a pointer swap. Thus, the heterogeneous versions of

HS shows reduced performance. LUD involves triangular matrix operations and has many row-wise and column-wise dependencies [7]. The heterogeneous versions make a lot of non-coalesced accesses to the device memory since the device cache or shared memory is not big enough to hold the entire matrix involved in the computation, which leads to reduced performance in GPU computation. The CUDA version of LUD implemented tiling which improves the cache performance. The heterogeneous versions of NN do not parallelize enough part of the kernel, thereby leading to a slower performance compared to the CUDA version. The heterogeneous versions of SC suffer from cyclic CPU-GPU data communication and thus become inefficient. The extraordinary performance of LC with CUDA is obtained by using a technique called persistent blocking [3,6] wherein all the iterations are performed in a single device kernel call and all cells are processed concurrently with one thread block allocated to each cell. In the kernel of heterogeneous HW, each thread loads data from memory in a loop which causes a lot of non-coalesced global memory loads. The number of misses in L2 cache of the GPU in the heterogeneous version are also about 48X as compared to the CUDA version. In case of LMD, heterogeneous version perform very little computation for the number of device global memory accesses it performs, which results in bad performance.

Focusing on OpenMP vs. heterogeneous versions will give a comparative perspective of the speedups that could be obtained using directive-based parallel programming techniques that exploit parallelism from the CPU and the GPU. We can observe that for 9 benchmarks, at least one heterogeneous version has performed better than its corresponding OpenMP version. However there are certain benchmarks whose heterogeneous versions do not perform as well. The slow performance of the heterogeneous versions of KM, SC, LUD, HW, and LMD has been already explained. In case of PFDR, the CPU-GPU data communication itself in both the CUDA and heterogeneous versions takes more time than the whole OpenMP program, so communication/computation ratio is quite bad for GPU approach.

7 Conclusions

In this paper, we have evaluated the effectiveness of two directive-based compilers, PGI and Cray, in: (i) dependence analysis and automatic application of transformations (ii) the programming effort to transform OpenMP programs to heterogeneous versions (iii) performance as compared to OpenMP and CUDA.

From the dependence analysis, we found that out of the 6 transformations and 3 idioms studied, both compilers were only able to privatize and generate code for reduction. Thus, the PGI and Cray compilers still seem to rely on the programmer to expose the parallelism.

We have proposed a sequence of steps to transform OpenMP programs to their heterogeneous versions. In this analysis, we observed that the Cray compiler was able to automatically inline most functions inside the parallel regions as opposed to the PGI compiler, which led to considerably reduced programmer efforts. The difficulty of programming with the directive-based compilers is closer to OpenMP programming than to CUDA programming.

In terms of performance, the versions compiled Cray performed faster than the ones of PGI compiler for 8 out of 15 Rodinia benchmarks. In comparison to fine-tuned CUDA versions, 6 out of 15 heterogeneous versions ran over the 85 % of the CUDA performance. This shows the potential of these heterogeneous directives-based compilers to produce efficient code and at the same time increase programmer productivity. In comparison to OpenMP, heterogeneous versions of the code ran faster in 9 out of 13 benchmarks at a similar programming effort to OpenMP. Degradation in performance of heterogeneous versions occurred because the compilers produced inefficient code and we could not overcome such inefficiencies due to not being able to express low-level optimizations using the directive-based compilers in the way CUDA versions did.

As a final remark, notice that the PGI and Cray compiler versions used correspond to the most up-to-date versions of early 2012. Current versions of these compilers now support OpenACC 2.0, which differs from the OpenACC 1.0 version that we used in the evaluation of this paper. New API routines have been added and the default behavior of some directives might have changed.

Acknowledgments. This research is part of the Blue Waters sustained-petascale computing project, which is supported by NSF (award number OCI 07-25070) and the state of Illinois. It was also supported by NSF under Award CNS 1111407 and by grants TIN2007-60625, TIN2010-21291-C02-01 and TIN2013-64957-C2-1-P (Spanish Government and European ERDF), gaZ: T48 research group (Aragon Government and European ESF).

References

1. Amini, M., Coelho, F., Irigoin, F., Keryell, R.: Static compilation analysis for host-accelerator communication optimization. In: Rajopadhye, S., Mills Strout, M. (eds.) LCPC 2011. LNCS, vol. 7146, pp. 237–251. Springer, Heidelberg (2013)
2. Bordawekar, R., Bondhugula, U., Rao, R.: Can CPUs match GPUs on performance with productivity?: Experiences with optimizing a flop-intensive application on CPUs and GPU. Technical report RC25033, IBM, August 2010
3. Boyer, M., Tarjan, D., Acton, S.T., Skadron, K.: Accelerating leukocyte tracking using cuda: a case study in leveraging manycore coprocessors. In: Proceedings of IPDPS, pp. 1–12 (2009)
4. CAPS Enterprise: HMPP workbench (2011). http://www.caps-entreprise.com/technology/hmpp/
5. CAPS Enterprise and Cray Inc. and NVIDIA and the Portland Group: The openacc application programming interface, v1.0, November 2011. http://www.openacc-standard.org/
6. Che, S., et al.: Rodinia: a benchmark suite for heterogeneous computing. In: IISWC 2009. pp. 44–54, October 2009
7. Che, S., et al.: A characterization of the rodinia benchmark suite with comparison to contemporary CMP workloads. In: Proceedings of IISWC, pp. 1–11 (2010)

8. Cloutier, B., Muite, B.K., Rigge, P.: A comparison of CPU and GPU performance for fourier pseudospectral simulations of the navier-stokes, cubic nonlinear schrodinger and sine gordon equations. ArXiv e-prints, June 2012

9. CRAY: Cray Compiler Environment (2011). http://docs.cray.com/books/S-2179-52/html-S-2179-52/index.html

10. Grauer Gray, S., Xu, L., Searles, R., Ayalasomayajula, S., Cavazos, J.: Auto-tuning a high-level language targeted to GPU codes. In: Proceedings of InPar, pp. 1–10 (2012)

11. Hacker, H., Trinitis, C., Weidendorfer, J., Brehm, M.: Considering GPGPU for HPC Centers: Is It Worth the effort? In: Keller, R., Kramer, D., Weiss, J.-P. (eds.) Facing the Multicore-Challenge. LNCS, vol. 6310, pp. 118–130. Springer, Heidelberg (2010)

12. Han, T., Abdelrahman, T.: HiCUDA: high-level GPGPU programming. IEEE Trans. Parallel Distrib. Syst. **22**(1), 78–90 (2011)

13. Henderson, T., Middlecoff, J., Rosinski, J., Govett, M., Madden, P.: Experience applying fortran GPU compilers to numerical weather prediction. In: Proceedings of SAAHPC, pp. 34–41, July 2011

14. Hernandez, O., Ding, W., Chapman, B., Kartsaklis, C., Sankaran, R., Graham, R.: Experiences with high-level programming directives for porting applications to GPUs. In: Keller, R., Kramer, D., Weiss, J.-P. (eds.) Facing the Multicore - Challenge II. LNCS, vol. 7174, pp. 96–107. Springer, Heidelberg (2012)

15. Enos, J., et al.: Quantifying the impact of GPUs on performance and energy efficiency in HPC clusters. In: Internatioanl Green Computing Conference, pp. 317–324, August 2010

16. Jablin, T.B., et al.: Automatic CPU-GPU communication management and optimization. SIGPLAN Not. **47**(6), 142–151 (2011)

17. Jin, H., Kellogg, M., Mehrotra, P.: Using compiler directives for accelerating CFD applications on GPUs. In: Chapman, B.M., Massaioli, F., Müller, M.S., Rorro, M. (eds.) IWOMP 2012. LNCS, vol. 7312, pp. 154–168. Springer, Heidelberg (2012)

18. Kennedy, K., Allen, J.R.: Optimizing Compilers for Modern Architectures: A Dependence-Based Approach. Morgan Kaufmann Publishers Inc., San Francisco (2002)

19. Khronos Group: Opencl - the open standard for parallel programming of heterogeneous systems (2011). http://www.khronos.org/opencl

20. Lee, S., Eigenmann, R.: OpenMPC: extended OpenMP programming and tuning for GPUs. In: Proceedings of SC 2010 (2010)

21. Lee, S., Min, S.J., Eigenmann, R.: OpenMP to GPGPU: a compiler framework for automatic translation and optimization. In: Proceedings of PPoPP 2009 (2010)

22. Lee, S., Vetter, J.S.: Early evaluation of directive-based GPU programming models for productive exascale computing. In: Proceedings of SC2012. IEEE Press, Salt Lake City (2012)

23. Leung, A., Vasilache, N., Meister, B., Baskaran, M., Wohlford, D., Bastoul, C., Lethin, R.: A mapping path for multi-GPGPU accelerated computers from a portable high level programming abstraction. In: Proceedings of GPGPU (2010)

24. Membarth, R., Hannig, F., Teich, J., Korner, M., Eckert, W.: Frameworks for GPU accelerators: a comprehensive evaluation using 2D/3D image registration. In: Proceedings of SASP, pp. 78–81, June 2011

25. NVIDIA: Compute Command Line Profiler. NVIDIA Whitepaper

26. NVIDIA: The Benefits of Multiple CPU Cores in Mobile Devices. NVIDIA Whitepaper. http://www.nvidia.com/content/PDF/tegra_white_papers/Benefits-of-Multi-core-CPUs-in-Mobile-Devices_Ver1.2.pdf

27. NVIDIA: Bring high-end graphics to handheld devices. NVIDIA White Paper (2011). http://www.nvidia.com/content/PDF/tegra_white_papers/Bringing_High-End_Graphics_to_Handheld_Devices.pdf
28. NVIDIA Corporation: NVIDIA CUDA programming guide version 4.0 (2011). http://developer.download.nvidia.com
29. OpenMP: Openmp: Complete specification v4.0 (2013). http://openmp.org/wp/resources/
30. The Portland Group: PGI compiler reference manual (2011). http://www.pgroup.com/doc/pgiref.pdf
31. Website, B.W.: (2011). http://www.ncsa.illinois.edu/BlueWaters/
32. Wienke, S., Springer, P., Terboven, C., an Mey, D.: OpenACC — first experiences with real-world applications. In: Kaklamanis, C., Papatheodorou, T., Spirakis, P.G. (eds.) Euro-Par 2012. LNCS, vol. 7484, pp. 859–870. Springer, Heidelberg (2012)

GLES: A Practical GPGPU Optimizing Compiler Using Data Sharing and Thread Coarsening

Zhen Lin, Xiaopeng Gao$^{(\boxtimes)}$, Han Wan, and Bo Jiang

School of Computer Science and Engineering, Beihang University, Beijing, China
gxp@buaa.edu.cn

Abstract. Writing optimized CUDA programs for General Purpose Graphics Processing Unit (GPGPU) is complicated and error-prone. Most of the former compiler optimization methods are impractical for many applications that contain divergent control flows, and they failed to fully exploit optimization opportunities in data sharing and thread coarsening. In this paper, we present GLES, an optimizing compiler for GPGPU programs. GLES proposes two optimization techniques based on divergence analysis. The first one is data sharing optimization for data reuse and bandwidth enhancement. The other one is thread granularity coarsening for reducing redundant instructions. Our experiments on 6 real-world programs show that GPGPU programs optimized by GLES achieve similar performance compared with manually tuned GPGPU programs. Furthermore, GLES is not only applicable to a much wider range of GPGPU programs than the state-of-art GPGPU optimizing compiler, but it also achieves higher or close performance on 8 out of 9 benchmarks.

Keywords: GPGPU · Optimization · Compiler

1 Introduction

General Purpose Graphics Processing Unit (GPGPU) has become one of the most popular accelerators in parallel computing area. Nowadays, the Compute Unified Device Architecture (CUDA) [11], is the most widely used programming model for GPU applications. Since CUDA exposes too many architectural related details, developing and maintaining a highly efficient CUDA program is very difficult.

In recent years, there are some work on automatic optimizing GPGPU programming at compile time. CUDA-lite [14] is the first source-to-source optimizing compiler for GPGPU programs. In order to improve GPU memory bandwidth, CUDA-lite takes programmer's annotation to perform GPU memory hierarchy optimization. Because CUDA-lite cannot automatically check memory access pattern, it still needs programmer's knowledge on GPU's complex memory hierarchy to provide annotations. Gcompiler [19] is another source-to-source optimizing compiler for GPGPU programs. It takes naive GPU kernels as input,

© Springer International Publishing Switzerland 2015
J. Brodman and P. Tu (Eds.): LCPC 2014, LNCS 8967, pp. 36–50, 2015.
DOI: 10.1007/978-3-319-17473-0_3

through a series of optimization methods on memory bandwidth and thread granularity, Gcompiler outputs a highly optimized GPU kernel. Gcompiler has achieved impressive performance gain on some examples of dense matrix computation, however, there are still some disadvantages on Gcompiler. Firstly, the applicable scope of Gcompiler is very small, it is not safe for applications that contain divergent control flows. Secondly, on-chip shared memory is only used to enhance memory bandwidth in Gcompiler, thus many opportunities of data sharing are ignored. CREST [15] is an optimizing and tuning framework for exploiting inter-thread locality by thread coarsening optimization. Compared with Gcompiler, CREST involves safety analysis in its optimizing process. However, CREST's coarsening strategy only focuses on improving data locality thus cannot effectively reduce redundant instructions for GPGPU programs.

In this paper, we present a practical compiler framework that can better exploit data sharing and performs thread coarsening for reducing redundant instructions. At first, we show that divergent variable analysis is critical to ensure the safety of both optimizations. In this paper, we use the definition of divergent variable in [5]. Based on the divergence information, GLES applies data sharing optimization and thread coarsening optimization. In data sharing optimization, the compiler analyses data access space of global memory, then it loads shareable data to on-chip shared memory with coalesced access. In thread coarsening optimization, GLES determines which statements can be shared between threads based on divergence analysis. Then it performs thread coarsening transformation on most profitable dimension.

We present experiments on NVIDIA GTX 480 and GTX 680 GPUs with 6 GPU kernels chosen from real-world applications like IMPATIANT MRI Toolset [7,18]. The results show that our compiler can achieve average 3.8X speedup over naive kernels and 1.1X speedup compared with hand-optimized kernels on average. In our experiments, we also compared with Gcompiler in 9 cases. The results show that our compiler is superior to Gcompiler in 4 out of 9 cases.

This paper makes the following contributions: (1) We propose a more aggressive and profitable optimizing method for data reuse and bandwidth improvement via caching data onto shared memory. (2) Our compiler correctly placing loading operations inside divergent control flows, thereby fixing erroneous implementation described by prior art. (3) We propose a novel method for thread coarsening, which can reduce issued instructions as well as memory accesses.

2   Motivation Examples

GLES is motivated by prior GPGPU optimizing techniques, CUDA-lite [14], Gcompiler [19] and CREST [15]. We will discuss these work in depth with 2 typical examples.

2.1   Example 1: Matrix Multiplication

In Fig. 1a, we show the naive kernel of matrix multiplication that supports arbitrary input size. In this paper, *gidx*, *gidy* and *gidz* refer to the global thread

```
                                __shared__ float sharedA[DIMY][TS];
                                if (in_boundary) {
                                  sum = 0.0;
                                  for (i = 0; i < WA; i += TS) {
                                    tile = MIN(WA - i, TS);
                                    __syncthreads();
                                    load_to_smem(); // unsafe loading
if (in_boundary) {                  __syncthreads();
  sum = 0.0;                        for (j = 0; j < tile; j++) {
  for (i = 0; i < WA; i++) {          // failed to share data in B
    sum+=A(gidy,i)*B(i,gidx);         sum+=sharedA(lidy,j)*B(i+j,gidx);
  }                                 } }
  C(gidy, gidx) = sum;            C(gidy, gidx) = sum;
}                               }
```

        (a) Naive kernel   **(b)** Coalesced kernel

Fig. 1. Coalescing transformation of matrix multiplication in a divergent control flow

coordinate in a thread grid, and $lidx$, $lidy$ and $lidz$ refer to the local thread coordinate in a thread block. In coalescing optimization of Gcompiler, the compiler can detect the global access of $A(gidy, i)$ is not coalesced, so it determines to move data of matrix A to shared memory. After loop tiling, the compiler declares shared memory for matrix A, loads data from global memory to shared memory with coalesced access, changes access of matrix A to corresponding shared memory, and inserts synchronization barriers before and after loading procedure. Figure 1b shows the optimized kernel after coalescing optimization.

There are two problems in this transformation process.

The first is safety issue. In loading procedure, the compiler requires a number of continuous threads to load global data onto shared memory. However, because the control flow statement filters some threads, which may not be determined at compile time, it is hard to predict which threads can reach the loading procedure. So the loading procedure is unsafe in this case. Besides, according to [11,17], synchronization barriers must be visible to all threads in a thread block, otherwise the kernel execution may cause deadlock or undefined errors. In Fig. 1b, the two synchronization barriers may not be seen by all threads in a thread block due to the divergent control flow. Since loading procedure is always accompanied with synchronization barriers, we call the place where compiler inserts these operations as loading point. Based on the above two reasons, the loading point cannot be placed inside in a divergent control flow.

The second is efficiency issue. There are two benefits of caching data onto shared memory, one is for data reuse, the other is for transforming non-coalesced accesses into coalesced ones. In this optimizing process, shared memory is only used for coalescing transformation. In this example, matrix A is loaded to shared memory for coalescing transformation, data in B is not loaded to shared memory because the access of matrix B already conforms with the coalescing requirements. However, it is still profitable to load data in B to shared memory because all threads in Y direction within a thread block access the same location of matrix B.

2.2   Example 2: MRI-GRID

In Fig. 2, we show a naive kernel snippet of MRI-GRID [7], which is a hotspot kernel in IMPATIENT MRI Toolset [18]. The original kernel is heavily optimized, we rewrote the kernel to its naive version. Now, we describe how prior compilers coarsen this kernel along X direction. And we define coarsening factor CF as the output granularity of the optimizing process.

```
1    for (k = kL; k <= kH; k++) {
2      for (j = jL; j <= jH; j++) {
3        delta = compute_delta(j, k);
4        for (i = 0; i < delta; i++) {
5          real = real_g[start + i];
6          //...
7          v0 = foo(gidx, gidy);
8          v = bar(v0, gidz);
9          if (v < cutoff) {
10             w = kernel_value(v);
11             pt += compute_pt(w);
12    } } } }
13   result(gidz, gidy, gidx) = pt;
```

Fig. 2. Naive kernel snippet of MRI-GRID

Gcompiler [19] proposes to share all control flow statements in the coarsening process. It is not applicable for divergent control flows. In this example, the variable v in S8 is dependent on $threadID$ of all three dimensions. Thus the conditional evaluates differently in if statement of S9, hence the if statement cannot be shared among threads. In addition, the aim of thread coarsening of Gcompiler is to improve global-to-register reuse. Thus it doesn't consider the benefit of instruction sharing when determining the granularity of coarsening.

Another thread coarsening strategy is proposed by CREST [15]. It proposes to insert a loop in the kernel, and iterate the loop multiple times to execute each thread's work one by one. The data locality can be increased after such transformation. But it fails to share redundant operations among threads. For example, in this case, S1 to S6 are identical for all threads, if we can share these statements among threads, the total instruction number can be significantly reduced.

As a consequence, in order to reduce the redundant operations as much as possible, the compiler should share identical statements as many as possible. One the other hand, the compiler must save all statements that are differently executed on each thread to ensure the safety of coarsening.

3   Compiler Framework

The overall framework of GLES is showed in Fig. 3. The input of GLES is the source code of a naive CUDA kernel, which doesn't use shared memory and has the finest thread granularity. We also assume the input kernels don't contain synchronization barrier. GLES outputs an optimized kernel source code, which

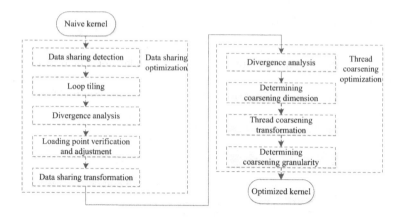

Fig. 3. The overall framework of GLES

will be further compiled by NVCC (NVIDIA CUDA compiler). GLES is composed of two optimizing phases: data sharing optimization and thread coarsening optimization. Divergence analysis plays a fundamental role for both optimizing phases.

3.1 Divergence Analysis

In Sect. 2, we have shown that the compiler should determine which statements, including control flows, are differently executed on each thread. To do so, we first apply divergence analysis algorithm proposed in [5] to find all divergent variables. A variable is divergent if it has different values at the same moment during kernel execution. The algorithm traverses a converted data dependence graph to find all variables that are data dependent or sync dependent (similar to control dependent) on thread ID. Because CUDA implements a single program multiple data (SPMD) model, only the statements that are data dependent on divergent variables may produce different results during kernel execution. Otherwise, the statements are identically executed among all threads, we call them as redundant statements. A control flow is divergent if its condition is data dependent on any divergent variables. Statements inside a divergent control flow may not be executed by all threads.

In Fig. 2, for example, variable v is divergent because it is dependent on $gidx$, $gidy$ and $gidz$. S9 is dependent on v, so it is a divergent control flow. S1-S5 are redundant statements because they do not dependent on any divergent variables.

3.2 Data Sharing Optimization

In data sharing optimization, at first, the compiler analyses the profit to load global data into shared memory. For profitable cases, the compiler verifies the validity of data loading point based on divergence analysis. If the loading point is invalid, the compiler tries to perform equivalent transformation to ensure the validity of loading point. At last, the compiler applies data sharing transformation to the kernel.

3.2.1   Data Sharing Detection

There are three patterns of global data accesses that can be improved through loading to shared memory. (1) Inter-thread shareable, the data access space of one thread is overlapped with other threads' access spaces. (2) Inner-thread shareable, one section of global data can be further used by the same thread. (3) Non-coalesced access of one continuous data space.

We define shareable factor SF to help GLES determine which global accesses are more profitable to be cached on shared memory.

$$SF = \frac{TBAT}{TBAS/WARP}$$

In which, $TBAT$ is the access times of an array by all threads in a thread block, $TBAS$ is the access space of an array by all threads in a thread block and $WARP$ is the warp size of GPU. $TBAS$ is the data space which will be loaded to shared memory with coalesced access if the compiler determines to perform data sharing optimization on the array. We assume only one access operation is issued for $WARP$ size of data by coalesced access, so $TBAS/WARP$ is the access times of a thread block in loading procedure. It is profitable to perform data sharing optimization if SF is larger than 1. When shared memory is not enough for all shareable data, GLES will load data in arrays with greater SF values.

Thread block access times $TBAT$ is defined as

$$TBAT = \sum_i \left(\sum_t TAT_{t,i} \times C_i \right)$$

$$C_i = \begin{cases} 1/WARP & \text{access } i \text{ is a coalesced access} \\ 1 & \text{access } i \text{ is a non-coalesced access} \end{cases}$$

In which $TAT_{t,i}$ denotes to the access times of statement i accessed by thread t. In our implementation, GLES obtains $TAT_{t,i}$ by counting the loop times of statement i.

Thread block access space $TBAS$ is defined as the union of all access spaces for one array.

$$TBAS = Volume\left(\bigcup_i AS_i \right)$$

In which, AS_i denotes to the space of statement i accessed by a thread block.

In order to determine the access space of statement i, we decompose each dimension of array index into the summation of 3 types of variables and set each variable's range based on its type. The first type is loop iterator, a loop iterator's range can be determined by its initiation and boundary condition. For example, in Fig. 1a, the range of loop index i is $[0 : WA - 1]$. The second type is $threadID$, the range of $gidx$ in a thread block is $[gidx - lidx : gidx - lidx + DIMX - 1]$, in which $DIMX$ refers to thread block size in X dimension. The third type is plain variable, the range of plain variable v is $[v : v]$. After GLES get each variable's range, by accumulating them together, the compiler gets thread block access space AS of a global access.

In the example of Fig. 1a, the AS of $B(i, gidx)$ is $[0 : WA - 1][gidx - lidx : gidx - lidx + DIMX - 1]$, so the $TBAS$ of matrix B is $WA * DIMX$. Because the access is coalesced and block size is $DIMX * DIMY$, $TBAT$ of matrix B is $WA * DIMX * DIMY/WARP$. Then SF is $DIMY$, i.e. it is profitable to load data in matrix B if thread block size in Y dimension is larger than 1.

GLES tiles the loop if $TBAS$ is larger than shared memory size. SF remains the same after loop tiling.

```
if (cond) {
  S1;
  for (cond_long) {
// invalid loading point
    for (cond_tile)
      gmem;
  }
  S2;
}
```

```
if (cond)
  S1;
for (cond_long) {
// valid loading point
  if (cond)
    for (cond_tile)
      gmem;
}
if (cond)
  S2;
```

(a) Before   (b) After

Fig. 4. A typical situation of loading point adjustment

3.2.2   Loading Point Verification and Adjustment

As discussed in Sect. 2.1, the compiler must ensure the loading point is visible for all threads. Loading point denotes to the place where GLES inserts loading procedure and barriers. So the loading point is valid if and only if it is not contained in any divergent control flow. Through equivalent code transformation, some invalid loading points can be adjusted.

Figure 4a presents a typical invalid loading situation that can be adjusted. Statement $gmem$ is a code block that contains shareable global memory accesses, it can either be a global access statement or a control flow statement which contains global accesses. We assume that the conditional expression $cond$ in if statement doesn't contain assignment expression.

In this situation, the access space of $gmem$ is larger than shared memory size, so the loop is tiled by the compiler. In fact, Fig. 1b is an example of this situation. In general, if $cond$ is non-divergent, the loading point of this situation is between two for loops. But the loading point is no longer valid if $cond$ is divergent. In this circumstance, to get valid loading point, GLES tries to split the divergent flow into Fig. 4b.

3.2.3   Data Sharing Transformation

The first step of data sharing transformation is declaring shared memory array. Array size to be declared in shared memory equals with the value $TBAS$ we analysed in Sect. 3.2.1. For example, shared memory for matrix B can be declared as $sharedB[TS][DIMX]$. Then the compiler inserts loading procedure to the verified loading point and adds barrier synchronizations before and after loading procedure. The loading procedure is composed of boundary checking statements and a series of assignment expressions. The base address of global memory is the lower bound of $TBAS$ determined in Sect. 3.2.1. After shareable data has been loaded, the compiler replaces global memory access with corresponding shared memory access.

3.3   Thread Coarsening Optimization

In thread coarsening optimization, first, the compiler updates the divergence information and checks which variables and statements cannot be shared among threads. Then the compiler performs thread coarsening transformation according to determined coarsening dimension.

3.3.1   Checking Variables and Statements to Be Duplicated

As shown in Sect. 2.2, the key to thread coarsening for reducing redundant instructions is to share the identical statements among threads. On the other hand, in order to ensure the safety of transformation, the compiler should duplicate variables and statements which cannot be shared among threads. Through divergence analysis, the output set V and S are variables and statements to be duplicated respectively. Because there are three dimensions in a GPU kernel, GLES performs this algorithm on each dimension. The following are the sets to be duplicated in the example of Fig. 2.

$$V_x = \{lidx, gidx, v0, v, w, pt\}$$
$$V_y = \{lidy, gidy, v0, v, w, pt\}$$
$$V_z = \{lidz, gidz, v, w, pt\}$$
$$S_x = S_y = \{S7, S8, S9, S13\}$$
$$S_z = \{S8, S9, S13\}$$

3.3.2   Thread Coarsening Strategy

Since GLES has detected variables and statements to be duplicated on each dimension. The next problem is to determine on which dimension and granularity the compiler performs thread coarsening transformation. GLES chooses the dimension which contains the least statements in its corresponding S set. In the case of Fig. 2, dimension Z is chosen because S_z contains less statements than the other two sets. Considering different statements may contribute differently to the execution time. A more careful strategy can be given by analysing the cost of each statement in S sets, and chooses the dimension with least cost. This will be our future work.

After coarsening dimension has been determined, GLES doubles kernel granularity by performing thread coarsening transformation, which is described in

```
1    for (k = kL; k <= kH; k++) {
2      for (j = jL; j <= jH; j++) {
3        delta = compute_delta(j, k);
4        for (i = 0; i < delta; i++) {
5          real = real_g[start + i];
6          //...
7          v0 = foo(gidx, gidy);
8          v_0 = bar(v0, gidz_0);
9          v_1 = bar(v0, gidz_1);
10         if (v_0 < cutoff) {
11           w_0 = kernel_value(v_0);
12           pt_0 += compute_pt(w_0);
13         }
14         if (v_1 < cutoff) {
15           w_1 = kernel_value(v_1);
16           pt_1 += compute_pt(w_1);
17    } } } }
18    result(gidz_0, gidy, gidx) = pt_0;
19    result(gidz_1, gidy, gidx) = pt_1;
```

Fig. 5. Coarsened MRI-GRID kernel on Z dimension with granularity of 2

Sect. 3.3.3, on determined dimension. After each time of doubling granularity, GLES calls NVCC to feedback register number used by the kernel. If the register usage has exceeded the maximum of GPU, GLES stops the doubling and returns the last kernel as output. Otherwise, GLES keeps doubling the kernel's granularity.

3.3.3   Thread Coarsening Transformation

Based on the determined coarsening dimension, we get corresponding set V and S. In the case of Fig. 2, GLES chooses to perform thread coarsening on Z dimension, so we get S_z and V_z. First, the compiler duplicates the declarations of all variables in V CF times and assigns each version a different symbol name. For $threadID$ in V, the ith version of id is initialized as $id + i * DIM$. Then the compiler duplicates each statement in S for CF times. When duplicating the ith version of a statement, the compiler replaces variables in V with its ith version. At last, the duplicated versions of statements are inserted to replace the original statements. The coarsened MRI-GRID kernel by granularity 2 on Z dimension is showed in Fig. 5.

Another benefit of thread coarsening is the improvement of instruction-level parallelism (ILP). It occurs when multiple versions of a non-control-flow statement are generated. For example, the instructions in S8 are independent with the instructions in S9, so they can be simultaneously performed.

4   Evaluation

GLES is implemented with Cetus [6] compiler infrastructure. We experiment on NVIDIA Fermi GTX 680 and Kepler GTX 480 GPUs. Both machines hosted on Intel Core i5 CPU. The programs are compiled with CUDA NVCC 5.0 and GCC 4.6 with -O2 option.

4.1   Overall Performance

Table 1 shows the benchmarks we experiment in this section. The first 5 benchmarks are heavily optimized, to get the naive version, we remap all shared memory references to global memory and change it to finest granularity if necessary. We also undo some other optimizations like loop unrolling and constant memory usage. We believe the naive version is much more readable and straightforward than manually optimized ones. In Table 1 we compare the code complexity, measured in lines of code (LOC), of naive kernels and manually optimized kernels.

Table 1. Benchmarks selected from real-world applications

Benchmark	Description	Naive LOC	Manual LOC
CUTCP	Coulombic potential	64	159
MRI-GRID	MRI gridding	76	156
MRI-Q	MRI matrix Q	37	52
FT	Fourier transformation	73	300
NBODY	N-body simulation	79	144
MMA	Matrix multiplication	12	unknown
Average		57	162

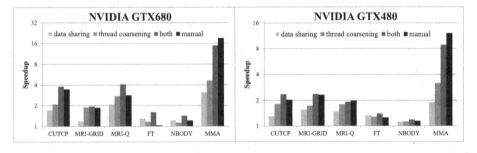

Fig. 6. Performance gain over naive kernels, experiment on NVIDIA GTX 680 and GTX 480

Each kernel has 4 optimized kernel versions: pure data sharing optimization, pure thread coarsening optimization, both sharing and coarsening optimizations and manual optimization. Figure 6 shows the performance gains over naive kernels on selected benchmarks.

CUTCP computes short-range electronic potentials induced by point charges in a 3D volume [13]. GLES generated kernels achieve better performance on both GPUs because it applied more profitable coarsening dimensions and granularities on each GPU. MRI-GRID, MRI-Q and FT are three major kernels in IMPATIENT MRI Toolset [7,18], which is a CUDA implementation for iterative MR image reconstruction. The result shows that GLES optimized kernel is similar with manually optimized kernel because we apply similar optimizations.

MRI-Q is used in 3D MRI reconstruction algorithm. Manually optimized kernel leverage constant cache for sharing an array, which achieves better performance than our method on GTX 680. FT implements the Fourier transformation. The manually optimized kernel only applies loop unroll optimization. NBODY is a N-body simulation selected from CUDA SDK. The overall speedup is limited because NBODY is compute intensive and the operations are different for all threads except for the loop. MMA is a matrix multiplication implementation that support arbitrary input size. Both optimizations can greatly increase data reuse in this case. Thread coarsening is even more effective after the data sharing because more shareable operations are exposed after loading point adjustment. We choose CUBLAS 5.0, a highly optimized math library, as the manual version.

In general, thread coarsening optimization tends to achieve better performance gains on GTX 680 because its register number is twice as many as in GTX 480, coarsening for GTX 680 can benefit from greater granularity.

4.2   Case Study: MRI-GRID

MRI-GRID kernel has three nested loops and the innermost loop of MRI-GRID contains 6 shareable global accesses and 56 float operations, in which 10 operations are independent on divergent variables.

Figure 7 shows more performance details of MRI-GRID kernel on GTX 480. In the experiment, we first optimize the kernel with data sharing optimization, for both the optimized and original kernels, we coarsen its granularity from 1 to 2, 4, 8 and 16. Then we run the 16 kernel versions with NVIDIA Visual Profiler to collect 4 performance metrics.

Global load requests can be reduced with both data sharing and thread coarsening. The gap between shared and non-shared versions decreases as the increase of granularity. But the granularity cannot be very large due to the limit of register number. So data sharing is still the dominant method for reducing global access. The metric of issued instructions shows data sharing reduces instruction number although the compiler inserts codes for transformation. That is because global memory access costs more instructions that shared memory access. As expected, issued instruction number decreases as we increase the granularity, but the shared version hits bottom at granularity of 4 and non-shared version hits bottom at granularity of 8. This phenomenon can be explained as local memory begins to spill on these points. As showed in L1 local cache miss metric, local memory begins to spill to L2 cache when granularity are 8 and 16 for shared and non-shared versions. Shared version tends to incur more local memory spills because data sharing optimization demands extra register usage.

The last three metrics contribute to the kernel execution time. Before local spilling points, the execution time of two versions decreases and the gap becomes smaller as the granularity increases. After spilling points, execution time begins to increase and the increasing speed of shared version is greater than non-shared version.

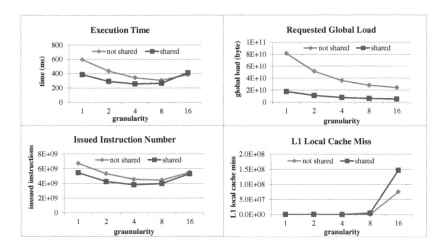

Fig. 7. Performance metrics of MRI-GRID on GTX480 for varying granularities

4.3   Performance Result Compared with Gcompiler

We compared GLES with Gcompiler with its own benchmarks, the details of the benchmark can be found in [19]. Note that these kernels are very simple and doesn't contain any divergent control flows, the average line of kernel code is 11.

In Fig. 8 we present the performance result compared with Gcompiler, the inputs are $4K \times 4K$ matrices and/or $4K$ vectors. We used recommended optimizing options of Gcompiler. And since both Gcompiler and GLES generate multiple versions of optimized kernels, varying granularity and thread block size. We compared the kernels with maximum performance.

We outperform Gcompiler in 4 benchmarks, MM, MV, CONV and STRSM.

In MM, data reuse of matrix B can improved by GLES with both data sharing and thread coarsening. However, Gcompiler only reuses matrix B with thread coarsening. Because thread coarsening can greatly increase register pressure of the kernel, the granularity is limited. Data reuse of matrix B can be improved to 64X with GLES, whereas 16X with Gcompiler. The access pattern of STRSM is similar to MM. In both cases, GLES outperforms Gcompiler due to improved data sharing strategy.

MV contains numerous non-coalesced accesses. Limited by shared memory size, each thread block can only allocate 32 computing threads. In our naive kernel, we allocate 256 threads for each block and add boundary check statement for actual compute. Boundary check is not supported by Gcompiler, so the thread block size is 32 for Gcompiler. After loading point adjustment, GLES uses more threads in the loading procedure and better exploits global load pipeline in GPU.

All data accesses in CONV are non-coalesced, so both GLES and Gcompiler transform global accesses with shared memory accesses. After that, Gcompiler doesn't perform thread coarsening in this case because its aim of coarsening is to

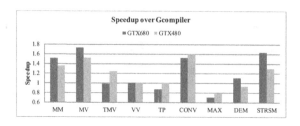

Fig. 8. Performance result compared with Gcompiler in 4k input size

reuse global-to-register accesses. But with our thread coarsening strategy, GLES can further reducing data accesses and issued instructions.

GLES achieves only about 70 % performance in MAX mainly because Gcompiler takes advantage of detecting data sharing among different iterations of different thread blocks.

5   Related Work

We have compared our work with most related previous studies [14,15,19] in Sects. 1 and 2. This section reviews other work on productive techniques for GPGPU programs.

OpemMPC [9,10] compiler translates OpenMP program to CUDA, it also extends traditional OpenMP to better fit GPU features. CUDA C [4] describes some optimizing methods implemented in NVCC. The memory space analysis in CUDA C is to distinguish specific memory access (local, shared, global) from generic access. They also perform divergence analysis, which can support two optimizing techniques in our paper. hiCUDA [8] defines a directive based interface for CUDA programming, programmers use directives for memory management and task assignment. OpenACC [12] is also a OpenMP-like programming standard for simplifying programming on heterogeneous systems. Although OpenMPC, hiCUDA and OpenACC have simplified GPGPU programming to a certain extent, programmer are still obliged to use the low-level operations they provide in order to achieve high performance. They mainly focus on optimization of data transfer and task assignment, so our kernel optimizing techniques can be complementary with their work.

Baskaran et al. [1–3] applied polyhedral model for C-to-CUDA generation and optimization. Their compiler performs optimizations on memory hierarchy and empirical search for optimal unroll factors. Compared with their data reuse strategy, we unified data reuse and access coalescing into one optimization and considered safety check in data loading procedure. PPCG [16] is a new polyhedral compiler for GPGPU, it extended prior work by supporting imperfectly nested loops. The basic idea of polyhedral compilers is to divide a polyhedral space into small blocks and assign them to threads. While GLES starts from finest granularity and coarsen workload of threads along optimization. In this manner, GLES can exploit instruction sharing resources.

6 Conclusion

This paper points out some drawbacks of prior GPGPU optimizing compilers and shows that divergent analysis is fundamental for both data sharing and thread coarsening optimizations. Based on divergence analysis, two novel optimization techniques are proposed. One is data sharing with shared memory, the other is thread coarsening for instruction sharing. The experiment results show that our compiler can be applied to more realistic applications and the performance is higher than most manually optimized programs. And we achieve higher or close performance compared with a state-of-art GPGPU optimizing compiler in 8 out of 9 benchmarks.

Acknowledgement. Thank Lujun Wang, Fan Ni and anonymous reviewers for reviewing and commenting on this paper. Thank Huiyang Zhou's suggestions and encouragement. This work is supported in part by Innovation Foundation of Huawei Company under grant no. IRP-2012-02-15, the National Natural Science Foundation of China (project no. 61202077) and the CCF-Tencent Open Research Fund (project no. CCF-TencentAGR20130111).

References

1. Baskaran, M.M., Ramanujam, J., Sadayappan, P.: Automatic C-to-CUDA code generation for affine programs. In: Gupta, R. (ed.) CC 2010. LNCS, vol. 6011, pp. 244–263. Springer, Heidelberg (2010)
2. Baskaran, M.M., Bondhugula, U., Krishnamoorthy, S., Ramanujam, J., Rountev, A., Sadayappan, P.: A compiler framework for optimization of affine loop nests for gpgpus. In: ICS (2008)
3. Baskaran, M.M., Bondhugula, U., Krishnamoorthy, S., Ramanujam, J., Rountev, A., Sadayappan, P.: Automatic data movement and computation mapping for multi-level parallel architectures with explicitly managed memories. In: PPOPP (2008)
4. Chakrabarti, G., Grover, V., Aarts, B., Kong, X., Kudlur, M., Lin, Y., Marathe, J., Murphy, M., Wang, J.-Z.: Cuda: compiling and optimizing for a gpu platform. In: ICCS (2012)
5. Coutinho, B., Sampaio, D., Pereira, F.M.Q., Meira Jr., W.: Divergence analysis and optimizations (2011)
6. Dave, C., Bae, H., Min, S.-J., Lee, S., Eigenmann, R., Midkiff, S.P.: Cetus: a source-to-source compiler infrastructure for multicores. IEEE Comput. **42**, 36–42 (2009)
7. Gai, J., Obeid, N., Holtrop, J.L., Wu, X.-L., Lam, F., Fu, M., Haldar, J.P., Hwu, W.-M.W., Liang, Z.-P., Sutton, B.P.: More impatient: a gridding-accelerated toeplitz-based strategy for non-cartesian high-resolution 3d mri on gpus. JPDC **73**(5), 686–697 (2013)
8. Han, T.D., Abdelrahman, T.S.: hiCUDA: High-Level GPGPU Programming. TPDS **22**, 78–90 (2011)
9. Lee, S., Eigenmann, R.: OpenMPC: extended OpenMP programming and tuning for gpus. In: SC (2010)

10. Lee, S., Min, S.-J., Eigenmann, R.: Openmp to gpgpu: a compiler framework for automatic translation and optimization. In: PPOPP (2009)
11. NVIDIA Corporation. CUDA C Programming Guide (2012)
12. OpenAcc. The OpenACC Application Programming Interface (2013)
13. Rodrigues, C.I., Hardy, D.J., Stone, J.E., Schulten, K., Hwu, W.-M.W.: Gpu acceleration of cutoff pair potentials for molecular modeling applications. In: CF (2008)
14. Ueng, S.-Z., Lathara, M., Baghsorkhi, S.S., Hwu, W.W.: CUDA-lite: reducing gpu programming complexity. In: Amaral, J.N. (ed.) LCPC 2008. LNCS, vol. 5335, pp. 1–15. Springer, Heidelberg (2008)
15. Unkule, S., Shaltz, C., Qasem, A.: Automatic restructuring of gpu kernels for exploiting inter-thread data locality. In: O'Boyle, M. (ed.) CC 2012. LNCS, vol. 7210, pp. 21–40. Springer, Heidelberg (2012)
16. Verdoolaege, S., Carlos Juega, J., Cohen, A., Ignacio Gómez, J., Tenllado, C., Catthoor, F.: Polyhedral parallel code generation for CUDA. TACO 9, 54 (2013)
17. Wong, H., Papadopoulou, M.-M., Sadooghi-Alvandi, M., Moshovos, A.: Demystifying GPU microarchitecture through microbenchmarking. In: ISPASS (2010)
18. Wu, X.-L., Gai, J., Lam, F., Fu, M., Haldar, J.P., Zhuo, Y., Liang, Z.-P., Hwu, W.-M., Sutton, B.P.: Impatient mri: Illinois massively parallel acceleration toolkit for image reconstruction with enhanced throughput in mri. In: IEEE International Symposium on Biomedical Imaging: From Nano to Macro (2011)
19. Yang, Y., Xiang, P., Kong, J., Zhou, H.: A GPGPU compiler for memory optimization and parallelism management. In: PLDI (2010)

Evaluating Performance Portability of OpenACC

Amit Sabne[1]([✉]), Putt Sakdhnagool[1], Seyong Lee[2], and Jeffrey S. Vetter[2,3]

[1] Purdue University, West Lafayette, IN 47907, USA
{asabne,psakdhna}@purdue.edu
[2] Oak Ridge National Laboratory, Oak Ridge, USA
{lees2,vetter}@ornl.gov
[3] Georgia Institute of Technology, Atlanta, USA

Abstract. Accelerator-based heterogeneous computing is gaining momentum in High Performance Computing arena. However, the increased complexity of the accelerator architectures demands more generic, high-level programming models. OpenACC is one such attempt to tackle the problem. While the abstraction endowed by OpenACC offers productivity, it raises questions on its portability. This paper evaluates the performance portability obtained by OpenACC on twelve OpenACC programs on NVIDIA CUDA, AMD GCN, and Intel MIC architectures. We study the effects of various compiler optimizations and OpenACC program settings on these architectures to provide insights into the achieved performance portability.

Keywords: OpenACC · Performance portability · High performance computing

1 Introduction

Recent years have seen a growing trend in the adoption of heterogeneous computing across many areas including mobile and high performance computing (HPC) [15]. Presently, NVIDIA CUDA GPUs, AMD GPUs, and Intel Xeon Phi are the prominent heterogeneous architectures. While all of these devices possess tremendous computational power, they have significant differences in their architectures as compared to traditional, latency-optimized CPUs. Furthermore, even within architectural families (e.g., CUDA GPUs), new generations of each architecture often differ significantly from their predecessor. Indeed, these devices are being more tightly-integrated into node architectures, eliminating limitations like the high-latency PCIe bus, and frequently changing the device memory model [14], adding on-chip programmer-managed caches, and having a lower number of core registers.

So far, many device-specific programming models and optimization strategies have been developed to exploit these architectures: CUDA [10] for NVIDIA GPUs, and Intel Language Extensions for Offload (LEO) [1] for Xeon Phi are two such architecture-specific programming models. However, despite the availability of these relatively high-level programming models, programming heterogeneous

© Springer International Publishing Switzerland 2015
J. Brodman and P. Tu (Eds.): LCPC 2014, LNCS 8967, pp. 51–66, 2015.
DOI: 10.1007/978-3-319-17473-0_4

systems requires considerable expertise and architectural knowledge to obtain high performance.

Ultimately, the goal of any programming system is to maintain a reasonable level of *performance portability*, where, ideally, programmers can write their application once, and execute it *efficiently* on any architecture without manual intervention. Unfortunately, current solutions like CUDA and LEO are not even *functionally portable* across devices. So, programmers are forced to have multiple versions of the code for each device that they must maintain and validate, which is tedious, error prone, and generally unproductive. The first programming model to allow such functional portability was OpenCL [12]. However, due to the low-level nature of this model, programming in OpenCL was tedious. OpenACC [11] was therefore proposed to address two major issues: (i) allow functional portability across various heterogeneous architectures, and (ii) ease the process of porting a serial or OpenMP application to individual heterogeneous devices.

OpenACC provides a set of directives, or *pragmas* that allow programmers to port an existing serial/OpenMP (C or FORTRAN) application to a heterogeneous system. The programmer must determine the compute intensive, parallel regions in the application, and insert the OpenACC directives on these regions. The underlying compiler framework is then responsible for generating executable instructions for the target devices, while the runtime system is responsible for coordinating code execution and data movement among the multiple devices in the node. OpenACC offers the benefit that programmers can incrementally offload and control computation with these directives. Still, even with this level of abstraction in OpenACC, the compiler and runtime system must make many accurate decisions to ensure that the generated code executes with performance comparable to an expert's manually written version of the application.

Beyond the functional portability, *performance portability* is vital to the success of any programming system because code optimizations for specific architectural features can be evasive. While many researchers have provided systems to offload an application written in a high-level language with programmer annotations onto a specific heterogeneous architecture [5,7,13], we are unaware of any studies on understanding the performance portability aspects of a high-level programming model across heterogeneous architectures, like GPUs and Xeon Phis. We believe that this question is of high importance, since an optimization that yields significant benefits on one architecture may be inconsequential on another architecture. The understanding of performance impacts of various optimizations is crucial to an OpenACC programmer.

In this paper, we study the performance portability of several OpenACC applications across different heterogeneous devices. Due to the architectural differences across current heterogeneous architectures, a tuned OpenACC application that runs efficiently on one architecture may not run efficiently on other architectures. Since performance is an outcome of the OpenACC program settings and compiler optimizations, it becomes necessary to understand how each program setting and optimization performs on each target architecture, in order to reason about performance portability. To this end, we use various optimizations instrumented in our

OpenARC [9] compiler to measure these trade-offs empirically. Then, using OpenARC's auto-tuning system, we obtain the best performing application configuration on each architecture. Next, to evaluate the OpenACC performance portability, we perform a cross-comparison experiment using the best performing application configuration for application/architecture pair against the other architectures. In the process, we highlight the effects of important program settings and compiler optimizations on each architecture, which, in turn, provide insights on realized performance.

To summarize, we make the following contributions:

- We evaluate the performance portability of the OpenACC programming model across NVIDIA GPUs, AMD GPUs, and Intel Xeon Phi coprocessor architectures on 12 OpenACC applications in an effort to understand the effects of various OpenACC program settings and compiler optimizations.
- From this evidence, we highlight the role of specific optimizations for individual architectural features, and provide a performance portability matrix showing the potential benefits (or costs) of highly-optimized applications.

The remainder of this paper is organized as follows: Sect. 2 gives a brief introduction to the target architectures and OpenACC programming model. Section 3 describes the OpenARC compiler framework. Section 4 evaluates performance portability of OpenACC. We conclude our work and present our future plan in Sect. 5.

2   Background

2.1   Target Architectures

We now briefly describe the architectural details of NVIDIA's Kepler GPUs, AMD's Graphics Core Next (GCN) GPUs and Intel Xeon Phi (MIC) Coprocessors. The high-performing cards of all these architectures come with their own device memories. Since their primary focus is on achieving massive parallelism, they resort to simpler in-order cores. On Kepler, the individual cores are distributed across Streaming Multiprocessors. GCN distributes them across Compute Units. Being evolved as GPUs, Kepler and GCN provide texture memories that can be used for caching read-only data. Kepler and GCN rely upon the underlying runtime to perform SIMD operations. On the other hand, being evolved from CPU cores, the wider SIMD units on MIC enable it to obtain its peak performance. The compiler has to perform vectorization to make use of the SIMD units on MIC, unless SIMD intrinsics are explicitly inserted by programmers. SIMD width on GCN and MIC is 16, while on CUDA, it is 32 (warp size). MIC distributes parallelism across cores; each core runs four hardware threads. Despite being a coprocessor, MIC runs an Operating System that handles the thread scheduling. Table 1 provides further comparative details of these architectures.

Table 1. Comparison of heterogeneous architectures

Property	CUDA	GCN	MIC
Programming models	CUDA, OpenCL	OpenCL, C++ AMP	OpenCL, Cilk, TBB, LEO, OpenMP
Thread scheduling	Hardware	Hardware	Software
Programmer managed cache	Yes	Yes	No
Global synchronization	No	No	Yes
L2 Cache type	Shared	Private per core	Private per core
L2 Total size	Upto 1.5 MB	Upto 0.5 MB	25 MB
L2 Line-size	128	64	64
L1 Data cache	Read-only + Read-write	Read-only	Read-write
Native mode	No	No	Yes

2.2 OpenACC Programming Model

The OpenACC [11] programming model provides a high-level, functionally portable programming approach for accelerators. It requires the programmer to insert directives, or, *pragmas*, on the compute-intensive parallel regions that can be offloaded to an accelerator. Optionally, the programmer can also prescribe the data movements between the CPU and the accelerator.

In general, many OpenACC constructs are similar to those of OpenMP. A major distinguishing factor is the parallelism deployment. While OpenMP supports just a single level, OpenACC parallelism manifests in three levels. (The offloading model in the latest version of OpenMP (V4.0) supports multi-level parallelism similar to OpenACC, but existing compilers do not support the offloading model yet.) A parallel section can be split into gangs, which can further be split into workers, which can in turn control vectors. The presence of multiple levels helps in making use of the massive parallelism in the heterogeneous architectures. Secondly, these levels make it easier to map the parallelism to different architectures, e.g., in CUDA, the gangs can be mapped to thread-blocks and workers can be mapped to threads of a threadblock. OpenACC allows the programmer to write a code without explicit memory transfer clauses, but for enhancing the performance, programmer can provide additional clauses, such as data copy-in and copy-out.

3   Overview of OpenARC Framework

OpenARC [9] is an open-source compiler framework for C-based OpenACC programs. It is built on top of Cetus [4] infrastructure, a C-based source-to-source translation framework. The OpenARC Intermediate Representation (IR) [2] is

Table 2. Optimizations performed by OpenARC (Partial list)

Optimization	Architecture
Data transfer optimization	Common
Parallel loop swap	Common
Tree-based reduction generation	Common
Aligned memory access generation	Common
Loop unrolling	Common
Texture memory loading	CUDA
Automatic shared memory loading	CUDA, GCN
Pitched memory allocation	CUDA

Table 3. OpenACC program settings that affect performance

Setting	Description
Num_gangs	Number of gangs that operate on a parallel region
Num_workers	Number of worker threads that belong to a gang
num_vectors	Number of vector threads that belong to a worker[a]
1D blocking	Using a single parallel loop
2D blocking	Using nested parallel loops
Loop collapse	Collapse nested loops so as to increase the iteration space
Tiling	Tile the parallel loops to gain cache benefits
Data operations	Creation, destruction and copies

[a] OpenARC currently does not support *vectors*, as most CUDA/OpenCL devices support only two-level parallelism.

derived from the very high-level, human-readable IR of Cetus. OpenARC currently supports OpenACC version 1.0, and some features of version 2.0a [11]. Current OpenARC version supports three architectures, namely, NVIDIA CUDA GPUs, AMD GPUs and Intel Xeon Phi coprocessors.

3.1 Compiler and Runtime

OpenARC compiler is a source-to-source translation system. It translates the input OpenACC program into a CUDA program for NVIDIA CUDA GPUs, and into OpenCL programs for AMD GCN GPUs and Intel MICs. OpenARC contains a runtime system that handles offloading of code sections on the accelerators and maintains data mappings between the CPU and accelerators.

The compiler, along with the runtime system support brings out certain optimizations as shown in Table 2. While some optimizations are architecture-dependent, others are common.

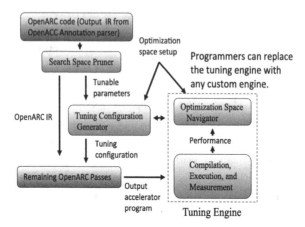

Fig. 1. A built-in OpenARC tuning framework. The figure shows that the tuning-related passes are invoked after the OpenACC annotation parser in the overall compilation flows.

3.2 Automatic Tuning

Apart from compiler instrumented optimizations, programmer-specified program settings can affect the performance of an OpenACC program. Table 3 shows a description of such program settings. The programmer must choose the suitable program settings and compiler optimizations to obtain high performance. Due to a large search space, the task of tuning an OpenACC program is a non-trivial. OpenARC compiler therefore assists the programmer by providing an automatic tuning system, as shown in Fig. 1. The overall tuning process is as follows:

(1) *Search Space Pruner* automatically prunes the exponential search space by choosing certain compiler optimizations and program settings that can affect the program performance. (2) With the resultant compiler optimizations and program settings, *Tuning Configuration Generator* generates all possible program configurations, each containing different compiler optimizations and program settings. These configurations guide the rest of the OpenARC compilation passes to generate configuration-specific output accelerator programs. (3) Then, the *Tuning Engine* compiles and executes these code variants to find the best performing configuration. Note that the best performing configuration is specific to a given program on a given architecture.

4   Performance Portability Evaluation

In this section, we evaluate the performance portability of OpenACC. To do so, we analyse the effects of different program settings and compiler optimizations on different architectures. With an automatic tuning system provided by OpenARC, we find the best performing configurations on each architecture, and analyse how these configurations perform on other architectures.

Table 4. System setup used in the evaluation

Accelerator	Card	Host CPU	Driver	OS	Memory
NVIDIA CUDA	GTX 680 (Kepler)	Intel Xeon E5520, 4 cores, 8 threads	CUDA 5.0, OpenCL 1.1	Scientific Linux 6.4	12 GB
AMD GPU	Radeon HD 7970 (GCN)	2 ×Intel Xeon E5520, 4 cores, 8 threads	OpenCL 1.2	Scientific Linux 6.4	12 GB
Intel Xeon Phi	Knights Corner (MIC)	2 ×Intel Xeon E5-2670, 8 cores, 16 threads	OpenCL 1.2	CentOS 6.2	256 GB

4.1   Experimental Setup

Table 4 describes the system setup used for this evaluation. We use twelve OpenACC programs in the evaluation, which were manually ported from OpenMP. *JACOBI* , *LAPLACE, MATMUL* and *SPMUL* are four kernels, while *SRAD, HOTSPOT, NW, LUD, BFS, BACKPROP, KMEANS* and *CFD* are applications from the Rodinia benchmark suite [3]. These OpenACC programs were automatically ported to three different architectures (CUDA, GCN, and MIC) by the OpenARC compiler. Table 5 describes the input sizes used for the evaluation. The focus of our evaluation is to provide insights into the architectural aspects of OpenACC portability, but not to compare the performance of individual architectures. We first describe the effects of various program settings and compiler optimizations on different architectures, which evaluates their performance portability. We next present results of the achieved overall OpenACC performance portability.

Table 5. Benchmarks - input specification

Benchmark	Input	Benchmark	Input
JACOBI	grid: 8192 × 8192, 10 iterations	LAPLACE	grid: 8192 × 8192, 1000 iterations
MATMUL	matrix size 4096 × 4096	SPMUL	kkt_power
SRAD	grid : 4096 × 4096	HOTSPOT	gird 4096 × 4096
NW	Matrix size : 4096	LUD	Matrix size : 2048
BACKPROP	Input weights : 655360	KMEANS	819200 data points
CFD	232K elements	BFS	No. of nodes : 16 million

4.2   Arranging OpenACC Parallelism

In this section, we describe how the arrangement of parallelism impacts performance in OpenACC programs with nested parallel loops. To do so, we use three different versions. 1D and 2D versions are similar to the ones shown in listings 1.1 and 1.2. The third version uses the loop collapsing clause, which essentially provides a larger iteration space to exploit more parallelism.

Listing 1.1. Single-level (1D) Parallel Version of Jacobi

```
#pragma acc parallel num_gangs(1024) num_workers(64)
{
    #pragma acc loop gang worker
    for (j = 1; j <= SIZE; j++) {
        for (i = 1; i <= SIZE; i++)
            a[i][j] = (b[i - 1][j] + b[i + 1][j]
                + b[i][j - 1] + b[i][j + 1]) / 4.0f;
    }
}
```

Listing 1.2. Two-level (2D) Parallel Version of Jacobi

```
#pragma acc parallel num_gangs(1024) num_workers(64)
{
    #pragma acc loop gang
    for (i = 1; i <= SIZE; i++) {
        #pragma acc loop worker
        for (j = 1; j <= SIZE; j++)
            a[i][j] = (b[i - 1][j] + b[i + 1][j]
                + b[i][j - 1] + b[i][j + 1]) / 4.0f;
    }
}
```

Figures 2, 3 and 4 depict the performance of 1D, 2D and loop collapsed program versions when the number of workers is varied on three benchmarks that contain nested parallel loops. The execution times for a benchmark are normalized with respect to the best execution time of the corresponding benchmark on a target architecture. In these experiments, the number of gangs was fixed to a large constant number (1024), and the number of workers was varied. Figure 2 shows the effects of such variation on CUDA, while Fig. 3 shows the effects on GCN. For both these architectures, if the number of workers used is low (i.e. 8 or 16), the performance is poor owing to the resource underutilization, since the SIMD width on CUDA is 32, while on GCN, it is 16. Since the outer parallel loop in these benchmarks has a high iteration count, parallelizing only the outer loop can suffice, especially if the loop body is small, e.g., in the *JACOBI* benchmark. On *JACOBI*, 1D and 2D versions perform almost equivalently on both GCN and CUDA. However, if the loop body is bigger, which is the case in *SRAD* and *HOTSPOT* benchmarks, the 1D versions perform poorer, compared to the 2D and collapsed versions. Resource underutilization is the reason for this behavior. As an example, consider the case with 1024 gangs and 16 workers, leading to 16384 total threads. In the 1D version, since only the outer loop is parallelized, 4096 iterations of *SRAD* would be scheduled on 16384 threads, with only the first 4096 threads performing useful work. This leads to resource underutilization. Note that on all these benchmarks, as the no. of workers grows large, the execution times saturate on CUDA and GCN. A deviating behavior to this observation is the performance of 1D *HOTSPOT* with 512 workers, on the GCN architecture - the higher number of workers leads to resource contention, resulting in poorer performance.

While the trends on the GPU architectures are almost similar, behavior on Intel MIC is quite different (Fig. 4). Notice that as the number of workers is increased, 1D versions perform much worse, while the 2D versions maintain the same performance. This unintuitive behavior is explained due to the software-thread management that MIC employs. At the beginning of execution, 240 threads are launched by the MIC driver, owing to the presence of 240 hardware threads. OpenCL workgroups are scheduled on these threads at runtime. When 16 workers are used, with 1024 gangs, to distribute 8192 iterations of the *JACOBI* kernel's outer loop, the total threads, as seen by the OpenACC programmer, are $1024 \times 16 = 16384$. Since the loop iteration count is less than this number, only the first 8192 threads would perform useful work. The first 8192 threads are placed in $8192/16 = 512$ workgroups (gangs), which in turn run on

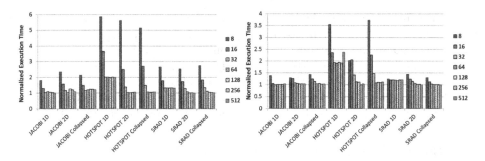

Fig. 2. NVIDIA CUDA   **Fig. 3.** AMD GCN

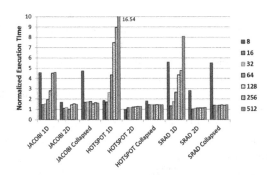

Fig. 4. Intel MIC

240 software threads, leading to a considerably good performance. However, if the number of workers is 512, then only the first $8192/512 = 16$ workgroups would be placed on the 240 software threads, leading to a huge resource under-utilization. So, despite of the number of workgroups being high, as suggested by the Intel OpenCL guide [6], the performance can be low, depending upon the workgroup size. In the 2D case, however, the outer loop of 8192 iterations is always split across 1024 gangs, leading to every workgroup performing useful work. Therefore, on MIC, for 1D versions, the lower the number of workers, better is the performance. Note however that when the number of workers falls below 16 (SIMD width on MIC), the performance reduces due to the lack of vectorization. Intel compiler performs scalarization of the kernel in such cases.

4.3 Effects of Memory Access Coalescing

Most heterogeneous architectures display enhanced performance if consecutive threads access consecutive memory locations in a parallel program. Loop ordering has a high impact on determining the nature of memory accesses. Loop interchange is therefore a primary optimization on heterogeneous architectures [8]. Figure 5 shows effects of such contiguous memory accesses on three benchmarks, *JACOBI*, *HOTSPOT* and *SRAD*. These benchmarks work on a grid, and accesses are made primarily to the neighboring elements. To measure the memory effects, we manually interchanged the loop order to obtain two versions. First version consisted of consecutive threads accessing contiguous elements in a matrix row (coalesced accesses). The second one did so for contiguous elements in a matrix column (non-coalesced accesses). It can be clearly observed from Fig. 5 that coalesced accesses are crucial to high-performance on all accelerators. The performance impact is relatively less on MIC, owing to its large L2 cache (25 MB).

4.4   Effects of Aligned Memory Accesses

Because all tested accelerators are based on SIMD architectures, their memory interfaces are most efficient when data are accessed in an aligned manner. Misaligned accesses will incur unrequested data being transferred, but the amount of the unnecessarily transferred data differs in each architecture. Moreover, the additional data may be used by later threads through L2 cache, having a prefetching effect. Therefore, the overall penalty of the misaligned accesses may not be statically predictable. Figure 6 shows the effects of the aligned memory accesses on both regular (*MATADD* - a synthetic kernel demonstrating regular, continuous accesses) and irregular (*SPMUL*) benchmarks, where input data for misaligned versions are manually padded and shifted, and corresponding array index expressions are also shifted accordingly. The results indicate that memory access alignment have noticeable performance impact on programs with regular, continuous access patterns (*MATADD*), but less important than memory coalescing, as shown in Fig. 5. To verify the prefetching effect through L2 cache, we created no-caching versions of the translated CUDA programs by manually modifying PTX codes to bypass L2 cache (*CUDA (no-HW caching)*). Comparing caching versions (*CUDA*) with no-caching versions (*CUDA(no-HW caching)*) suggests that aligned accesses are less important in architectures with hardware caching, due to prefetching effects. The figure also shows that MIC has different behavior than CUDA and GCN; on MIC, irregular programs (*SPMUL*) may also have some benefits from aligned accesses due to large L2 caches. The abnormal performance drop *MATADD2D* is caused by too much prefetching; profiling results show that MIC performs more aggressive hardware prefetching (a built-in hardware feature in MIC) on aligned version of *MATADD2D*, but that causes more L2 cache conflicts, incurring more L2 cache misses.

4.5   Tiling Transformation

The traditional tiling transformation is intended at increasing the temporal locality of data. It does so by blocking the computation and working on one block at a time, so that this block can fit in the cache. The transformation comprises loop stripmining, followed by loop interchange. OpenACC standard version 2.0 supports tiling with an additional clause that can be placed on loops.

Figure 8 shows the performance impact of tiling on *JACOBI* and *MATMUL* kernels for three different tile sizes. Tile sizes used are 32×32, 64×64, 128×128, respectively, except for *MATMUL* on MIC where they were 64×2, 64×4 and

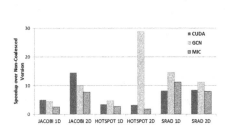

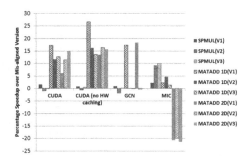

Fig. 5. Memory coalescing benefits on different architectures: MIC is impacted the least by the non-coalesced accesses

Fig. 6. Benefits of aligned memory accesses on different architectures, where each benchmark is configured with different thread mappings. (The number of gangs decreases in v1, v2, and v3 order, while the number of workers is fixed.)

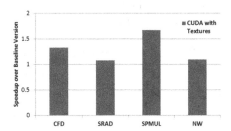

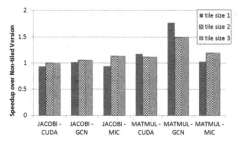

Fig. 7. Effects of caching read-only data on texture memory in CUDA

Fig. 8. Impact of tiling transformation: *MATMUL* shows higher benefits than *JACOBI* owing to more contiguous accesses

64×8. Since all these architectures have a relatively small L1 cache, which is shared among many gangs, tiling can fail to provide performance benefits owing to the unpredictable cache accesses made by different gangs. However, on L2 cache, due to its larger size, we could observe a reduction in misses, resulting in performance improvements. The performance benefits are larger in *MATMUL* than in *JACOBI* owing to a more regular access pattern. The stellar performance improvement (1.7x) was seen on GCN on *MATMUL*, with about 30 % reduction in cache misses. The overheads of tiling transformation include the extra loops and their corresponding conditions, which can outweigh caching benefits in certain cases. Using tiling transformation along with the programmer-managed cache can improve the tiling performance further.

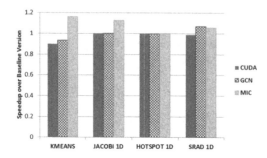

Fig. 9. Effects of loop unrolling - MIC shows benefits on unrolling

4.6   Exploiting Device-Specific Memories

In order to maintain generality, the OpenACC standard fails to provide constructs to make use of device-specific memories, like textures, on CUDA and AMD GPUs. To atone for this limitation, the OpenARC compiler can automatically detect the presence of read-only data structures and can place these data elements on device-specific memories. Figure 7 shows the performance effects of placing read-only data structures on CUDA texture memory on four benchmarks, namely, *CFD*, *SRAD*, *SPMUL* and *NW*. The performance gain can be as high as 67 % due to the utilization of texture memory.

4.7   Loop Unrolling

Loop unrolling is a common compiler optimization. By unwinding the loop body, the overhead of index calculation and branching can be reduced. With the help of OpenARC, we unrolled the loops inside kernel regions by various factors and analysed the effects. Figure 9 shows the unrolling effects on four different benchmarks, which contained loops inside kernel bodies. The largest benefits are seen on MIC, with the speed-up being as high as 17 %. We observed that on CUDA, the underlying nvcc compiler performs unrolling itself, leading to no performance benefits due to further unrolling.

4.8   Performance Portability Evaluation Using OpenARC Auto-Tuning

We now evaluate the achieved OpenACC performance portability by our compiler and runtime system. To do so, we execute the best performing program configuration of one architecture on other architectures and compare the obtained performance with the best possible performance that could be obtained on those architectures. We therefore must generate the best performing configuration of every benchmark on each architecture. We generate these program configurations, which consist of program settings and compiler optimizations, using the OpenARC tuning system.

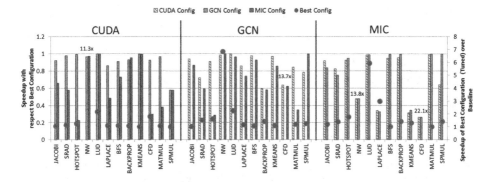

Fig. 10. Performance portability evaluation: best performing OpenACC program on one architecture may not produce best performance on another architecture. Tuning can be highly beneficial over the baseline translated codes.

Figure 10 displays the cross-architecture performance comparison of the individual benchmarks. The results on the left are run on CUDA, the ones in the middle are run on GCN, while the rightmost ones are run on MIC. On CUDA, for a given benchmark, we found out the best configuration through the tuning system, and then compared its performance against the best configuration of the same benchmark on GCN and MIC architectures. The process was repeated for GCN and MIC. Figure 11 shows the performance portability achieved across all benchmarks. The numbers in this figure are calculated by taking a geometric mean of the speedups achieved by every benchmark in Fig. 10. Each entry in the box represents the percentage of the best performance achieved on the corresponding architecture. The primary reasons for the performance gap were seen to be: (i) parallelism arrangement, (ii) usage of device-specific memories, and (iii) other architecture-specific optimizations, e.g., using pitched malloc on CUDA. It is worthwhile to note that the performance portability is higher among the GPU architectures. Note that the data transfer optimizations are completely architecture-independent for the evaluated devices; these optimizations, which optimize data allocations and transfers, are equally beneficial on all architectures.

The dots in Fig. 10 correspond to the secondary vertical axis (on the right). They display the performance improvement achieved by OpenARC automatic tuning over the baseline translated versions, for each benchmark on every architecture. The baseline versions are the default versions obtained from the compiler which uses heuristics to set the compiler options and program settings. The benefits of tuning are evident, with the maximum speedup being as high as 22x.

4.9 Performance Comparison Against Hand-Written Codes

We now present the performance comparison of hand-written CUDA/OpenCL programs against OpenARC generated versions on different architectures (Fig. 12). For this comparison, we used those benchmarks from Rodinia suite that provided

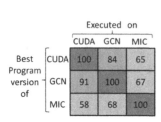

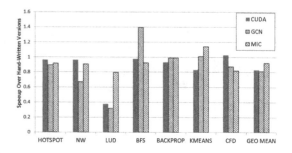

Fig. 11. Performance portability achieved across benchmarks: number in each box represents percentage of the best performance obtained

Fig. 12. Comparison of hand-written CUDA/OpenCL programs against auto-tuned OpenARC code versions. Tuned OpenACC programs perform reasonably well against hand-written codes

both CUDA and OpenCL versions. On benchmarks that benefit less from the programmer-managed caches, the performance of hand-written versions matches that of the OpenARC versions. Such benchmarks include *BFS*, *BACKPROP* and *CFD*. OpenARC version of *BFS* outperforms the hand-written OpenCL program due to the sub-optimal parallelism arrangement. In the case of *LUD* benchmark, which benefits highly due to the programmer-managed caches, the hand-written versions outperform since the automatic shared memory loading is not possible. However, since MIC lacks programmer-managed caches, OpenARC performs decently with respect to the hand-written OpenCL program on *LUD*. On *KMEANS*, OpenARC performs better than the hand-written code on MIC due to the compiler instrumented unrolling. The out-performance of *CFD* on CUDA is due to the automatic texture memory usage instrumented by OpenARC. The geometric mean bars in Fig. 12 indicate that OpenARC can reach 82 %, 81 % and 92 % of the hand-written codes' performance on CUDA, GCN and MIC architectures respectively.

5   Conclusion and Future Work

Programming models have remained a key obstacle in the widespread adoption of accelerators for general purpose computing. While different high-level programming models have been proposed, there has been a little understanding on the portability aspects of such models. This paper has tried to analyse the portability of one such programming model, OpenACC. The paper gauged the performance portability of the OpenACC programming model across three major accelerators: NVIDIA CUDA GPUs, AMD GCN GPUs, and Intel Xeon Phi Coprocessors (MIC). The evaluation was performed by running program configurations achieving the top performance on one architecture on another architecture to see if the top performance could be achieved. Our analysis shows that while code portability is achievable, performance portability eludes a common programming model, owing to the diversity in the architectures that necessitates architecture-specific optimizations. We are tackling this issue in our ongoing work. Our plan is to use automatic runtime-instrumentation to achieve performance portability across different architectures.

Acknowledgements. The paper has been authored by Oak Ridge National Laboratory, which is managed by UT-Battelle, LLC under Contract #DE-AC05-00OR22725 to the U.S. Government. Accordingly, the U.S. Government retains a non-exclusive, royalty-free license to publish or reproduce the published form of this contribution, or allow others to do so, for U.S. Government purposes. This research is sponsored by the Office of Advanced Scientific Computing Research in the U.S. Department of Energy. This research is sponsored by the Office of Advanced Scientific Computing Research in the U.S. Department of Energy.

References

1. The heterogeneous offload model for intel many integrated core architectures. http://software.intel.com/sites/default/files/article/326701/heterogeneous-progr-amming-model.pdf. Accessed 25 June 2014

2. OpenARC: Open Accelerator Research Compiler. http://ft.ornl.gov/research/openarc. Accessed 25 June 2014

3. Che, S., Boyer, M., Meng, J., Tarjan, D., Sheaffer, J.W., Ha Lee, S., Skadron, K.: Rodinia: a benchmark suite for heterogeneous computing. In: Proceedings of the IEEE International Symposium on Workload Characterization (IISWC) (2009)

4. Dave, C., Bae, H., Min, S.J., Lee, S., Eigenmann, R., Midkiff, S.: Cetus: a source-to-source compiler infrastructure for multicores. IEEE Comput. **42**(12), 36–42 (2009)

5. Han, T.D., Abdelrahman, T.S.: hiCUDA: a high-level directive-based language for GPU programming. In: GPGPU-2: Proceedings of 2nd Workshop on General Purpose Processing on Graphics Processing Units, pp. 52–61. ACM (2009)

6. Intel: OpenCL Design and Programming Guide for the Intel Xeon Phi Coprocessor. http://software.intel.com/en-us/articles/opencl-design-and-programming-guide-for-the-intel-xeon-phi-coprocessor. Accessed 25 June 2014

7. Lee, S., Eigenmann, R.: OpenMPC: extended OpenMP programming and tuning for GPUs. In: SC 2010: Proceedings of the 2010 ACM/IEEE Conference on Supercomputing. IEEE Press (2010)

8. Lee, S., Min, S.J., Eigenmann, R.: OpenMP to GPGPU: a compiler framework for automatic translation and optimization. In: ACM SIGPLAN Symposium on Principles and Practice of Parallel Programming (PPoPP), pp. 101–110. ACM, February 2009

9. Lee, S., Vetter, J.S.: Openarc: open accelerator research compiler for directive-based, efficient heterogeneous computing. In: Proceedings of the 23rd International Symposium on High-Performance Parallel and Distributed Computing, HPDC 2014, pp. 115–120. ACM, New York (2014). http://doi.acm.org/10.1145/2600212.2600704

10. NVIDIA: CUDA (2013). https://developer.nvidia.com/cuda-zone. Accessed 25 June 2014

11. OpenACC: OpenACC: directives for Accelerators (2011). http://www.openacc-standard.org. Accessed 25 June 2014

12. OpenCL: OpenCL (2013). http://www.khronos.org/opencl/. Accessed 25 June 2014
13. Ravi, N., Yang, Y., Bao, T., Chakradhar, S.: Apricot: an optimizing compiler and productivity tool for x86-compatible many-core coprocessors. In: Proceedings of the 26th ACM International Conference on Supercomputing, ICS 2012, pp. 47–58. ACM, New York (2012). http://doi.acm.org/10.1145/2304576.2304585
14. Spafford, K., Meredith, J.S., Lee, S., Li, D., Roth, P.C., Vetter, J.S.: The tradeoffs of fused memory hierarchies in heterogeneous architectures. In: ACM Computing Frontiers (CF). ACM, Cagliari (2012)
15. Vetter, J.S. (ed.): Contemporary High Performance Computing: From Petascale Toward Exascale. CRC Computational Science Series, vol. 1, 1st edn. Taylor and Francis, Boca Raton (2013)

NAS Parallel Benchmarks for GPGPUs Using a Directive-Based Programming Model

Rengan Xu$^{(\boxtimes)}$, Xiaonan Tian, Sunita Chandrasekaran, Yonghong Yan, and Barbara Chapman

Department of Computer Science, University of Houston, Houston, TX 77004, USA
{rxu6,xtian2,schandrasekaran,yyan3,bchapman}@uh.edu

Abstract. The broad adoption of accelerators boosts the interest in accelerator programming. Accelerators such as GPGPUs are optimized for throughput and offer high GFLOPS and memory bandwidth. CUDA has been adopted quite rapidly but it is proprietary and only applicable to GPUs, and the difficulty in writing efficient CUDA code has kindled the necessity to create higher-level programming approaches such as OpenACC. Directive-based programming models such as OpenMP and OpenACC offer programmers an option to rapidly create prototype applications by adding annotations to guide compiler optimizations. In this paper we study the effectiveness of a high-level directive based programming model, OpenACC, for parallelizing NAS Parallel Benchmarks (NPB) on GPGPUs. We present the application of techniques such as array privatization, memory coalescing, cache optimization and examine their impact on the performance of the benchmarks. The right choice or combination of techniques/hints are crucial for compilers to generate highly efficient codes tuned to a particular type of accelerator. Poorly selected choice or combination of techniques can lead to degraded performance. We also propose a new clause, 'scan', that handles scan operations for arbitrary input array size. We hope that the practices discussed in this paper will provide useful guidance to users to effectively migrate their sequential/CPU-parallel codes to GPGPU architectures and achieve optimal performance.

1 Introduction

Heterogeneous architectures that comprise of commodity CPU processors and computational accelerators such as GPGPUs have been increasingly adopted in both supercomputers and workstations/desktops for engineering and scientific computing. These architectures are able to provide massively parallel computing capabilities provided by accelerators while preserving the flexibilities of CPU accommodating computation of different workloads. However, effectively tapping their full potential is not straight-forward, largely due to the programmability challenges faced by users while mapping highly computation algorithms.

Programming models such as CUDA [7] and OpenCL [4] for GPGPUs offer users programming interfaces with execution models closely matching the GPU

© Springer International Publishing Switzerland 2015
J. Brodman and P. Tu (Eds.): LCPC 2014, LNCS 8967, pp. 67–81, 2015.
DOI: 10.1007/978-3-319-17473-0_5

architectures. Effectively using these interfaces for creating highly optimized applications require programmers to thoroughly understand the underlying architecture, as well as significantly change the program structures and algorithms. This affects both productivity and performance. Another approach that has been standardized are the high-level directive-based programming models, e.g. HMPP [14], OpenACC [3] and OpenMP [5]. These models require developers to insert directives and runtime calls into the existing source code, offloading portions of Fortran or C/C++ codes to be executed on accelerators.

Directives are high-level language constructs that programmers can use to provide useful hints to compilers to perform certain transformation and optimizations on the annotated code region. The use of directives can significantly improve programming productivity. Users can still achieve high performance of their program comparable to code written in CUDA or OpenCL, subjected to the requirements that a careful choice of directives and compiler optimization strategies are made. The choice of such strategies vary from one accelerator type to the other.

In this paper, we will discuss the parallelization strategies to port NAS Parallel Benchmarks (NPB) [10] to GPGPUs using high-level compiler directives, OpenACC. NPB are well recognized for evaluating current and emerging multi-core/many-core hardware architectures, characterizing parallel programming models and testing compiler implementations. The suite consists of five parallel kernels (IS, EP, CG, MG and FT) and three simulated computational fluid dynamics (CFD) applications (LU, SP and BT) derived from important classes of aerophysics applications. Together they mimic the computation and data movement characteristics of large scale computational CFD applications [10]. This is one of the standard benchmarks that is close to real world applications. We believe that the OpenACC programming techniques used in this paper can be applicable to other models such as OpenMP. Based on the application requirements, we will analyze the applicability of optimization strategies such as array privatization, memory coalescing and cache optimization. With vigorous experimental analysis, we will then analyze how the performance can be incrementally tuned.

The main contributions of this paper are:

- With GPUs as the target architecture, we highlight the critical techniques and practices required to parallelize benchmarks in NAS that are close to real-world applications.
- We analyze a number of choices and combinations of optimization techniques and study their impact on application performance. We learned that poorly selected options or using system default options for optimizations may lead to significant performance degradation. We share these findings in this paper.
- We also compare the performances of OpenACC NPB with that of the well-tuned OpenCL and CUDA versions of the benchmarks to present the reasoning behind the performance gap.

To the best of our knowledge, we are the first group to create an OpenACC benchmark suite for the C programs in NPB.

The organization of this paper is as follows: Sect. 2 provides an overview of GPU architecture and OpenACC. In Sect. 3 we discuss typical steps of parallelizing scientific application using OpenACC and some optimization techniques. Performance results are discussed in Sect. 4. Section 5 discusses the programmability and performance portability issues of using OpenACC. Section 6 highlights related work in this area. We conclude our work in Sect. 7.

2   GPU Architecture and OpenACC Directives

GPU architectures differ significantly from that of traditional processors. In this paper, GPU is always referred to **G**eneral **P**urpose **GPU**. Employing a Single Instruction Multiple Threads (SIMT) architecture, NVIDIA GPUs have hundreds of cores that can process thousands of software threads simultaneously. GPUs organize both hardware cores and software threads into two-level of parallelism. Hardware cores are organized into an array of SMs (Streaming Multiprocessors), each SM consisting of a number of core named as SPs (Scalar Processors). An execution of a computational kernel, e.g. CUDA kernel, will launch a set of (software) thread blocks. Each thread block can contain hundreds of threads. For programmers, the challenges to efficiently utilize the massive parallel capabilities of GPUs are to map the algorithms onto two-level thread hierarchy, and to lay out data on both the global memory and shared memory to maximize coalesced memory access for the threads. Using low-level programming models such as CUDA and OpenCL to do this has been known as not only time consuming but also the software created are not identical to its original algorithms significantly decreasing code readability.

Directive-based high-level programming models for accelerators, e.g. OpenACC and OpenMP accelerator extensions, have been created to address this programmability challenge of GPUs. Using these programming models, programmers insert compiler directives into a program to annotate portions of code to be offloaded onto accelerators for executions. This approach relies heavily on the compiler to generate efficient code for thread mapping and data layout. It could be potentially challenging to extract optimal performance using such an approach rather than using other explicit programming models. However, the model simplifies programming on heterogeneous systems thus saving development time, while also preserves the original code structure that helps in code portability. These models extend the host-centric parallel execution model for devices that reside in separate memory spaces. The execution model assumes that the main program runs on the host, while the compute-intensive regions of the main program are offloaded to the attached accelerator. The memory spaces on the host and the device are separate from one another. Host cannot access the device memory directly and vice versa.

OpenACC allows users to specify three levels of parallelism in a data parallel region: coarse-grain parallelism "gang", fine-grain parallelism "worker" and vector parallelism "vector", to map to the multiple-level thread hierarchy of GPUs. Mapping these three-level parallelism to the GPU threading structure will be left to the compiler and runtime systems, according to the hints given by the programmers. It can be a challenge for programmers, particularly on large programs with complex irregular data access pattern and thread synchronization.

There are already a number of compilers that provides support for OpenACC. Those include PGI, CAPS and Cray, open-source OpenACC compilers include accULL [22], OpenUH [24] and OpenARC [19]. Our focus in this paper is to use the NAS benchmarks to evaluate OpenACC support in our in-house OpenUH compiler.

3   Parallelization and Optimization Strategies

One of the main benefits of programming using a directive-based programming model is achieving performance by adding directives incrementally and creating portable modifications to an existing code. We consider the OpenMP version of NPB benchmarks as the starting point. Steps to parallelize legacy code using OpenACC are:

(1) Profile the application to find the compute intensive parts, which are usually loops.
(2) Determine whether the compute intensive loops can be executed in parallel. If not, perform necessary code transformations to make the loops parallelizable, if possible.
(3) Prepend `parallel/kernels` directives to these loops. The `kernels` directive indicates that the loop needs to be executed on the accelerator. Using the `parallel` directive alone will cause the threads to run the annotated code block redundantly, until a `loop` directive is encountered. The `parallel` directive is mostly effective for non-loop statements.
(4) Add `data` directives for data movement between the host and the device. This directive should be used with care to avoid redundant data movement, e.g. putting `data` directives across multiple compute regions. Inside the data region, if the host or device needs some data at the end of one compute region, `update host` directive could be used to synchronize the corresponding data from the device to host, or `update device` directive is used if the device needs some data from the host.
(5) Optimize data structures and array access pattern to efficiently use the device memory. For instance, accessing data in the global memory in a coalesced way, i.e. consecutive threads should access consecutive memory address. This may require some loop optimizations like loop permutation, or transforming the data layout that will change the memory access pattern.
(6) Apply loop scheduling tuning. Most of the OpenACC compilers provide some feedback during compilation informing users about how a loop is scheduled. If the user finds the default loop scheduling not optimal, the user should optimize the loop manually by adding more `loop` directives. This should lead to improvement in speedup.

```
for(k=0; k<N; k++){              for(k=0; k<N; k++){
    for(j=0; j<N; j++){             for(j=0; j<N; j++){
        for(i=0; i<N; i++){            for(i=0; i<N; i++){
            A[j][i] = ...                 AX[k][j][i] = ...
        }                             }
    }                             }
}                             }
```

Fig. 1. Array privatization example

(7) Use other advanced optimizations such as the `cache` directive, which defines the variables to be cached by the kernel. Usage of the `async` clause will initiate data movement operations and kernel execution as asynchronous activities, thus enabling an overlap with continuous execution by the host CPU.

Some of the above steps need to be applied repeatedly along with profiling and feedback information provided by compiler and profilers. The practices and optimization techniques applied vary depending on the original parallel pattern and code structures of an application. Some of those techniques are summarized in the following sections. While these techniques have been used for optimizing parallel program on CPUs, applying them on GPUs pose different challenges, particularly when using them in large code bases.

3.1 Array Privatization

Array privatization makes different threads access distinct memory addresses, so that different threads do not access the same memory address. It is a technique of taking some data that is common or shared among parallel tasks and duplicating it so that different parallel tasks can have a private copy to operate. Figure 1 shows an example for array privatization. If we parallelize the triple-nested loop on the left side of the figure using OpenMP for CPU and only parallelize the outermost loop, each thread handles the inner two loops. The array A could be annotated as OpenMP `private` clause to each thread, thus no modification is required to keep the memory usage minimal and improve the cache performance. However this is not the case with OpenACC. In OpenACC, if the compiler still only parallelizes the outermost loop, multiple threads will be reading and writing to the same elements of the array A. This will cause data race conditions, incorrect results and potential crashes. An option here is to use the OpenACC `private` clause which is described in [6]. However, if the number of threads is very large, as typically in GPUs, it is very easy that all copies of the array exceed the total memory available. Even though sometimes the required memory does not exceed the available device memory, it is possible that the assigned number of threads is larger than the number of loop iterations, and in this case some of the device memory will be wasted since some threads are idle. Also the life time of variable within a `private` clause is only for a single kernel instance. This limits our choice to apply loop scheduling techniques since only the outermost loop can be parallelized. If the triple nested loop can be parallelized and each

```
      #pragma acc kernels loop gang
80:   for (k = 0; k <= grid_points[2]-1; k++) {
        #pragma acc loop worker
81:     for (j = 0; j <= grid_points[1]-1; j++) {
          #pragma acc loop vector
82:       for (i = 0; i <= grid_points[0]-1; i++) {
83:         for (m = 0; m < 5; m++) {
84:             rhs[m][k][j][i] = forcing[m][k][j][i];
85:         }
86:       }
87:     }
88:   }
```

Fig. 2. Loop scheduling example

thread executes the innermost statements, thousands of threads still need to be created. Keeping the array A private to each thread will easily cause an overflow of memory available on the accelerator device. The right side of Fig. 1 shows the array privatized code that addresses this issue. This solution added another dimension to the original array so that all threads can access different memory addresses of the data and no data race will happen anymore.

3.2   Loop Scheduling Tuning

When parallelizing loops using OpenACC, `parallel/kernels` directives are inserted around the loop region. With the `parallel` directive, the user can explicitly specify how the loop is scheduled by setting whether the loop is scheduled in the level of `gang`, `worker` or `vector`. With the `kernels` directive, however, loop scheduling is usually left to the compiler's discretion. Ideally, the compiler performs loop analysis and determines an optimal loop scheduling strategy. Our simple experiments show that, when using the `kernels` directive, the compiler makes good choices most of the times. But the compiler often opts for the less efficient loop scheduling when the loop level is more than three. Figure 2 shows one of the scheduling techniques that delivers efficient loop scheduling. However the default scheduling by some compiler only applies to the loops in lines 82 and 83. The loops in line 80 and 81 are executed sequentially. This default option is very inefficient since the two outer most loops are not parallelized. Work in [24] discusses other loop scheduling mechanisms that could be applied in this context.

3.3   Memory Coalescing Optimization

The speedup from the parallel processing capability of GPU can be tremendous if memory coalescing is efficiently achieved. GPU has faster memory with unique data fetching and locality mechanism. In CPU, only one thread fetches consecutive memory data into the cache line, so the data locality is limited to only one thread. In GPU, however, consecutive threads fetch consecutive memory data into the cache line allowing better data locality. For instance, the code in Fig. 2 is already optimized for memory coalescing. The i loop is vectorized with the rightmost dimension of *rhs* and *forcing* is *i*. In the original serial code version, the memory access pattern of *rhs* and *forcing* are rhs[k][j][i][m] and forcing[k][j][i][m], respectively. But for memory coalescing purposes, we need to reorganize the data layout so that the dimension "m" is not on the farther right. Since C language is row-major, the right most dimension is contiguous in memory. We need the threads to access (i.e. the vector loop) the right most dimension. So after data layout reorganization, the memory access pattern becomes rhs[m][k][j][i] and forcing[m][k][j][i].

3.4 Data Motion Optimization

Data transfer overhead is one of the important factors to consider when determining whether it is worthwhile to accelerate a workload on accelerators. Most of the NPB benchmarks consist of many global variables that persist throughout the entire program. An option to reduce data transfer will be to allocate the memory for those global variables at the beginning of the program so that those data reside on the device until the end of the program. Since some portion of the code cannot be ported to the device, we could use **update** directive to synchronize the data between the host and device.

3.5 Cache Optimization

NVIDIA Kepler GPU memory hierarchy has several levels of memory, including global memory, then L2 cache for all SMs and the registers, L1 cache, shared memory and read-only data cache for each SM. In Kepler GPU, L1 cache is reserved only for local memory accesses such as register spilling and stack data. Global loads are cached in L2 cache only [8]. Here the usage of both L1 and L2 is controlled by the hardware and they are not manageable by the programmer. The shared memory can be utilized by the **cache** directive in OpenACC. Although the read-only data cache is also controlled by the hardware, the programmer can give some hints in the CUDA kernel file to tell the compiler what the read-only data list is. Since the read-only data cache is a device specific memory, OpenACC does not have any directive to utilize this cache. However, when the user specifies the device type when using OpenACC, the compiler can perform some optimizations specific to the specified device. We implemented this optimization in the compiler used so that the compiler can automatically determine the read-only data in a kernel by scanning all data in that kernel and then add "const __restrict__" for all read-only data and add "__restrict__" for other data that has no pointer alias issue. These prefix are required in CUDA if the user wants the hardware to cache the read-only data [8]. This compiler optimization can improve the performance significantly if the read-only data is heavily reused.

3.6 Array Reduction Optimization

Array reduction means every element of an array needs to do reduction. This is supported in OpenACC specification which only supports scalar reduction.

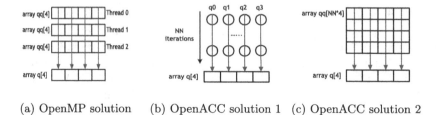

(a) OpenMP solution   (b) OpenACC solution 1   (c) OpenACC solution 2

Fig. 3. Solutions of array reduction in EP benchmark.

Different programming models solve this issue differently. As shown in Fig. 3, there are several ways to solve the array reduction in array q in EP benchmark. In the OpenMP version, each thread has its own private array qq to store the partial count of q, for the purpose of reducing the overhead of atomic update of shared variables. Thus, each thread only needs to perform an atomic update on q with its own partial sum qq. Since OpenACC does not support array reduction, Lee et al. [20] decomposes the array reduction into a set of scalar reductions which is shown in Fig. 3(b). This implementation is not scalable as it cannot handle large array reduction, and the size of the result array must be known at compile time. Our solution, as shown in Fig. 3(c), uses the array privatization technique to make a copy of q and expand it by another dimension with size NN (declared as new variable qq). In this way, each thread does its own work independently and writes the result into its own portion of the global memory. Finally, each element of q can be obtained by doing reduction just once with qq.

3.7   Scan Operation Optimization

The NAS IS benchmark has both inclusive and exclusive prefix-sum/scan operations. The inclusive scan takes a binary operator $\oplus$ and an array of N elements $[a_0, a_1, \ldots, a_{N-1}]$ and returns the array $[a_0, (a_0 \oplus a_1), \ldots, (a_0 \oplus a_1 \oplus \ldots \oplus a_{N-1})]$. Exclusive scan is defined similarly but shifts the output and uses an identity value I as the first element. The output array is $[I, a_0, (a_0 \oplus a_1), \ldots, (a_0 \oplus a_1 \oplus \ldots \oplus a_{N-2})]$. In scan loop, an element in the output array depends on its previous element, and because of such data dependence, it cannot be parallelized by the `loop` directive in OpenACC. To overcome such limitations, we provided some extensions to the OpenACC standard. We introduced a new `scan` clause to the `loop` directive followed by usage of recursive algorithm in [17] to handle the scan operation for arbitrary input array size. We implemented this optimization in OpenUH compiler.

4   Performance Evaluation

The experimental setup is a machine with 16 cores Intel Xeon x86_64 CPU with 32 GB main memory, and an NVIDIA Kepler GPU card (K20) with 5 GB global

Table 1. Comparing elapsed time for NPB-ACC, NPB-SER, NPB-OCL and NPB-CUDA (time in seconds), "-" implies no result due to "out ofmemory" issue. For NPB-CUDA, only LU, BT and SP are accessible. Data size increases from A to C, ~16x size increase from each of the previous classes. The "Techniques Applied" numbers refer to the optimizations described in corresponding sections. Other than listed techniques, we have optimized all of our OpenACC implementations including using data motion optimizations as well.

Benchmark	EP			CG			FT			IS		
Data size	A	B	C	A	B	C	A	B	C	A	B	C
NPB-SER	46.56	187.02	752.03	2.04	101.80	269.96	6.97	79.42	390.35	0.99	4.04	17.00
NPB-OCL	0.27	0.82	2.73	0.36	13.42	35.39	1.49	32.55	-	0.04	0.35	1.74
NPB-ACC	0.49	1.96	7.85	0.36	9.51	21.28	1.18	9.20	-	0.06	0.23	1.94
Techniques applied	3.1, 3.3, 3.6			3.5			3.1, 3.3			3.7		
Benchmark	MG			LU			BT			SP		
Data size	A	B	C	A	B	C	A	B	C	A	B	C
NPB-SER	2.57	11.48	99.39	60.38	264.71	1178.97	93.14	387.51	1626.33	52.17	225.26	929.85
NPB-OCL	0.13	0.61	5.48	5.32	16.70	54.88	46.12	167.48	-	11.84	54.35	288.40
NPB-ACC	0.24	1.12	7.55	6.64	26.12	103.97	15.25	63.61	226.70	3.45	15.90	57.46
NPB-CUDA	-	-	-	5.79	19.58	75.06	13.08	53.46	216.98	2.47	11.17	43.16
Techniques applied	3.1, 3.2, 3.5			3,1, 3.3, 3.5			3,1, 3,2, 3.3, 3.5			3,1, 3.2, 3.3		

memory. We use OpenUH compiler to evaluate the performance of C programs of NPB on GPUs. This open source compiler provides support for OpenACC 1.0 at the time of writing this paper. Although implementations for OpenACC 2.0 are beginning to exist, they are not robust enough to be used to evaluate NPB-type benchmarks. For evaluation purposes, we compare the performances of our OpenACC programs with serial and third-party well tuned OpenCL [23] and CUDA programs [1] (that we had access to) of the NAS benchmarks. All OpenCL benchmarks run on GPU rather than CPU. We used GCC 4.4.7 and -O3 flag for optimization purposes. The CUDA version used by the OpenACC compiler is CUDA 5.5. The OpenCL codes are compiled by GCC compiler and link to CUDA OpenCL library.

Table 1 shows the execution time taken by NPB-SER, NPB-OCL and NPB-ACC, which are the serial, OpenCL and OpenACC versions of the NPB benchmarks, respectively. For the FT benchmark, OpenCL and OpenACC could not execute for problem size Class C. The reason being, FT is memory limited; the Kepler card in use ran out of memory. Same to do with the OpenCL program for BT benchmark. However this was not the case with OpenACC. The reason being: OpenCL allocated the device memory for all the data needed in the beginning of the application. With OpenACC program, different solver routines have different memory coalescing requirements, as a result, different routines have different data layout. For those data, OpenACC program only allocates the device memory in the beginning of the solver routines and frees the device memory before exiting these routines. This explains that the data in the OpenCL program are active throughout the full application, but for the OpenACC program,

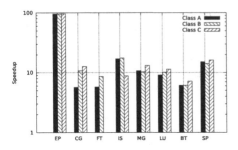

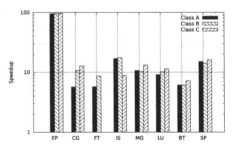

Fig. 4. NPB-ACC speedup over NPB-SER

Fig. 5. NPB-ACC Performance improvement after optimization

some data is only active in some of the routines, hence saving the total memory requirement at a given time.

Figure 4 shows the speedup of NPB-ACC over NPB-SER for the benchmarks that have been optimized. It is quite clear that all the benchmarks show significant speedup, especially EP. This is because EP is an embarrasingly parallel benchmark that has only few data transfers and our optimization technique enabled all the memory accesses to be nicely coalesced. Most of the benchmarks observed increase in speedup as the data problem size increased, except IS. This is because, IS uses buckets to sort an input integer array, the value of the bucket size is fixed as defined in the benchmark, no matter what the data size is. As a result, when the data size becomes larger, the contention to each bucket becomes more intense decreasing the performance to quite an extent. However this does not affect the numerical correctness due to atomic operations in place to prevent data races.

We measure the effectiveness of the potential optimizations applied in Fig. 5 by comparing the baseline and the optimized versions of the benchmarks. The baseline versions use only array privatization in order to parallelize the code and data motion optimization to eliminate unnecessary data transfer overhead and not any other optimizations discussed. The optimized versions exploit the optimizations discussed earlier.

IS benchmark demonstrates much improvement from the baseline version. This is due to the *scan* operation discussed earlier. CG mainly benefits from cache optimization, the rest of the optimizations all seem to have a major impact on the benchmark's performance. FT benchmark shows improvement due to Array of Structure (AoS) to Structure of Array (SoA) transformation since the memory is not coalesced in AoS data layout but coalesced in SoA data layout. Note that the execution time of the three pseudo application benchmarks LU, BT and SP are even less than 20 % of the time taken by the baseline version. LU and BT observed over ∼50 % and ∼13 % of performance improvement using cache optimization, since both the benchmarks extensively use read-only data.

LU, BT and SP benchmarks benefit significantly from memory coalescing optimizations since in the serial code the memory access is not coalesced at all for GPU architecture. Memory coalescing requires explicit data layout transformation.

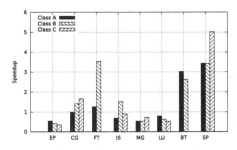

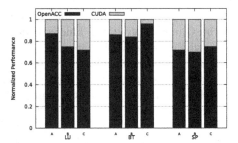

Fig. 6. NPB-ACC speedup over NPB-OCL

Fig. 7. NPB-ACC performance comparison with NPB-CUDA

We observed that tuning loop scheduling is very crucial for MG, BT and SP benchmarks since these benchmarks have three or more levels of nested loops. The compiler could not always identify the best loop scheduling option, requiring the user to intervene.

These analysis of benchmark results indicate that it is insufficient to simply insert directives to an application no matter how simple or complex it is. It is highly essential to explore optimization techniques, several of those discussed in this paper, to not only give the compiler adequate hints to perform the necessary transformations but also perform transformations that can exploit the target hardware efficiently.

To evaluate our optimizations further, we compare the NPB-ACC with well-tuned code written with the low-level languages OpenCL (NPB-OCL) and CUDA (NPB-CUDA). Figures 6 and 7 show the corresponding results. Figure 6 shows that the EP program using OpenACC is around 50 % slower than that of the OpenCL program. This is because the OpenACC version uses array privatization, which increases the device memory in turn exceeding the available memory limit. Therefore we use the blocking algorithm to move data chunk by chunk into the device. We launch the same kernel multiple times to process each data chunk. The OpenCL program, however, uses the shared memory in GPU and does not need to use array privatization to increase the GPU device memory, therefore it only needs to launch the kernel once. Faster memory access through shared memory and reduced overhead due to less number of kernel launches improved the results for OpenCL. Although OpenACC provides a `cache` directive that has similar functionalities to CUDA's shared memory, the implementation of this directive within OpenACC compiler is not technically mature enough yet. This is one of the potential areas where support in OpenACC can be improved.

Performance of OpenACC programs of benchmarks BT and SP are much better than that of the OpenCL programs. The reason is two-fold. First up, the OpenCL program does not apply the memory coalescing optimization; memory accesses are highly uncoalesced. Secondly, the program does not apply loop fission optimization; there are very large kernels. Although the large kernel contains many parallelizable loops, they are only executed sequentially inside the large kernel. On the contrary, the OpenACC program uses loop fission, thus breaking the large kernel into multiple smaller kernels and therefore exposing more parallelism.

The OpenACC program for benchmark MG appears to be slower than that of the OpenCL program. This is because former program uses array privatization, which needs to allocate the device memory dynamically in some routines, however the latter uses shared memory, which has faster memory access and no memory allocation overhead. The OpenACC program for benchmark FT is faster than OpenCL, since OpenACC transforms the AoS to SoA data layout to enable memory coalescing. The OpenACC program for benchmark LU is slower than OpenCL since the former privatizes small arrays into the GPU global memory, but OpenCL uses the small array inside the kernel as in they will be allocated in registers or possibly spilled to L1 cache. The memory access from either register or L1 cache is much faster than that from the global memory as used by OpenACC.

Figure 7 shows the normalized performance of NPB-ACC and NPB-CUDA. We found CUDA programs for only the pseudo applications, i.e. LU, BT and SP, hence we have only compared OpenACC results of these applications with CUDA. The result shows that OpenACC programs for LU, BT and SP benchmarks achieve $72\% - 87\%$, $86\% - 96\%$ and $72\% - 75\%$ to that of the CUDA programs, respectively. The range denotes results for problem sizes from CLASS A to C. We see that the performance gap between CUDA and OpenCL is quite small. The reasoning for the small performance gap is the same as that we have explained for the OpenCL LU benchmark. It is quite evident that careful choice of optimization techniques for high-level programming models can result in reaching performance very close to that of a well hand-written CUDA code. We believe that as the OpenACC standard and its implementation evolve, we might even be able to obtain better performance than CUDA. Thus successfully achieving portability as well.

5   Discussion

5.1   Programmability

Programming heterogeneous systems can be simplified using OpenACC-like directive-based approaches. An expected advantage is that they help maintain a single code base catering to multiple targets, leading to considerably lesser code maintenance. However, in order to achieve good performance, it is insufficient to simply insert annotations. The user's intervention is required to manually apply certain code transformations. This is because the compiler is not intelligent enough to determine the optimal loop scheduling for accelerated kernels and optimize the data movement automatically. With respect to memory coalescing requirement, currently there is no efficient mechanism to maintain different data layout for different devices, the user has to change the data layout. There is no compiler support that can effectively utilize the registers and shared memory in GPU that play an important role in GPUs. Data movement is one of the most important optimization techniques. So far it has been the user's responsibility to choose the necessary data clause and to move data around in order to get the best performance. If the compiler provides suitable hints, this technique can prove to be quite useful.

5.2 Performance Portability

Achieving performance portability can be quite tricky. Different architectures demand different programming requirements. Merely considering a CPU and a GPU; obtaining optimal performance from CPU largely depends on locality of references. This holds good for GPUs as well, but the locality mechanism of the two architectures are different. The amount of computation that a CPU and a GPU can handle also differs significantly. It is not possible to maintain a single code base for two different architectures unless the compiler automatically handles most of the optimizations internally. Performance portability is not only an issue with just the architecture, but also an issue that different compilers can provide a different implementation for a directive/clause. Moreover the quality of the compilation matters significantly. For example, the OpenACC standard allows the user to use either `parallel` or `kernels` in the compute region. The `kernels` directive allows the compiler to choose the loop scheduling technique to be applied i.e. analyze and schedule each loop level to `gang/worker/vector`. A compiler can use its own technique to schedule the loop nest to nested gang, worker and vector; this is typically not part of the programming model standard. As a result, the performance obtained using the `kernels` directive is different for different compilers. On the contrary, the code that uses `parallel loop` directive is more portable since this allows the user to have control over adopting the loop scheduling explicitly. Also the transformations of the `parallel` directive by most of the OpenACC compilers are similar.

6 Related Work

The performance of NPB benchmarks are well studied for conventional multi-core processor based clusters. Results in [18] show that OpenMP achieves good performance for a shared memory multi-processor. Other related works also include NPB implementations of High-Performance Fortran (HPF) [15], Unified Parallel C (UPC) [2] and OpenCL [23]. Pathscale ported an older version of NPB (NPB 2.3) using OpenACC [9], but only SP and IS could be compiled and executed successfully. Moreover their implementation of the benchmark, IS, does not use the challenging bucket sorting algorithm; this algorithm poses irregular memory access pattern challenges that is not straightforward to solve. However, we do use this sorting algorithm and overcome the challenges by using OpenACC's atomic and scan operation extensions. With high performance computing systems rapidly growing, hybrid programming models become a natural programming paradigm for developers to exploit hardware characteristics. Wu et al. [25] discuss a hybrid OpenMP + MPI version of SP and BT benchmarks. Pennycook et al. [21] describe the MPI + CUDA implementation of LU benchmark. The hybrid implementations commonly yield better performance if communication overhead is significant for MPI implementation and if computation for a single node is well parallelized with OpenMP. NAS-BT multi-zone benchmark was evaluated in [11] using OpenACC and OpenSHMEM hybrid model.

Grewe et al. [16] presented a compiler based approach that automatically translate OpenMP program to optimized OpenCL code for GPUs and they evaluated all benchmarks in NPB suite. Lee et al. [20] parallelized EP and CG from NPB suite using OpenACC, HMPP, CUDA and other models and compared the performance differences. But our implementation is different from theirs for these two benchmarks. Inspired by the similar subroutines of the benchmarks in NPB, Ding et al. [12,13] developed a tool that can conduct the source code syntactic similarity analysis for scientific benchmarks and applications.

7   Conclusion

This paper discusses practices and optimization techniques for parallelizing and optimizing NAS parallel benchmarks for GPGPU architecture using the OpenACC high-level programming model. We present performance and speedup obtained by using an open source OpenACC compiler. We believe these techniques can be generally applicable for other programming models and scientific applications. We also analyze the effectiveness of these optimizations and measure their impact on application performance. Poorly selected options or using system default options for optimizations may lead to significant performance degradation. We also compared the performance of OpenACC NPB with that of the well-tuned OpenCL and CUDA versions of the benchmarks. The results indicate we achieve performance close to that of the well-tuned programs. This shows that using high-level programming directives and with the right optimization techniques, we are not only achieving the much needed portability but also achieving performance close to that of well-tuned programs. We also investigated and implemented the scan and cache optimizations in the compiler used. As future work, we will identify strategies to automate optimizations that we have used in our compiler for better programmability and perhaps performance.

References

1. NPB-CUDA (2013). http://www.tu-chemnitz.de/informatik/PI/forschung/download/npb-gpu/
2. NPB-UPC (2013). http://threads.hpcl.gwu.edu/sites/npb-upc
3. OpenACC (2013). http://www.openacc-standard.org
4. OpenCL Standard (2013). http://www.khronos.org/opencl
5. OpenMP (2013). www.openmp.org
6. 11 Tricks for Maximizing Performance with OpenACC Directives in Fortran (2014). http://www.pgroup.com/resources/openacc_tips_fortran.htm
7. CUDA (2014). http://www.nvidia.com/object/cuda_home_new.html
8. CUDA C Programming Guide (2014). http://docs.nvidia.com/cuda/cuda-c-programming-guide/

9. Pathscale NPB2.3 OpenACC (2014). https://github.com/pathscale/NPB2.3-Open ACC-C
10. Bailey, D., et al.: The NAS Parallel Benchmarks. NASA Ames Research Center (1994)
11. Baker, M., Pophale, S., Vasnier, J.-C., Jin, H., Hernandez, O.: Hybrid programming using OpenSHMEM and OpenACC. In: Poole, S., Hernandez, O., Shamis, P. (eds.) OpenSHMEM 2014. LNCS, vol. 8356, pp. 74–89. Springer, Heidelberg (2014)
12. Ding, W., Hernandez, O., Chapman, B.: A similarity-based analysis tool for porting OpenMP applications. In: Keller, R., Kramer, D., Weiss, J.-P. (eds.) Facing the Multicore-Challenge III. LNCS, vol. 7686, pp. 13–24. Springer, Heidelberg (2013)
13. Ding, W., Hsu, C.-H., Hernandez, O., Chapman, B.M., Graham, R.L.: KLONOS: similarity-based planning tool support for porting scientific applications. Concurrency Comput. Pract. Experience **25**(8), 1072–1088 (2013)
14. Dolbeau, R., Bihan, S., Bodin, F.: HMPP: a hybrid multi-core parallel programming environment. In: Workshop on GPGPU (2007)
15. Frumkin, M., Jin, H., Yan, J.: Implementation of NAS parallel benchmarks in high performance fortran. NAS Techinical report NAS-98-009 (1998)
16. Grewe, D., Wang, Z., O'Boyle, M.F.: Portable mapping of data parallel programs to OpenCL for heterogeneous systems. In: 2013 IEEE/ACM International Symposium on CGO, pp. 1–10. IEEE (2013)
17. Harris, M., Sengupta, S., Owens, J.D.: Parallel prefix sum (scan) with CUDA. GPU Gems **3**(39), 851–876 (2007)
18. Jin, H., Frumkin, M., Yan, J.: The OpenMP implementation of NAS parallel benchmarks and its performance. Technical report, NAS-99-011, NASA Ames Research Center (1999)
19. Lee, S., Li, D., Vetter, J.S.: Interactive program debugging and optimization for directive-based, Efficient GPU Computing (2014)
20. Lee, S., Vetter, J.S.: Early evaluation of directive-based GPU programming models for productive exascale computing. In: SC 2012, pp. 23:1–23:11. IEEE Computer Society Press (2012)
21. Pennycook, S.J., Hammond, S.D., Jarvis, S.A., Mudalige, G.R.: Performance analysis of a hybrid MPI/CUDA implementation of the NAS LU benchmark. ACM SIGMETRICS Perform. Eval. Rev. **38**(4), 23–29 (2011)
22. Reyes, R., López-Rodríguez, I., Fumero, J.J., de Sande, F.: accULL: an OpenACC implementation with CUDA and OpenCL support. In: Kaklamanis, C., Papatheodorou, T., Spirakis, P.G. (eds.) Euro-Par 2012. LNCS, vol. 7484, pp. 871–882. Springer, Heidelberg (2012)
23. Seo, S., Jo, G., Lee, J.: Performance characterization of the NAS parallel benchmarks in OpenCL. In: IEEE International Symposium on IISWC, pp. 137–148. IEEE (2011)
24. Tian, X., Xu, R., Yan, Y., Yun, Z., Chandrasekaran, S., Chapman, B.: Compiling a high-level directive-based programming model for GPGPUs. In: Caşcaval, C., Montesinos-Ortego, P. (eds.) LCPC 2013 - Testing. LNCS, vol. 8664, pp. 105–120. Springer, Heidelberg (2014)
25. Wu, X., Taylor, V.: Performance characteristics of hybrid MPI/OpenMP implementations of NAS parallel benchmarks SP and BT on large-scale multicore clusters. Comput. J. **55**(2), 154–167 (2012)

Understanding Co-run Degradations on Integrated Heterogeneous Processors

Qi Zhu[1]([✉]), Bo Wu[2], Xipeng Shen[3], Li Shen[1], and Zhiying Wang[1]

[1] National Key Laboratory of High Performance Computing,
National University of Defense Technology, Changsha Hunan 410073, China
{qizhu,lishen,zywang}@nudt.edu.cn
[2] EECS, Colorado School of Mines, Golden, CO 80401, USA
bwu@mines.edu
[3] Department of Computer Science, North Carolina State University,
Raleigh, NC 27695, USA
xshen5@ncsu.edu

Abstract. Co-runs of independent applications on systems with heterogeneous processors are common (data centers, mobile devices, etc.). There has been limited understanding on the influence of co-runners on such systems. The previous studys on this topic are on simulators with limited settings.

In this work, we conduct a comprehensive investigation of the performance of co-running jobs on integrated heterogeneous processors. The investigation produces a list of interesting and counter-intuitive findings. It reveals some critical design issues in modern operating systems in supporting heterogeneous processors, and suggests some potential solutions at the levels of program transformation and OS design.

Keywords: Heterogeneous architecture · Performance analysis · CPU and memory contention · Optimization · GPGPU

1 Introduction

Recent years have seen a trend in processor development towards integrated heterogeneity, in which, CPU and Graphic Processing Units (GPU) are integrated into a single chip. Examples include Fusion processors from AMD and Ivy Bridge processors from Intel. The GPU in such systems is often called integrated GPU (iGPU). The integration is a double-edged sword. On one hand, it removes the need for data copying from the host memory to the GPU memory as discrete heterogeneous systems (e.g., NVIDIA Tesla GPU) require. The removal is appealing as such data copying usually goes through PCI-e interface, the limited bandwidth of which often throttles the benefits of co-processors substantially.

But on the other hand, the integration also deepens resource sharing between CPU and iGPU and hence intensifies their interplay. For instance, on an Ivy Bridge processor, the CPU and iGPU in a chip share the last level cache (LLC),

© Springer International Publishing Switzerland 2015
J. Brodman and P. Tu (Eds.): LCPC 2014, LNCS 8967, pp. 82–97, 2015.
DOI: 10.1007/978-3-319-17473-0_6

memory bus, and main memory. The sharing may lead to much severe co-run contention. The execution of a program on CPU may affect the performance of a co-running GPU program by polluting the cache or consuming the memory bus bandwidth, and vice versa. Understanding the influence of co-run contention is important for job scheduling, especially in a multi-programming system (e.g., data centerns and smartphones). Even though many prior studies have explored co-run contention in multicore CPUs [1–3,6–10], it has not been systematically studied on integrated heterogeneous processors. For the massive parallelism of GPU and its special execution models, co-run contentions on integrated processors could differ substantially from those on traditional multicore systems, in both degree and properties. For instance, when one memory access instruction is executed on a GPU, many memory access requests are issued at the same time from many threads, which intensifies the memory bus usage, but at the same time offers the opportunity for hiding the access latency by overlapping operations among threads. Results presented later in this paper confirm the large disparity between the co-run influences.

Recent years have seen some work on effectively utilizing both CPU and GPU [11–14], but they are all about job partition: mapping different portions of a single program to the computing elements for load balance rather than treating co-run contentions. An exception is a recent study by Grewe et al. [12], who built a machine learning model that considers GPU contention in job partition. But the contention they consider is actually time sharing of iGPU between different kernels, rather than the interplay between concurrently running tasks on CPU and iGPU. The only work we find directly on co-run contention between CPU and iGPU is by Mekkat et al. [15], who proposed a LLC management to alleviate co-run degradations in integrated heterogeneous processors. However, their study was conducted in a processor simulator. Later sections of this paper will show that there is a large disparity between what we observe on actual systems and their results and assumptions.

Overall, there is a lack of a comprehensive understanding of co-run contention on integrated heterogeneous processors; there are some important questions remaining open. How much performance degradation could be caused by the contention? Does the influence differ significantly on CPU and iGPU? What potential does scheduling have for alleviating the contention?

This paper presents a study trying to answer those questions through a set of systematic measurement on modern systems, a careful analysis, and a scheduling experiment for confirmation. We focus on co-runs of multiple independent programs rather than different portions of a single program, because the latter has been studied by many previous works [11–14] while the former has not. In Sect. 2, we describe our experiment settings on Intel IvyBridge.

The measurement results, reported in Sect. 3, leads to a set of observations. Some contradict the perceptions made in previous studies on simulators, and some contradict general intuitions. Examples include

– Prior studies [15] assume that iGPU, because of the benefits of its massive parallelism for hiding access latency, is less sensitive to co-run contentions

than CPU is in performance. But our measurement shows the opposite. On average, iGPU is subject to performance degradations by as much as several times—sometimes, orders of magnitude—more than CPU is.
- Prior studies on simulators focus on primarily the influence of memory contention. However, our study finds that the primary factor for co-run degradations of iGPU is actually context switches between the host thread of a GPU program and the threads of other CPU workload. In most cases, the effects of memory contention is negligible compared to that of context switches.

We provide a careful analysis of the results, and explain the major observations. Section 2 discribes the experiment settings. The analysis reveals a number of important insights, listed in Sect. 3. Section 3 also provides the implications of these insights for maximizing the computing efficiency of integrated heterogeneous processors. Section 4 reports some optimizations and experimental results, demonstrating the large performance potential of leveraging those insights for alleviating co-run contention.

In summary, this work makes the following major contributions:

- To the best of our knowledge, this is the first systematic measurement of the influence of co-run contention on integrated heterogeneous processors.
- It contributes a set of observations and insights that are critical for effective utilization of integrated heterogeneous processors, and corrects some existing misperceptions.
- It points out promising directions to explore for solving the co-run degradations issues by revealing the large potential of two optimizations, namely kernel fusion and accelerator-conscious scheduling.

2   Exeperiment Settings

In order to get a conherence understanding, we evaluate the performance of co-running programs acrossing hardware and software platforms.

2.1   Hareware Platforms

A lot of hardware vendors including AMD, Intel and NVIDIA, have proposed their multi-core heterogeneous architecture, e.g. APU, Ivy Bridge, Mic and Denver. In this work, we take Ivy Bridge as the example of multi-core heterogeneous architecture, illustrated in Fig. 1.

The i7-3770k [4] is an implementation of Ivy Bridge. On one chip of i7-3770k there are four CPU cores of 3.5 GHz and one HD 4000 iGPU of 1.6 GHz. Because of the hyper-threading technology, the number of CPU cores is 8 from the user's perspective. The LLC of the processor, 8MB in size, is shared among the CPU cores and the iGPU. The cores of CPU and iGPU and the ports of LLC are connected by a structure called *ring bus*.

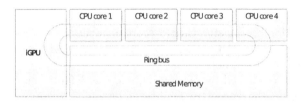

Fig. 1. Architecture of Ivy Bridge.

Table 1. Benchmarks

Name	Description
AESEncryptDecrypt (AESE)	AES for encryption and description
BinomialOption (Bino)	Modeling of price evolvement
Blackscholes (Blac)	Option pricing
DCT	Discrete Cosine Transform
Histogram (His)	Histogram construction
HistogramAtomics (HisA)	Histogram construction with atomic operations
MonteCarloAsian (Mont)	Monte Carlo simulation
RadixSort (Radi)	Radix sorting of numbers
SobelFilter (Sobe)	Sobel operator in edge detection
URNG	Image noise generation
BitonicSort (BS)	Bitonic sorting
FastWalshTransform (FWT)	Fast algorithm for WalshHadamard transform
FloydWarshall (FW)	Shortest path finding

2.2 OS, Driver, and Benchmark

Currently, on IvyBridge, only Intel OpenCL driver runs well and the OS must be Windows 7. We use AMD APP SDK [5] as the benchmark suite. As a carefully written set of benchmarks, the OpenCL SDK has been used in many prior studies. It consists of programs of a broad range of domains and computing patterns, and covers the key kernels used in many applications.

In this work, we co-run programs on differt platforms with each other to measure the performance degradation caused by contention. Table 1 lists the programs chosen from the AMD SDK. They are selected for the stableness of their performance across repetitive executions and their coverage of a variety of domains.

2.3 Timing Mechanisms

We employ two means for time measurement, named *host timer* and *device timer* respectively. The host timer starts right before a kernel gets enqueued for GPU to run, and stops when the GPU gives the notification of finished kernel execution.

It hence includes the time spent by the kernel itself, as well as the time to launch it and the delay for the master thread to realize the finish of the kernel. The device timer, on the other hand, is part of the OpenCL API and measures only the running time of the kernel.

To prevent biases caused by random noises, the default benchmarks contain a loop surrounding the kernel to facilitate repeated executions of the kernel for timing purpose. The number of iterations of the loop is set to 2000 in our experiments. The average time per iteration is used in our analysis.

3   Contention Analysis

We conduct all pair-wise co-runs of the programs. In each co-run, one of the OpenCL programs runs only on the multicore CPU, the execution of whose kernels utilizes all 8 CPU cores, while the other OpenCL program runs its kernels on the iGPU. We call them *CPU program* and *GPU program* respectively (even though they are both OpenCL programs that could run on both platforms). It is worth noting that by the default OpenCL execution model, the non-kernel parts of the GPU program still execute on CPU.

Our methodology for measuring co-run performance follows the practice that is common in prior co-run studies [17]. In measuring the performance of program A under co-runs with program B, we put program B into a infinite loop such that it continuously runs throughout the execution of program A. From now on, we call program A the *target program* or *the target*, and program B the *contender program* or the *contender*.

We next report the performance of the co-running programs measured by both the host timer and the device timer, which show some surprising performance degradations. We then provide a thorough analysis of the results and reveal some novel insights.

3.1   Counter-Intuitive Observations

Figure 2 shows the performance degradation of CPU programs when the contender runs on GPU. The baseline is their single-run performance on CPU, and the host timer is used. The X-axis indicates the names of the target programs and the Y-axis indicates the names of the contenders. The results show that most CPU programs are subject to minor performance degradations: 88 out of the 100 co-runs have degradation less than 5%. Program *DCT*, when co-running with *DCT* on GPU, exhibits the largest degradation, 14%.

In comparison, the degradations of GPU programs are much more significant. As Fig. 3 shows, compared to their single-run performance on GPU, the programs show dramatic performance degradations: 46 out of the 100 co-runs have degradation over 50%, with the maximum as much as 3976%.

The observations came in as a surprise. Prior studies [15] have argued that GPU is expected to be less sensitive than CPU is to co-run contentions: For its massive parallelism, GPU offers more opportunities than CPU for hiding memory

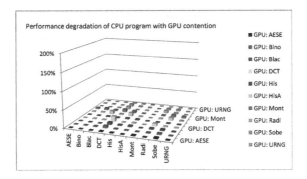

Fig. 2. Performance degradation of CPU programs with GPU contention (measured by host timer).

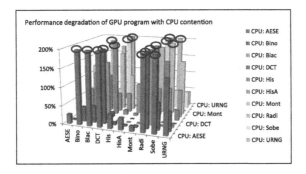

Fig. 3. Performance degradation of GPU programs with CPU contention (measured by host timer). The bars circled at the top have degradations over 200 %, detailed in Table 2.

Table 2. GPU programs with more than 200 % contention slowdown when running with CPU contenders

GPU_CPU	Bino_AESE	Blac_AESE	Blac_Mont	DCT_AESE	DCT_Bino	DCT_His
Slowdown	6.3x	7.0x	2.2x	20.1x	4.3x	10.1x
GPU_CPU	DCT_Sobe	DCT_URNG	Radi_AESE	Radi_Bino	Radi_Blac	Radi_His
Slowdown	4.2x	7.4x	39.8x	5.6x	2.8x	9.3x
GPU_CPU	Radi_Sobe	Radi_URNG	Sobe_AESE	Sobe_Mont	Sobe_URNG	-
Slowdown	6.1x	12.4x	8.4x	2.2x	2.0x	-

access latency by overlapping operations by different threads, and hence shall be more resilient to the memory system interferences caused by program co-runs. The argument is intuitive. But how to explain the observed results?

A Seemingly Reasonable but Actually Unsound Explanation. Our initially projected explanation is that due to the large memory footprint, memory accesses by GPU are easier to get evicted from cache. The negative effect somehow

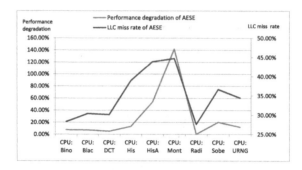

Fig. 4. The trends of LLC miss rate and performance degradation when AESE runs on GPU with other CPU programs running on CPU.

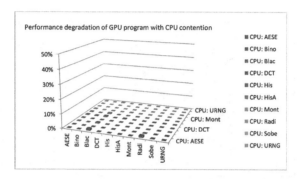

Fig. 5. Performance degradation of GPU programs with CPU contention (measured by device timer).

outweighs the effects of the communication overlapping. To confirm it, through hardware performance counters, we collect the miss rates of the last level cache (LLC) of some of the co-runs. Figure 4 shows the results of the co-runs of program AESE. The LLC curve exhibits similar trends as the co-run degradation curve.

It seems that all pieces of the puzzle fall into place—until we examined the performance reported by the device timer. As shown in Fig. 5, the co-runs do not lengthen the execution of the GPU kernels in any noticable degree for most programs. The largest co-run degradation appears on the kernels of program *Blac* while it co-runs with *AESE*, but the degradation is only as small as 2 %—a clear contrast with the up to 200 % degradations reported by the host timer. The results suggest that besides the contention in the memory systems, there is probably some other factor that is critical for explaining the large co-run degradations of GPU programs as measured by the host timer.

Demystification. Considering that a key difference between the two kinds of timers is the inclusion of the time to launch a kernel, we suspect that the primary factor for the large co-run degradation of GPU programs is the delay in launching kernels. Kernels are launched by the master CPU thread of the GPU program.

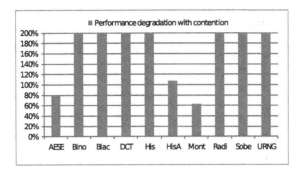

Fig. 6. The performance degradation of iGPU programs with contention of a mutex program.

In co-runs, the master thread time shares the CPU core with one of the threads of the contender program, the context switches incurred by which could trigger some delay in the kernel launches.

To verify the hypothesis, we conduct two measurements. First, we create a contender program that has the minimum memory footprint and hence incurs the minimum interference to the memory accesses by the GPU program. The contender program contains a mutex lock shared by all worker threads. No unlock operation exits in the microbenchmark. Therefore, if one worker thread gets the lock, all other workers start busy-waiting for the lock, keeping accessing just the same memory address. As Fig. 6 reports, the target GPU programs exhibit large slowdown, comparable to the slowdown observed in Fig. 3. Given that in these co-runs, the memory interference is minimal but the context switches are substantial, the results agree with our hypothesis.

Our second measurement directly examines the correlations between the numbers of context switches and the co-run degradations. Through the Performance Monitor of Windows 7, we collect the number of context switches when a GPU program runs with different contenders and with no contender. Figure 7 reports that a strong correlation exists between the numbers and the co-run degradations. Figure 7 shows the results on the first four benchmarks (others have similar trends, ommitted for legibility). Each curve is obtained in this way: We first sort all the (average context switch numbers per second, co-run degradations) tuples collected in all the co-runs of the program in an increasing order of the number of context switches. We then connect them together. Except for several local fluctuations, a clear monotonic increasing trend manifest in all the curves, indicating the strong correlations between context switches and co-run degradations.

Fine-grained timing further shows that the main delay is between the time when the kernel finishes and the resumption of the host thread. Because most GPU kernels are short (but repeated invoked), the delay casts a significant effect on the overall running time of those GPU programs. The differences of the co-run degradations of those GPU programs align well with the length of the kernels in those programs: The shorter the kernel is, typically the larger the co-run degradation is.

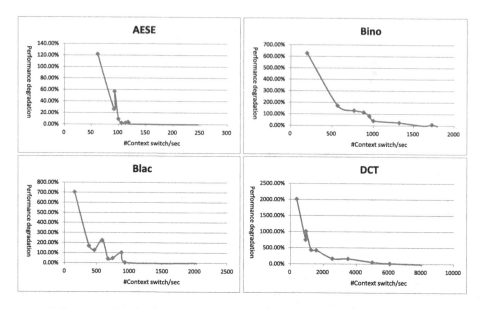

Fig. 7. The relationship between the number of context switches and the co-run degradations of GPU programs.

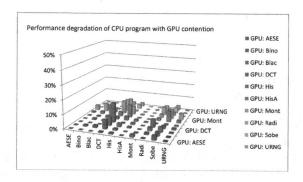

Fig. 8. Performance degradation of CPU programs with GPU contention (measured by device timer).

In addition to the two measurements, we tried to reduce the number of context switches through adjustment to the schedulers in the operating system. The results further validate that context switch is the primary reason for the co-run degradations. Details are given in the next section.

For completeness, Fig. 8 shows the co-run degradations of the CPU programs measured with the device timer. The results are not much different from those reported by the host timer. The context switch affects only one CPU thread, and does not have a large impact on the CPU program overall Performance. The degradations on CPU are mainly caused by the memory contention.

4 Optimizations

In this section, we explor the potential of two optimizations for alleviating the co-run degradations of GPU programs.

4.1 Kernel Fusion

Kernel fusion is a transformation that fuses two or more GPU kernel functions into one. It has been explored in previous studies [19–21], but mainly for the purpose of reducing data copying between CPU and GPU. On integrated GPU, CPU and GPU share the same address space and hence the saving of the data copy becomes irrelevant. In this work, we exploit this method to reduce the influence of context switches. The idea is that the fused code would require fewer kernel launches than the original and hence become less affected by the delay caused by the context switches. We are not aware of such a usage of kernel fusion in prior studies.

A barrier for fusing two kernels is the difficulty for global synchronization on GPU. A launch of a GPU kernel usually creates a large number of threads. Only part of them are active at one time point, the others have to wait till they are finished to get started running. So in the default execution mode of a GPU program, there is no way to synchronize all threads before the termination of the kernel execution.

But global synchronizations are sometimes necessary for kernel fusion. If the two kernel functions to fuse have data dependences, simply putting them into one could cause dependence violations and hence jeopardize the correctness of the execution; a global synchronization between them would ensure a correct execution order.

We circumvent the difficulty by leveraging the idea of *persistent threads* [22–25]. Persistent threads are a small number of threads that are created such that all of them can run simultaneuously on GPU. Since they are all active at the same time, a global synchronization among them is easy to enable through a shared variable in the global memory. With it, fusing multiple kernels becomes straightforward.

A limitation of kernel fusion is the limited number of kernels to fuse on some GPU programs. Among the AMD SDK benchmark, we find that kernel fusion is applicable to only some of them as others contains only one kernel. We manually applied kernel fusion to them. Table 3 lists their names, input parameters and numbers of kernels. We experiment with multiple inputs for each program as the number of kernels to fuse depends on the inputs.

Figure 9 reports the performance results. The contender program is *AESE*. On all four programs, the fusion dramatically reduces the co-run degradations. The benefits are consitently substantial across inputs.

4.2 Accelerator-Conscious Priority Control

Although kernel fusion helps the four programs substantially, its applicability is limited. In this part, we aim to explore the potential of scheduling control, a more general solution.

Table 3. The description of programs appling Kernel Combination.

Name	Input parameter	Number of kernels
Redixsort	16384	8
	32768	8
	65536	8
	131072	8
BitonicSort	1024	55
	2048	66
	4096	78
	8192	91
FastWalshTransform	512	9
	1024	10
	2048	11
	4096	12
FloydWarshall	64	64
	128	128
	256	256
	512	512

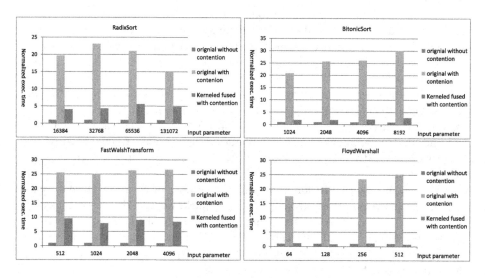

Fig. 9. Running time normalized by the time of the original benchmark's single runs.

Windows documentation shows that the default scheduling policy is round-robin (RR). In order to schedule processes fairly, RR generally employs time-sharing, giving each job a time slot or quantum (time slice), and interrupting the job if it is not completed by then. The job is resumed next time a time slice

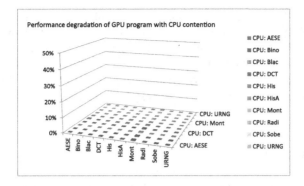

Fig. 10. The performance degradaton of GPU program with contention after accelerator-couscious priority control.

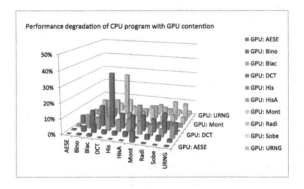

Fig. 11. The performance degradaton of CPU program with contention after accelerator-couscious priority control.

is assigned to that process. The scheduling is relatively fair for co-running CPU programs, but not for GPU programs as shown by the orders of magnitude larger slowdown of GPU programs than CPU programs as reported earlier.

In this work, we attempt to add the consciousness of accelerators into the scheduling policy by assigning a higher level of priority of the process of the GPU program (through the API "SetThreadPriority"). On Windows, threads are scheduled in the RR fashion at each priority level, and only when there are no executable threads at a higher level does scheduling of threads at a lower level take place. Therefore, the GPU host thread with a higher priority will obtain the possession of the CPU core even if there is another CPU thread is running on the core. It minimizes the delay between the launches of two GPU kernels. The priority of GPU host thread is set as *THREAD_PRIORITY_HIGHEST* which is 2 points above the default setting *THREAD_PRIORITY_NORMAL* for the priority class. The performance degradation of GPU and CPU programs after the priority control is shown in Fig. 10. The host timer is used. The performance degradation of the GPU programs are removed almost completely.

It demonstrates the promise of the solution, and at the same time, further confirms that context switch is the major reason for the large slowdown.

We acknowledge that the priority adjustment could potentially cause some unfairness in some special settings. In addition, after the priority adjustment, the CPU programs exhibit slightly larger slowdown as Fig. 11 shows (in comparison to Fig. 2). A complete design of the accelerator-conscious scheduler is part of our future studies.

5   Related Work

The earlier sections have already covered a number of related studies. Here, we just give a brief overview of the works related with shared cache and co-scheduling. Cache sharing exists in both homogeneous and heterogeneous system. It has drawn a lot of research interest, especially in cache management and process/thread scheduling. In cache management, many different methods (e.g., [29–33]) have been introduced to design shared cache to strike a good tradeoff between the destructive and constructive effects of cache sharing on multicore CPU.

In process/thread scheduling, the main focus on shared cache has been job co-scheduling including thread clustering. Many job co-scheduling studies [6–10] are on homogeneous architectures, attempting to alleviate shared-cache contention by placing independent jobs appropriately. Mars et al. propose "Whare-Map" [28] to exploit heterogeneity in Warehouse-Scale Computers and deploy programs on different machine according to the already in-place continuous profiling subsystems found in production environments. To the best of our knowledge, this current paper provides the first systematic study on the co-run degradations of CPU and GPU programs on integrated GPUs.

6   Conclusion

In this work, we conduct the first comprehensive investigation of the performance of co-running jobs on integrated heterogeneous processors. The investigation produces some novel findings and insights. For the first time, it points out the important role of context switch in affecting the co-run performance of GPU programs. It reveals some critical design issues in modern operating systems. It explores the potential of two kinds of optimizations, kernel fusion and accelerator-conscious priority control. Both significantly improve the computing efficiency on integrated heterogeneous processors, with the latter being more generally applicable. This study lays the foundation for future research towards maximizing the whole-system synergy on machines equipped with integrated accelerators.

Acknowledgments. We thank the reviewers for the helpful comments. This material is based upon work supported by DOE Early Career Award and the National Science

Foundation (NSF) under Grant No. 1320796 and CAREER Award. Any opinions, findings, and conclusions or recommendations expressed in this material are those of the authors and do not necessarily reflect the views of DOE or NSF. This work is also partially supported by 863 Program of China (2012AA010905), NSFC (61272144, 61272143) and NUDT/Hunan Innov. Fund. For PostGrad. (B120604, CX2012B029).

References

1. Markatos, E.P., LeBlanc, T.J.: Using processor affinity in loop scheduling on shared-memory multiprocessors. IEEE Trans. Parallel Distrib. Syst. **5**(4), 379–400 (1994)
2. Squillante, M.S., Lazowska, E.D.: Using processor-cache affinity information in shared-memory multiprocessor scheduling. IEEE Trans. Parallel Distrib. Syst. **4**(2), 131–143 (1993)
3. Gelado, I., Stone, J.E., Cabezas, J., et al.: An asymmetric distributed shared memory model for heterogeneous parallel systems. ACM SIGARCH Comput. Archit. News (ACM) **38**(1), 347–358 (2010)
4. George, V., Engineer, S.P., Piazza, T., et al.: Technology Insight: Intel Next Generation Microarchitecture Codename Ivy Bridge (2011)
5. Amd, APP SDK 2.4. http://developer.amd.com/amd-license-agreement/?f=AMD-APP-SDK-v2.4-Windows-64.exe
6. Jiang, Y., Shen, X., Chen, J., et al.: Analysis and approximation of optimal co-scheduling on chip multiprocessors. In: Proceedings of the 17th International Conference on Parallel Architectures and Compilation Techniques, pp. 220–229. ACM (2008)
7. Tian, K., Jiang, Y., Shen, X.: A study on optimally co-scheduling jobs of different lengths on chip multiprocessors. In: Proceedings of the 6th ACM Conference on Computing Frontiers, pp. 41–50. ACM (2009)
8. Jiang, Y., Tian, K., Shen, X.: Combining locality analysis with online proactive job co-scheduling in chip multiprocessors. In: Patt, Y.N., Foglia, P., Duesterwald, E., Faraboschi, P., Martorell, X. (eds.) HiPEAC 2010. LNCS, vol. 5952, pp. 201–215. Springer, Heidelberg (2010)
9. Fedorova, A., Seltzer, M., Smith, M.D.: Improving performance isolation on chip multiprocessors via an operating system scheduler. In: Proceedings of the 16th International Conference on Parallel Architecture and Compilation Techniques, pp. 25–38. IEEE Computer Society (2007)
10. El-Moursy, A., Garg, R., Albonesi, D.H., et al.: Compatible phase co-scheduling on a CMP of multi-threaded processors. In: Proceedings of the 20th International Parallel and Distributed Processing Symposium (IPDPS 2006), p. 10. IEEE (2006)
11. Grewe, D., Wang, Z., O'Boyle, M.F.P.: OpenCL task partitioning in the presence of GPU contention. In: Cascaval, C., Montesinos-Ortego, P. (eds.) LCPC 2013 - Testing. LNCS, vol. 8664, pp. 87–101. Springer, Heidelberg (2014)
12. Luk, C.K., Hong, S., Qilin, K.H.: Exploiting parallelism on heterogeneous multiprocessors with adaptive mapping. In: 42nd Annual IEEE/ACM International Symposium on Microarchitecture (MICRO-42), pp. 45–55. IEEE (2009)
13. Grewe, D., O'Boyle, M.F.P.: A static task partitioning approach for heterogeneous systems using OpenCL. In: Knoop, J. (ed.) CC 2011. LNCS, vol. 6601, pp. 286–305. Springer, Heidelberg (2011)

14. Ravi, V.T., Ma, W., Chiu, D., et al.: Compiler and runtime support for enabling generalized reduction computations on heterogeneous parallel configurations. In: Proceedings of the 24th ACM International Conference on Supercomputing, pp. 137–146. ACM (2010)

15. Mekkat, V., Holey, A., Yew, P.C., et al.: Managing shared last-level cache in a heterogeneous multicore processor. In: Proceedings of the 22nd International Conference on Parallel Architectures and Compilation Techniques, pp. 225–234. IEEE Press (2013)

16. Liu, Y., Zhang, E.Z., Shen, X.: A cross-input adaptive framework for GPU program optimizations. In: IEEE International Symposium on Parallel and Distributed Processing (IPDPS 2009), pp. 1–10. IEEE (2009)

17. Tuck, N., Tullsen, D.M.: Initial observations of the simultaneous multithreading Pentium 4 processor. In: Proceedings of the 12th International Conference on Parallel Architectures and Compilation Techniques (PACT 2003), pp. 26–34. IEEE (2003)

18. Ding, C., Zhong, Y.: Predicting whole-program locality through reuse distance analysis. ACM SIGPLAN Not. (ACM) **38**(5), 245–257 (2003)

19. Fousek, J., Filipovi, J., Madzin, M.: Automatic fusions of CUDA-GPU kernels for parallel map. ACM SIGARCH Comput. Archit. News **39**(4), 98–99 (2011)

20. Wang, G., Lin, Y.S., Yi, W.: Kernel fusion: an effective method for better power efficiency on multithreaded GPU. In: 2010 IEEE/ACM International Conference on Cyber, Physical and Social Computing (CPSCom), Green Computing and Communications (GreenCom), pp. 344–350. IEEE (2010)

21. Wu, H., Diamos, G., Wang, J., et al.: Optimizing data warehousing applications for GPUs using kernel fusion, fission. In: 2012 IEEE 26th International Parallel and Distributed Processing Symposium Workshops & PhD Forum (IPDPSW), pp. 2433–2442. IEEE (2012)

22. Aila, T., Laine, S.: Understanding the efficiency of ray traversal on GPUs. In: Proceedings of the Conference on High Performance Graphics, pp. 145–149. ACM (2009)

23. Chen, L., Villa, O., Krishnamoorthy, S., et al.: Dynamic load balancing on single- and multi-GPU systems. In: 2010 IEEE International Symposium on Parallel and Distributed Processing (IPDPS), pp. 1–12. IEEE (2010)

24. Gupta, K., Stuart, J.A., Owens, J.D.: A study of persistent threads style GPU programming for GPGPU workloads. In: Innovative Parallel Computing (InPar), pp. 1–14. IEEE (2012)

25. Xiao, S., Feng, W.: Inter-block GPU communication via fast barrier synchronization. In: 2010 IEEE International Symposium on Parallel and Distributed Processing (IPDPS), pp. 1–12. IEEE (2010)

26. http://unixhelp.ed.ac.uk/CGI/man-cgi?sched_setscheduler+2

27. Zahedi, S.M., Lee, B.C.: REF: resource elasticity fairness with sharing incentives for multiprocessors. In: Proceedings of the 19th International Conference on Architectural Support for Programming Languages and Operating Systems (ASPLOS) (2014)

28. Mars, J., Tang, L., Hundt, R.: Whare-Map: heterogeneity in homogeneous warehouse-scale computers. In: Proceedings of the 40th Annual International Symposium on Computer Architecture (ISCA), pp. 1–12 (2013)

29. Zhang, E.Z., Jiang, Y., Shen, X.: Does cache sharing on modern CMP matter to the performance of contemporary multithreaded programs? ACM Sigplan Not. (ACM) **45**(5), 203–212 (2010)

30. Chang, J., Sohi, G.S.: Cooperative cache partitioning for chip multiprocessors. In: Proceedings of the 21st Annual International Conference on Supercomputing, pp. 242–252. ACM (2007)
31. Rafique, N., Lim, W.T., Thottethodi, M.: Architectural support for operating system-driven CMP cache management. In: Proceedings of the 15th International Conference on Parallel Architectures and Compilation Techniques, pp. 2–12. ACM (2006)
32. Suh, G.E., Devadas, S., Rudolph, L.: A new memory monitoring scheme for memory-aware scheduling and partitioning. In: Proceedings of the Eighth International Symposium on High-Performance Computer Architecture, pp. 117–128. IEEE (2002)
33. Qureshi, M.K., Patt, Y.N.: Utility-based cache partitioning: a low-overhead, high-performance, runtime mechanism to partition shared caches. In: Proceedings of the 39th Annual IEEE/ACM International Symposium on Microarchitecture, pp. 423–432. IEEE Computer Society (2006)

Algorithms for Parallelism

Simultaneous Inspection: Hiding the Overhead of Inspector-Executor Style Dynamic Parallelization

Daniel Brinkers[(✉)], Ronald Veldema, and Michael Philippsen

Programming Systems Group, Friedrich-Alexander University Erlangen-Nürnberg
(FAU), Erlangen, Germany
{daniel.brinkers,ronald.veldema,michael.philippsen}@fau.de

Abstract. A common approach for dynamic parallelization of loops at runtime is the inspector-executor pattern. The inspector first runs the loop without any (side) effects to analyze whether there are data dependences that would prevent parallel execution. Only if no such dependences are found, does the executor phase actually run the loop iterations in parallel. In previous works, the overhead of the inspection must either be amortized by the parallel execution or is completely wasted if the loop turns out to be non-parallelizable.

In this paper we propose to run the inspection phase simultaneous to an instrumented sequential version of the loop. This way we can reduce and hide the overhead in case of a non-parallelizable loop. We discuss what needs to be done so that the sequentially executed iterations do not invalidate the inspector's concurrent work (in which case sequential execution is needed for the whole loop).

Our measurements show that if a loop cannot be executed in parallel there is an overhead below 1.6 % compared to the runtime of the original sequential loop. If the loop is parallelizable, we see speedups of up to a factor of 3.6 on a quad core processor.

1 Introduction

Processors no longer get faster on sequential code. Hence, to improve performance, we need to exploit parallelism, preferably from loops as most time is spent there. But loop parallelization has to be conservative as any data dependence between loop iterations may cause a race condition that prevents parallelization. A challenge are computed dependences, e.g., if a data structure is accessed with a level of indirection as in `A[B[i]]` or in linked data structures that allow duplicate elements (i.e., hash tables, maps, graphs). Pointer arithmetics or function pointers further complicate the programmer's (or the compiler's) analysis as it must conservatively include any address that may be accessed. Finally for functions called (directly or indirectly) from dynamically loaded libraries, the actual code to run is chosen at runtime instead of at compile-time, voiding any static compiler analysis unless the analysis works with an unrealistic "closed world assumption". Hence, for many loops it cannot be statically decided whether they

© Springer International Publishing Switzerland 2015
J. Brodman and P. Tu (Eds.): LCPC 2014, LNCS 8967, pp. 101–115, 2015.
DOI: 10.1007/978-3-319-17473-0_7

are parallelizable. Auto-parallelization can only be performed at runtime as only then all memory accesses and dependences can be resolved.

Most inspector-executor systems for loop parallelization work in two phases. When they dry-run a candidate loop in their first phase they avoid side effects by skipping I/O statements and by writing to (and reading from) a software cache that stores tuples of memory addresses and values instead of working on real application data. If a loop iteration reads from an address that another iteration has written to, there is a data dependence and the original loop must run sequentially. Without such and other cross-iteration data dependences the executor phase can run the loop iterations in parallel.

There is no widespread use of this technique as there are not enough parallelizable loops in general-purpose code, given the cost of the inspection. Assume that a loop's inspection takes time K and the sequential execution takes time S. For a parallelizable loop, the total execution time on Processors is $K + \frac{S}{P}$. As $K + \frac{S}{P} \ll S$ parallel execution can often amortiz the inspection cost K. But since in the non-parallelizable case it takes $K + S$, the cost is a show-stopper. Even though some auto-parallelization systems parallelize the inspector itself [10,13] the slowdown of $\frac{K}{P} + S$ for non-parallelizable loops is still prohibitive.

This paper achieves both a good performance for parallelizable loops and a low overhead for non-parallelizable loops. The proposed (parallel) inspector runs simultaneous to the sequential loop that already makes progress. Once the inspector finishes and determines that the loop is parallelizable, the sequential loop is halted and execution continues in parallel. Otherwise the non-parallelizable loop proceeds sequentially. Hence we try to hide the inspector's overhead for non-parallelizable loops and aim at $max(\frac{K}{P}, S)$ which is S in practice.

The sequential loop needs to be instrumented to detect cross-iteration dependences to memory that the dry-run of the concurrent inspectors would also touch. We keep the instrumentation overhead c low ($<1.6\%$ on benchmarks) and thus achieve a worst case runtime of $(1 + c) \cdot S$ for a non-parallelizable loop and $\frac{K}{P} + \frac{(1+c) \cdot S}{P}$ otherwise. This is better than a speculative execution of the unmodified sequential loop with a full rollback in case of a dependence.

Section 2 explains the new simultaneous inspector. Section 3 outlines the optimizations that make our implementation efficient. We remove superfluous access checks to memory locations and perform load balancing between the sequential iterations and the inspectors. Section 4 presents the performance of the system on benchmarks. Section 5 discusses related work before we conclude.

2   Inspection While Sequential Progress is Being Made

Due to the conditional assignment in Fig. 1 and also as there may be aliasing among the arrays in the C-like language that we use, it is statically unknown whether the loop is parallelizable, especially as there is indirect

```
1    for(int i = 0 .. 1000):
2        a[b[i]] = c[i] + 1;
3        if i == 50 : b[400] = 0;
```

Fig. 1. Non-parallelizable loop.

addressing. Below we first cover (a parallelized version of) traditional loop auto-parallelization. We then extend this to run simultaneously to the sequential loop.

2.1 Parallel Inspection as a Pre-processing Step

Figure 2 shows the transformation of the sample loop into a basic inspector-executor version. A `parfor` loop in our pseudo code runs all its iterations in parallel. A `par` block runs all of its comprised statements in parallel. After a `parfor` or `par` all changes to memory are made visible to all other threads. Single word reads and writes to main memory are atomic. The details of the parallelized inspection phase are described in [13] where we also present the bit operations that cut down on system cycles.

The code (conceptually) uses three global hash tables and three macros to do its work, see Fig. 3. `Reg` (short for 'registration') records the loop iteration that writes to an address, `written` tracks whether the current iteration has already written to an address before, and `epoch` records the logical time when the address was written to. By incrementing `time` before analyzing a loop there is no need to reset all data structures as we can identify outdated entries.

To simplify the explanation, let us ignore the `written` table for now. There are two situations that render a parallel execution of the loop illegal: (A) if an iteration reads from a memory address before or after another iteration writes to it (flow- or anti-dependence), and (B) if an iteration writes to a memory address that another iteration already wrote to (output-dependence).

The parallel inspector works in two phases. The *registration phase* registers in the `reg` hash table which loop index writes to which address. The `REG` macro

```
1   INIT ();
2
3   // inspector: registration
4   parfor(int i = 0 .. 1000) :
5       REG(i , &a[b[i]]);
6       if i == 50 : REG(i, &b[400]);
7
8   // inspector: checking
9   parfor(int i = 0 .. 1000):
10      CR(i , &c[i]); CR(i, &b[i]);
11      CW(i , &a[b[i]]);
12      if i == 50 : CW(i, &b[400]);
13
14  // executor
15  parfor(int i = 0 .. 1000) :
16      a[b[i]] = c[i] + 1;
17      if i == 50 : b[400] = 0;
18  goto end;
19
20  // sequential loop
21  sequential_loop:
22      kill_threads ();
23      for(int i = 0 .. 1000):
24          a[b[i]] = c[i] + 1;
25          if i == 50 : b[400] = 0;
26
27  end:
```

Fig. 2. Basic pre-processing inspector-executor for Fig. 1.

```
1   int reg [];
2   threadprivate bool written [];
3   int time = 0;
4   int epoch [];
5
6   def INIT () :
7       time++
8
9   def REG(i , addr) :
10      reg[hash(addr)] = i;
11      epoch[hash(addr)] = time;
12      written[hash(addr)] = false;
13
14  def CR(i , addr) :
15      a = hash(addr)
16      if time == epoch[a] :
17          if i != reg[a] :
18              goto sequential_loop;
19          if written[a] :
20              goto sequential_loop;
21
22  def CW(i , addr) :
23      a = hash(addr);
24      if i != reg[a] :
25          goto sequential_loop;
26      written[a] = true;
27
```

Fig. 3. Inspection macros.

in Fig. 3 also records in `epoch` the logical `time` of each write. Additionally, the `written` table entry is reset here to avoid a global initialization.

The *checking phase* finds loop carried dependences as follows. The `CR` macro of Fig. 3 finds the dependences of type A. If within the current epoch, `REG` has registered a different iteration count for an address that is now read, then there is a flow- or anti-dependence that disallows parallel execution. Entries of an earlier epoch are irrelevant. We discuss the racing issues later. The `CW` macro finds dependences of type B. If two iterations write to the same address, at least one of the checking threads finds the other iteration count in `reg`. When analyzing a write access, `CW` does not need to consult the `epoch` table as the prior *registration phase* has surely written the current `time` to the `epoch` table for that address. As soon as `CR` or `CW` find a dependence, the inspector jumps to the sequential loop (where `kill_threads` stops all other inspecting threads).

For the example of Fig. 1 assume non-aliasing arrays and unique values for `b[i]`. Only the conditional assignment causes a dependence as iteration 50 writes to `a[400]` that iteration 400 later reads. The *registration phase* adds (50, `&b[400]`) to the `reg` table. The *checking phase* for iteration 400 finds $50 \neq 400$ in `reg` and correctly flags the loop as non-parallelizable.

Let us now discuss the `written` table. Conceptually the inspector's dry-run must use a (software) cache to keep the values that a real execution would write to memory. Although in the running example line 2 updates `a[b[i]]`, the inspector was still correct even though it did not store updated values anywhere. The reason is that it did *not use* the updated values. But assume that the condition in line 3 would be `a[b[i]]==50` instead of `i==50`. Then the dry-run needs the updated value to decide which memory address to read and whether to inspect the branch. A (software) cache could provide this value.

Unfortunately, software caches are too costly. The `written` table is an efficient approximation. The idea is that a bit is set in `written` whenever a cache would hold an updated value for an address. If `CR` reads from an address that `CW` has written to before, there is a potential threat that either the control flow or the used address depends on an updated value. If another iteration had updated this value, it is a regular dependence of type A or B that is detected by means of `reg`. If, however, an iteration i had updated the value itself, then `reg` does not help as it only stores this iteration number i. With `written` the inspector can conservatively give up and flag the loop as non-parallelizable on such an *non-inspectable dependence* (type C). In the altered example, the iteration 50 that sets `a[b[i]]` in line 2, also sets the corresponding `written` bit. When it later *uses* `a[b[i]]` in the condition it finds its own iteration count in `reg`, which is ok. But the extra bit flags the type C dependence.[1] The bit vector is much faster than a software cache. But the price is that loops with un-inspectable dependences are flagged as non-parallelizable even if the updated value does not influence the control flow.

---

[1] Note that as inspectors do not modify memory, the dry-run does not set `b[400]` to 0. This tricks the inspector to work with a wrong `a[b[400]]`. But what matters is that the loop is flagged as non-parallelizable since the dependence on `&b[400]` is found instead.

The parallel registration and the parallel checking work on `reg` and `epoch` without any costly synchronization. But this does not affect correctness. While all parallel registration threads write the same values to the `epoch` tables, they may concurrently register the same address with different iteration counts in the `reg` table. Only one of those entries may survive. The subsequent *checking phase* detects such lost hash table updates because at least one of the checking threads finds the other iteration count in `reg`. As the *checking phase* only reads the `epoch` and `reg` table there are no races. The `written` bits are thread private and cannot cause any races.

2.2 Simultaneous Parallel Inspection

The novel idea of this paper is to run the (parallel) inspector while the sequential loop already starts to do real work on one core. As the sequential loop may change data that the concurrent inspectors read, it must be instrumented with the (REG, CR, CW) macros.

Figure 4 shows the (simplified) transformed code for a quad core that runs the sequential loop on one core and simultaneously assigns three threads to both the *registration* and the *checking phase*. The *head* strip of the sequential loop (lines 4–9) runs concurrently to the *registration phase*. It has added REG macros. The *middle* strip (lines 16–21) runs concurrently to the *checking phase*, with added new flavors of the CR and CW macros. Note that the if-statement is optimized away in some of the (par)for loops.

The simplified load balancing in Fig. 4 assumes that it takes the same time to execute and inspect a loop iteration. Section 3.2 will show how to better load-balance between the sequential loop and the parallel inspectors. In line 35, `kill_threads` now also terminates the sequential strip at some iteration *k* from where the final for-loop in line 36–38 continues if the loop is flagged as non-parallelizable.

```
1   INIT();
2   par:
3      // sequential head
4      for(k = 0 .. 250):
5         REG(k, &a[b[k]]);
6         a[b[k]] = c[k] + 1;
7         if k == 50 :
8            REG(k, &b[400]);
9            b[400] = 0;
10     // inspection: registration
11     parfor(i = 251 .. 1000):
12        REG(i, &a[b[i]]);
13        // if i == 50 : REG(i, &b[400]);
14  par:
15     // sequential middle m-iterations
16     for(k = 251 .. 500):
17        CR_STRICT(k, &c[k]);
18        CR_STRICT(k, &b[k]);
19        CW_LAZY(k, &a[b[k]]);
20        a[b[k]] = c[k] + 1;
21        // if k == 50 : CW_LAZY(k, &b[400]);
22     // inspection: checks:
23     parfor(i = 0 .. 250, 501 .. 1000):
24        CR(i, &c[i]); CR(i, &b[i]);
25        CW(i, &a[b[i]]);
26        if i == 50 : CW(i, &b[400]);
27     // executor (tail)
28     parfor(i = 501 .. 1000):
29        a[b[i]] = c[i] + 1;
30        // if i == 50 : b[400] = 0;
31  goto end;
32
33  // sequential loop
34  sequential_loop:
35     kill_threads();
36     for(;k < 1000; ++k):
37        a[b[k]] = c[k] + 1;
38        if k == 50 : b[400] = 0;
39
40  end:
```

Fig. 4. Simultaneous inspection.

The sequential strips may change application data while the inspectors are registering and checking memory accesses. Because of the resulting potential race conditions we must now be more conservative and give up on parallelizing in case of *any* reads from data that was updated in the loop, even for cases in which the written bit has helped before. The trade-off is that by being more conservative, we may flag more loops as non-parallelizable (which we will mitigate in Sect. 3.1), but on the other hand we gain the ability to run the sequential loop with a simultaneous inspection, i.e., we can hide inspection overhead.

We need to give up on parallelizing in case of an intra-iteration dependence because the approximation of the software cache with written may now cause the inspector to miss loop carried anti-dependences. For the running example now assume a=c and b[i]=i but b[0]=300. Iteration 0 then writes to a[300] and iteration 300 reads from a[300]. Hence there is a loop carried dependence. The value registered for &a[300] is racy and either 0 or 300. If iteration 300 is registered, the anti-dependence is missed because in the *checking phase* of iteration 300 written only suggests an intra-iteration anti-dependence.

Instead of the anti-dependence the pre-processing inspector from Sect. 2.1 detects an output-dependence in iteration 0 and gives up on parallelizing. Fortunately, the simultaneous inspector can detect a (potentially racy) read from an address that was written to by one of the sequential *head* iterations. In such a situation the inspector gives up on parallelizing because otherwise the *registration* and *checking* phases may read different values from memory for an address (and may use these values for indirect addresses or for control-flow decisions).

To implement this, the CR_STRICT macro (see Fig. 5) is more strict in checking dependences and it foregoes parallelization on any address that was registered as being written to. As the less strict written is no longer needed, the CW_LAZY macro can lazily refrain

```
1   def CR_STRICT(i, addr):
2       if time == epoch[hash(addr)]  :
3           goto sequential_loop;
4   def CW_LAZY(i, addr):
5       if i != reg[hash(addr)]  :
6           goto sequential_loop
```

Fig. 5. More macros.

from updating it. A beneficial effect of the simpler macros in Fig. 5 is that they lower the overhead of the instrumentation.[2] To avoid the intra-iteration anti-dependence in other iterations that prevent parallelization, it suffices to use the new flavor of the macros in the *middle* strip. This is especially relevant for the optimization of Sect. 3.1 that removes some of the checks in the *middle* strip that may falsely prevent parallelization.

Finally, we must ensure that the sequential loop only writes to addresses that have previously been registered. In other words, assume address X to be written by iteration Y. When the sequential *middle* strip then executes iteration Y, it needs to write to address X. If the sequential *middle* strip were to update a different memory address, it means that the inspector has to give up on parallelizing as there is no proper software cache to maintain all effects.

By construction, the *registration phase* must have already registered any write access of the *middle* strip. There is an inductive argument that the reg

---

[2] Note that the gotos in the macros of Figs. 3 and 5 are slightly different for the simultaneous inspection: they are delayed until the interrupted iteration finishes.

array is maintained correctly, even in the presence of the sequential *head* and *middle* strips and the resulting potential race conditions. Before the *middle* strip starts with its first iteration, the `reg` table holds an entry for each address to which the *head* strip has written to. The induction is that if the `reg` table holds an entry for every write access before iteration n of the *middle* strip, it also holds entries for all accesses before iteration $n + 1$ since otherwise a dependence is found. This is achieved by the CR_STRICT macro that checks that all values that the *middle* sequential strip reads in iteration n are independent of writes in previous iterations. If no dependence is found all values that the *middle* strip reads are the same as they were in the *registration* of the same iteration. So the addresses for the write accesses have to be the same. At the end of iteration n and thus at the start of iteration $n + 1$ all executed write accesses are properly registered in the `reg` table.

Hence, after the *registration phase*, all addresses that are written to have been registered (including those from the sequential *head*). However, some entries may have been overwritten. In the *checking phase* we detect such output-dependences because all writes are double-checked, even those writes that the sequential *head* has already performed on application data.

3   Optimizations

3.1   Removing Superfluous Checks

To allow a simultaneous inspection, we needed to be overly conservative in that no read operation may read data written in the loop. We can relax this a little using static analysis. The key insight is that read-checks in the *middle* sequential strip can be removed if the value read is not used elsewhere, either directly or indirectly (to perform control-flow decisions or to compute addresses). Reads on the right hand

```
1   par:
2     // inspection: checks of h-iterations
3     parfor(i = 0 .. 250):
4       // removed CR(i, &c[i]), CR(i, &b[i])
5       CW_LAZY(i, &a[b[i]]); // instead of CW
6       if i == 50 : CW_LAZY(i, &b[400]);
7
8     // sequential middle of m-iterations
9     for(k = 251 .. 500):
10      // removed CR(k, &c[k])
11      CR_STRICT(k, &b[k]);
12      CW_LAZY(k, &a[b[k]]);
13      a[b[k]] = c[k] + 1;
14      // if k == 50 : CW_LAZY(k, &b[400]);
15
16    // inspection: checks of rest
17    parfor(i = 501 .. 1000):
18      CR(i, &c[i]); CR(i, &b[i]);
19      CW(i, &a[b[i]]);
20      if i == 50 : CW(i, &b[400]);
```

Fig. 6. Optimized replacement for the *checking phase* (lines 16–21) of Fig. 4.

side of an assignment, arguments of calls, etc., fit in this category and their read-checks can almost all be removed as explained below. Read-checks in the *checking phase* for iterations which are executed in the *head* sequential strip are always removed.

For the running example now assume a=c and b[i]=i but b[0]=1. Then there is a flow-dependence between iteration 0 and iteration 1. But since the sequential *head* executes both iterations in the correct order we can ignore this dependence and remove the *checking* for it. The check responsible for finding this dependence is the CR(i,&c[i]) in line 24 of Fig. 4. The same argument applies to CR(i,&b[i]). Figure 6 shows the result. The checking of the iterations 0 to 250 is factored out into a separate **parfor** loop in lines 3–6. After removing all CR macros for these iterations, **written** is no longer checked. Hence, the faster CW_LAZY macro that does not set **written** can replace CW in lines 5 and 6.

Let us now examine the general case. We call iterations that are executed in the sequential *head h-iterations.* Analogously, *m-iterations* form the sequential *middle.* There are three ways in which updated values can reach a read access of a variable in the middle loop: (1) the variable was written before the loop, (2) the variable was written in an *h-iteration* or an *m-iteration* prior to the current *m-iteration,* or (3) the variable is marked for write access in a later iteration.

Case (1) effectively creates a read-only variable for the loop and we do not need a read-check. Case (2) sequentially executes the code in the *m-iterations* as the programmer intended. Any reads and writes are therefore already in the correct order and we do not need to check them. In case (3) a later iteration than those in the *m-iterations* writes the data that is now read in the *m-iteration.* This is also OK as it follows the same semantics as the original sequential loop.

Hence, in all three cases in which a write can affect an *m-iteration*'s read, its read-checks can be removed. The only exception is if a read is from an address that can be changed as explained above. This would cause the inspector's registered addresses to become invalid. Read-checks for *h-iterations* can be removed for the same reason. We can even remove all read-checks because the exception does not apply.

The *m-iterations* are also executed in the correct order. But when CR_STRICT checks these iterations it also verifies that the *registration* and the sequential *middle* execution of this iterations use the same values for address calculations or control-flow decisions. Hence, CR_STRICT macros can be removed for addresses that a static analysis for unused values finds in the *registration phase.*

The example in Fig. 4 calls the CR_STRICT macro twice: for (k,&c[i]) and (k,&b[i]) in lines 17 and 18. Of these addresses the *registration phase* only uses b[i] in line 12. Since c[i] is not used to change an address anywhere, the *m-iterations* no longer need to call the macro, see line 10 of Fig. 6. (We can ignore the different variable names for the loop iterator.)

3.2   Dynamic Load Balancing

Ideally, all the iterations in a sequential *head* strip take the same time as the (parallel) *registration* of the remaining iterations. The same holds for the *middle* strip and the (parallel) *checking.* Otherwise either the core that works on the sequential strip or the threads that do the parallel inspection have to wait at the implicit barrier after the phases (before lines 17 and 27 of Fig. 4). In Fig. 4 we have used a naive load balancing by splitting the iteration space into

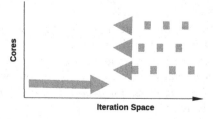

Fig. 7. Iteration space partitioning.

quarters. A better load balancing must take the actual runtime of the sequential iteration into account. But unfortunately, these are unknown.

We manually searched for a good ratio but the optimum varies for different loops as the ratio between the runtime of an iteration in the inspectors and the execution varies. Especially the *registration* of an iteration can be much faster than the execution as only writes matter. Since in general it is undecidable to statically determine the runtime of code without executing it, we use a dynamic load balancing instead.

The key idea is to have the inspectors work from the upper end of the iteration space as shown in Fig. 7. They are done as soon as they reach the iteration that has just been executed by the sequential loop, that then also comes to an end. As the inspectors can do their work in parallel they can also do it backwards.

Figure 8 shows the loop with all optimizations applied. There is no need for expensive synchronization. Inspection and sequential execution may overlap causing some iterations to be registered or checked even though they have just been executed sequentially.

Let us explain why for both barriers such an overlap does not influence the inspection. First, since only the sequential execution writes application data, an additional inspection does not interfere. If the inspector threads stop too late at the barrier between the *registration* phase and the *checking phase* they may overwrite some entries in the **reg** table. As we already detect overwritten entries in the **reg** table, a race is not a prob-

```
1    INIT();
2    par: {  // execution thread
3       for (X = 0 .. 1000):
4          if done == THREADS-1: break;
5          REG(X, &a[b[X]]);
6          a[b[X]] = c[X]+1;
7          if X == 50:
8             REG(X, &b[400]);
9             b[400] = 0;
10         P = X;
11         barrier();
12         done = 0;
13         for (; X < 1000; ++X):
14            if done == THREADS-1: break;
15            CR_STRICT(X, &b[X]);
16            CW_LAZY(X, &a[b[X]]);
17            a[b[X]] = c[X]+1;
18            if X == 50:
19               CW_LAZY(X, &b[400]);
20               b[400] = 0;
21      }
22      // inspection threads
23      parfor (k = 0 .. THREADS-1):
24         for (i = part(k, 1000..0)):
25            REG(i, &a[b[i]]);
26            if i == 50: REG(i, &b[400]);
27            if i < X: done++; break;
28         barrier();
29         for (i = part(k, 0, P)):
30            CW_LAZY(i, &a[b[i]]);
31            if i == 50: CW_LAZY(i, &b[400]);
32         for (i = part(k, 1000..X)):
33            CR(i, &c[i]); CR(i, &b[i]);
34            CW(i, &a[b[i]]);
35            if i == 50: CW(i, &b[400]);
36            if i < X: done++; break;
37      // executor tail
38      parfor (i = X .. 1000):
39         a[b[i]] = c[i]+1;
40      goto end;
41
42      // sequential_loop
43      for ( ; X < 1000; ++X):
44      sequential_loop:
45         a[b[X]] = c[X]+1;
46         if X == 50: b[400] = 0;
47      end:
```

Fig. 8. Optimized version.

lem. In fact, it is more likely that the same iteration count will be registered twice for an address. Hence, the races to the **reg** table because of inspectors that overlap some iterations of the sequential *head* are harmless.

Second, at the barrier between the *m-iterations* and the checking inspectors, overlaps are also unproblematic. At this point `reg` does no longer change. Only the *m-iterations* can change application data and only the parallel inspectors can change `written`. There is thus no overlap in reads from and writes to the inspectors' data structures. As discussed before, whenever the parallel inspection reads changed application data, a dependence is found.

4 Performance

There are two hypotheses that we need to prove. First, that a failed attempt to parallelize a loop does not add much cost (compared to running the loop sequentially from the start) and second, that a parallelized loop achieves good performance. Furthermore, we need to evaluate the impact of the two optimizations from Sect. 3. All measurements were performed on a quad-core Intel CPU at 3.4 GHz running Linux 3.4. We use GCC 4.8 and have enabled all optimizations (-O3) for all measurements. We use four benchmarks with prallelizable loops, two of which *cannot* be statically parallelized (and also a programmer would a have difficulties). In these cases only a runtime parallelization is viable. To measure the overhead of inspecting non-parallelizable loops we artificially injected dependences into the iteration space of these benchmarks. The benchmarks are:

Spec-norm calculates the spectrum norm of a parameterized matrix with a matrix-vector product as the hot loop. This parallelizable benchmark demonstrates that our technique is even applicable to typical numeric problems and achieves good performance. **3D-morph** is a statically parallelizable 3D graphics algorithm that does (slow) trigonometric computations in its hot loop. In contrast to **Spec-norm**, there are only write operations. **Bi-cube** calculates a bi-cubic interpolation of a 2D data field. The interpolated values are written to the same data field and the offsets are read from memory. A precise static data-dependence analysis is impossible. **Graph** calculates euclidean distances in a graph which is stored in a data structure with indirections. It computes the distance between pairs of 2D points. But to get the 2D coordinates, the algorithm has to resolve two layers of indirection. This makes a precise static analysis impossible. The indirection also makes the inspection expensive.

The most important result is the runtime overhead of non-parallelizable loops. This overhead depends on which iteration carries the artificially injected dependence. If the inspector finds a dependence early, the overhead is small. The accumulated overhead is large if the injected dependence is found in the last inspected iteration.

Figure 9(a) shows the overhead of the inspection for non-parallelizable loops. On the x-axis is the fraction of the iteration space that is free of dependences, i.e., the x-axis shows where in the iteration space we injected the artificial dependence. The plot shows the overhead incurred by doing the inspection, giving up on parallelizing, and continuing with the pure sequential loop, compared to running the un-instrumented loop completely sequentially.

The overhead of pre-processing inspector (Sect. 2.1) shows the saw tooth pattern in Fig. 9(b). Each of the four tooths is caused by its inspector thread.

If the dependence is injected in a late iteration, the inspector takes longer to find it. In the worst case an inspector thread finds the dependence in its last iteration. This wastes much time. For the benchmarks the overhead reaches up to 36 %.

The more costly the inspection is compared to the executor, the larger is the tooth. The inspection phase of **3D-morph** skips the expensive trigonometric functions. Therefore even running the whole inspection before the sequential execution does not add much to the overall runtime. The *registration phase* for the matrix-vector-multiply of **spec-norm** skips 4864 reads per registered written address. Hence, inspecting is still cheap compared to the execution phase. **Bi-cube** needs about the same time to calculate the addresses of neighboring cells (both in the *registration phase* and the *checking phase*) and to do the numerics. The benchmark's

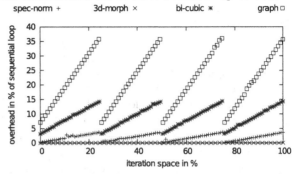

(a) Overhead of pre-processing inspector (Sec. 2.1)

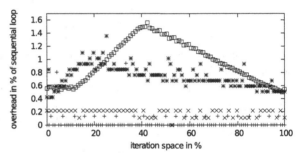

(b) Overhead of simultaneous inspector (Sec. 3.2)

Fig. 9. Inspection overhead.

inspection is therefore similarly expensive as its execution phase. **Graph** also needs to resolve indirections caused by the graph data structure in all phases. Moreover, as each iteration performs only little work (an euclidean distance calculation) the inspection overhead is relatively large.

The overhead of the simultaneous inspector (with both optimizations of Sect. 3 engaged) is much better, see Fig. 9(b). There is a maximal overhead of just 1.6 % compared to running the un-instrumented loops sequentially. **3D-morph** and **spec-norm** have near zero overheads because of the same reason as before. Actually their overhead is even lower as the sequential *middle* can skip most of the read-checks because the memory addresses are neither involved in address calculations nor in control flow decisions. **Bi-cube** and **graph** show a more distinct pattern. There are ripples in the beginning followed by a triangular behavior. The ripples are caused by dependences found by the parallel inspector that are triggered by writes in the *head* strip. The up-going edge of the triangle is caused by dependences found in the *middle* strip, the down-going edge shows dependences found during the parallel *checking*. Later iterations are inspected earlier, since the inspectors start from the upper end of the iteration space, see Sect. 3.2.

Let us examine the performance for parallelizeable loops (without dependences). Figure 10 shows the speed-up normalized to the un-instrumented sequential loop. The first bar shows the runtime of the benchmarks with the pre-processing (parallel) inspector (Sect. 2.1). Then follow the naive simultaneous inspector (Sect. 2.2), the version with superfluous read-checks removed (Sect. 3.1), and finally the fully opti-mized version (Sect. 3.2). For the two middle bars in each group there is no dynamic load balancing. Instead of

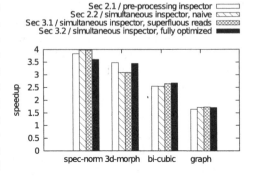

Fig. 10. Runtime of the full parallel version of the benchmarks with different optimizations enabled.

splitting the iteration space in quarters, we manually hand-crafted a benchmark specific splitting that minimizes idle times. We achieve a speedup of up to 3.6 on a quad core processor for the parallelizeable loops. Simultaneous inspection is a gain for non-parallelizable loops and it does not negatively affect speedups for parallelizable loops.

As the inspection overhead is low for **spec-norm** and **3D-morph** the opti-mizations cannot buy more speedup. For the benchmarks with more expensive inspectors (**graph** and **bi-cubic**) the simultaneous inspection, the optimizations of Sect. 3, and the fact that by merging execution and inspection in the sequential strips avoids some recalculations even improve the achievable speedups slightly (although the main reason for the optimizations was to cut down the overhead for non-parallelizable loops). Section 3.1 is allowing more loops to be parallelizeable we also see a small gain in performance for the **graph** and **bi-cubic** benchmarks.

Let us explain the beneficial effect of the dynamic load balancing (Sect. 3.2) in more detail. Figure 11 shows that dynamic load balancing assigns different fractions of the iteration space to the *head* strip, to the *middle* strip, and to the parallel *tail*. In Fig. 10 the two inner bars of each group use the hand-crafted benchmark-specific load balancing. Dynamic load balancing is competitive (**spec-norm** is the worst case with a slowdown of 12 %) and it even out-performs the handcrafted version in the other bench-marks. Of course a benchmark-specific splitting is not practical. If we had used the averages of Fig. 11 to split the iteration space instead of benchmark-specific boundaries, the speedups of the inner two bars would go down up to 40 %.

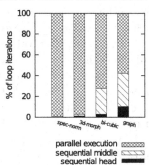

Fig. 11. Partitioning of the dynamic load balancer.

5   Related Work

We discuss three avenues of related work, namely work related to inspector-executor systems, systems using transactions to parallelize loops, and auto-parallelization systems in general.

Inspector-Executor Systems. As far as we know, this paper is the first work that simultaneously inspects a loop for parallelizability while one core already starts to execute the loop sequentially. While there is our earlier work that parallelizes the pre-processing inspection to reduce the overhead [13], little has been done to remove or hide the cost of the inspection.

Liao et al. [10] present another parallelized inspector. Their system can parallelize loops that are only partially parallelizable (only subsets of the iteration space can run in parallel). Our system cannot do this. But the downside of their approach is that they require the loop to use arrays only. They cannot handle indirect addressing at all.

Arenaz et al. [1] present a promising way to achieve a better load balancing for the parallel execution of the loop. Their inspector counts the frequency of write accesses and uses this data to estimate the runtime of the iterations. Our inspector could be extended with similar heuristics to improve the load balancing of the fully parallel *tail* of the iteration space. This is an aspect that is orthogonal to the problems we address here.

Another orthogonal idea to reduce the inspection overhead is to run the inspector for a loop only once [14]. If the control-flow later hits the loop again, there is no repeated inspection. Instead the previous decision is reused. The inspection cost is hence easier to amortize. But this is only possible if the structure of the inspected data and the indirections are known to be static, i.e., no pointer may be changed. Otherwise, the inspector has to run again.

Optimistic loop parallelization with transactions is an alternative approach. Similar to our work there are checks that determine if the parallel execution is valid. But while our sequential strips are guaranteed to make progress, the optimistic parallelization starts a transaction that tentatively runs the loop in parallel. In case of a non-parallelizable loop the transaction aborts. All changes to memory are then discarded and control is passed to the sequential loop that starts from scratch. The time spent in a speculative parallel execution is completely wasted. There is hardware support for transactions [3–5]. But it has many restrictions, e.g., the number of memory accesses allowed in one transaction is severely limited (currently about 64 cache lines in Intel CPUs). Software transactions [12] are more flexible but are known to be slow. Moreover their overhead cannot be avoided (in contrast to inspector-executor systems or hardware transactions).

Other specialized support to revert memory changes include checkpoints [8] that store copies of changed data for restoration in case of failure [16], or shadowing by means of a local copy of the data used in a loop iteration [7]. However, these approaches make all memory accesses more expensive and need extra work for the revocation of written memory in case of a non-parallelizable loop.

Auto-Parallelization Systems. Qian [15] surveys automatic parallel programming tools, including auto-parallelizing compilers. Most of the work mentioned relies on the ability to statically analyze the dependences. If full automatic parallelization does not work, Garcia et al. [6] suggest to provide the programmer with recommendations for manual parallelization. With profile data such recommendations can be further improved [9,11,17]. All the remaining complex cases are left to inspector-executor, such as the one presented here.

Campanoni et al. [2] propose to parallelize the instructions of a single iteration, instead of running the iterations in parallel. This is orthogonal to our work and can be applied to loops with loop carried dependences. The effect of this parallelization is more fine-grained.

6   Conclusions

We presented an auto-parallelization technique for loops that is based on the inspector-executor pattern. The novel idea is to run the inspector concurrently to the sequential execution of the loop it investigates. Even if the loop turns out to be non-parallelizable, partial results stay. Instead of having wasted time on a pre-processing inspection, most of the overhead of the simultaneous inspection is hidden.

The performance section shows that the sequential loop only needs little instrumentation to allow a simultaneous inspection. By inspecting the loop from the upper end of the iteration space, a dynamic load balancing can further reduce the overhead as it avoids idling. In total, the simultaneous inspector-executor still achieves a good speedup (up to a factor of 3.6 on a quad core) for a parallelizable loop. But more importantly, it has only a small overhead of at most 1.6 % for non-parallelizable loops. This is much better than the overhead of a (parallel) pre-processing inspection on non-parallelizable loops (up to 36 % overhead).

References

1. Arenaz, M., Touriño, J., Doallo, R.: An inspector-executor algorithm for irregular assignment parallelization. In: Cao, J., Yang, L.T., Guo, M., Lau, F. (eds.) ISPA 2004. LNCS, vol. 3358, pp. 4–15. Springer, Heidelberg (2004)
2. Campanoni, S., Jones, T., Holloway, G., Reddi, V.J., Wei, G.-Y., Brooks, D.: Helix: automatic parallelization of irregular programs for chip multiprocessing. In: Proceedings of the International Symposium on Code Generation and Optimization (CGO 2012), pp. 84–93, San Jose, CA, March 2012
3. Chen, M.K., Olukotun, K.: The Jrpm system for dynamically parallelizing java programs. In: Proceedings of the International Symposium on Computer Architecture (ISCA 2003), pp. 434–446, San Diego, CA, June 2003
4. DeVuyst, M., Tullsen, D.M., Kim, S.W.: Runtime parallelization of legacy code on a transactional memory system. In: Proceedings of the International Conference on High-Performance and Embedded Architectures and Compilers (HiPEAC 2011), pp. 127–136, Heraklion, Greece, January 2011

5. Du, Z.-H., Lim, C.-C., Li, X.-F., Yang, C., Zhao, Q., Ngai, T.-F.: A cost-driven compilation framework for speculative parallelization of sequential programs. In: Proceedings of the Conference on Programming Language Design and Implementation (PLDI 2004), pp. 71–81, Washington DC, June 2004
6. Garcia, S., Jeon, D., Louie, C.M., Taylor, M.B.: Kremlin: rethinking and rebooting Gprof for the multicore age. In: Proceedings of the International Conference on Programming Language Design and Implementation (PLDI 2011), pp. 458–469, San Jose, CA, June 2011
7. García-Yáguez, Á., Llanos, D.R., González-Escribano, A.: Exclusive squashing for thread-level speculation. In: Proceedings of the International Symposium on High Performance Distributed Computing (HPDC 2011), pp. 275–276, San Jose, CA, June 2011
8. Gupta, M., Nim, R.: Techniques for speculative run-time parallelization of loops. In: Proceedings of the International Conference on Supercomputing (SC 1998), pp. 1–12, San Jose, CA, November 1998
9. Larsen, P., Ladelsky, R., Lidman, J., McKee, S.A., Karlsson, S., Zaks, A.: Parallelizing more loops with compiler guided refactoring. In: Proceedings on the International Conferences on Parallel Proceesing (ICPP 2012), pp. 410–419, Pittsburg, PA, September 2012
10. Leung, S.-T., Zahorjan, J.: Improving the performance of runtime parallelization. In: Proceedings of the Symposium on Principles and Practice of Parallel Programming (PPoPP 1993), pp. 83–91, San Diego, CA, May 1993
11. Liao, S.-W., Diwan, A., Bosch, R.P., Jr., Ghuloum, A., Lam, M.S.: Suif explorer: an interactive and interprocedural parallelizer. In: Proceedings of the Symposium on Principles and Practice of Parallel Programming (PPoPP 1999), pp. 37–48, Atlanta, GA, May 1999
12. Mehrara, M., Hao, J., Hsu, P.-C., Mahlke, S.: Parallelizing sequential applications on commodity hardware using a low-cost software transactional memory. In: Proceedings of the International Conference on Programming Language Design and Implementation (PLDI 2009), pp. 166–176, Dublin, Ireland, June 2009
13. Philippsen, M., Tillmann, N., Brinkers, D.: Double inspection for run-time loop parallelization. In: Rajopadhye, S., Mills Strout, M. (eds.) LCPC 2011. LNCS, vol. 7146, pp. 46–60. Springer, Heidelberg (2013)
14. Ponnusamy, R., Saltz, J., Choudhary, A.: Runtime compilation techniques for data partitioning and communication schedule reuse. In: Proceedings of the International Conference on Supercomputing (SC 1993), pp. 361–370, Portland, OR, November 1993
15. Qian, Y.: Automatic parallelization tools. In: Proceedings of the World Congress Engineering and Computer Science (WCECS 2012), pp. 97–101, San Francisco, CA, October 2012
16. Rauchwerger, L., Padua, D.: The LRPD test: speculative run-time parallelization of loops with privatization and reduction parallelization. In: Proceedings of the International Conference on Programming Language Design and Implementation (PLDI 1995), pp. 218–232, La Jolla, CA, June 1995
17. Tournavitis, G., Wang, Z., Franke, B., O'Boyle, M.F.P.: Towards a holistic approach to auto-parallelization: integrating profile-driven parallelism detection and machine-learning based mapping. In: Proceedings of the International Conference on Programming Language Design and Implementation (PLDI 2009), pp. 177–187, Dublin, Ireland, June 2009

Tiled Linear Algebra a System for Parallel Graph Algorithms

Saeed Maleki[✉], G. Carl Evans, and David A. Padua

Department of Computer Science, University of Illinois at Urbana-Champaign,
201 North Goodwin Avenue, Urbana, IL 61801-2302, USA
{maleki1,gcevans,padua}@illinois.edu

Abstract. High performance parallel kernels for solving graph problems
are complex and difficult to write. Some systems have been developed to
facilitate the implementation of these kernels but the code they produce
does not always perform as well as custom software. In this space, we
propose Tiled Linear Algebra (TLA), a multi-level system based on linear algebra but with explicit parallel extensions. Programs can be first
written in a conventional manner using linear algebra and then tuned
for parallel performance using our extension. This separation allows programmers with different expertise to focus on their strengths with writing
original codes that can then be tuned by parallel experts.

This paper presents the background on using linear algebra to express
graph algorithms and describes the extensions TLA provides to implement their parallel versions. The key extensions supported by TLA are:
data distribution, partial computation, delaying updates, and communication. With these extensions to the traditional linear algebra operators, we could produce linear algebra based versions of several problems
including single source shortest path that should preform close to custom implementations. We present results on several single source shortest
path algorithms to demonstrate the features of TLA.

1 Introduction

In recent years, the importance of graph algorithms has been on the rise. While
graph algorithms have always been a part of computer science, graph analytics
have become increasingly important in the recent past. Graph analytics is used
for the analysis of large network systems, capturing the interactions in social networks, natural language analysis, and cyber-security algorithms. Furthermore,
in many cases, the size of the graphs to be analyzed has grown and continues
to grow. For example, Facebook as a social network graph (with users as vertices and friendships as edges) has grown from 1 million to 845 million users in 7
years (2004–2011). Analysis of graphs of this size requires large parallel machines
whose programming is a complex task due to correctness and performance.

Linear algebra operators can represent many graph algorithms in a concise
and clear manner as discussed in [3, 12]. The use of this notation allows for rapid
development of complex algorithms. Today, the power and flexibility of using

J. Brodman and P. Tu (Eds.): LCPC 2014, LNCS 8967, pp. 116–130, 2015.
DOI: 10.1007/978-3-319-17473-0_8

linear algebra primitives comes with drawbacks. Standard sparse linear algebra kernels do not always take advantage of the structure of the graphs or parameters of the target machine and, as a result, fall short of the performance of custom implementations. To address this, we propose *Tiled Linear Algebra (TLA)* that is a multi-level parallel system with high-level linear algebra structure. In TLA, linear algebra primitives are used to construct a correct program and then performance features controlled by "knobs" are used to tune the kernels. These features include controlling distribution and communication frequency.

We organize this paper as follows. Section 2 describes the use of linear algebra for graph algorithms and Sect. 3 describes our extensions. We describe the algorithms to solve the Single Source Shortest Path (SSSP) problem and our experiments in Sect. 4. We wrap up with a discussion of related work in Sect. 5 and our conclusions in Sect. 6.

2   Graph Algorithms Using Linear Algebra

Using linear algebra as an abstraction for programming parallel graph algorithms is not new. CombBLAS [3] is perhaps the best known system using this approach. This section overviews linear algebra for representing graph algorithms.

There is a correspondence between a graph and a matrix. A graph $G = (V, E)$ with n vertices (set V) and m edges (set E) can be represented by its adjacency matrix A which is an $n \times n$ matrix such that $A(i, j) = 1$ if there is an edge e_{ij} from vertex v_i to vertex v_j and $= 0$ otherwise. This allows for directed and undirected graphs and can be extended to weighted graphs by using the weight rather than 1 to represent an edge. This representation is at the core of using linear algebra to describe graph algorithms. It should be noted that typically this matrix will be sparse and performance efficiency will depend, just as in conventional linear algebra, on how sparsity is handled.

Reachability Example: Reachability is the problem of finding all the reachable vertices in a directed graph $G = (V, E)$ from a source vertex $s \in V$. More formally, $Reach(G, s) = \{v \in V | \exists v_1, v_2, \ldots, v_k \in V, v_i v_{i+1} \in E, v_1 = s, v_k = v\}$. There exists a duality between reachability and matrix vector multiplication. Consider a vector r with $|V|$ elements (i.e. one element per vertex of the graph) with values $r(s) = 1$ and 0 everywhere else and the adjacency matrix A of graph G. All neighbors of s reachable in 1 step correspond to the non-zero entries of the vector $A^T \cdot r$. Consider Fig. 1 which shows a graph with its transposed adjacency matrix, A^T, with non-zeros shown as dots. Vertex 7 is the source vertex, s, of the reachability problem and as just mentioned, r has only one non-zero element (represented by the dot in position 7 for s). The result of the matrix vector multiplication will produce a vector r' with non-zeros represented by dots which corresponds to the non-zeros in the matrix shown by unfilled dots in the figure. $r' = A^T \cdot r$ computes the vertices that can be reached from 7 by traversing one edge (shown by dotted arrows in the figure). $r'' = r + r' = r + A^T \cdot r$ represents all vertices that can be reached in 1 or fewer (0) edge traversals. In general,

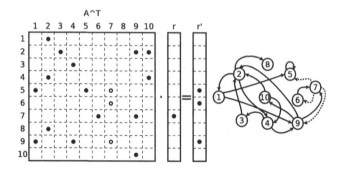

Fig. 1. Matrix-vector multiplication for reachability.

if r_0 includes 7 as a reachable vertex, an iterative matrix-vector multiplication $r_{i+1} = r_i + A \cdot r_i$ will find all of the vertices which are in $i + 1$ or fewer edge traversals. The algorithm would terminate when a fixed point has been reached which in this case means that r_{i+1} and r_i has non-zeros in the same positions. These non-zeros in the final vector corresponds to all vertices reachable in any number of edge traversals. Note that, the elements of r_i could have different (positive) values and these values do not have a clear meaning. However, if we had a different algebra and replaced 1 and 0 by *true* and *false*, regular multiplication by $\wedge$, and regular addition by $\vee$, the result would have been the same except that all the non-zeros would all have been *true*.

A **semiring** is a five-tuple $(D, \oplus, \otimes, \mathbb{0}, \mathbb{1})$, where D is the set of elements of the semiring and D is closed under $\oplus$ and $\otimes$. $\mathbb{1} \in D$ is the identity for $\otimes$ which means that $\forall x \in D : x \otimes \mathbb{1} = \mathbb{1} \otimes x = x$ and $\mathbb{0} \in D$ is the identity for $\oplus$ which means that $\forall x \in D : x \oplus \mathbb{0} = \mathbb{0} \oplus x = x$. Also, $\mathbb{0}$ nullifies any elements of D with $\otimes$: $\forall x \in D : x \otimes \mathbb{0} = \mathbb{0} \otimes x = \mathbb{0}$. Given two matrices, $A_{l,m}$ and $B_{m,n}$, with elements from a semiring, D, their product is denoted $A \odot B$ and results in an $l \times n$ matrix defined such that

$$(A \odot B)(i, j) = A(i, 1) \times B(1, j) + A(i, 2) \times B(2, j) + \ldots + A(i, m) \times B(m, j)$$

In this notation, the semiring $(\mathbb{R} \cup \{\infty\}, \min, +, \infty, 0)$ with the real numbers extended with ∞ as the domain, min as the additive operation $\oplus$, and $+$ as the multiplicative operation $\otimes$ is called the **tropical** semiring. Tropical semiring is specifically useful for computing single source shortest path from a source vertex to every other vertex in a graph which is discussed in more details below. The other useful semirings for other algorithms are the real field $(\mathbb{R}, +, \times, 0, 1)$ for page-rank computation or the boolean semiring $(\{0, 1\}, \vee, \wedge, 0, 1)$ which, as mentioned in the example above, is a natural algebra for reachability problems.

A directed and weighted graph $G = (V, E)$ can be represented by its adjacency matrix A_G of size $n \times n$ where $|V| = n$ and whose values are $A_G(i, j) = weight(v_iv_j)$ if $v_iv_j \in E$ and $A_G(i, j) = \infty$ otherwise. That is, the elements of A_G are from the tropical semiring. A_G is a sparse matrix where the sparsity comes from the $\mathbb{0} = \infty$ elements in the matrix which represent the non-existent edges in the graph. Let d be an $n \times 1$ vector where its ith element, $d(i)$ is the distance to v_i, then $d' = A_G^T \odot d$ would also be a distance vector where $d'(i) = \min_{v_j v_i \in E(G)} (d(j) + weight(v_j v_i))$. $d'' = d \oplus A_G^T \odot d = d \oplus d'$ is another distance vector where in the computation of $d''(i)$, $\forall j : d(j) + w(v_j v_i)$ are considered as well $d(i)$ itself. This is equivalent to first, computing a new distance $d'(i)$ for each vertex v_i considering distance d of its incoming neighbors and the weight of corresponding edge $(\forall j : d(v_j) + w(v_j v_i))$ and second, comparing this new $d'(i)$ distance with $d(i)$ and setting $d''(i)$ to the smaller one.

Using adjacency matrix representation, one can express algorithms to find the shortest path using matrix-vector product in tropical semiring. For example, assuming that d_0 is a distance vector where $d_0(s) = 0$ and $\forall v \in V(G) \backslash \{s\}$: $d_0(v) = \infty$. At step i, the well known Bellman-Ford algorithm computes $d_{i+1} = d_i \oplus A_G^T \odot d_i$ and it iterates for $|V(G)| - 1$ times. In Sect. 3.2, we will explain how linear algebra can be used to express other algorithms.

3   Tiled Linear Algebra

One of the most important aspects of linear algebra for graph algorithms is that the adjacency matrix of a graph G, A_G, is sparse and the system needs to use sparse algorithms. Otherwise, for example, a matrix-vector multiplication will require $O(|V|^2)$ operations instead of $O(|E|)$. Furthermore, different ways of representing a sparse matrix can impact the performance. Therefore, we believe that it is important for the programmer to have control over the representation.

Papers [3,8] discuss how graph algorithms can be represented in terms of matrix operations on different semirings. However, there are many ways to parallelize a matrix operation. In particular, the parallelization of matrix operations can be represented using *tiling* which partitions an array into subarrays by dividing each of the dimensions of the original array into segments. Each tile is assigned to a processor which will be responsible for the values of that tile. This assignment is done by a mapping function from tiles to processors.

In our notation, we tile and assign tiles to processors at the same time. Let's say matrix A is read from file `input.txt` (which, for example, contains the edge list of a graph) and we want to divide the rows and columns into two segments. We will use command `A = ReadAndTile('input.txt', 2, 2, f);` to read from the file and tile it accordingly. `f` is a function that assigns each tile to a processor. Therefore, there are four tiles which we denote by $A_{1,1}$, $A_{1,2}$, $A_{2,1}$ and $A_{2,2}$. Each tile is conceived as having the size equal to the whole matrix, but contain non-0 only in the regions associated with the tile. Therefore, $A_{1,1} \oplus A_{1,2} \oplus A_{2,1} \oplus A_{2,2} = A$. To create a vector of size $n \times 1$ and tile it into 2 segments, we will use command `v = CreateArray(n,2,f2);` where `f2` is another mapping function. Even though we explicitly ask the user for a tiling pattern, we do not explicitly use the tiling when representing operations.

3.1   Delaying Updates

As is well known, we can use the tiling to control where each component of the computation occurs and how the processors communicate. In regular parallel

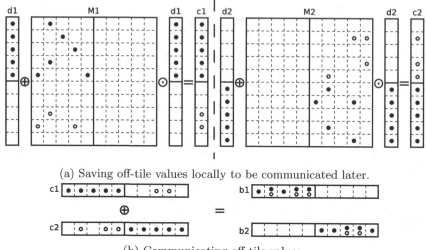

(a) Saving off-tile values locally to be communicated later.

(b) Communicating off-tile values.

Fig. 2. Sparse matrix vector multiplication with delaying updates.

linear algebra, updates need to be visible by all the processors as soon as they occur. However, the updates can be postponed as, for example, is done in asynchronous algorithms [1,9].

Let A_G be the adjacency matrix of G and $M = A_G^T$. As discussed above, if d is a distance vector for the vertices of G, $c = d \oplus M \odot d$ will be another distance vector with distances updated by traversing 0 or 1 edges. Figure 2a represents the computation of $c = d \oplus M \odot d$. Let M be tiled 1×2 and $f(x, y) = y$ be the tile to processor mapping function such that tile $(1, 1)$ is assigned to processor p_1 and tile $(1, 2)$ is assigned to processor p_2. Also assume that d and c are vectors of size $n \times 1$ ($n = |V(G)|$ which is 10 in Fig. 2a) and they are tiled 2×1 and $f_2(x, y) = x$ is their mapping function. Figure 2a shows these tilings and distributions of M, d and c. The dots in the Figure represent the non-zeros. Processor 1 stores M1, d1 and c1 and processor 2 stores M2, d2 and c2. Notice that M1 and M2 are each the size of the original matrix M, but with zeros outside the tile each of them represents. d1 and d2 have the same property. On the other hand, c1 and c2 are the size of the original vector c but there are non-zeros outside of the tiles that they are representing shown by unfilled dots.

It is easy to see that $c = d \oplus M \odot d = (d_1 \oplus M_{1,1} \odot d_1) \oplus (d_2 \oplus M_{1,2} \odot d_2)$. Therefore, without any communication, p_1 can compute $d_1 \oplus M_{1,1} \odot d_1$ and p_2 can compute $d_2 \oplus M_{2,1} \odot d_2$. However, since c_1 and c_2 have non-zeros everywhere, it is necessary to do a global computation to prepare for the next iteration. The value of d in the next iteration is $c = (d_1 \oplus M_{1,1} \odot d_1) \oplus (d_2 \oplus M_{1,2} \odot d_2)$ which requires adding c_1 and c_2.

To save communication time, we assign c_1 to d_1 and c_2 to d_2 before going to the next iteration. In this way, we do not carry out a global reduction. In other words, we do not add c_1 to c_2 to get c. Instead, the values in the second tile of c_1 and the first tile of c_2 continue accumulating separately. At some point in time a global reduction is performed. As discussed below, by avoiding numerous global reductions, the performance of the algorithm improves. Postponing the reduction as just described is useful in the cases where it is not necessary to communicate the computed values immediately. This is the case of the reachability problem in which a processor can compute multiple iterations locally and find more reachable vertices before it communicates the remote reachable vertices.

To be able to postpone updates using our notation, we introduce $\leftarrow$ as an assignment operand which computes the linear algebra operation using only local values on the processor. In the case where an element on the left hand side of $\leftarrow$ is assigned to a different process, that value is only updated locally. For example, c <*and then a global*- d+M*d will perform the local computation and will produce values that go to another processor. These values are the unfilled dots shown in Fig. 2a for both processors involved.

For communicating the values saved locally to the processor which owns the value, we introduce the $\oplus$ = operation which communicates all of the saved values to the owner processor where they are accumulated to the local copies of the elements using $\oplus$ as Fig. 2b depicts it. In the figure, b1 and b2 are the values assumed by c1 and c2 in the next iteration. After the owner processors update their values, communicated values become $\mathbb{0}$.

3.2   Partial Computation

In the simple version of reachability described in Sect. 2, all the reached vertices are processed in each iteration. Processing a vertex v in this problem means that marking all neighbors of v as reachable. This is clearly suboptimal since after one iteration all neighbors of a vertex have been reached. To improve upon this, we limit the processing to only vertices who were reached for the first time in the previous iteration. To be able to support this feature, we propose using mask vectors with $\mathbb{0}$ representing false and $\mathbb{1}$ representing true from the boolean semiring. Mask vectors are not different from other vectors except for the purpose they are used. A mask vector is used with *element-wise multiplication* represented by the operator "$\otimes$.". If a and b are two vectors in a semiring, $a \otimes .b$ is another vector where $(a \otimes .b)(i) = a(i) \otimes b(i)$. Now if b is a mask vector, $a \otimes .b$ will be a sparse subvector of a with some elements set to $\mathbb{0}$.

Note that mask vectors are used to avoid unnecessary computation. Therefore, the system should be aware of the fact that a vector can be sparse. For example, in the case of $A \odot v$ where A is a sparse matrix and v is a sparse vector, only a corresponding columns of non-zero elements of v should be considered.

Partial computation is important for many algorithms where an update to a vertex will only affect a few neighboring vertices. For example, in the case of SSSP, if a vertex is updated, an algorithm needs only to update its outgoing neighbors. Another example is the PageRank problem where if an update to a vertex is higher than the threshold, it only affects the neighbors of that vertex.

4   Single Source Shortest Path

The Single-Source Shortest Path (SSSP) problem finds the shortest distance from a source vertex to every other vertex in a graph. An instance of the problem is denoted by (G, w, s) where $G = (V, E)$ is a graph with the set of vertices, V, and the set of edges, E, and a source vertex, $s \in V$. Each edge $vu \in E$ has a tail, $v \in V$, and a head, $u \in V$. The map $w : E \rightarrow \mathbb{R}$ associates a weight for each edge $vu \in E$. Vertex $s \in V$ is the source whose distances to all other vertices is desired. This section assumes that all the weights are positive. The shortest distance from s to v is denoted by $d(s, v)$.

There are several algorithms to solve SSSP which we will discuss about how some of them can be expressed in TLA. In spite of their differences, the main operation in these algorithms is matrix-vector multiplication in tropical semiring.

4.1   Algorithms

The four best-known algorithms to solve SSSP problem are: Dijkstra [6], Bellman-Ford [2], Chaotic-Relaxation [5], and Δ-Stepping [13]. Bellman-Ford is the only algorithm that is capable of solving SSSP with negative edge weights but this aspect will not be discussed further in this paper and we assume all the graphs have positive edge weights. The basic operation that all four algorithm use is **relaxation** which takes an edge vu and **checks** if $d(s, v) + w(vu) < d(s, u)$ where d is not necessarily the final minimum distance but the shortest path "so-far" in the computation. If the check condition is true, $d(s, u)$ is updated with $d(s, v) + w(vu)$. The difference between the algorithms mentioned above is in the **order** in which relaxations are applied which directly affects the amount of work each algorithm performs. We measure the amount of work done by each algorithm in terms of the number of checks (for $d(s, v) + w(vy) < d(s, u)$) which is equal to the total number of relaxations.

Below, we assume that $G = (V, E)$ is the input graph and that the transpose of its adjacency matrix is M. Initially, in all four algorithm $d(s, v) = \infty$ for all $v \in V - \{s\}$ and $d(s, s) = 0$. The values of d are stored in a tiled vector. Next, we will explain each algorithm and express them in TLA.

Bellman-Ford: Our implementation of the Bellman-Ford algorithm in TLA (shown in Fig. 3) relaxes all the vertices during each iteration. The algorithm terminates after $|V| - 1$ iterations. As we discussed in Sect. 2, d+M*d which corresponds to the formula $d \oplus M \odot d$ computes a new distance vector for G by relaxing all the edges. Parallelizing this algorithm is straightforward by partitioning the vertices and having each processor relax one or more of the resulting subsets. As shown in Fig. 3, in every iteration of the for loop, each processor relaxes its own portion of edges assignment ("<-" in line 2) and then a global communication (operation +=) sends remote updates (line 3).

```
1   for (int i = 0; i < n-1; i++){
2             d <- d + M*d;
3             d += d;   }
```

Fig. 3. Bellman-Ford algorithm main loop using TLA.

Chaotic-Relaxation: The Chaotic-Relaxation algorithm is the same as the Bellman-Ford algorithm except that at each iteration, it only relaxes those vertices which changed distances in the previous iteration. TLA code for this algorithm is shown in Fig. 4. This algorithm is a small improvement over Bellman-Ford obtained by avoiding redundant relaxations. To this end, we use the mask vector r which has one element for each vertex and is used to keep track of the vertices whose distances did not change in the previous iteration. The vector r is initialized so that it is false everywhere except for the position corresponding the vertex s. The element-wise multiplication ($*.$) on line 2 prunes elements which did not change their distance and sparse matrix-sparse vector multiplication ($M*(d*.r)$) takes advantage of it.

In the following algorithms, the scalar `notDone` (replicated across processors) is used to decide when to terminate the algorithm. The last iteration is that in which $d(s, v)$ remain constant for all $v \in V$. In other words, the algorithm is finished when r (set on line 4) is all 0 (all false) for each tile. Note that `r <- b != d` sets `r(i)` to 1 if `b(i) != d(i)` and sets it to 0 otherwise. Finding out when r is all 0 is done by the local reduction `notDone <- any(r)` on line 6 followed by the global reduction `notDone += notDone` on line 7. If `notDone` is 0, it means that there was at least one 0 in one of the tiles of r.

```
1   do {
2             c <- d + M*(d*.r);
3             b += c;
4             r <- (b != d);
5             d <- b;
6             notDone <- any(r);
7             notDone += notDone; /* global reduction */
8   } while (notDone != 0);
```

Fig. 4. Chaotic-Relaxation main loop using TLA.

Dijkstra's Algorithm: Dijkstra's algorithm is the fastest sequential SSSP algorithm. At each iteration in this algorithm, only one vertex is **processed** which is the vertex with minimum distance among the vertices not processed before. Processing a vertex means relaxing all of its outgoing edges. The TLA code for this algorithm is shown in Fig. 5.

The major difference between this algorithm and the previous two algorithms is that the matrix-vector multiplication for this algorithm (line 3) is with a vector which has only one non-0 element in it ($d *. r$) and that element corresponds to the vertex with the minimum distance among the unprocessed vertices. Finding the element with minimum distance is done with the help of vector m which keeps track of the processed vertices (line 5). Lines 6 and 7 find the index and

```
1    m <- 0;
2    for (int i = 0; i < n; i++){
3            d <- d + M*(d*.r);
4            d += d;
5            m <- m+r;
6            ind <- argmin(d*.(!m));
7            minVal <- min(d*.(!m));
8            globalMinVal += minVal; /* global reduction */
9            r <- 0;
10           if (minVal == globalMinVal)
11                   r(ind) = 1;          }
```

Fig. 5. Dijkstra's algorithm main loop using TLA.

the minimum distance vertex in each processor locally and it is communicated globally on line 8. Lines 10 and 11 determines in each processor if the local minimum value is equal to the global minimum value and, if so, sets r accordingly. The algorithm terminates after all n vertices are processed.

Δ-Stepping: Δ-Stepping is another SSSP algorithm which is half way between the Dijkstra's and the Chaotic relaxation algorithms. Δ-Stepping processes a bucket of vertices in each iteration not just one as in the case of Dijkstra's algorithm nor all vertices as in the case of the Chaotic relaxation algorithm. Δ-Stepping distributes vertices into buckets $\{b_0, b_1, b_2, \dots\}$ where bucket $b_i = \{v | \Delta i \le d(v) < \Delta(i + 1)\}$. Note that $d(v)$ is dynamic and as the algorithm advances, it changes value. Therefore, the algorithm should update the bucket for each vertex that is updated. In iteration i, Δ-Stepping only considers vertices from bucket b_i. Since relaxing outgoing edges of a vertex from b_i may add more vertices in it, this process has to continue until there are no more vertices in b_i whose outgoing edges are not relaxed. The algorithm terminates when there are no vertices to process. Note that if b_i is completely processed and the algorithm advances to b_{i+1}, it will never again need to process vertices from b_i since all the weights are positive.

Our version of Δ-Stepping in TLA code is shown in Fig. 6. It is similar to the code in Fig. 4 with a few modifications. First, the main matrix-vector multiplication for relaxation is different which is shown on line 2. There are two mask vectors for this algorithm: (1) r which is similar to r from in Fig. 4 and it holds the vertices that needs to be processed; (2) bucket which is set on line 6 and contains the vertices that belong to bucket b_i. Initially, it contains vertices that are in the range of $[0 \dots \Delta)$. To find out whether there are more vertices in bucket b_i to relax, the scalar notDoneBucket is used on line 7. Similar to notDone scalar from Fig. 4, a reduction on array bucket*.r determines if i should be incremented (line 10) and bucket is set accordingly (line 11).

None of these 4 algorithms required delaying updates and all of them could have been done by fusing local computation with global communication. Next, we will describe our parallel SSSP algorithm which takes advantage of this feature.

Partially Asynchronous Δ-Stepping: This algorithm is similar to Δ-Stepping with the exception that Δ-Stepping algorithm is used locally only. In other words,

```
1  do {
2          c <- d + M*((d*.r)*.bucket);
3          c += c;
4          r <- (c != d);
5          d <- c;
6          bucket <- d >= i*Δ & d < (i+1)*Δ;
7          notDoneBucket <- any(bucket*.r);
8          notDoneBucket += notDoneBucket;
9          if (!notDoneBucket){
10                 i++;
11                 bucket <- d >= i*Δ & d < (i+1)*Δ;
12         }
13         notDone <- any(r);
14         notDone += notDone;
15 } while (notDone != 0);
```

Fig. 6. Δ-Stepping main loop using TLA.

each processor applies Δ-Stepping to process its own vertices. Local relaxation occurs for multiple iterations (for **pipeline** iterations) and after that a global communication exchanges the distance updates. The invariant from Δ-Stepping algorithm explained before does not hold in here; in a processor, a global distance update may add vertices for processing from lower buckets since other processors may have been processing vertices from lower buckets. Therefore, after a global update, each processor needs to start from the smallest bucket which has unprocessed vertices.

The TLA code for this algorithm is shown in Fig. 7. As described above, the algorithm applies a local Δ-Stepping for its vertices as shown in lines 2–10. The code in this loop is similar to the one from the original Δ-Stepping except that every computation is local (note that only <- is used). After this loop, a global update exchanges distances and updates mask vector r (line 12). After that, the variable minDist will be computed which is the minimum distance among all of the local unprocessed vertices. Line 15 finds the minimum bucket with unprocessed vertices in it. The rest of the code is similar to the other SSSP algorithms.

4.2   Performance Comparison

This Section compares the parallel performance of each of the SSSP algorithms described in Sect. 4.1. We will also how each feature of TLA affects the performance.

Figure 8 shows the parallel performance of Chaotic Relaxation, Dijkstra, Δ-Stepping and Partially Asynchronous Δ-Stepping. We excluded Bellman-Ford from this figure since it is significantly slower than the other four algorithms ($\sim 2000\times$). The X axis in this figure represents different number of processors and the Y axis is for running time. Each algorithms is specified by its color: blue for Chaotic Relaxation, gray for Dijkstra, red for Δ-Stepping and purple for Δ-Stepping with pipelining (Partially Asynchronous Δ-Stepping). The orange color is for the communication cost. Therefore, each group of 4 bars represents

```
1    do {
2              for (int j = 0; j < pipeline; j++){
3                      b <- d + M*((d*.r)*.bucket);
4                      r <- (b != d);
5                      d <- b;
6                      bucket <- d >= i*Δ & d < (i+1)*Δ;
7                      notDoneBucket <- any(bucket*.r);
8                      if (!notDoneBucket){
9                              i++;
10                             bucket <- d >= i*Δ & d < (i+1)*Δ; }}
11            b += d;
12            r <- (b != d);
13            d <- b;
14            minDist <- min(d*.r);
15            i = minDist / Δ;
16            notDone <- any(r);
17            notDone += notDone;
18   } while (notDone != 0);
```

Fig. 7. Partially Asynchronous Δ-Stepping algorithm in TLA.

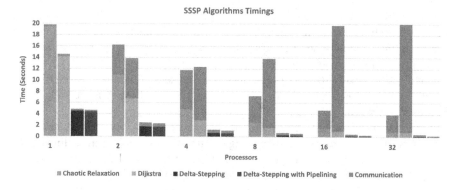

Fig. 8. SSSP algorithms performance comparison

the running time for each algorithm with one specific number of processors. The input graph is an R-MAT graph with $SCALE = 20$.

The fact that Bellman-Ford is significantly slower than Chaotic-Relaxation (order of 2000×) shows that how crucial is partial computation for SSSP algorithms. On the other hand, Chaotic Relaxation algorithm does not scale well because of the communication cost. But as it can be seen, just the blue portion of running time is scaling well. This is because the algorithm is massively parallel and the work is balanced well since each processor owns roughly the same number of edges.

Dijkstra algorithm in Fig. 8 has a better sequential performance than Chaotic relaxation but since it only processes one vertex at a time, the parallel performance is poor and most of the communication cost is just the idle time. However, Δ-Stepping is performing faster than both Dijkstra and Chaotic Relaxation and it is providing decent speed up. Δ-Stepping with pipelining is almost as fast as Δ-Stepping for 1, 2 and 4 processors. It is hard to see in Fig. 8 how they compare with higher number of processors. Therefore, Fig. 9 directly compares them.

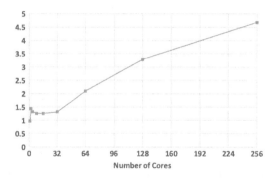

Fig. 9. Delaying updates speed up.

Figure 9 shows the speed up of Partially Asynchronous Δ-Stepping over Δ-Stepping for different number of processors. As it can be seen, up to 16 processors, it does not provide significant improvement but for larger number of processors, it is certainly effective which in this case is more than 4× faster. This shows the importance of delaying updates feature in TLA. Next Section, will study how pipeline factor itself can control the performance of our algorithm.

4.3 Delaying Updates Impact on Partially Asynchronous Δ-Stepping

Our Partially Asynchronous Δ-Stepping has two tunable parameters: the Δ factor and the *pipeline* factor. The best Δ value can be experimentally found and it will neither be affected by the number of processors used nor by the source vertex. On the other hand, the **pipeline** factor which impacts the total number of relaxations, has different best values for different number of processors. Again, each relaxation is a **check** to find whether we can reach a vertex with a shorter distance. We will use the number of checks as a measurement for the amount of work the algorithm does. `pipeline` is a variable as shown in Fig. 7 that controls the number of iterations of local Δ-Stepping between each global communication for updating distances. In other words, it controls the frequency of global communication which impacts the performance in two ways. If the intercommunication interval is too long, a processor almost always computes distances of paths that go through local vertices. This may result in useless checks and updates for those vertices whose shortest path goes through vertices owned by different processors. Thus, it is better for the exchange of relaxation requests not to be too infrequent so that vertices can reach their final distance sooner. However, updating too frequently may add significant overhead because of the initial cost of each communication.

Figure 10a and b show the execution of Partially Asynchronous Δ-Stepping algorithm of Fig. 7 with an R-MAT graph [4] with $SCALE = 20, a = 0.55, b = 0.1, c = 0.1, d = 0.25, M = 8 \times N$ and $\Delta = 2^{16}$ on a shared memory machine with 40 cores as the value of the pipeline factor changes. Figure 10a shows the

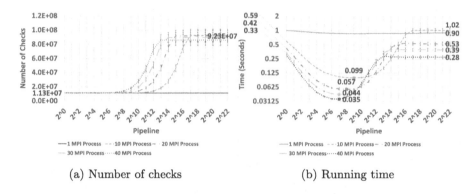

(a) Number of checks   (b) Running time

Fig. 10. Pipeline factor impact on the number of checks and the running time.

number of checks and Fig. 10b shows the running times. Each line corresponds to a different number of processor. We use a value of $\Delta = 2^{16}$, as it results in the lowest execution time independent of the number of processors. Numbers are computed by averaging the running times of the algorithm for 16 randomly chosen source vertices. All axes are logarithmic. The error bars represent the standard deviation. The marked points on the plot in Fig. 10b show the best performing value of the pipeline factor.

The number of checks, increases with the pipeline factor, however, it is almost constant at first and then increases drastically. The left most points represent frequent global updates. On the other hand, a high pipeline factor has the same effect as if there were no pipelining at all. With low pipeline factor the numbers of checks is the same for all number of processors. As the pipeline factor increases, there is a factor of ~ 8 increase in the number of checks for all number of processes (except, of course, for the case of 1 processor where it remains constant). As it can be seen in Fig. 10b, low values for pipeline factor do not deliver the best performance because for these values, the algorithm sends many short messages. In fact, for low values, the algorithm is 6× slower than the optimal. On the other hand, high values of the pipeline factor slows down the algorithm because of the large number of checks (relaxations). In fact, for high pipeline values the algorithm is $\sim 8\times$ slower than the best execution times. This tracks the factor of 8 increase in the number of checks. The point at which the pipeline factor delivers the best performance is different for each number of processors. The best pipeline factors for different graphs are different but the optimum is never at too low or too high values. This suggests that using the idea of delaying updates is effective and it increases the performance by multiple factors.

5   Related Work

Our work is most similar to the combinatorial BLAS [3] but we differ in that where they handle the parallelism entirely under the abstraction of linear algebra but we make the parallelism and distribution explicit. In TLA, the programmer can write the same type of program that was expressible in the combinatorial BLAS since we are both based on the linear algebra but in TLA the programmer can directly control distribution, communication, and grain size. These features allow an expert programmer to take code and tune it to take advantage of hardware and algorithmic features that are not exposed in a system.

Another model of parallel graph computation is the vertex programing model. This model is used by PowerGraph [7], Pregl [11], and GraphLab [10]. In this model, the programmer thinks of graph algorithms as running in parallel and interaction on the edges between vertices. Also, the very fine grained work is aggregated by the runtime system and not under programmer control. It also lacks the ability to restrict computation when available under programmer control. These limitations would prevent expressing algorithms such as Δ-Stepping where the work does flow directly from neighboring vertices.

6   Conclusion

In this paper, we presented TLA, a system for graph algorithms using linear algebra. We have demonstrated the express-ability of our library with implementations of several SSSP algorithms. Our experiments have shown that by using the extensions in TLA, we achieve performance comparable to custom implementations of the same algorithms.

In the future, we intend to develop TLA in to a full featured library with more included semirings as well as support for user defined ones. We believe that as we implement more algorithms with TLA, we will find more extensions to the underlaying liner algebra. Extensions that we have considered included asynchronous messaging, control over updating, and support for dynamic graphs.

References

1. Arnal, J., Migallón, V., Penadés, J.: Synchronous and asynchronous parallel algorithms with overlap for almost linear systems. In: Hernández, V., Palma, J.M.L.M., Dongarra, J. (eds.) VECPAR 1998. LNCS, vol. 1573, pp. 142–155. Springer, Heidelberg (1999)
2. Bellman, R.: On a routing problem. Q. Appl. Math. **16**, 87–90 (1958)
3. Buluç, A., Gilbert, J.R.: The combinatorial blas: design, implementation, and applications. Int. J. High Perform. Comput. Appl. **25**(4), 496–509 (2011)
4. Chakrabarti, D., Zhan, Y., Faloutsos, C.: R-mat: a recursive model for graph mining. In: SDM (2004)
5. Chazan, D., Miranker, W.: Chaotic relaxation. Linear Algebra Appl. **2**(2), 199–222 (1969)
6. Dijkstra, E.: A note on two problems in connexion with graphs. Numerische Mathematik **1**(1), 269–271 (1959)
7. Gonzalez, J.E., Low, Y., Gu, H., Bickson, D., Guestrin, C.: Powergraph: distributed graph-parallel computation on natural graphs. In: Proceedings of the 10th USENIX Conference on Operating Systems Design and Implementation, OSDI 2012, pp. 17–30, USENIX Association, Berkeley(2012)

8. Kepner, J., Gilbert, J. (eds.): Graph Algorithms in the Language of Linear Algebra. Society for Industrial and Applied Mathematics, Philadelphia (2011)

9. Krishnamoorthy, S., Baskaran, M., Bondhugula, U., Ramanujam, J., Rountev, A., Sadayappan, P.: Effective automatic parallelization of stencil computations. In: Proceedings of the 2007 ACM SIGPLAN Conference on Programming Language Design and Implementation, PLDI 2007, pp. 235–244, ACM, New York (2007)

10. Low, Y., Bickson, D., Gonzalez, J., Guestrin, C., Kyrola, A., Hellerstein, J.M.: Distributed graphlab: a framework for machine learning and data mining in the cloud. Proc. VLDB Endow. 5(8), 716–727 (2012)

11. Malewicz, G., Austern, M.H., Bik, A.J., Dehnert, J.C., Horn, I., Leiser, N., Czajkowski, G.: Pregel: A system for large-scale graph processing. In: Proceedings of the 2010 ACM SIGMOD International Conference on Management of Data, SIGMOD 2010, pp. 135–146, ACM, New York (2010)

12. Mattson, T., Bader, D.A., Berry, J.W., Buluç, A., Dongarra, J., Faloutsos, C., Feo, J., Gilbert, J.R., Gonzalez, J., Hendrickson, B., Kepner, J., Leiserson, C.E., Lumsdaine, A., Padua, D.A., Poole, S., Reinhardt, S., Stonebraker, M., Wallach, S., Yoo, A.: Standards for graph algorithm primitives. In: HPEC, pp. 1–2 (2013)

13. Meyer, U., Sanders, P.: Delta-stepping: a parallelizable shortest path algorithm. J. Algorithms 49(1), 114–152 (2003)

An Approach for Proving the Correctness of Inspector/Executor Transformations

Michael Norrish[1]([⊠]) and Michelle Mills Strout[2]

[1] NICTA, Canberra, Australia
michael.norrish@nicta.com.au
[2] Colorado State University, Fort Collins, USA
michelle.strout@colostate.edu

Abstract. To take advantage of multicore parallelism, programmers and compilers rewrite, or transform, programs to expose loop-level parallelism. Showing the correctness, or legality, of such program transformations enables their incorporation into compilers. However, the correctness of inspector/executor strategies, which develop parallel schedules at runtime for computations with nonaffine array accesses, rests on the correctness of the inspector code itself. Since inspector code is often provided in a run-time library, showing the correctness of an inspector/executor transformation in a compiler requires proving the correctness of any hand-written or compiler-generated inspector code as well. In this paper, we present a formally defined language (called PseudoC) for representing loops with indirect array accesses. We describe how using this language, where the reads and writes in array assignments are distinguished, it is possible to formally prove the correctness of a wavefront parallelism inspector in HOL4. The key idea is to reason about the equivalence of the original code and the inspector/executor code based on operational semantics for the PseudoC grammar and properties of an executable action graph representation of the original and executor loops.

1 Introduction

Inspector/executor strategies refer to a category of program transformations that apply to loop nests with non-affine memory references and loop bounds. The executor is a transformed version of the original code, and the inspector code implements parallelization and/or run-time reordering by performing a data reordering and/or a reordering of loop iterations into a new schedule. The new schedules and/or data orderings are created to parallelize the loop and/or improve the data locality.

In this paper, we focus on reordering iterations of a sequential loop into a sequence of wavefronts, where all of the iterations within a wavefront can be executed in parallel. A wavefront parallelism inspector/executor transformation consists of the compile-time transformation of loops with non-affine array accesses, like the one in Fig. 1, into an inspector and an executor as shown in Fig. 2. Assuming that the index arrays h, g, and f from Fig. 1 are not modified

© Springer International Publishing Switzerland 2015
J. Brodman and P. Tu (Eds.): LCPC 2014, LNCS 8967, pp. 131–145, 2015.
DOI: 10.1007/978-3-319-17473-0_9

```
// ==== original executor
for (i=lb; i<ub; i++ ) {
    A[h[i]]=...A[g[i]]
              ...A[f[i+1]]...
}
```

```
// ==== inspector
// Code that generates the data
// structures to represent
// iterations in each wavefront.


// ==== transformed executor
for (w=0; w<numwave; w++) {
    parfor ( i in wavefront(w) ) {
        A[h[i]]=...A[g[i]]
                  ...A[f[i+1]]...
    }
}
```

Fig. 1. Example original code with indirect array accesses and an example action graph.

Fig. 2. The inspector and executor code after applying the wavefront parallelism transformation.

in the loop being transformed, the dependencies between iterations in the original loop can be determined at runtime immediately before the execution of the loop itself.

Figure 1 also illustrates what we call an *action graph* for the example loop given that lb = 0, ub = 6, h[] = {4,3,3,5,1,7}, g[] = {1,3,0,0,6,6}, and f[] = {-1,2,1,5,5,4,7}. Each node in the action graph contains all of the read and write access information for a statement instance and enough information about the statement to enable execution of that statement. The read and write information as well as original execution order is used to connect nodes with data dependence edges. The action graph differs from a dependence graph in that a data-flow dependence graph just indicates the partial ordering between iterations and is not executable.

Inspector strategies are quite prevalent in the literature [1–10]. They are implemented manually [9], with code generators for specific kernels [10], and with compilers inserting calls to run-time library inspectors [11]. The main difference between these approaches and the one we are presenting is that we give formal, mechanically checked proofs of the correctness of both the inspector, and also the data dependence analysis that the inspector depends on. The inspector code is non-trivial because its efficiency often derives from specializing the implementation for a specific kernel and/or a restricted set of kernels with certain characteristics, such as the sparse matrix data structure being used.

In this paper, we present a formal strategy for proving the correctness of inspectors that we are in the process of applying to the wavefront parallelization inspector/executor transformation. The first realization is that we can break out the reads and writes in the representation of the original computation, providing a convenient picture of a program's memory behavior. This leads to our language PseudoC, which is given a formal small-step operational semantics (one that allows for interleaving across concurrent computations). We continue with a general theorem connecting our formalization of the action graph view of a program to its realization in PseudoC. This connection allows proofs of program equivalence in the presence of iteration reordering and/or parallelization. Preconditions on such results then serve as the formal specification of inspectors. Using the HOL4 theorem prover [12], we then show the correctness of a simple inspector that uses wavefronts. The methods and advantages of mechanized proof (simply, a much stronger assurance of correctness) are discussed further in Sect. 3.2. Mechanizing the full wavefront parallelization inspector/executor is ongoing work. We ultimately aim to provide a library of verified inspector/executor parallelization transformations.

Section 2 describes the applicability and limitations of a wavefront parallelization micro-benchmark. Section 3 indicates why the typical approach to showing the legality of auto-parallelization and other program transformations using data dependence abstractions is problematic when applying this approach to inspector/executor strategies. Section 4 presents the PseudoC grammar that breaks out reads and writes to enable formal reasoning about data dependencies. Section 5 describes how the proof is done in HOL4 using the action graph and small-step operational semantics for PseudoC. Section 6 summarizes related work, and Sect. 7 concludes.

2   Applicability of Wavefront Parallelization

Wavefront parallelization has been applied to applications such as sparse triangular solvers [13], `doacross` loops in PERFECT benchmarks [14], and more recently in various benchmarks and a proxy application called UMT (Unstructured Mesh for Transport code) [15]. We developed a microbenchmark and wavefront inspector/executor to use as an initial case study for developing an approach to formally proving the correctness of inspector/executor transformations. This section describes the micro-benchmark and presents some experimental results to illustrate the applicability of the wavefront parallelization transformation.

The micro-benchmark, with the original code and executor shown in Fig. 3, reads in a square, sparse matrix and uses the pattern of non-zero entries in the sparse matrix to provide a `do across` loop dependence pattern[1]. For each non-zero entry, the benchmark performs a parameterized summation involving exponent calls to enable experimentation with the arithmetic intensity (flops/byte). If the amount of work is set to zero, then no `exp()` calls will occur but at least four adds will occur each iteration. The particular summation in the inner loop was selected because it converges to a small number, which enables easy testing. The result of the summation is added to the data array as indexed by the row and column of the non-zero entries.

The wavefront executor is shown in Fig. 3. The initial inspector for our case study is serial, but we also plan to implement the parallel wavefront inspectors by Rauchwerger et al. [14] and Zhuang et al. [15]. The serial inspector code in

---

[1] If there is a non-zero at location A_{ij} in the sparse matrix and $i < j$, then there is a dependence between iteration i and j (i must execute before j).

```
// =========== Original Code ===========
// foreach non-zero A_ij in sparse matrix:
for (int p=0; p<nnz; p++) {

  // sum = Σ_{k=0}^{w-1} 1 / exp( k * data[row[p]] * data[col[p]] )
  double sum = 0.0;
  for (int k=0; k<workPerIter; k++) {
    sum += 1.0/exp((double)k*data[row[p]]*data[col[p]]);
  }
  data[row[p]] += 1.0 + sum;
  data[col[p]] += 1.0 + sum;
}


// =========== Executor =======
// for each wavefront
for (int w=0; w<=max_wave; w++) {
  // foreach non-zero A_ij in sparse matrix in wavefront
  #pragma omp parallel for shared(data)
  for (int k=wavestart[w]; k<wavestart[w+1]; k++) {
    int p = wavefronts[k];

    // same loop body as in Original Code
  }
}
```

Fig. 3. The wavebench micro-benchmark original code and executor.

our case study visits each iteration of the original loop in order and keeps track of the last write and read for each data element in an array. This information is used to determine the earliest wavefront in which to place an iteration while still satisfying data dependencies.

We ran wavebench on an HP-Z800-Xeon E5520-SATA, 8 core 2.26 GHz with 12 GB of RAM, 32 KB L1, 256 KB L2, and two 8 MB L3 caches, where each L3 cache is shared by 4 cores. The sparse matrices used are from the Davis Florida Collection [16] and range from 3.1 to 8.5 million non-zeroes.

Figure 4 shows the speedup of the executor for the five matrices we ran when the number of exp() calls were set to 4. The average parallelism in the action graph for each sparse matrix is shown in parentheses next to the sparse matrix name. Average parallelism is the number of iterations divided by the number of wavefronts, or critical path length. The inspector overhead was less than running the executor once. Note that the 1d5pt.mm does not have any parallelism to exploit, so wavefront parallelization only adds additional loop overhead.

As an exemplar, this micro-benchmark has many benefits. We can determine when wavefront parallelism will be beneficial by modifying the amount of work being performed in the inner loop. When the number of exp() calls is 4 or above, all of the input matrices with parallelism have a speedup of 2 or higher. This indicates that for this machine a computation would require a lot of work

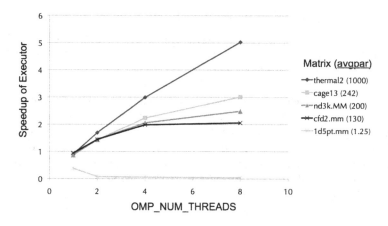

Fig. 4. Speedup of the wavebench micro-benchmark on a Xeon 2x quad core.

within the loop for wavefront parallelism to be useful. The other benefit of this micro-benchmark is that the dependencies between iterations in the loop are not artificially generated. They derive from sparse matrices applicable to real applications.

The limitation of the benchmark is that it is an artificial computation kernel and we are only performing one inspector/executor strategy to it, specifically wavefront parallelism. The simplicity of the computational kernel and the single, non-parallel inspector ease the process of developing an approach to performing formal verification of inspector/executor transformation correctness.

3   The Legality of Program Transformations

In the compilers research area, the legality of auto parallelization and program transformations are determined by performing a data dependence analysis and then checking whether the transformed representation of the program still satisfies the original dependencies [17–20]. In this Section, we review how dependence analysis has been used in the past to determine transformation legality and indicate issues that arise when applying this approach to inspector/executor transformations.

3.1   Using Data Dependence Analysis to Argue Correctness

The data dependencies between computations (*i.e.*, iterations in a loop) are derivable from how each iteration reads and writes data. Data dependence analysis represents such data dependencies with various levels of precision [21]. For computations with indirect array accesses, Wonnacott and Pugh [22] introduced the idea of using uninterpreted function symbols to represent dependence relations in such codes at compile time. They used this representation to improve the detection of fully parallel loops at compile-time, and they also suggested using the approach to create run-time checks to determine parallelism. Hybrid Analysis [23,24] uses a "uniform set representation" to perform as much data dependence analysis for parallelism detection at compile time as possible, with generated code that performs any necessary dynamic checks.

The Sparse Polyhedral Framework [25,26] took the use of uninterpreted functions in data dependence relations further than just detecting parallelization to the determination of constraints on index arrays generated by inspector/executor strategies. Performing a data dependence analysis with petit (a tool available with the Omega project [27]) and specifying the transformations as relations, a manual proof of correctness using pre and post conditions was performed for the full sparse tiling transformation applied to the Gauss-Seidel computation [28].

As an example of deriving such constraints, the data dependence relation for the original kernel in the wavebench micro-benchmark in Fig. 3 is:

$$\{[p] \rightarrow [p'] \mid (p < p') \wedge (0 \leq p, p' < nnz) \wedge ((row(p) = row(p'))$$
$$\vee (row(p) = col(p')) \vee (col(p) = row(p')) \vee (col(p) = col(p')))\},$$

where $row()$ and $col()$ are uninterpreted function symbols representing the corresponding index arrays. Note that the variable sum is privatizable. It would also be possible to detect that the full loop is a reduction, but for simplicity of the micro-benchmark we ignore that and derive the dependencies caused by the increment on the accesses to the data array.

The wavefront parallelization transformation can be expressed in the Sparse Polyhedral Framework using the following relation: $\{[p] \rightarrow [w, p] \mid w = wave(p)\}$, where w is the iterator over wavefronts in Fig. 3 and the p loop in the transformed code is parallel. The transformed space $[w, p]$ is executed in lexicographical order except for the p loop, which since it has been specified as parallel, will execute in parallel for each instance of w. The waves loop with iterator w is executed in sequential order. Applying this transformation to the data dependence relation for the original loop results in the transformed dependencies:

$$\{[w, p] \rightarrow [w', p'] \mid w = wave(p) \wedge w' = wave(p') \wedge (p < p') \wedge (0 \leq p, p' < nnz)$$
$$\wedge ((row(p) = row(p')) \vee (row(p) = col(p'))$$
$$\vee (col(p) = row(p')) \vee (col(p) = col(p')))\}.$$

The transformed data dependence relation, and thus the transformation that created it, is legal if the dependencies are all lexicographically positive. For this example, this leads to the constraint that if there was an original dependence between iteration p and p', then it must be the case that $wave(p)$ is strictly less than $wave(p')$, ensuring that iteration p is executed before iteration p' in the new wavefront parallel schedule.

Current inspector/executor implementations of wavefront schedules such as [14,15] present their inspector algorithms and argue that they place iterations from the original loop into wavefronts so that the original dependencies are satisfied. This approach for determining the correctness of inspector/executor transformations assumes that the data dependence analysis (often performed manually for a particular class of computations) is correct, and also uses informal arguments to show the inspector implementation is correct.

3.2 Why Mechanized Proofs

Yang *et al.*'s experience [29] is a strong suggestion that the only way to avoid bugs in C compilers is through formal verification. Their work found code generation ("middle end") bugs in 10 different C compilers (*e.g.*, 202 in LLVM; 79 in GCC, including 25 classed as release-blocking). In contrast, the only bugs found in the mechanically verified CompCert compiler [30] were in its at-the-time-unverified front-end, and in the interface to its assembler.

There is no reason to suppose that inspector-executor optimizations should be immune to bugs; if anything, the optimizations' complexity likely provides lots of hiding places for bugs. The only tools capable of verifying compilers at the requisite level of detail are interactive theorem-proving systems, such as ACL2, Coq (used for CompCert), Isabelle, PVS and HOL4 (used in this work). These systems are capable of defining the relevant semantics (*e.g.*, for C and for the instruction set of the CPU), defining the functions that transform syntax, and proving that the functions are actually correct.

Performing such verifications is extremely labor-intensive (see Sect. 5.5 below on how this might be ameliorated), but there seems to be no better way towards high assurance.

4   Expressing Codes in PseudoC

Our approach enables formal proofs of the correctness of an inspector/executor transformation without assuming correct data dependence analysis, or a correct inspector implementation. We start with a representation for the original code and the executor that separates the reads from the writes in assignment statements. This is the PseudoC language, for which we have defined a small-step operational semantics capturing possible interleaving concurrent execution.

In addition to the operational semantics for PseudoC, we have also defined a function that maps a PseudoC program into an action graph representation that tracks all reads and writes (Sect. 5.2). This action graph representation is used only during proofs: it is a mathematical artifact, albeit one that inspectors may try to approximate with their own runtime analyses.

Figure 5 shows the grammar for PseudoC, which is rich enough to represent original code with for-loops and indirect array references, and the case study inspector and executor. The operational semantics for some example PseudoC statements are shown in Fig. 6. The semantics relates pairs of memories and pieces of PseudoC syntax.

The original code and the executor perform assignments to array elements via the Assign production rule where the reads are represented as $\langle dexpr\rangle$s so that the operational semantics can indicate the ability for reads and writes from different iterations within a parallel loop to be interleaved. The first inference rule in Fig. 6 is for the `Assign` statement, which assigns a value to an array element. Given that the conditions above the horizontal rule are true, then the memory state m_0 will be updated to the memory state m and the `Assign` statement will be replaced with the `Done` assignment, representing successful termination. The value $V(i)$ is an expression that has been fully evaluated to an integer i, in this case representing the index at which the array will be updated.

When a `ForLoop` or a `ParLoop` is interpreted, the loop body is replicated as many times as there are loop iterations. (In the original code and the executor, we assume that all loops are bounded). Each copy of the loop body has instances of the iterator variable replaced the appropriate value from the iteration's domain. The copies are then collected underneath a `Seq` or `Par` construct (Fig. 6 shows a `ForLoop` and therefore a `Seq` construct).

The final two rules in Fig. 6 illustrate how loop bodies then evaluate with `Seq` and `Par` constructors. In the `Seq`, the first iteration has to evaluate to completion before any others can evaluate. In the `Par`, any loop body can take a step at any stage, representing the possible interleaving that parallel loops afford.

$\langle value \rangle ::= $ `Int` $\langle int \rangle$
    | `Real` $\langle real \rangle$
    | `Bool` $\langle bool \rangle$
    | `Array` $\langle value\ list \rangle$
    | `Error`

$\langle expr \rangle ::= $ `VarExp` $\langle ident \rangle$
    | `ISub` $\langle ident \rangle \langle expr \rangle$
    | $\langle expr \rangle \langle binop \rangle \langle expr \rangle$
    | $\langle unaryop \rangle \langle expr \rangle$
    | `Value` $\langle value \rangle$

$\langle dexpr \rangle ::= $ `DValue` $\langle value \rangle$
    | `ARead` $\langle ident \rangle \langle expr \rangle$
    | `VRead` $\langle ident \rangle$

$\langle domain \rangle ::= $ `D` $\langle expr \rangle \langle expr \rangle$

$\langle stmt \rangle ::= $ `Assign` `(` $\langle ident \rangle$, $\langle expr \rangle$ `)` $\langle dexpr\text{-}list \rangle$
      $\langle rhs\text{-}f \rangle$
    | `AssignVar` $\langle ident \rangle \langle dexpr\text{-}list \rangle \langle rhs\text{-}f \rangle$
    | `IfStmt` $\langle expr \rangle \langle stmt \rangle \langle stmt \rangle$
    | `Malloc` $\langle ident \rangle \langle int \rangle \langle value \rangle$
    | `ForLoop` $\langle ident \rangle \langle domain \rangle \langle stmt \rangle$
    | `ParLoop` $\langle ident \rangle \langle domain \rangle \langle stmt \rangle$
    | `Seq` $\langle stmt\text{-}list \rangle$
    | `Par` $\langle stmt\text{-}list \rangle$
    | `Abort`
    | `Done`

Fig. 5. The abstract syntax tree grammar for the PseudoC language. To break out the reads from the writes, the array element assignment `Assign` and the variable assignment `AssignVar` statements include a list of $\langle dexpr \rangle$s and then a lambda function called the right-hand side function $\langle rhs - f \rangle$ that can map a list of $\langle value \rangle$s to a single value.

5   Proof of Correctness

5.1   Original Code and Executor Equivalence

The heart of the correctness problem is verifying that, after the inspector has done its work, the original code and the executor have the same effect. However, the original code and the executor may execute their array assignments in radically different orders. To formally capture the equivalence between old and new programs we map their syntax into a domain where non-conflicting assignments can be executed in any order and compare the results there.

$$\frac{(\forall r \in reads.\ \mathsf{isValue}(r))\quad \mathsf{upd\_array}(m_0, id, i, rhsf(reads)) = m}{(m_0, \mathtt{Assign}((id, \mathsf{V}(i)), reads, rhsf)) \longrightarrow (m, \mathtt{Done})}$$

$$\frac{\mathsf{evalexpr}(m, e_1) = l\quad \mathsf{evalexpr}(m, e_2) = u}{(m, \mathtt{ForLoop}(id, \mathsf{D}(e_1, e_2), s)) \longrightarrow (m, \mathtt{Seq}[s[id := l], s[id := l+1], \ldots, s[id := u-1]])}$$

$$\frac{(m_0, s_1) \longrightarrow (m, s)}{(m_0, \mathtt{Seq}\ [s_1, s_2, \ldots, s_n] \longrightarrow (m, \mathtt{Seq}\ [s, s_2, \ldots, s_n])}$$

$$\frac{(m_0, c_0) \longrightarrow (m, c)}{(m_0, \mathtt{Par}\ [p, \ldots, c_0, \ldots, s] \longrightarrow (m, \mathtt{Par}\ [p, \ldots, c, \ldots, s])}$$

Fig. 6. Example operational semantic rules for PseudoC.

The domain we choose is the *nested action graph*. The nodes of these graphs are either (recursively) sub-graphs themselves, or at the base case, pending array assignments. Each node of the latter sort contains a list of read locations, a write location and a function for turning the read values into a value to be written. The read list of a sub-graph node is the union of all the reads in the sub-graph. Sub-graph nodes also contain write lists, consisting of all the writes made in the sub-graph. There is an edge between two nodes if they have overlapping write lists, or if one has a read contained in the other's write list. Given such a pair of nodes, the direction of the edge depends on the ordering between those nodes' assignments in the original program.

We refer to a node containing a pending assignment as *atomic*. Though such a node contains memory reads and an eventual write that might interleave with other nodes' execution, such a node can only be executed when the dependence edges allow it, meaning that modeling its execution as atomic is justified.

The behavior of graph on an input memory is computed by repeatedly removing nodes with no incoming edges, and executing their assignments. Though non-deterministic in its choice of nodes, this behaviour can only result in one possible output memory. Similarly, parallel programs may exhibit transient non-determinism, but if they are race-free, their execution will have only one possible eventual result. If a program is not race-free, the action graph semantics categorizes this as an error: such a program has no corresponding action graph.

5.2   Creating Action Graphs from PseudoC

The function graphOf maps PseudoC programs to graphs. It is defined recursively over the syntax of an executor program. Not all forms of PseudoC program are convertible to action graphs; in particular, original code and executors cannot include unbounded loops (*e.g.*, while loops), nor Malloc calls.

Because the execution of graphOf must both unwind executors with parameterized (but bounded) loops, and decide which branch of if-statements is taken, the graphOf function takes an initial memory value as a parameter. It also computes the memory that will result from the execution of the graph, so that updated memory values can be passed through the program recursively. This can be seen in the clause for the ForLoop mapping in Fig. 7.

$$
\begin{aligned}
&\mathsf{graphOf}\ m_0\ (\mathtt{ForLoop}\ vnm\ d\ body)\ =\\
&\quad \mathsf{do}\\
&\qquad dvs\ \leftarrow\ \mathsf{dvalues}\ m_0\ d;\\
&\qquad \mathsf{FOLDL}\ (\lambda acc\ v.\\
&\qquad\qquad \mathsf{do}\\
&\qquad\qquad\quad (m,g)\ \leftarrow\ acc;\\
&\qquad\qquad\quad (m',sg)\ \leftarrow\ \mathsf{graphOf}\ m\ (body[vnm := v]);\\
&\qquad\qquad\quad \mathsf{SOME}(\,m',\\
&\qquad\qquad\qquad\qquad g\ \oplus\ \langle\ \mathsf{reads} := \mathsf{greads}(sg); \mathsf{writes} := \mathsf{gwrites}(sg);\\
&\qquad\qquad\qquad\qquad\qquad\qquad \mathsf{data} := sg\rangle)\\
&\qquad\qquad \mathsf{od})\\
&\qquad\quad (\mathsf{SOME}(m_0,\varepsilon))\\
&\qquad\quad dvs\\
&\quad \mathsf{od}
\end{aligned}
$$

Fig. 7. Calculating the graph of a **for** loop. This is a simplified version of the function defined in HOL4. The FOLDL folds (or "reduces") the computation of the graph. It begins with the input memory m_0 and an empty graph (ε). Each iteration over the loop values (dvs) then returns an updated version of each, calculating a sub-graph (sg), embedding this into a node (between the angle-brackets), and adding that node to the accumulating graph.

The treatment of **for**-loops also demonstrates the use of and need for *nested* action graphs: a loop's body may contain multiple atomic assignments, or indeed more, nested loops. When we perform our wavefront analysis, we want to schedule entire loop bodies as a unit. The unit of computation with action graphs is a single node, so loop bodies consisting of multiple atomic actions need to have those actions bundled together into a sub-graph that is then treated as a single node at the higher level. The graph construction for parallel loops is given in Fig. 8.

Theorem 1. *For all PseudoC programs p, if there exists a nested action-graph g such that g = graphOf(p), then the program has only one possible behavior, which is the same as that obtained by executing the graph g.*

5.3   Characterizing Equivalence

With a correct action graph semantics in hand, the next step in our approach to showing inspector/executor correctness is to characterize the conditions under which the equivalence will hold. In essence, the task is to prove a theorem of the form ⟨inspector post-condition⟩ ⇒ graphOf(*old*) = graphOf(*new*). We have not

graphOf m_0 (**ParLoop** $vnm\ d\ body$) $=$
  do
      dvs $\leftarrow$ dvalues $m_0\ d$;
      ns $\leftarrow$ MAP ($\lambda v.$ do (m, sg) $\leftarrow$ graphOf m_0 ($body[vnm := v]$);
                            SOME($\langle$ reads $:=$ greads(sg); writes $:=$ gwrites(sg);
                                      data $:=$ $sg\rangle$)
                  od) dvs;
      assert($\forall i\,j.\ \ i < j < |ns| \Rightarrow ns_i \not\curvearrowright_t ns_j$);
      g $\leftarrow$ SOME(FOLDR($\lambda a\,g.\ a \oplus g$) $\varepsilon\ ns$);
      m $\leftarrow$ nagEval g (SOME m_0);
      SOME(m, g)
  od

Fig. 8. Calculating the action graph of a **ParLoop**. The sub-graphs are calculated independently, under the MAP, which iterates over the loop's domain values dvs. The memory resulting from each sub-graph computation (m) is ignored rather than being the basis for the execution of the next iterations as in the handling of **ForLoop**. The assert checks that none of the calculated sub-graphs have a dependence between each other. The final graph is assembled by adding all of the nodes in ns to an empty graph, and the final memory is calculated by evaluating that final graph with the graph evaluation function, nagEval.

yet proved a theorem of this shape for the parallelizing wavefront transformation, but we can illustrate our approach with a simple example that *has* been mechanically verified. This iteration reordering imagines a loop with a body of the form `A[W(i)]` `=` ... `A[R₁(i)]` ... `A[Rₙ(i)]` ..., where the assignment target is a function W of the iteration index (perhaps *via* an indirection array), and where the n reads are mediated through the various R_i functions (again, possibly indirection arrays).

We have mechanically proved the following:

Theorem 2. *With W and R specifying the program's write and read information as above, let $\mathsf{ddepR}(W, R, i, j)$ be true iff iteration i comes before iteration j and they have the same write, or if one writes to one of the other's reads. Then*

$$(\forall i\,j.\ i < j < N \wedge \mathsf{ddepR}(W, R, i, j) \Rightarrow \delta^{-1}(i) < \delta^{-1}(j)) \wedge$$
$$\delta : \{0 \ldots N-1\} \to \{0 \ldots N-1\}\ \text{a bijection}$$
$$\Rightarrow$$
$$(\texttt{for(i=0;i<N;i++)}\ \{A[W(i)] = \ldots A[R_j(i)] \ldots\}) =$$
$$(\texttt{for(i=0;i<N;i++)}\ \{A[W(\delta(i))] = \ldots A[R_j(\delta(i))] \ldots\})$$

Alternatively: as long as the inverse of the new indirection array/function does not change the order of iterations that are connected with a data dependence, the new executor will be equivalent to the old.

The proof of this result depends heavily on the existence of the action graph domain into which the `for`-loops are mapped.

5.4   Verifying the Inspector

When a theorem of the above form has been proved, the final stage of the verification can be performed. That is, we must now confirm that the inspector establishes the desired post-condition. Note that, as in the example above, we aim to prove as general a post-condition as possible. If this is done, correct inspectors may compute different reorderings or parallelizations.

Continuing our iteration reordering example, we have mechanically verified that a permissible inspector is one that orders iterations by their wavefront number. This is our last mechanically verified theorem:

Theorem 3. *Sorting the iterations of a simple for loop with respect to the iterations' wavefront number generates a δ-function that is both a bijection over the for-loop's domain, and respects the dependence relation. This δ can then be used to correctly reorder iterations, as per the equivalence of Sect. 5.3.*

Even this much leaves aspects of the inspector's implementation under-specified. For example, the inspector must generate iterations' wave numbers without access to the complete action graph. Handling these sorts of details will move what is verified ever closer to the code that actually executes.

5.5   Limitations and Future Work

We do not expect that correct transformations will ever be easy to verify. Rather, our goal is to establish a verified library, one that couples verified executor transformations with families of verified inspectors. These inspectors will have been to shown to meet the transformations' preconditions, allowing programmers and compilers to deploy them safely.

The transformations will need to be as general as possible in two ways: with general preconditions allowing multiple inspector strategies, and embodying general patterns of code transformations.

Our mechanization effort is still ongoing, but we are confident that the approach sketched here is a viable strategy. There is still more to be done: (1) we want to express inspector implementations in a higher level language than PseudoC, one where relevant notions such as binary relations and the operations on them are first-class; (2) nonetheless, such a high-level language should have a verified translation to PseudoC; and (3) we would like to formally capture the compile-time syntactic analysis that leads to the inspector's static knowledge of where reads and writes occur are possible.

6   Related Work

Inspector/executor strategies were developed to find shared-memory, partial parallelism in `doacross` loops [1,2] and to implement distributed memory parallelism between `doall` loops that accessed distributed data [3]. Later data reordering transformations [4–7] and sparse tiling [8–10] was developed.

Other related work includes formally showing the correctness of compilers and translators, which is an exciting area of recent research progress. The CompCert compiler by Leroy [30] has been formally shown to correctly translate a mildly restricted subset of C to x86 assembly code with equivalent semantics. The CompCert compiler performs register allocation, instruction scheduling, and some data-flow optimizations, but does not include any parallelization.

In the context of irregular applications with indirect array accesses, Gilad and Bodik [31] have developed a domain-specific language LL for transforming dense matrices into various sparse matrix formats and showing the equivalence of computations on the sparse matrix format to the corresponding computation on the dense matrix format. This work is relevant to inspector/executor strategies as the conversion between sparse matrix formats is typically done with an inspector. However, this work does not look at parallelization transformations.

7   Conclusions

Parallelization transformations in compilers are typically determined correct based on data dependence analysis and reasoning about how parallelization, possibly in combination with other transformations, continue to satisfy such dependencies. This approach assumes too much, especially in the context of irregular applications with indirect memory references where it is necessary to assume both that the data dependence analysis is correct and that the inspector code is correct as well.

In this paper, we present a new approach for determining the correctness of an inspector/executor strategy, ultimately aiming to provide a library of verified inspector/executor parallelization transformations. All code (the original code, inspector, and executor) are represented in our PseudoC language, which separates reads from writes. This language has two formal semantics: a small-step operational semantics where reads and writes in separate iterations of a parallel loop can execute concurrently, and one in terms of action graphs. The action graph semantics allows the proof of program equivalences subject to certain conditions. Inspector correctness then depends on showing that these conditions are met. Important preliminaries and simple examples have already been fully mechanized in HOL4; and work toward a fully verified wavefront parallelization transformation is ongoing.

Acknowledgements and Availability. This project is supported by a Department of Energy Early Career Grant DE-SC0003956. NICTA is funded by the Australian Government through the Department of Communications and the Australian Research Council through the ICT Centre of Excellence Program.

Our source code is available from github at https://github.com/mn200/inspector-strategies.

References

1. Saltz, J.H.: Aggregation methods for solving sparse triangular systems on multiprocessors. SIAM J. Sci. Stat. Comput. **11**(1), 123–144 (1990)
2. Koelbel, C., Mehrotra, P.: Compiling global name-space parallel loops for distributed execution. IEEE Trans. Parallel Distrib. Syst. **2**(4), 440–451 (1991)
3. Saltz, J., Chang, C., Edjlali, G., Hwang, Y.S., Moon, B., Ponnusamy, R., Sharma, S., Sussman, A., Uysal, M., Agrawal, G., Das, R., Havlak, P.: Programming irregular applications: runtime support, compilation and tools. Adv. Comput. **45**, 105–153 (1997)
4. Mitchell, N., Carter, L., Ferrante, J.: Localizing non-affine array references. In: Proceedings of the International Conference on Parallel Architectures and Compilation Techniques (PACT), pp. 192–202, October 1999
5. Ding, C., Kennedy, K.: Improving cache performance in dynamic applications through data and computation reorganization at run time. In: Proceedings of the ACM SIGPLAN Conference on Programming Language Design and Implementation, pp. 229–241, May 1999
6. Han, H., Tseng, C.W.: Efficient compiler and run-time support for parallel irregular reductions. Parallel Comput. **26**(13–14), 1861–1887 (2000)
7. Mellor-Crummey, J., Whalley, D., Kennedy, K.: Improving memory hierarchy performance for irregular applications using data and computation reorderings. Int. J. Parallel Prog. **29**(3), 217–247 (2001)
8. Douglas, C.C., Hu, J., Kowarschik, R., Rüde, U., Weiß, C.: Cache optimization for structured and unstructured grid multigrid. Electron. Trans. Numer. Anal. **10**, 21–40 (2000)
9. Strout, M.M., Carter, L., Ferrante, J., Freeman, J., Kreaseck, B.: Combining performance aspects of irregular Gauss-Seidel via sparse tiling. In: Pugh, B., Tseng, C.-W. (eds.) LCPC 2002. LNCS, vol. 2481, pp. 90–110. Springer, Heidelberg (2005)
10. Mohiyuddin, M., Hoemmen, M., Demmel, J., Yelick, K.: Minimizing communication in sparse matrix solvers. In: Supercomputing (2009)
11. Das, R., Uysal, M., Saltz, J., Hwang, Y.S.S.: Communication optimizations for irregular scientific computations on distributed memory architectures. J. Parallel Distrib. Comput. **22**(3), 462–478 (1994)
12. Slind, K., Norrish, M.: A brief overview of HOL4. In: Mohamed, O.A., Muñoz, C., Tahar, S. (eds.) TPHOLs 2008. LNCS, vol. 5170, pp. 28–32. Springer, Heidelberg (2008). http://hol.sourceforge.net
13. Saltz, J.H.: Automated problem scheduling and reduction of communication delay effects. Technical report, Yale University (1987)
14. Rauchwerger, L., Amato, N.M., Padua, D.A.: A scalable method for run-time loop parallelization. Int. J. Parallel Prog. **23**(6), 537–576 (1995)
15. Zhuang, X., Eichenberger, A., Luo, Y., O'Brien, K., O'Brien, K.: Exploiting parallelism with dependence-aware scheduling. In: International Conference on Parallel Architectures and Compilation Techniques (PACT), pp. 193–202 (2009)
16. Davis, T.A., Hu, Y.: The University of Florida sparse matrix collection. ACM Trans. Math. Softw. **38**(1), 1:1–1:25 (2011)
17. Banerjee, U., Eigenmann, R., Nicolau, A., Padua, D.A.: Automatic program parallelization. Proc. IEEE **81**(2), 211–243 (1993)
18. Lengauer, C.: Loop parallelization in the polytope model. In: Best, E. (ed.) CONCUR 1993. LNCS, vol. 715, pp. 398–416. Springer, Heidelberg (1993)

19. Feautrier, P.: Automatic parallelization in the polytope model. In: Perrin, G.-R., Darte, A. (eds.) The Data Parallel Programming Model. LNCS, vol. 1132, pp. 79–103. Springer, Heidelberg (1996)
20. Kennedy, K., Allen, J.R.: Optimizing Compilers for Modern Architectures: A Dependence-based Approach. Morgan Kaufmann Publishers Inc., San Francisco (2002)
21. Yang, Y.Q., Ancourt, C., Irigoin, F.: Minimal data dependence abstractions for loop transformations: extended version. Int. J. Parallel Prog. **23**(4), 359–388 (1995)
22. Pugh, W., Wonnacott, D.: Nonlinear array dependence analysis. In: Third Workshop on Languages, Compilers, and Run-Time Systems for Scalable Computers, Troy, New York, May 1995
23. Rus, S., Hoeflinger, J., Rauchwerger, L.: Hybrid analysis: static & dynamic memory reference analysis. Int. J. Parallel Program. **31**(4), 251–283 (2003)
24. Oancea, C.E., Rauchwerger, L.: Logical inference techniques for loop parallelization. In: Proceedings of the 33rd ACM SIGPLAN Conference on Programming Language Design and Implementation, PLDI 2012, pp. 509–520 (2012)
25. Strout, M.M., Carter, L., Ferrante, J.: Compile-time composition of run-time data and iteration reorderings. In: Proceedings of the ACM SIGPLAN Conference on Programming Language Design and Implementation (PLDI). ACM, New York, June 2003
26. Strout, M.M., LaMielle, A., Carter, L., Ferrante, J., Kreaseck, B., Olschanowsky, C.: An approach for code generation in the sparse polyhedral framework. Technical report CS-13-109, Colorado State University, December 2013
27. Kelly, W., Maslov, V., Pugh, W., Rosser, E., Shpeisman, T., Wonnacott, D.: The Omega calculator and library, version 1.1.0, November 1996
28. Strout, M.M., Carter, L., Ferrante, J.: Proof of correctness for sparse tiling of Gauss-Seidel. Technical report, UCSD Department of Computer Science and Engineering, Technical report #CS2003-0741, April 2003
29. Yang, X., Chen, Y., Eide, E., Regehr, J.: Finding and understanding bugs in C compilers. In: Hall, M.W., Padua, D.A. (eds.) PLDI, pp. 283–294. ACM, New York (2011)
30. Leroy, X.: Formal verification of a realistic compiler. Commun. ACM **52**(7), 107–115 (2009)
31. Arnold, G., Hölzl, J., Köksal, A.S., Bodík, R., Sagiv, M.: Specifying and verifying sparse matrix codes. In: Proceedings of the 15th ACM SIGPLAN International Conference on Functional Programming (ICFP), ICFP 2010, pp. 249–260 (2010)

Fast Automatic Heuristic Construction Using Active Learning

William F. Ogilvie[1]([⊠]), Pavlos Petoumenos[1], Zheng Wang[2],
and Hugh Leather[1]

[1] School of Informatics, University of Edinburgh, Edinburgh, UK
s0198982@sms.ed.ac.uk, {ppetoume,hleather}@inf.ed.ac.uk
[2] School of Computing and Communications, Lancaster University, Lancaster, UK
z.wang@lancaster.ac.uk

Abstract. Building effective optimization heuristics is a challenging task which often takes developers several months if not years to complete. Predictive modelling has recently emerged as a promising solution, automatically constructing heuristics from training data. However, obtaining this data can take months per platform. This is becoming an ever more critical problem and if no solution is found we shall be left with out of date heuristics which cannot extract the best performance from modern machines.

In this work, we present a low-cost predictive modelling approach for automatic heuristic construction which significantly reduces this training overhead. Typically in supervised learning the training instances are randomly selected to evaluate regardless of how much useful information they carry. This wastes effort on parts of the space that contribute little to the quality of the produced heuristic. Our approach, on the other hand, uses active learning to select and only focus on the most useful training examples.

We demonstrate this technique by automatically constructing a model to determine on which device to execute four parallel programs at differing problem dimensions for a representative CPU–GPU based heterogeneous system. Our methodology is remarkably simple and yet effective, making it a strong candidate for wide adoption. At high levels of classification accuracy the average learning speed-up is 3x, as compared to the state-of-the-art.

Keywords: Machine learning · Workload scheduling

1 Introduction

Building effective program optimization heuristics is a daunting task because modern processors are complicated; they have a large number of components operating in parallel and each component is sensitive to the behaviour of the others. Creating analytical models on which optimization heuristics can be based has become harder as processor complexity has increased, and this trend is bound to

© Springer International Publishing Switzerland 2015
J. Brodman and P. Tu (Eds.): LCPC 2014, LNCS 8967, pp. 146–160, 2015.
DOI: 10.1007/978-3-319-17473-0_10

continue as processor designs move further towards heterogeneous parallelism [1]. Compiler developers often have to spend months if not years to get a heuristic right for a targeted architecture, and these days compilers often support a wide range of disparate processors. Whenever a new processor comes out, even if derived from a previous one, the optimizing heuristics need to be re-tuned for it. This is typically too much effort and so, in fact, most compilers are out of date [2].

Machine Learning based predictive modelling has rapidly emerged as a viable means to automate heuristic construction; by running example programs (optimized in different ways) and observing how the variations affect program runtime automatic machine learning tools can predict good settings with which to compile new, as yet unseen, programs. There are many studies showing that machine learning outperforms human based approaches [2,3]. Recent work also illustrates that it can be used to automatically port across architecture spaces [4] and can find more appropriate ways of mapping program parallelism to various platforms [5]. This new research area is promising, having the potential to fundamentally change the way compiler heuristics are designed; that is to say, compilers can be automatically tuned for new hardware without the need for months of compiler experts' time; however, before the potential of predictive modelling based heuristic construction can be realized there remain many hurdles which must be tackled. One major concern is the cost of collecting training examples. While machine learning allows us to automatically construct heuristics with little human involvement, the cost of generating training examples (that allow a learning algorithm to accumulate knowledge) is often very expensive.

This paper presents a novel, low-cost predictive modelling approach that can significantly reduce the overhead of collecting training examples without sacrificing prediction accuracy. Traditionally in predictive modelling training examples are randomly selected for labelling where, in the context of machine learning based compilers and run-time systems, labelling involves profiling code under varying conditions. This is inefficient because random selection often provides redundant data to the learner. In effect a cost is paid for training but little or no benefit is actually received. We tackle this problem by using *active learning* [6] to select and only focus on useful training instances, which greatly reduces the training overhead. Specifically, we build a number of initial distinct models with a small set of randomly selected training examples. We ask those models to make predictions on unseen data points, and the points for which the models 'disagree' the most are profiled. We then rebuild the models by re-running the learning algorithm with the new training example together with the existing ones, and repeat this process until a completion criterion is met after which a final heuristic is produced. In this way, we profile and collect training examples that provide the most information to the algorithm, thereby enabling it to improve the prediction accuracy of the learned models more quickly.

We demonstrate the effectiveness of our approach by using active learning to automatically construct a heuristic to determine which processor will give the better performance on a CPU–GPU based heterogeneous platform at differing problem sizes for a given program. More specifically, our approach is evaluated by building heuristics to predict the better processor to use for 4 benchmarks which have equivalent OPENMP and OPENCL implementations; where OPENMP is used for the CPU since it has a more mature implementation than OPENCL. Comparing our work to a typical random sampling technique, widely used in prior work, reveals that our methodology speeds up training by a factor of 3x on average: saving weeks of intensive compute time.

The research presented in this paper makes the following contributions. It

- shows that the training overhead of machine learning based heuristic design can be significantly reduced without sacrificing prediction accuracy;
- demonstrates how active learning can be used to automatically derive a heuristic to map OPENMP and OPENCL programs on a CPU–GPU based heterogeneous platform;
- provides detailed analysis of active learning based heuristic tuning.

The rest of this paper is organized as follows: in Sect. 2 we give a motivating example for this research, in Sect. 3 we discuss our approach and the implementation details of our system, in Sect. 4 we outline the methodology used to validate our technique, Sect. 5 provides our results and accompanying analysis, Sect. 6 references related work, and we conclude in Sect. 7.

2   Motivation

To motivate our work, we demonstrate how much unnecessary effort is involved in the traditional random-sampling based learning techniques, and point out the extent to which a better strategy can improve matters. In Fig. 1(a) we show for HotSpot, from the Rodinia [7,8] suite, when it is better to run on the CPU *versus* the GPU for maximum performance. The benchmark accepts two independent program inputs, and their values form the axes of the graph. The graph data itself was generated by randomly selecting 12,000 input combinations and running them on both the CPU and GPU enough times to make a statistically sound decision about which device is better for each, where a boundary line approximately separates the regions at which either device should be chosen.

Machine learning has been shown to be a viable option for creating heuristics for this type of problem [9,10]. To build such a heuristic, a machine learning algorithm typically requires a set of training examples to learn from. In our case, we need to use a set of profiled program inputs to find a model that is a good estimate of the boundary as shown in Fig. 1(a). The quality of the training examples will have a significant impact on the accuracy of the resultant model.

In Fig. 1(b) a random selection of 200 inputs to HotSpot is chosen, as might be typical in a standard 'passive' learning technique[1]. From this data a heuristic is

---

[1] In passive learning techniques, the training examples are selected without feedback as to the quality of the machine learned heuristic. Most usually, this will mean that all training examples are generated ahead of time and then a heuristic is learned once. In active learning, by contrast, the selection of training examples is an iterative process which is driven by feedback about the quality of the heuristic.

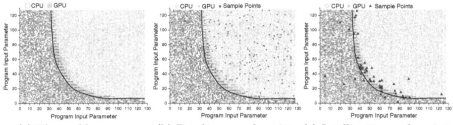

(a) The problem space   (b) Random sample points (c) Intelligent sample points

Fig. 1. Learning with randomly selected inputs versus carefully chosen inputs. Figure (a) shows the problem space of the Rodinia `HotSpot` benchmark. 12,000, 2-dimensional program inputs are run to discover which device (CPU or GPU) gives the better performance. A boundary line approximately separates the parts of the space where CPU and GPU are better. Figure (b) shows a random selection of 200 inputs. Using RandomCommittee to learn a heuristic with these inputs achieves an accuracy of 95 %. Figure (c) shows an intelligent selection of 31 inputs near to the boundary line. Using RandomCommittee to learn a heuristic with these inputs achieves an accuracy of 97 %, representing a 6x speed-up in training time.

created with the RandomCommittee machine learning algorithm from the Weka tool-kit [11], and the heuristic achieves a respectable 95 % accuracy. Machine learning can clearly learn good heuristics in this case, but our intuition insists that the majority of the randomly selected inputs offer little useful information. In fact, we would expect that only those points near to the boundary line in Fig. 1(a) should be required to accurately define a model.

We prove this intuition in Fig. 1(c) where we have instead selected just 31 inputs close to the boundary line and once again asked the RandomCommittee algorithm to learn a heuristic. Using fewer than 15 % as many observations as the standard passive learning technique we achieve an accuracy of 97 %. There is, therefore, significant potential to reduce the training cost for the machine learned heuristics if we could only choose the right inputs to train over. Unfortunately, without already knowing the shape of the space it is impossible to tell what the best inputs should be, but nevertheless we will show that it is possible to approximate their location.

In this paper we present a simple active learning technique that maintains a set of training inputs, adding to the set incrementally by selecting inputs that look likely to improve the heuristic quality based on what has already been seen. For the `HotSpot` benchmark, our approach avoids nearly all of the unimportant inputs, quickly focussing in on the best inputs to choose. The following section describes our methodology in detail.

3 Our Approach

As a case study, this work aims to train a predictor to determine the best processor to use for a given program input. We wish to avoid profiling inputs that provide little or no information for the learning algorithm to train over so that we

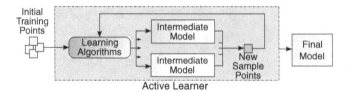

Fig. 2. An overview of our active learning approach. Initially, we use a few random samples to construct several intermediate models. Those models are utilized to choose which new data point is to be profiled next. The new sampled data point is then used to update the models. We repeat this process until a certain termination criterion is met where a final model will be produced as the outcome.

can minimize the overhead of collecting training examples. We achieve this by using active learning which carefully chooses each input to be profiled in turn. At each step, our algorithm attempts to choose a new input that will most improve the machine learned heuristic when it is added to the training set of examples.

Figure 2 provides an overview of how our approach can be applied to this case study problem. First, some number of program inputs are chosen at random to 'seed' the algorithm and these are then profiled to determine the better device for them – CPU or GPU. What follows is a number of steps which progressively add to the set of training examples until some termination criterion are met. To select which program input to add to the training set for profiling, a number of different, intermediate models are created using the current training set and different machine learning algorithms. Our method then searches for an input for which the intermediate models or heuristics most disagree on whether it should be run on the CPU or the GPU. The intuition is that the more these models agree on an input, the less likely it is able to improve the prediction accuracy of the learned heuristic.

The technique for choosing new training inputs is called *Query by Committee* (QBC) [12] and is described in Sect. 3.1, whilst Sect. 3.3 details how the inputs are profiled: particularly, how the decision about whether the input should be run on the CPU or on the GPU is made statistically sound.

3.1   Query by Committee

The key idea behind active learning is that a machine learning algorithm can perform better with fewer training examples if it is allowed to choose the data from which it learns. There are a number of approaches available [13] but we employ a heterogeneous implementation of *Query by Committee* (QBC), a widely utilized active learning technique.

The 'committee' in our QBC implementation consists of a number of distinct learning algorithms that are initially trained with a small set of randomly collected examples. In our case, each training example is a set of program inputs with a label indicating which processor gives better performance when these inputs are profiled. As these models are initially built from a small set of examples they are unlikely to be highly accurate at first, but we are able to iteratively improve these models with the following steps using new, carefully chosen, training examples.

The challenge in active learning lies in how to select those training examples that are most likely to improve the prediction accuracy of a model out of all the potential examples we could use. In QBC this is achieved by asking each distinct model to make predictions on a random collection of program inputs not currently present in the training set - called the *candidate set*. Since each model is built using a different algorithm they may or may not reach consensus as to whether a particular program input should be run on a particular device. We then only profile those inputs for which the 'committee' *disagrees* the most to discover the true, best-performing processor, and then add those new training examples into the training set. The learning loop begins again by creating its distinct intermediate models using the new information it has gathered and carefully selects another informative example to learn from. This procedure repeats until some completion criterion are met.

The insight behind QBC is that we do not want to create new training instances from parts of the problem-space which are already collectively understood by the committee of algorithms, but rather would like to sample those regions which are least well defined. The idea being that if we reduce the regions of disagreement between the committee members, by choosing training instances from within those regions, we incrementally get closer to the true boundary over which the processor choice should be altered and hence increase the accuracy of our final heuristic.

An Example: Figure 3 provides a hypothetical example to demonstrate how new training points are selected by QBC in our methodology. In Fig. 3(a) we are presented with an input-space which is fully described by two parameters and has some training examples already shown. In this case, our committee consists of two distinct classification algorithms that we will call X and Y. Based upon the location of these examples within the input-space, and which device is faster under these conditions (represented by different shapes), the two classification algorithms give rise to different models, as illustrated in Fig. 3(a) and (b). If we overlap the classification boundaries of the two models, as in Fig. 3(c), we can see that there are parts of the space that classifiers X and Y are in agreement about and a region of disagreement. Knowing the location of disagreement regions, we can then select a new training example that is least well defined by the committee. The technique for finding the disagreement regions and selecting a new training example is described in the next section.

3.2   Assessing Disagreement

We use information entropy (1) [14] to evaluate the level of disagreement for each potential set of inputs that could be added to the training set next, i.e., those that have not been profiled so far, where $p(x_i)$ is the proportion of committee

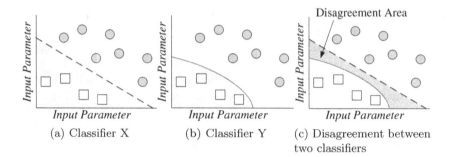

(a) Classifier X   (b) Classifier Y   (c) Disagreement between
                                                    two classifiers

Fig. 3. A simplified input space with two input parameters and the locations of profiled training examples. We use two different learning algorithms to build two different classifiers – (a) and (b). We then combine these models, as in (c), to find the region of disagreement between them and use this information to better choose where future training examples should be drawn from.

members that predict that the instance (set of inputs) x is fastest on device i of n. From within all the candidate instances found to have the maximum entropy value in a given iteration of the learning loop one example is randomly chosen to be profiled next. This means the inputs associated with that instance are run on the CPU and GPU kernels and it is determined which processor is faster under those conditions. The relevant label is given to the instance and the information added to the training set. The learning loop begins another iteration and the intermediate models formed again, but this time the new information is taken into account.

$$H\left(x\right) = -\sum_{i=1}^{n} p(x_i) \log p(x_i) \tag{1}$$

3.3 Statistically Sound Profiling

Since computer timings are inherently noisy we use statistics to increase the reliability of our models. In particular, we record a minimum number of timings from each device, as specified by the user. We use Interquartile Range [15] outlier removal then apply Welch's t-test [16] to discover if one hardware device is indeed faster than the other. If we cannot conclude from the t-test that this is the case, then we perform an equivalence test. Both devices are said to be 'equivalent' if the difference between the higher mean plus its 95 % confidence interval minus the lower mean minus its confidence is within some threshold of indifference. In our system this threshold was set to be within 1 % of the minimum of the two means. If the fastest device cannot be determined and they are not equivalent an extra set of observations are obtained and the tests applied again, up until some user defined number of tries. In the case of equivalence or the threshold of attempts being reached the CPU is chosen as the preferred device since it is more energy-efficient.

Table 1. The sizes of the input-space for each benchmark. Each dimension has a value of between *Min* and *Max*, inclusive, and a step value of *Stride*. *Size* gives the total number of points in each input-space, and *Cand* is the number of points in the candidate set for each benchmark.

Benchmark	#Dimentions	Min	Max	Stride	Size	Cand
HotSpot	2	1	128	1	$16,384$	10,000
Matrix Mult.	3	1	256	1	$1.6x10^7$	10,000
PathFinder	2	2	1024	1	$1.0x10^6$	10,000
SRAD	2	128	1024	16	$3,136$	2,636

4   Experimental Setup

This section describes the details of the experimental case studies that we undertook, starting with the platform and benchmarks used, moving on to the particular QBC settings, and finally discussing the evaluation methodology.

4.1   Platform and Benchmarks

We evaluated our approach on a CPU–GPU based heterogeneous platform with an Intel Core i7 7770 4-core CPU (8 Hardware threads) @ 3.4 GHz and an NVIDIA Geforce GTX Titan GPU (6 GB memory). The machine runs Open-Suse v12.3 Linux and we used gcc v4.7.2 and the NVIDIA CUDA Toolkit v5.5 for compilation. We used 3 benchmarks from the Rodinia suite, HotSpot, PathFinder, and SRAD, and we also included a simple Matrix Multiplication application. These benchmarks were specifically chosen because they have equivalent OPENCL and OPENMP versions available, and each has multiple program inputs which affect the workload of their respective parallel kernels.

4.2   Active Learning Settings

Machine Learning Models: Our active learning framework uses 12 unique algorithms from the Weka tool-kit to form the committee, each executed with default parameter values. They are Logistic, MultilayerPerceptron, IB1, IBk, KStar, LogitBoost, MultiClassClassifier, RandomCommittee, NNge, ADTree, Random Forest, and RandomTree. These were selected because they can produce a binary predictor from numeric inputs and have been widely used in prior work.

Program Input Space: The dimensions of the input-space for each benchmark were chosen to give realistic values to learn over – see Table 1.

Initial Training Set and Candidate Set Sizes: For all experiments the training set was initialised with a single randomly chosen instance – the minimum possible. The effect of changing this parameter is discussed in Sect. 5.3. The candidate set size was either 10,000 inputs not already present in the training and test sets or the maximum number of points not in the training and test sets, whichever was smaller – see Table 1.

Termination Criterion: The learning iterations were halted at 200 steps since it was found experimentally that the learning improvement had plateaued by that time.

4.3 Evaluation Methodology

Runtime Measurement and Device Comparison: To determine if a benchmark is better suited to the CPU or GPU for a given input it is run on each device at least 10 times and at most 200 times. As mentioned in Sect. 3, we employ interquartile-range outlier removal, Welch's t-test, and equivalence testing to ensure the statistical soundness of the gathered program execution times.

Testing: For testing purposes, a set of 500 inputs were excluded from any training and candidate sets. Both our active and passive learning experiments were run 10 times for each benchmark and the arithmetic mean of the accuracy (or other metrics) were recorded. For both active and passive learning, the accuracy was taken as the average accuracy of all 12 models. That is to say, we compared the average accuracy achieved using a 12-member QBC algorithm *versus* the same 12 algorithms trained using random data as the number of QBC-chosen or randomly-chosen training sets increased in size.

5 Experimental Results

In this section we begin by presenting the overall results of our experiments, showing that our active learning approach can significantly reduce the training time by a factor of 3 when compared to the random sampling technique. We then move on to examine the performance exhibited by our system for each benchmark in turn. Finally, we discuss how the change in two user supplied parameters (i.e. initial training set and candidate set sizes) can affect the performance of our methodology.

5.1 Overall Learning Costs

Figure 4 shows the average learning speed-up of our approach over the passive, random-sampling technique traditionally used in heuristic construction. The speed-up values are based on the number of inputs which need to be profiled in order to train a predictor to an accuracy of at least 85 %. As can be seen from this figure, our approach constantly outperforms the classical random-sampling technique for all benchmarks, which in real terms means a saving of weeks to train these heuristics.

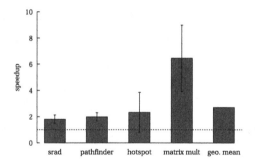

Fig. 4. On average our methodology requires 3x fewer training examples to create a high quality heuristic than the traditional random-sampling technique, proving that this simple algorithm can save weeks, and potentially months, of compute time.

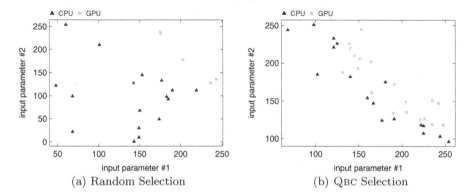

(a) Random Selection   (b) QBC Selection

Fig. 5. Since the `Matrix Multiplication` input-space is three-dimensional and not as simply defined as the other benchmarks it is difficult for a human to visualise the separation between CPU and GPU regions; to make it a little easier the graph above was flattened so that the z-axis has values $122 \leq z \leq 144$. Active learning was over six times faster than random sampling at producing a high quality model for this code, quicker than the other programs tested and likely due to the additional dimension reducing the effectiveness of random selection.

5.2   Analysis of Training Point Selection

If we look at Figs. 5, 6, 7 and 8 we can see clearly where the cost savings associated with QBC are coming from. That is, in all cases the algorithm quickly chooses points surrounding the boundary between the CPU and the GPU optimum regions, giving it the ability to more accurately approximate its shape in less time.

5.3   Sensitivity to Parameters

As well as confirming the validity of our approach we also conducted two further experiments to determine the impact that some user defined parameters might

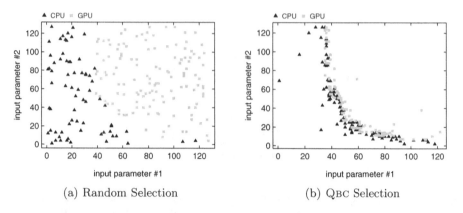

Fig. 6. The difference between QBC and random sampling is stark for the HotSpot code. In particular, the QBC algorithm is able to quickly converge and define the boundary between the two devices whilst random selection trains on redundant or less informative points, proved by the fact it takes twice as long as QBC.

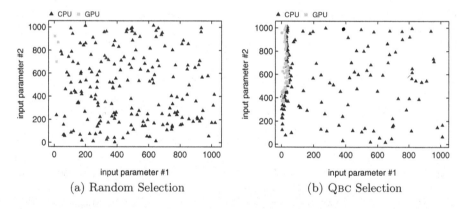

Fig. 7. The PathFinder QBC graph displays more randomness than the previous two. The probable reason for this, judging by the location of the boundary line, is that the active learner cannot initially locate the GPU region. Nevertheless, active learning is still twice as fast at generating a good quality heuristic compared with the random sampling technique.

have on the effectiveness of the system. The first experiment (Fig. 9) involved altering how many randomly selected training examples were initially supplied to the QBC algorithm to get it started. The second experiment (Fig. 10) investigated the extent to which changing the candidate set size would have an effect on the speed of heuristic construction.

In Fig. 9 it is clear that increasing the number of random training instances used to seed the QBC algorithm for HotSpot has no significant effect in the long-term performance but is detrimental in the short term, however, one can

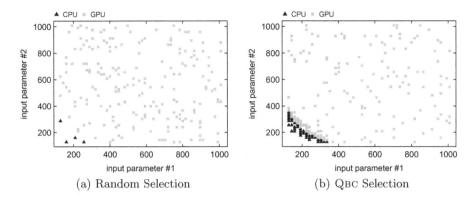

(a) Random Selection   (b) QBC Selection

Fig. 8. Similarly, the SRAD input-space appears to show that QBC initially searches randomly because it has difficulty approximating the location of the comparitively small CPU region. However, once the algorithm has an idea of where this region is located it quickly concentrates on the boundary and forms a high-quality heuristic in half the time of the passive learning methodology.

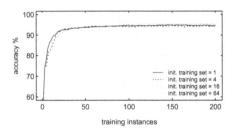

Fig. 9. This graph shows that increasing the number of random examples given initially to the QBC algorithm for HotSpot is at first detrimental to its performance, however, in a complex space increased randomness may help discover complex localized features.

imagine a case where a complex space with many localized features may be better explored through an initially random approach followed-up by active learning.

Figure 10 shows how changing the size of the candidate set for the HotSpot benchmark affects the performance of the system. In particular, the data indicates a smaller candidate set size may be more beneficial. Presumably this is because a larger candidate set increases the likelihood that the learner receives redundant information from neighbouring high entropy points.

6   Related Work

Analytic Modelling: Analytic models have been widely used to tackle complex optimization problems, such as auto-parallelization [17, 18], runtime estimation [19–21], and task mappings [22]. A particular problem with them, however, is the model has to be re-tuned whenever it is targeted at new hardware [23].

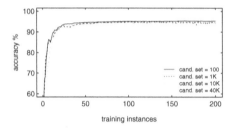

Fig. 10. This graph shows that choosing a lower candidate set size may be more beneficial than a larger one.

Predictive Modeling: Predictive modeling has been shown to be useful in the optimization of both sequential and parallel programs [9,10,24,25]. Its great advantage is that it can adapt to changing platforms as it has no *a priori* assumptions about their behaviour but it is expensive to train. There are many studies showing it outperforms human based approaches [2,3,26–29]. Prior work for machine learning in compilers, as exemplified by the MilePost GCC project [30], often uses random sampling or exhaustive search to collect training examples. The process of collecting training examples could be expensive, taking several weeks if not months. Using active learning, our approach can significantly reduce the overhead of collecting training examples. This accelerates the process of tuning optimization heuristics using machine learning. The Qilin compiler [31] uses runtime profiling to predict a parallel program's execution time and map work across the CPU and GPU accordingly; however, where their approach is designed to work after deployment ours can be performed ahead of time, thereby reducing any slow-downs experienced by the end-user.

Active Learning for Systems Optimization: A recent paper by Zuluaga *et al.* [32] proposed an active learning algorithm to select parameters in a multi-objective problem. Their work is not concerned with single-objective workload scheduling and does not consider statistical soundness of raw data. Balaprakash *et al.* [33,34] used active learning to reduce execution time of scientific codes but they only consider code variants and OPENCL parameters as inputs; they do not discuss the impact of problem size on performance.

Problem Size Optimization: Optimizing code for different problem sizes in heterogeneous systems is discussed by Liu *et al.* [35] where they give an implementation of a compiler which uses a combination of regression trees and representative GPU kernels, but their approach uses exhaustive search. Adaptic is a compilation system for GPUs [36] and uses analytical models to map an input stream onto the GPU at runtime but their technique is not easily portable, where ours tackles that problem directly by making learning cheaper.

7   Conclusions

We have presented a novel, low-cost predictive modelling approach for machine learning based automatic heuristic construction. Instead of building heuristics based on randomly chosen training examples we use active learning to focus on those instances that improve the quality of the resultant models the most. Using QBC to construct a heuristic to predict which processor to use for a given program input our approach speeds up training by a factor of 3x, saving weeks of compute time.

Acknowledgements. This work was funded under the EPSRC grant, ALEA (EP/H0 44752/1).

References

1. Power, J., Basu, A., Gu, J., Puthoor, S., Beckmann, B.M., Hill, M.D., Reinhardt, S.K., Wood, D.A.: Heterogeneous system coherence for integrated cpu-gpu systems. In: Proceedings of MICRO 2013
2. Kulkarni, S., Cavazos, J.: Mitigating the compiler optimization phase-ordering problem using machine learning. In: Proceedings of OOPSLA 2012
3. Dubach, C., Jones, T., Bonilla, E., Fursin, G., O'Boyle, M.F.P.: Portable compiler optimisation across embedded programs and microarchitectures using machine learning. In: Proceedings of MICRO 2009
4. Cavazos, J., Fursin, G., Agakov, F., Bonilla, E., O'Boyle, M.F.P., Temam, O.: Rapidly selecting good compiler optimizations using performance counters. In: Proceedings of CGO 2007
5. Grewe, D., Wang, Z., O'Boyle, M.F.: Portable mapping of data parallel programs to OpenCL for heterogeneous systems. In: Proceedings of CGO 2013
6. Settles, B.: Active learning literature survey, University of Wisconsin-Madison, Computer Sciences Technical report 1648 (2009)
7. Che, S., Boyer, M., Meng, J., Tarjan, D., Sheaffer, J., Lee, S.-H., Skadron, K.: Rodinia: a benchmark suite for heterogeneous computing. In: Proceedings of IISWC 2009
8. Che, S., Sheaffer, J., Boyer, M., Szafaryn, L., Wang, L., Skadron, K.: A characterization of the rodinia benchmark suite with comparison to contemporary cmp workloads. In: Proceedings of IISWC 2010
9. Cooper, K.D., Schielke, P.J., Subramanian, D.: Optimizing for reduced code space using genetic algorithms. In: Proceedings of LCTES 1999
10. Wang, Z., O'Boyle, M.F.: Mapping parallelism to multi-cores: a machine learning based approach. In: Proceedings of PPoPP 2009
11. Hall, M., Frank, E., Holmes, G., Pfahringer, B., Reutemann, P., Witten, I.H.: The WEKA data mining software: an update. SIGKDD Explor. **11**(1), 10–18 (2009)
12. Seung, H.S., Opper, M., Sompolinsky, H.: Query by committee. In: Proceedings of COLT 1992
13. Bishop, C.M.: Pattern Recognition and Machine Learning (Information Science and Statistics). Springer-Verlag New York Inc., Secaucus (2006)
14. Dagan, I., Engelson, S.P.: Committee-based sampling for training probabilistic classifiers. In: Proceedings of ICML 1995
15. Moore, D.S., McCabe, G.P.: Introduction to the Practice of Statistics. W.H. Freeman, New York (2002)
16. Welch, B.L.: The Generalization of "Student's" Problem when Several Different Population Variances are Involved. Biometrika **34**, 28–35 (1947)

17. Bastoul, C.: Code generation in the polyhedral model is easier than you think. In: Proceedings of PACT 2004
18. Pouchet, L.-N., Bastoul, C., Cohen, A., Cavazos, J.: Iterativeoptimization in the polyhedral model: part II, multidimensional time. In: Proceedings of PLDI 2008
19. Clement, M., Quinn, M.: Analytical performance prediction on multicomputers. In: Proceedings of SC 1993
20. Wilhelm, R., Engblom, J., Ermedahl, A., Holsti, N., Thesing, S., Whalley, D., Bernat, G., Ferdinand, C., Heckmann, R., Mitra, T., Mueller, F., Puaut, I., Puschner, P., Staschulat, J., Stenström, P.: The worst-case execution-time problem - overview of methods and survey of tools. ACM TECS **7**, 1–53 (2008)
21. Hong, S., Kim, H.: An analytical model for a GPU architecture with memory-level and thread-level parallelism awareness. In: Proceedings of ISCA 2009
22. Hormati, A.H., Choi, Y., Kudlur, M., Rabbah, R., Mudge, T., Mahlke, S.: Flextream: adaptive compilation of streaming applications for heterogeneous architectures. In: Proceedings of PACT 2009
23. Stephenson, M., Amarasinghe, S., Martin, M., O'Reilly, U.-M.: Meta optimization: improving compiler heuristics with machine learning. In: Proceedings of PLDI 2003
24. Wang, Z., O'Boyle, M.F.: Partitioning streaming parallelism for multi-cores: a machine learning based approach. In: PACT 2010
25. Grewe, D., Wang, Z., O'Boyle, M.F.P.: OpenCL task partitioning in the presence of GPU contention. In: Caşcaval, C., Montesinos-Ortego, P. (eds.) LCPC 2013 - Testing. LNCS, vol. 8664, pp. 87–101. Springer, Heidelberg (2014)
26. Grewe, D., Wang, Z., O'Boyle, M.: A workload-aware mapping approach for data-parallel programs. In: HiPEAC 2011
27. Zuluaga, M., Krause, A., Milder, P., Püschel, M.: "Smart" design space sampling to predict pareto-optimal solutions. In Proceedings of LCTES 2012
28. Emani, M.K., Wang, Z., O'Boyle, M.F.P.: Smart, adaptivemapping of parallelism in the presence of external workload. In: CGO 2013
29. Wang, Z., O'Boyle, M.F.P.: Using machine learning to partition streaming programs. ACM TACO **10** (2013)
30. Fursin, G., Miranda, C., Temam, O., Namolaru, M., Yom-Tov, E., Zaks, A., Mendelson, B., Bonilla, E., Thomson, J., Leather, H., Williams, C., O'Boyle, M., Barnard, P., Ashton, E., Courtois, E., Bodin, F.: In: Proceedings of the GCC Developers' Summit
31. Luk, C.-k., Hong, S., Kim, H.: Qilin: exploiting parallelism on heterogeneous multiprocessors with adaptive mapping. In: Proceedings of MICRO 2009
32. Zuluaga, M., Krause, A., Sergent, G., Püschel, M.: Active learning for multi-objective optimization. In: Proceedings of ICML 2013
33. Balaprakash, P., Gramacy, R.B., Wild, S.M.: Active-learning-based surrogate models for empirical performance tuning. In: Proceedings of CLUSTER 2013
34. Balaprakash, P., Rupp, K., Mametjanov, A., Gramacy, R.B., Hovland, P.D., Wild, S.M.: Empirical performance modeling of GPU kernels using active learning. In: Proceedings of ParCo 2013
35. Liu, Y., Zhang, E.Z., Shen, X.: A Cross-input adaptive framework for GPU program optimizations. In: Proceedings of IPDPS 2009
36. Samadi, M., Hormati, A., Mehrara, M., Lee, J., Mahlke, S.: Adaptive input-aware compilation for graphics engines. In: Proceedings of PLDI 2012

Jagged Tiling for Intra-tile Parallelism and Fine-Grain Multithreading

Sunil Shrestha[1]([⊠]), Joseph Manzano[2], Andres Marquez[2], John Feo[2],
and Guang R. Gao[1]

[1] CAPSL, University of Delaware, Newark, DE 19716, USA
sunil@udel.edu, ggao@capsl.udel.edu
[2] Pacific Northwest National Laboratory, Richland, WA 99354, USA
{joseph.manzano,andres.marquez,john.feo}@pnnl.gov

Abstract. In this paper, we have developed a novel methodology that takes into consideration multithreaded many-core designs to better utilize memory/processing resources and improve memory residence on tileable applications. It takes advantage of polyhedral analysis and transformation in the form of PLUTO [6], combined with a highly optimized fine grain tile runtime to exploit parallelism at all levels. The main contributions of this paper include the introduction of multi-hierarchical tiling techniques that increases intra tile parallelism; and a data-flow inspired runtime library that allows the expression of parallel tiles with an efficient synchronization registry. Our current implementation shows performance improvements on an Intel Xeon Phi board up to 32.25 % against instances produced by state-of-the-art compiler frameworks for selected stencil applications.

1 Introduction

With the increasing number of cores in current computing systems and the massive computational power they offer, one of the bottlenecks in achieving higher performance has been the access to the memory. Along with the computation power, memory speed has increased as well, however at a much slower pace. Memory access latency is determined by many factors such as bandwidth, interconnect delay, memory bank contention, memory paging overhead and unbalanced task distribution. Taking advantage of the locality principle, multiple efforts [13], have been made so far to minimize the access time to memory in an integrated framework, such as by storing recently used data in cache, efficient reuse of cached data through tiling, data percolation using communication-avoiding algorithms [9], code transformations and prefetching. Although, these approaches work very well in pushing the "memory wall" farther, data movements end up being performed in most cases for the benefit of a single thread or computational unit.

An important class of optimization approaches tackling the "memory wall" maximizes memory reuse inside the most computational expensive parts of an applications – commonly nested loops. One of the most successful techniques to

© Springer International Publishing Switzerland 2015
J. Brodman and P. Tu (Eds.): LCPC 2014, LNCS 8967, pp. 161–175, 2015.
DOI: 10.1007/978-3-319-17473-0_11

date involves the concept of a "tile". A tile is a sub-partition of a loop nests' iteration space into blocks with the purpose of increasing the data locality and reducing communication overhead across them. This approach is very effective as we
can see in classical tiling approaches where tile sizes are based on cache sizes. In
these techniques, a single thread effectively maximizes reuse from caches before
heading back to the main memory. As effective as this approach is, there are few
things that need consideration: Firstly, when processing resources are in abun-
dance and optimization is highly coarse grained, this may lead to idle resources.
One of the main reasons that this pathology has persisted is of the limited memory bandwidth assumption. However, this assumption ignores the possibility of
memory reuse across processing units, especially when they share different levels
of the memory hierarchy. Secondly, when each thread performs data movements
for itself without a priori knowledge of concurrent thread execution and data
movement pattern, they can interfere with each other to their performance's
detriment. This could take the form of increased caches misses and a higher
strain on the entire memory subsystem.

In addition, the trend of increasing the number of processing elements in a
chip seems to be the norm for many years to come. In order to take advantage of
additional processing resources, current and new software stacks need to provide
concurrent units the ability to (re)act based on other threads execution and
the application data movement pattern. In other words, these stacks need to
update their machine models to reflect modern platforms. With the axiom that
the base optimization technique used would be tiling, memory reuse needs to
be considered in both the inter, as well as, the intra tile so that the strain
or underuse of resources can be alleviated. For the simple for-loop in Fig. 1,
a classical approach produces tiling as shown in Fig. 2. This is a very efficient
way of tiling as it is designed for minimal communication and coarse-grained
parallelism. However, given the enormous amount of processing power, can we
do better and utilize available resources while keeping communication overhead
relatively low? In this paper, we attempted to answer this question with an
approach that maximizes parallelism and improve locality for threads working
together in a highly synchronous fashion.

Firstly, in order to maximize available processing resources while keeping
memory bandwidth strain low, we have developed a technique to exploit intra-
tile parallelism without compromising inter-tile parallelism. Using the existing
polyhedral framework PLUTO [6] and the code generator CLOOG [4], we create
a multi-hierarchical highly parallel tiles that reside at the lowest level cache and
communicate with minimal overhead. Sets of these inner tiles form outer level

```
for  (int  i=1;  i<=n; i++){
    for  (int  j=1;  j<=n; j++){
        A[i][j] = A[i-1][j] + A[i][j-1];
    }
}
```

Fig. 1. Stencil example

tiles that can also run in parallel. Secondly, in order to execute these highly parallel tiles, we have developed a data-flow inspired fine grained execution mechanism in which threads sync using atomic operations. Using locality provided by higher level caches (e.g. L2 cache) and parallelism provided by our tiling technique, we are able to improve locality and reuse, thus improving the overall system performance.

The main contributions of this paper include multi-hierarchical tiling technique that increase intra tile parallelism; and a data-flow inspired runtime library that allows the expression of intra tile parallelism. The rest of the paper is organized as follows. Section 2 provides related work. Section 3 explains our framework in detail. Sections 4 and 5 showcases experiments, results and discussion. Section 6 presents our future work. Finally, Sect. 7 does the conclusion.

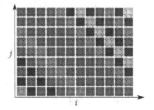

Fig. 2. Classical tiling

2   Related Work

The technique of Iteration Space Tiling proposed by Michael Wolfe [26,27], has been widely used to aggregate different dimensions of loop iterations to improve locality and reuse [25]. It improves performance by exploiting reuse beyond innermost loops. Such approach works very well for perfectly nested loops, although it can be extended beyond. With the advancement made by the linear algebra community, hierarchical tiling code can be generated automatically using tools like PLUTO [6]. Using the polyhedral framework proposed by Feautrier [11,12], PLUTO attempts to generate communication minimal tiling code. The main idea here is to have efficient space and time mapping [15] while extracting multiple degree of parallelism that can be tiled with cost efficient hyperplanes.

One of the difficulty of tiling is to find right shapes and sizes that can map well to the iteration space and is also cost efficient [17]. Apart from classical rectangular or cubical shaped tiles, other shaped tiling shapes (e.g. diamond, hexagonal) has also been studied. These tiling shapes are selected based on the access patterns of the loop nest such that communication becomes minimal and/or allows parallel start for certain types of applications [2,16]. These techniques are very effective, however are normally limited to tiling for only one level of memory hierarchy.

Data centric approach used by Kodukula [20], uses blocking of data based on its flow through memory hierarchy. His approach selects sequence of blocks that is touched by a processor and executes statements associated with those blocks. However, depending on dependence such transformation can be very complex.

Mitigating long latency cache miss penalties by overlapping data movement with computation is another avenue for memory latency optimization. In order to do so, memory access pattern needs to be known a priori to the actual use of data. However, prefetching has to be timed such that data stay in cache and do not get evicted before the use happens. Techniques such as loop splitting/loop peeling [22] to divide the loop in multiple phases where one can be used to prefetch data has been attempted before. However, loop peeling is not obvious for all nested loops. Prefetch when done unnecessarily, becomes just an extra overhead. To alleviate these shortcomings, systems like APACS [21] provide an integrated solution for cache and prefetching with adaptive partitioning, prefetch pipelining and prefetch buffer management techniques. Although such solutions are promising, they require substantial hardware support. Moreover, techniques like Intel helper threads [19] and Gan's data percolation [14] allows "special" threads to improve locality.

Bikshandi [5] introduced hierarchical tiled array (HTAs) that manipulates tiles using array operations such that parallel computation takes array form in distributed tiles. Baskaran [3] used explicit data movement and index transformation to improve locality on scratchpad. These techniques benefit block of threads when contiguous memory is used but they are less efficient when dealing with strided or irregular accesses.

Current fine grain runtime concentrate on the interaction of many threads and had dealt with memory bandwidth and contention problems in many interesting ways. The Efficient Architecture for Running THreads (EARTH) [23] uses the un-interruptable fine grain threads, called fibers, which shares their activation frames. The SWARM framework developed by ET International [18] has similar concepts as EARTH, but added support for direct access shared memory structures, placement information and different "codelet" pattern operations that allow more efficient use of data. Finally, the most recent development is Rice's Open Community Runtime (OCR) [7] system. It is designed as a fertile ground to experiment with new techniques and systems.

Most of the original compiler work presented here has a single thread focus or starkly favors coarse grain parallelism. Improving on this, a fine-grain collaborative view on code generation for multiple threads can yield significant improvements. This thread collaboration can extend beyond scheduling techniques and encompass data restructuring as well; a topic that was not considered in the fine-grain multithreaded work presented above. The approach presented in [10] aims to solve these issues with a hierarchical tiling framework for multicore clusters. They exploit inter and intra (with threading) node parallelism using tiling. Moreover, they exploit NUMA aware allocation and take advantage of vector register blocking to further increase performance. Stencil codes are used to showcase benefits. Although their approach is similar to our framework, key differences in our favor are the creation of more intra-tile parallelism (similar to their intra-node parallelism) with our jagged tiling technique.

3   Framework

The overview of the framework is shown in Fig. 3. The framework is designed to maximize the use of parallel processing resources while keeping runtime overhead low. It uses PLUTO [6] and CLOOG [4] as a compiler toolchain for highly

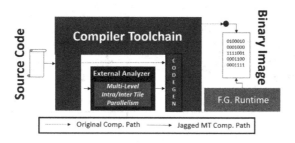

Fig. 3. Framework

parallel tiled code generation as shown in Sect. 3.1. It is followed by data-flow like execution where threads working in close proximity in time and space form a thread group $ThGrp$ and collaborate within with minimal overhead. Such grouping is designed to take advantage of locality on L2 tiles while executing in highly parallel and synchronous fashion.

3.1 Overview of Polyhedral Code Generation

In this subsection, we provide a brief overview of PLUTO, CLOOG and some of the polyhedral terminologies used in this paper.

PLUTO takes a C code as an input and transforms it into a coarse-grain parallel OpenMP code that is optimized for data locality. Using its affine transformation framework, statement wise transformations are done to minimize communication across boundaries. A cost function is used to reduce the communication distance and volume between tiling hyperplanes.

Under polyhedral terminology, a hyperplane $\phi(\boldsymbol{v})$ is a $n-1$ dimensional affine subspace in n dimensional space. For statements S, a hyperplane $\phi_s(\boldsymbol{v})$ with dimensionality m and normal $(c_1 c_2 ... c_m)$ represents an affine transformation in the form,

$$\phi_s(\boldsymbol{v}) = (c_1 c_2 ... c_m).\boldsymbol{v} + c_0 \tag{1}$$

For given 'k' statements, in order for statement-wise hyperplane $(\phi_{s_1}, \phi_{s_2} ... \phi_{s_k})$ to be a legal tiling hyperplane, the following has to be satisfied between source 's' and target 't' along all dependence edge.

$$\phi_{S_i}(\boldsymbol{t}) - \phi_{S_j}(\boldsymbol{s}) \geq 0 \tag{2}$$

When a combination of 'm'[1] hyperplanes, represented by $\phi^1, \phi^2 ... \phi^m$, form tiles, they are self-contained i.e. dependencies for statements within tiles are either satisfied or can be satisfied within.

PLUTO finds communication minimal tiling hyperplanes and uses them for multiple level tiling targeting different levels of the memory hierarchy. Such tiling creates supernodes for each different tiling levels. It uses CLOOG, which

---

[1] Where m is less or equal to the number of dimensions of the iteration space.

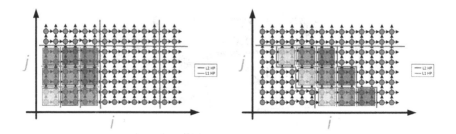

(a) Two level hierarchical Tiling with (1,0) and (0,1) Tiling Hyperplanes

(b) Two level hierarchical Tiling with (1,1) and (0,1) Tiling Hyperplanes

Fig. 4. Two level hierarchical Tiling: Classical and Jagged

is a code generation tool that scans the polyhedra in a global lexicographic ordering. Such scanning is performed as specified by the scattering function, which is an affine transformation function. The code generator is oblivious to any information about the dependencies and, in absence of a scattering function, scans the polyhedra in the lexicographic order as specified by the original iterator. It uses PolyLib [24] for its polyhedral operations. Interested readers are strongly encouraged to read references [6] and [4] for more information about PLUTO and CLOOG respectively.

Our framework leverages the existing transformation framework, parallelization and locality optimization that PLUTO uses for code generation. In order to generate parallel inner tiles, our framework uses an external analyzer that calls PLUTO using a modified *Domain* (iteration space polytope) and a updated *Scattering function* (scanning order of polyhedra). We explain our algorithm in the next section.

3.2 Jagged Tiling for Intra-tile Parallelism

Our framework uses the tiling hyperplanes generated by PLUTO for the lowest level memory hierarchy i.e. (L1 cache). These tiling hyperplanes are designed to be communication minimal using a cost function that reduces the communication distance and volume. Under the PLUTO framework, these hyperplanes are used for tiling multiple level of memory hierarchy. However, using the same tiling hyperplanes for both levels come at the cost of sequential or pipeline parallel execution of inner L1 tiles as shown in Fig. 4(a). In our framework, we solve this by constructing outer tiles in which at least one face of the polytope has concurrent start. Given 'm' hyperplanes, we create at least one parallel hyperplane and use it together with the other hyperplanes to create the L2 tiles. For clarity, we represent all original hyperplanes by ϕ, L1 hyperplanes by φ and L2 hyperplanes by Φ. The condition for such tiling is shown in equations below,

$$\varphi^1_{S_i}(t) - \varphi^1_{S_j}(s) \geq 1 \quad for\ one\ hyperplane \tag{3}$$

$$\varphi^l_{S_i}(t) - \varphi^l_{S_j}(s) \geq 0 \quad for\ l\ hyperplanes\ where\ 1 < l \leq m \tag{4}$$

The algorithm to generate such tiles is shown in Algorithm 1. Once the level 1 tiles are created, we use the $L1$ supernode hyperplanes $\varphi i_{L1s}, \varphi^{i+1}_{L1s}...\varphi^{i+m-1}_{L1s}$ to create the outer L2 tiles. The iteration space matrix representing the *Domain* is updated to reflect the new L2 tile domain and its scattering function is updated to mark outer and inner tiles parallel. Figure 4(b) shows the pictorial view of jagged tiling.

For our stencil example, the tiling hyperplanes are (1,0) and (0,1). Using these hyperplanes, we create L1 tiles and iterators 'i' and 'j' with tile size of 32. Once the supernode iterator 'I' and 'J' are created, hyperplanes (1,0) and (0,1) are added and thus hyperplanes $(1,1)^2$ and (0,1) are used to create L2 tiles using the tile size of 8 (which gives L2 size 8*32). The resulting scattering functions are used to create parallel code. The *Domain* and *Scattering functions* produced by this process are shown below[3] for the example stencil in Fig. 1.

Domain	Scattering
$1 \leq i \leq n-1$	$c1_{L2} = I_{L2} + J_{L2}$
$1 \leq j \leq n-1$	$c2_{L2} = J_{L2}$
$32I_{L1} \leq i \leq 32I_{L1} + 31$	$c1_{L1} = I_{L1} + J_{L1}$
$32J_{L1} \leq j \leq 32J_{L1} + 31$	$c2_{L1} = J_{L1}$
$8I_{L2} \leq I_{L1} + J_{L1} \leq 8I_{L2} + 7$	$c1 = i$
$8J_{L2} \leq J_{L1} \leq 8J_{L2} + 7$	$c2 = j$

3.3 Fine-Grain Execution

Codes that are designed to run at a very fine grain level suffer from communication overhead, reflected in its performance. With jagged tiling we have created a highly parallel code that is capable of running multiple level of tiles in parallel. In order to exploit available parallelism, we use a data-flow inspired low overhead dependency and task update scheme, based on bit masking, that enables multiple threads to work synchronously within a tile. Figure 5 shows the overview of our fine grain execution approach. These mechanisms allows high performance, low overhead communication within thread groups during the program execution.

Each group of threads grab a L2 task and initial dependency mask associated with it. Such masks are repeatable across different L2 tiles for regular applications. Dependencies among the lowest level tiles are represented by different sets of bits which are collectively updated by a group of threads working together

---

[2] The parallel hyperplane.

[3] Where n is the size of a dimension in the iteration space. For our example, both dimensions are the same.

Algorithm 1. Generating Jagged Tiles

Input: Given tiling hyperplanes $\phi_s^i, \phi_s^{i+1}...\phi_s^{i+m-1}$, Domain D_s, L1 tile sizes $tL1_i, tL1_{i+1}...tL1_{i+m-1}$ and L2 tile sizes $tL2_i, tL2_{i+1}...tL2_{i+m-1}$

1: $TS_1 = \{tL1_i, tL1_{i+1}...tL1_{i+m-1}\}$ ▷ A set of all L1 Tile sizes
2: $TS_2 = \{tL2_i, tL2_{i+1}...tL2_{i+m-1}\}$ ▷ A set of all L2 Tile sizes
3: $\phi = \{\phi_s^i, \phi_s^{i+1}...\phi_s^{i+m-1}\}$ ▷ A set of the original tiling hyperplanes
4: PLUTO_TILING_ALGORITHM(ϕ, D_s, TS_1) ▷ At this point, all $\varphi_{L1s(s)}$ are created
5: Update *Domain* constraint to get parallel hyperplane $\varphi_{L1s}^1 \rightarrow \varphi_{L1s}^1 + \varphi_{L1s}^2$ such that $\varphi_{L1s(t)}^1 - \varphi_{L1s(s)}^1 \geq 1$ leaving other hyperplanes as is
6: $\varphi = \{\varphi_{L1s}^i, \varphi_{L1s}^{i+1}...\varphi_{L1s}^{i+m-1}\}$
7: PLUTO_TILING_ALGORITHM(φ, D_s, TS_2) ▷ At this point, all $\Phi_{L2s(s)}$ are created
8: Perform Unimodular transformation on L1 scattering supernode: $\varphi T_{L1s}^1 \rightarrow \varphi T_{L1s}^1 + \varphi T_{L1s}^2$ to extract inner parallelism.
9: Perform Unimodular transformation on L2 scattering supernodes: $\Phi T_{L2s}^1 \rightarrow \Phi T_{L2s}^1 + \Phi T_{L2s}^2$ to extract outer parallelism.

Output: Updated domain and scattering function

inside the highest level tile. Each thread perform atomic bit-wise operations on the dependency masks and creates a task mask that represents all the tasks ready to execute. If the task mask is non-zero, thread finds the task, execute, update dependencies and update the task. This happens in a highly parallel fashion such that every thread is aware of the status of the tasks within the assigned tile. The implementation of this approach of synchronization between threads is done solely using atomic operations to keep the overhead low. This process is shown in Fig. 5, where the initial bit-mask is updated during the execution until all tasks are completed.

Our goal is to exploit the parallelism for a given architecture. With such an approach, threads can work in a collaborative fashion while reducing contention and hence improving overall performance.

4   Experimental Setup

The experiments were done on Intel Xeon Phi 7110P coprocessor. Each coprocessor is equipped with 61 cores running at 1.1 GHz connected with FDR infiniband interconnect. Each core can support up to 4 hyper-threads, totaling up to 244 threads. Each core has 32 KB L1 cache per thread and 512 KB L2 cache shared by 4 threads. In addition to the private L2, cores in this system also have access to L2s of all other cores via a ring topology. Only when there is a private L2 cache miss as well as ring L2 caches miss (shared L2s), the request is served by the memory.

On the software side, we divided our experiments into three different sections. In the first section, we selected an example stencil to explore the behavior of parallelism at fine granularity. We ran the example stencil with sweeps from 4 to 128 threads with 4 threads per group with two workloads: 8k by 8k and 16k by 16k elements, as shown in Fig. 6.

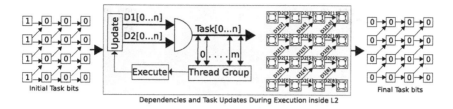

Fig. 5. Fine grain execution example

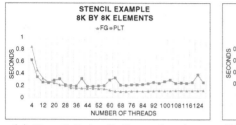

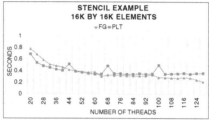

(a) Stencil 8k by 8k Execution time   (b) Stencil 16k by 16k Execution time

Fig. 6. Stencil Example Execution times for PLUTO generated code (PLT) and our framework (FG)

In addition, we implemented two versions (1D and 2D) of the Seidel solver loop, a well known scientific algorithm that computes the solution of a set of linear equations. We selected these examples to showcase our framework against PLUTO generated code using OpenMP as their parallel target. We selected arrays of 4 million elements and 8 millions elements running 4k and 16k times respectively for the one dimensional Seidel. The execution time for these runs are presented in Fig. 7. For our 2D Seidel, our selected workloads are a 4k by 4k array of elements ran over 2 K times and a 10k by 10 K element array ran over 6k times. The results of these runs are shown in Fig. 8.

In the final section, we chose one Seidel example, the biggest 2D case, to characterize the memory and remote cache misses. These results are shown in Fig. 9 for caches and in Fig. 10 for memory.

All our experiments were designed to utilize all 4 hyperthreads provided by our target architecute. In order to do so, we did 'compact pinning' such that hyperthreads form a thread group in our fine-grain execution. Similary, we set 'KMP_AFFINITY' to compact for OpenMP code. Our experiments show better runtime for fine grain execution compared to PLUTO generated parallel code using OpenMP as a baseline – denoted as 'PLT' in figures. In addition, our results shows that when threads collaborate, we gain in performance. All our codes were compiled using Intel's icc version 13.1.1 and use the Linux Perf tool [1] to collect the memory and cache related performance counter information. The performance counters collected from our experiments are presented in Table 1.

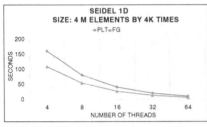
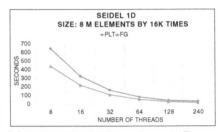

(a) Seidel 1D 4 Million elements Execution time

(b) Seidel 1D 8 Million elements Execution time

Fig. 7. Seidel 1D Execution times for PLUTO generated code (PLT) and our framework (FG)

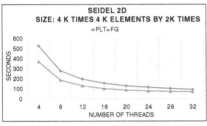
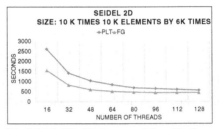

(a) Seidel 2D 4 thousand by 4 thousand elements Execution time

(b) Seidel 2D 10 thousand by 10 thousand elements Execution time

Fig. 8. Seidel 2D Execution times for PLUTO generated code (PLT) and our framework (FG)

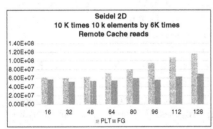
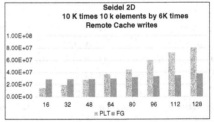

(a) Seidel 2D Remote Cache misses for Reads

(b) Seidel 2D Remote Cache misses for Writes

Fig. 9. Seidel 2D Remote Cache misses for PLUTO generated code (PLT) and our framework (FG)

5   Discussion

The benefit of execution with locality consideration comes from the amount of reuse an application offers. The stencil in example in Fig. 1 does not have much reuse. Thus, when smaller number of threads are used, the generated PLUTO

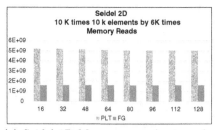
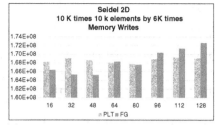

(a) Seidel 2D Memory-served misses for Reads

(b) Seidel 2D Memory-served misses for Writes

Fig. 10. Seidel 2D Memory-served misses for PLUTO generated code (PLT) and our framework (FG)

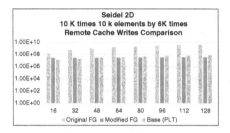

Fig. 11. Seidel 2D write serviced by memory for PLUTO generated code (PLT) our framework plus overhead and our framework without overhead. Note that the Y axis is in logarithmic scale.

code (represented as PLT in the charts) can outperform fine-grain execution with jagged tiling (represented as FG in the charts) since only limited amount of data is reused in few cores L2 caches and it is not enough to overcome the slow start introduced by coarser outer L2 tiles. However, as number of threads are incremented, FG show better execution time. This trend is visible in Fig. 6.

Figures 7 and 8, on the other hand, have much better reuse since the Seidel loops (for both 1D and 2D) have time dimensions in which the entire arrays are reused. When L2 locality is not considered as is the case with the PLUTO generated code, eviction rates increases and this is reflected in the performance of this approach. However with FG, threads working as a group execute different tiles within L2 in a synchronous fashion exploiting both parallelism and reuse offered within outer tiles. In all these approaches, the performance gains are clearly visible up to a number of threads and afterward the performance stay constant. This plateau is reached when the available parallelism is exhausted and the rest of the threads do not have any useful work. In Figs. 7(a) and 8(a), the plateau is reached at 64 and 32 threads respectively. When increasing the workload sizes (as in Figs. 7(b) and 8(b)), the plateau is pushed further (to 240 threads for the first case and 128 for the second).

Table 1. Performance Counters collected for the Largest Seidel Example

Performance Counter	Description
L2_DATA_READ_MISS_CACHE_FILL	Level 2 Cache misses for reads serviced by a remote cache
L2_DATA_WRITE_MISS_CACHE_FILL	Level 2 Cache misses for writes serviced by a remote cache
L2_DATA_READ_MISS_MEM_FILL	Level 2 Cache misses for reads serviced by the memory
L2_DATA_WRITE_MISS_MEM_FILL	Level 2 Cache misses for writes serviced by the memory

In Intel Xeon Phi, when a thread misses a read or a write access to local L2 caches, it first checks if data is available in neighboring L2 caches and goes to the memory only if there is both local and remote L2 misses. These events include both demand fills as well as prefetches and is hence a close approximation for demands hits and misses in local L2 caches. In the Intel Xeon Phi, the remote cache accesses might be as expensive as an access to memory; thus, having a large number of remote cache access might greatly affect performance [8]. Figure 9(a) and (b) show amount of reads and write shared among caches within the L2 ring for the largest Seidel loop example (c.f. Fig. 8(b)). Similarly, Fig. 10(a) and (b) show amount of data brought from memory for the same test case.

The information extracted from Figs. 9(a) and 10(a) show that the PLUTO generated code has a higher number of remote cache accesses and memory serviced reads compared with the Fine grained approach. This tells us that for the same workload, fine grained data is reused more often than its PLUTO counterpart (i.e. low memory misses and low remote cache misses for the same data set).

In the case of writes, Figs. 9(b), 10(b) and 11, show interesting results. The remote cache misses for the writes shows an inflection point around 64 threads. After 64 threads, the FG approach shows improvements over the PLUTO generated code. However, before the inflection point, our approach incurs in more share writes. The reason is that when using more cores more core caches can participate into the computation.

Figure 11 show the original overhead for memory writes for our framework. The Y axis in this figure is in log-scale to better show the differences between the approaches. The original framework suffers from a large number of writes to memory. This effect is due to a synchronization variable inside the framework. However, the number of writes in this application are an order magnitude lower than reads. Thus, their effect in performance is small. However, to obtain the application's memory-serviced writes, we modified the framework to bypass the synchronization variable. This data is presented in Fig. 10(b). In this case, we have an increase on writes, but as expressed before, the sheer number of more reads than writes, means that reads have a larger influence in the performance of the application for this application. However, we are investigating how to reduce this write pressure on the main memory.

These charts show that for application with plenty of reuse, threads can take advantage of accesses by threads within group and hence collaborate to maximize memory residence in nearby memory with minimal interference.

The balance between granularity of tasks and the amount of parallelism is very crucial to maximize performance. Coarse grain execution can lead to underutilization of resources whereas fine grain can lead to more conflicts and contentions at different levels of memory hierarchy. Most of current architectures offer vast amount of computing resources, some with hyperthreads sharing caches and some with non-uniform memory access where accessing some address ranges are cheaper than others. In such cases, taking advantage of shared resources such as caches or address range in close proximity by threads working together as a unit can have significant effect on performance.

6   Future Work

With our jagged tiling technique and fine grain execution, we improve both locality and parallelism of an application. However, current implementation of our jagged tile creation is limited to pipeline parallel applications. We plan to extend our apporoach to include highly parallel algorithms that has parallel start such that both inner and outer tile parallelism can be exploited. Also, the concept of grouping of thread to improve locality with thread collaboration can benefit many other applications besides stencils. We plan to look into different applications with reuse and architectures that can take advantage of thread and memory mapping. In addition, we plan to reduce synchronization overhead that our framework currently incurs to make our framework more efficient.

7   Conclusion

Today's systems poses tremendous computational power, however memory sub-systems haven't been able to keep up with the accelerating pace of computing resources. Many optimization techniques over the years have provided significant boosts in performance by reducing memory access latency. These techniques, although very effective, often stay blindfolded towards collaboration chances that processing resources in massively parallel systems present. This can lead to resource underutilization and missed opportunities to maximize reuse among threads working in close proximity in time and space. With our novel tiling approach that exploits multi-level parallelism along with our fine grain execution framework, we showed that when parallel threads collaborate, it leads to higher cache reuse and better resource utilization.

References

1. perf: Linux profiling with performance counters
2. Bandishti, V., Pananilath, I., Bondhugula, U.: Tiling stencil computations to maximize parallelism. In: Proceedings of the International Conference on High Performance Computing, Networking, Storage and Analysis, SC 2012, Los Alamitos, CA, USA, pp. 40:1–40:11 (2012)
3. Baskaran, M.M., et al.: Automatic data movement and computation mapping for multi-level parallel architectures with explicitly managed memories. In: Proceedings of the 13th ACM SIGPLAN Symposium on Principles and Practice of Parallel Programming, pp. 1–10. ACM (2008)
4. Bastoul, C.: Generating loops for scanning polyhedra: cloog users guide. Polyhedron 2, 10 (2004)
5. Bikshandi, G., et al.: Programming for parallelism and locality with hierarchically tiled arrays. In: Proceedings of the Eleventh ACM SIGPLAN Symposium on Principles and Practice of Parallel Programming, PPoPP 2006, pp. 48–57. ACM, New York (2006)
6. Bondhugula, U., Ramanujam, J.: Pluto: a practical and fully automatic polyhedral parallelizer and locality optimizer (2007)
7. Intel Open Source Technology Center. Open community runtime (2012)
8. Cepeda, S.: Optimization and performance tuning for Intel Xeon Phi coprocessors, part 2: understanding and using hardware events (2012)
9. Datta, K., Kamil, S., Williams, S., Oliker, L., Shalf, J., Yelick, K.: Optimization and performance modeling of stencil computations on modern microprocessors. Siam Rev. (2008)
10. Dursun, H., et al.: Hierarchical parallelization and optimization of high-order stencil computations on multicore clusters. J. Supercomput. 62(2), 946–966 (2012)
11. Feautrier, P.: Some efficient solutions to the affine scheduling problem. i. one-dimensional time. Int. J. Parallel Program. 21(5), 313–347 (1992)
12. Feautrier, P.: Some efficient solutions to the affine scheduling problem. part ii. multidimensional time. Int. J. Parallel Program. 21(6), 389–420 (1992)
13. Frigo, M., Leiserson, C.E., Prokop, H., Ramachandran, S.: Cache-oblivious algorithms. In: Proceedings of the 40th Annual Symposium on Foundations of Computer Science, FOCS 1999, p. 285. IEEE Computer Society, Washington, DC (1999)
14. Gan, G., Wang, X., Manzano, J., Gao, G.R.: Tile percolation: an OpenMP tile aware parallelization technique for the cyclops-64 multicore processor. In: Sips, H., Epema, D., Lin, H.-X. (eds.) Euro-Par 2009. LNCS, vol. 5704, pp. 839–850. Springer, Heidelberg (2009)
15. Griebl, M., Lengauer, C., Wetzel, S.: Code generation in the polytope model. In: Proceedings 1998 International Conference on Parallel Architectures and Compilation Techniques, pp. 106–111. IEEE (1998)
16. Grosser, T., Verdoolaege, S., Cohen, A., Sadayappan, P.: The relation between diamond tiling and hexagonal tiling. In: HiStencils 2014, p. 65 (2014)
17. Högstedt, K., Carter, L., Ferrante, J.: Selecting tile shape for minimal execution time. In: Proceedings of the Eleventh Annual ACM Symposium on Parallel Algorithms and Architectures, pp. 201–211. ACM (1999)
18. ET International. Swarm (swift adaptive runtime machine) (2012)
19. Kim, D., et al.: Physical experimentation with prefetching helper threads on intel's hyper-threaded processors. In: Proceedings of the International Symposium on Code Generation and Optimization: Feedback-directed and Runtime Optimization, CGO 2004, p. 27. IEEE Computer Society, Washington, DC (2004)

20. Kodukula, I., Ahmed, N., Pingali, K.: Data-centric multi-level blocking, pp. 346–357 (1997)
21. Lewis, J., et al.: An automatic prefetching and caching system. In: 2010 IEEE 29th International Performance Computing and Communications Conference (IPCCC), pp. 180–187, December 2010
22. Massachusetts Institute of Technology: Laboratory for Computer Science and D.O.J. Tanguay. Compile-time Loop Splitting for Distributed Memory Multiprocessors. Massachusetts Institute of Technology, Department of Electrical Engineering and Computer Science (1993)
23. Theobald, K.B.: Earth: An Efficient Architecture for Running Threads. McGill University, Montreal (1999)
24. Wilde, D.K.: A library for doing polyhedral operations, Technical report (1997)
25. Wolf, M.E., Lam, M.S.: A data locality optimizing algorithm. In: Proceedings of the ACM SIGPLAN 1991 Conference on Programming Language Design and Implementation, PLDI 1991, pp. 30–44. ACM, New York (1991)
26. Wolfe, M.: More iteration space tiling. In: Proceedings of the 1989 ACM/IEEE Conference on Supercomputing, Supercomputing 1989, pp. 655–664. ACM, New York (1989)
27. Wolfe, M.: Iteration space tiling for memory hierarchies. In: Proceedings of the Third SIAM Conference on Parallel Processing for Scientific Computing, pp. 357–361. Society for Industrial and Applied Mathematics, Philadelphia (1989)

The STAPL Skeleton Framework

Mani Zandifar$^{(\boxtimes)}$, Nathan Thomas, Nancy M. Amato,
and Lawrence Rauchwerger

Parasol Lab, Department of Computer Science,
Texas A&M University, College Station, USA
{mazaninfardi,nthomas,amato,rwerger}@cse.tamu.edu

Abstract. This paper describes the STAPL Skeleton Framework, a high-level skeletal approach for parallel programming. This framework abstracts the underlying details of data distribution and parallelism from programmers and enables them to express parallel programs as a composition of existing elementary skeletons such as map, map-reduce, scan, zip, butterfly, allreduce, alltoall and user-defined custom skeletons.

Skeletons in this framework are defined as parametric data flow graphs, and their compositions are defined in terms of data flow graph compositions. Defining the composition in this manner allows dependencies between skeletons to be defined in terms of point-to-point dependencies, avoiding unnecessary global synchronizations. To show the ease of composability and expressivity, we implemented the NAS Integer Sort (IS) and Embarrassingly Parallel (EP) benchmarks using skeletons and demonstrate comparable performance to the hand-optimized reference implementations. To demonstrate scalable performance, we show a transformation which enables applications written in terms of skeletons to run on more than 100,000 cores.

1 Introduction

Facilitating the creation of parallel programs has been a concerted research effort for many years. Writing efficient and scalable algorithms usually requires programmers to be aware of the underlying parallelism details and data-distribution. There have been many efforts in the past to address this issue by providing higher-level data structures [6,29], higher-level parallel algorithms [8,19,21], higher-level abstract languages [5,19,27], and graphical parallel programming languages [25]. However, most of these studies focus on a single paradigm and are limited to specific programming models.

This research supported in part by NSF awards CNS-0551685, CCF-0833199, CCF-0830753, IIS-0916053, IIS-0917266, EFRI-1240483, RI-1217991, by NIH NCI R25 CA090301-11, by DOE awards DE-AC02-06CH11357, DE-NA0002376, B575363, by Samsung, Chevron, IBM, Intel, Oracle/Sun and by Award KUS-C1-016-04, made by King Abdullah University of Science and Technology (KAUST). This research used resources of the National Energy Research Scientific Computing Center, which is supported by the Office of Science of the U.S. Department of Energy under Contract No. DE-AC02-05CH11231.

© Springer International Publishing Switzerland 2015
J. Brodman and P. Tu (Eds.): LCPC 2014, LNCS 8967, pp. 176–190, 2015.
DOI: 10.1007/978-3-319-17473-0_12

Algorithmic skeletons [9], on the other hand, address the issue of parallel programming in a portable and implementation-independent way. Skeletons are defined as polymorphic higher-order functions, that can be composed using function composition and serve as the building blocks of parallel programs. The higher-level representation of skeletons provides opportunities for formal analysis and transformations [26] while hiding underlying implementation details from end users. The implementation of each skeleton in a parallel system is left to skeleton library developers, separating algorithm specification from execution. A very well-known example of skeletons used in distributed programming is the *map-reduce* skeleton, used for generating and processing large data sets [10].

There are many frameworks and libraries based on the idea of algorithmic skeletons [14]. The most recent ones include Müesli [23], FastFlow [2], SkeTo [20], and the Paraphrase Project [15] that provide implementations for several skeletons listed in [26], such as *map, zip, reduce, scan, farm*. However, there are two major issues with existing methods that prevent them from scaling on large systems. First, most existing libraries provide skeleton implementations only for shared-memory systems. Porting such codes to distributed memory systems usually requires a reimplementation of each skeleton. Therefore, the work in this area, such as [1], is still very preliminary. Second, in these libraries, composition of skeletons is not projected into the implementation level, requiring skeleton library developers to provide either new implementations for composed skeletons [23] or insert global synchronizations between skeleton invocations resulting in a Bulk Synchronous Parallel (BSP) model, as in [20] which generally cannot achieve optimal performance.

In this work, we introduce the STAPL Skeleton Framework, a framework that enables algorithmic skeletons to scale on distributed memory systems. Skeletons in this framework are represented as parametric data flow graphs that allow parallelism to be expressed explicitly. Therefore, skeletons specified this way are inherently ready for parallel execution regardless of the underlying runtime execution model. These parametric data flow graphs are expanded over the input data and are executed in the STAPL data flow engine known as the **PARAGRAPH**. We show that parallel programs written this way can scale on more than 100,000 cores.

Our contributions in this paper are as follows:

☐ a skeleton framework based on parametric data flow graphs that can easily be used in both shared and distributed memory systems.
☐ a direct mapping of skeleton composition as the composition of parametric data flow graphs, allowing skeletons to scale on large supercomputers without the need for global synchronizations.
☐ an extensible framework to which new skeletons can be easily added through composition of existing skeletons or adding new ones.
☐ a portable framework that can be used with data flow engines other than the STAPL **PARAGRAPH** by implementing an execution environment interface.

This paper is organized as follows: In Sect. 2, we present the related work in the area of algorithmic skeletons. In Sect. 3, we provide an overview of the STAPL

Skeleton framework where we show how to break the task of writing parallel programs into algorithm specification and execution. In Sect. 4, we show a transformation that allows fine-grain skeletons to execute and perform well in a parallel environment. In Sect. 5, we present a case study showing expressivity and composability using the NAS EP and IS benchmarks. We evaluate our framework using experiments over a wide set of skeletons in Sect. 6. Conclusions and future work are presented in Sect. 7.

2   Related Work

Since the first appearance of skeleton-based programming in [9], several skeleton libraries have been introduced. The most recent efforts related to our approach are Müesli [23], FastFlow [2], Quaff [11], and SkeTo [20].

The Münster skeleton library (Müesli) is a C++ library that supports polymorphic task parallel skeletons such as *pipeline*, *farm*, and data parallel skeletons such as *map*, *zip*, *reduce*, and *scan* on array and matrix containers. Müesli can work both in shared and distributed memory systems on top of OpenMP and MPI, respectively. Skeleton composition in Müesli is limited in the sense that composed skeletons require redefinitions and cannot be defined directly as a composition of elementary skeletons.

FastFlow is a C++ skeleton framework targeting cache-coherent shared-memory multi-cores [2]. FastFlow is based on efficient Single-Producer-Single-Consumer (SPSC) and Multiple-Producer-Multiple-Consumer (MPMC) FIFO queues which are both lock-free and wait-free. In [1] the design and the implementation of the extension of FastFlow to distributed systems has been proposed and evaluated. However, the extension is evaluated on only limited core counts (a 2×16 core cluster). In addition, the composition is limited to task parallel skeletons with intermediate buffers, which limits their scalability.

Quaff is a skeleton library based on C++ template meta-programming techniques. Quaff reduces the runtime overhead of programs by applying transformations on skeletons at compile time. The skeletons provided in this library are *seq*, *pipe*, *farm*, *scm* (split-compute-merge), and *pardo*. Programs can be written as composition of the above patterns. However, Quaff only supports task parallel skeletons and is limited to shared-memory systems.

SkeTo is another C++ skeleton library built on top of MPI that provides parallel data structures:*list*, *matrix*, and *trees*, and a set of skeletons *map*, *reduce*, *scan*, *zip*. SkeTo allows new skeletons to be defined in terms of successive invocations of the existing skeletons. Therefore, the approach is based on a Bulk Synchronous Parallel model and requires global synchronization in between skeleton invocations in a skeleton composition. In our framework, we avoid global synchronizations by describing skeleton compositions as point-to-point dependencies between their data flow graph representations.

3   STAPL Skeleton Framework

The STAPL Skeleton Framework is built on top of the Standard Template Adaptive Parallel Library (STAPL) [6,7,16,29] and is an interface for algorithm developers as depicted in Fig. 7. STAPL is a framework for parallel C++ code development with interfaces similar to the (sequential) ISO C++ standard library (STL) [24]. STAPL hides the notion of processing elements and allows asynchronous communication through remote method invocations (RMIs) on shared objects. In addition, STAPL provides a data flow engine called the PARAGRAPH, which allows parallelism to be expressed explicitly using data flow graphs (a.k.a. task graphs). The runtime system of STAPL is the only platform specific component of STAPL, making STAPL programs portable to different platforms and architectures without modification Fig. 1.

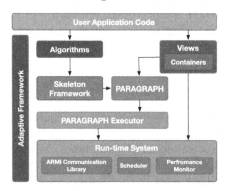

Fig. 1. The STAPL library component diagram.

Using the STAPL Skeleton Framework, algorithm developers only focus on defining their computation in terms of skeletons. As we will see in this section, each skeleton is translated to a parametric data flow graph and is expanded upon the presence of input data. The data flow representation of skeletons allows programs to run on distributed and shared memory systems. In addition, this representation formulates skeleton composition as point-to-point dependencies between parametric data flow graphs, allowing programs to execute without the need for global synchronization.

3.1   Algorithm Specification

Parametric Dependencies. In our framework, skeletons are defined in terms of parametric data flow graphs. We name the finest-grain node in a parametric data flow graph a *parametric dependency (pd)*. A parametric dependency defines the relation between the input and output elements of a skeleton as a parametric coordinate mapping and an operation.

The simplest parametric dependency is defined for the *map* skeleton:

$$map(\oplus)[a_1 \ldots a_n] = [\oplus(a_1) \cdots \oplus (a_n)]$$
$$map\text{-}pd(\oplus) \equiv \{< i > \mapsto < i >, \oplus\} \tag{1}$$

In other words, the element at index i of the output is computed by applying $\oplus$ on the element at index i of the input. This representation carries spatial information about the input element. As we will see later, it is used to build data flow graphs from parametric dependencies.

The zip_k skeleton is a generalization of the *map* skeleton over k lists:

$$zip_k(\oslash)[a_1^1, \ldots, a_n^1] \ldots [a_1^k, \ldots, a_n^k] = [\oslash(a_1^1, \ldots, a_1^k), \ldots, \oslash(a_n^1, \ldots, a_n^k)]$$

$$zip\text{-}pd_k(\oslash) \equiv \{< \underbrace{i, \ldots, i}_{k} > \mapsto < i >, \oslash)\} \tag{2}$$

Elem Operator. Parametric dependencies are expanded over the input size with the data parallel *elem* compositional operator. An *elem* operator receives a parametric dependency (of type δ) and expands it over the given input, with the help of *span* (of type ψ), to form a list of nodes in a data flow graph:

$$elem :: \psi \to \delta \to [\delta]$$

$$elem_{span}(parametric\text{-}dependency) \tag{3}$$

For ease of readability in Eq. 3, we show *span* as a subscript and the *parametric dependency* in parenthesis.

A *span* is defined as a subdomain of the input. Intuitively, the default *span* is defined over the full domain of the input and is omitted for brevity in the default cases. As we will see later in this section, there are other *spans*, such as *tree-span* and *rev-tree-span*, used to define skeletons with tree-based data flow graphs.

With the help of the *elem* operator, *map* and *zip* skeletons are defined as:

$$map(\oplus) = elem(map\text{-}pd(\oplus))$$

$$zip_k(\oslash) = elem(zip\text{-}pd_k(\oslash)) \tag{4}$$

Given an input, these parametric definitions are instantiated as task graphs in the STAPL Skeleton Framework.

Repeat Operator. Many skeletons can be defined as tree-based or multilevel data flow graphs. Our *repeat* operator allows such skeletons to be expressed simply as such. The *repeat* operator is a function receiving a skeleton and applying it to a given input successively for a given number of times specified by a unary operator of type $\beta \to \beta$ called ξ:

$$repeat :: [\alpha] \to [\alpha] \to (\beta \to \beta) \to [\alpha] \to [\alpha]$$

$$repeat(S, \xi)[a_1, \ldots, a_n] = (\underbrace{S \ldots (S(S[a_1, \ldots, a_n])))}_{\xi(n) \ times} \tag{5}$$

An example of the *repeat* operator is a tree-based data flow graph definition of the *reduce* skeleton (Fig. 2). In a tree-based *reduce*, each element at level j depends on two elements at level $j - 1$. Therefore, the parametric dependency for each level of this skeleton can be specified as:

$$reduce\text{-}pd(\otimes) \equiv \{(< 2i, j - 1 >, < 2i + 1, j - 1 >) \mapsto < i, j >, \otimes\} \tag{6}$$

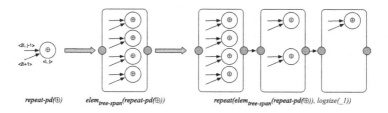

repeat-pd(⊕)   *elem*$_{tree-span}$*(repeat-pd(⊕))*   *repeat(elem*$_{tree-span}$*(repeat-pd(⊕))), logsize(_1))*

Fig. 2. The process of creating the tree-based representation of the *reduce* skeleton.

Each level of this tree representation is then expanded using the *elem* operator. However, the expansion is done in a different way than the default case used in Eqs. 1 and 2. In a tree, the *span* of the *elem* operator at each level is half of its previous level, starting from the *span* over the domain of the input at level 0. We name this *span* a *tree-span* and we use it to define a tree-based *reduce*:

$$reduce(\otimes) = repeat(elem_{tree-span}(reduce\text{-}pd(\otimes)), log_2(n)) \qquad (7)$$

Similarly, other skeletons can be defined using the *elem* and *repeat* operators such as *scan*, *butterfly*, *reverse-butterfly*, and *broadcast* as shown in Fig. 4. For brevity, we show only the simultaneous binomial tree implementation of the *scan* skeleton in Figs. 3(a) and 4. However, we support two other scan implementations in our framework, namely the exclusive scan implementation introduced in [4] and the binomial tree scan [28], which are expressed in a similar way.

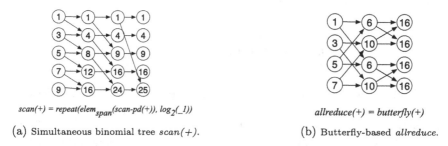

scan(+) = repeat(elem$_{span}$*(scan-pd(+)), log*$_2$*(_1))*

(a) Simultaneous binomial tree *scan(+)*.

allreduce(+) = butterfly(+)

(b) Butterfly-based *allreduce*.

Fig. 3. Data flow representation of the binomial *scan* and *butterfly* skeletons.

Compose Operator. In addition to the data flow graph composition operators presented above, we provide a skeleton composition operator called *compose*. The *compose* operator, in its simplest form, serves as the functional composition used in the literature for skeleton composition and is defined as:

$$compose(S_1, S_2, \ldots, S_n)\, x = S_n \circ \ldots \circ S_2 \circ S_1 x = S_n(\ldots(S_1 x))) \qquad (8)$$

The *map-reduce* and the *allreduce* skeleton are skeletons which can be built from the existing skeletons (Fig. 4) using the *compose* operator.

The binomial tree representation of the _scan_ skeleton

$$scan\text{-}pd(\oplus) \equiv \begin{cases} \{(< i, level - 1 >, < i - 2^{level}, level - 1 >) \mapsto < i, level >, \oplus\} & \text{if } i \geq 2^{level} \\ \{(< i, level - 1 > \mapsto < i, level >), id\} & \text{if } i < 2^{level} \end{cases}$$

$$scan(\oplus) = repeat(elem(scan\text{-}pd(\oplus)), log_2(size))$$

The k-ary _tree_ and _reverse-tree_ skeletons:

$$tree_k(pd) = repeat(elem_{tree-span_k}(pd), log_k(n))$$

$$rev\text{-}tree_k(pd) = repeat(elem_{rev\text{-}tree\text{-}span_k}(pd), log_k(size))$$

The _broadcast_ skeleton:

$$broadcast\text{-}pd \equiv \{(< i/2 > \mapsto < i >), \lambda x.x\}$$

$$broadcast = rev\text{-}tree(broadcast\text{-}pd)$$

The _butterfly_ and _reverse-butterfly_ skeletons:

$$butterfly\text{-}pd(\otimes) \equiv \{(< i, level - 1 >, < i \pm 2^{n-level-1} >) \mapsto < i, level >, \otimes)\}$$

$$rev\text{-}butterfly\text{-}pd(\otimes) \equiv \{(< i, level - 1 >, < i \pm 2^{level} >) \mapsto < i, level >, \otimes\}$$

$$butterfly(\otimes) = repeat(elem(butterfly\text{-}pd(\otimes)), log_2(size))$$

$$rev\text{-}butterfly(\otimes) = repeat(elem(rev - butterfly\text{-}pd(\otimes)), log_2(size))$$

Skeletons composed from the existing skeletons:

$$allreduce_1(\oplus) = butterfly(\oplus)$$

$$allreduce_2(\oplus) = broadcast \circ reduce(\oplus)$$

$$alltoall(\star) = butterfly(\star)$$

$$fft\text{-}DIT = butterfly(fft\text{-}DIT\text{-}op)$$

$$fft\text{-}DIF = ref\text{-}butterfly(fft\text{-}DIF\text{-}op)$$

$$map\text{-}reduce(\oplus, \otimes) = reduce(\otimes) \circ map(\oplus)$$

The _do-while_ skeletons:

$$while\ p\ S\ x = if\ p\ x$$
$$then\ while\ p\ S\ (S\ x)$$
$$else\ x$$

Fig. 4. A list of skeletons compositions

Do-While Operator. The compositional operators we mentioned so far cover skeletons that are static by definition. A _do-while_ skeleton is intended to be used in dynamic computations which are bounded by a predicate p as in [17]. The _do-while_ skeleton applies the same skeleton S to a given input until the predicate is satisfied. It is defined as shown in Fig. 4.

The execution of the _do-while_ skeleton requires its corresponding data flow graph to be dynamic, as the number of iterations are not known a priori. This functionality is allowed in our framework with the help of the _memento_ design pattern [12], as we will see later in Sect. 3.2.

Flows. So far, we have only showed the skeletons that are composed using _repeat_ and _compose_ using simple functional composition. In these compositions, a skeleton's output is passed as the input to the subsequent skeleton. Similar to the _let_ construct in functional programming languages, input/output dependencies between skeletons can be defined arbitrarily as well (e.g., Fig. 5). To represent such compositions in our internal representation of skeletons, we define one input and one output port (depicted as red filled circles in Figs. 2 and 5) for each skeleton. We formulate the skeleton composition as the connections between these ports and refer to them as *flows*. Flows are similar to the notion of flows in flow-based programming [22].

With the help of *ports* and *flows*, skeleton composition is directly mapped to point-to-point dependencies in data flow graphs, avoiding unnecessary global synchronizations commonly used in BSP models. As a concrete example, Fig. 5 shows a customized flow used for NAS IS skeleton-based representation.

3.2   Algorithm Execution

In the previous section we looked at algorithm specification. In this section, we explain how an input-size independent algorithm specification is converted to a data flow graph through the *spawning* process.

Skeleton Manager. The Skeleton Manager orchestrates the spawning process in which a skeleton composition is traversed in a pre-order depth-first-traversal, in order to generate its corresponding data flow graph. The nodes of this data flow graph correspond to the parametric dependency instances in a composition. If a PARAGRAPH environment is used, these data flow graphs will represent a taskgraph and will be executed by the data flow engine of STAPL called the PARAGRAPH. The creation and execution of taskgraphs in a STAPL PARAGRAPH can progress at the same time, allowing overlap of computation and communication.

Environments. An environment defines the meaning of data flow graph nodes generated during the spawning process. As we saw earlier, in a PARAGRAPH environment each data flow graph node represents a task in a taskgraph. Similarly, other environments can be defined for execution or additional purposes, making our skeleton framework portable to other libraries and parallel frameworks.

For example, we used other environments in addition to the PARAGRAPH environment for debugging purposes such as (1) a GraphViz environment which allows the data flow graphs to be stored as GraphViz dot files [13], (2) a debug environment which prints out the data flow graph specifications on screen, and (3) a graph environment which allows the data flow graphs to be stored in a STAPL parallel graph container [16]. Other environments can also be easily defined by implementing the environment interface.

Memento Queue. The Skeleton Manager uses the memento design pattern [12] to record, pause, and resume the spawning process allowing the incremental creation of task graphs, and execution of dynamic skeletons. For example, the continuation and the next iteration of a *do-while* skeleton are stored in the back and the front of the memento queue, respectively, in order to allow input-dependent execution.

4   Skeleton Transformations

As mentioned earlier, various algorithms can be specified as compositions of skeletons. Since skeletons are specified using high-level abstractions, algorithms written using skeletons can be simply analyzed and transformed for various purposes, including performance improvement.

In this section, we define the coarsening transformation operator $\mathcal{C}$ which enables efficient execution of skeletons using hybrid (a.k.a. macro) data flow graphs [18] instead of fine-grained data flow graphs.

4.1   Definitions

Before explaining the coarsening transformation, we need to explain a few terms that are used later in this section.

Dist and Flatten Skeletons. A *dist* skeleton [17] partitions the input data and a *flatten* (*projection*) skeleton unpartitions the input data. They are defined as:

$$dist \ [a_1, \ldots, a_n] \ = \ [[a_1, \ldots, a_k], \ldots, [a_j, \ldots, a_n]]$$
$$flatten \ [[a_1, \ldots, a_k], \ldots, [a_j, \ldots, a_n]] \ = \ [a_1, \ldots, a_n] \qquad (9)$$

Homomorphism. A function $\mathscr{F}$ on a list is a homomorphism with respect to a binary operator $\oplus$ iff on lists x and y we have [26]:

$$f(x + \!\!+ \ y) = f(x) \oplus f(y) \qquad (10)$$

in which $+\!\!+$ is the list concatenation operator.

The skeletons that are list homomorphisms can be defined as a composition of the *map* and the *reduce* skeletons, making them suitable for execution in parallel systems. However, as mentioned in [26], finding the correct operators for the *map* and *reduce* can be difficult even for very simple computations. Therefore, in our transformations of skeletons which are list homomorphisms, we use their *map-reduce* representation only when the operators can be devised simply, and in other cases we define a new transformation.

4.2   Coarsening Transformations ($\mathcal{C}$)

As we saw earlier, skeletons are defined in terms of parametric data flow graphs. Although fine-grained data flow graphs expose maximum parallelism, research has shown [18] that running fined-grained data flow graphs can have significant overhead on program execution on Von Neumann machines. This is due to the lack of spatial and temporal locality and the overhead of task creation, execution, and pre/post-processing. In fact, the optimum granularity of data flow graphs depends on many factors, one of the most important being hardware characteristics. Therefore, we define the coarsening transformation in this section as a transformation which is parametric on the input size where granularity can be tuned per application and machine.

The coarsening transformations, listed in Eq. 11, use *dist* skeleton to make coarser chunks of data (similar to the approach used in [17]). Then they apply an operation on each chunk of data (e.g., $map(map(\oplus))$ in $\mathcal{C}(map(\oplus))$). Subsequently, they might apply a different skeleton on the result of the previous phase to combine the intermediate results (e.g., $reduce(\otimes)$ in $\mathcal{C}(reduce(\otimes))$). Finally, they might apply a *flatten* skeleton to put the result in its original fine-grain format:

$$\mathcal{C}(map(\oplus)) = flatten \circ map(map(\oplus)) \circ dist$$
$$\mathcal{C}(zip(\oslash)) = flatten \circ zip(zip(\oslash)) \circ dist$$
$$\mathcal{C}(reduce(\otimes)) = reduce(\otimes) \circ map(reduce(\otimes)) \circ dist \qquad (11)$$
$$\mathcal{C}(butterfly(\otimes)) = flatten \circ map(butterfly(\otimes)) \circ butterfly(zip(\otimes)) \circ dist$$
$$\mathcal{C}(rev\text{-}butterfly(\otimes)) = flatten \circ butterfly(zip(\otimes)) \circ map(rev\text{-}butterfly(\otimes)) \circ dist$$

The coarsening transformation of the *map-reduce* can be defined in two ways:

$$\mathcal{C}(map\text{-}reduce(\oplus, \otimes)) = \mathcal{C}(reduce(\otimes) \circ map(\oplus)) = \mathcal{C}(reduce(\otimes)) \circ \mathcal{C}(map(\oplus))$$
$$\mathcal{C}(map\text{-}reduce(\oplus, \otimes)) = reduce(\otimes) \circ map(map\text{-}reduce(\oplus, \otimes)) \circ dist \qquad (12)$$

For performance reasons, it is desirable to choose the second method in Eq. 12 as the first one might require intermediate storage for the result of $\mathcal{C}(map(\oplus))$.

Similarly, the coarsening transformation for *scan* can be defined as:

$$\mathcal{C}(scan(\oplus)) = let \ r_1 \leftarrow scan(\oplus) \circ map(reduce(\oplus)) \circ dist$$
$$r_2 \leftarrow scan_{exclusive} \circ map(last) \ r_1$$
$$in \ flatten \circ zip(\Psi(\oplus)) \ r_1 \ r_2 \qquad (13)$$

In Eq. 13 Ψ is a function of type $\alpha \rightarrow [\alpha] \rightarrow [\alpha]$ and is defined as:

$$\Psi(\oplus) \ c \ [a_1, \ldots, a_n] = [a_1 \oplus c, \ldots, a_n \oplus c] \qquad (14)$$

The coarsening transformation in Eq. 13 is more desirable than the *map-reduce* transformation listed in [26]. The reason is that the *reduce* operation used in [26] is defined in an inherently sequential form while in Eq. 13 we define the transformation in terms of other parallel skeletons.

Limitation. Similar to the approach in [26], our coarsening transformation is currently limited to input-independent skeletons which are list homomorphisms.

5   Composition Examples

The goal in this section is to show the expressivity and ease of programmability of our skeleton framework. As a case study we show the implementation of two NAS benchmarks [3] (Embarrassingly Parallel (EP) and Integer Sort (IS)) in terms of skeletons.

5.1   NAS Embarrassingly Parallel (EP) Benchmark

This benchmark is designed to evaluate an application with nearly no inter-processor communication. The only communication is used in the pseudo-random number generation in the beginning and the collection of results in the end. This benchmark provides an upper bound for machine floating point performance. The goal is to tabulate a set of Gaussian random deviates in successive square annuli.

The skeleton-based representation of this benchmark is specified with the help of the *map-reduce* skeleton. The *map* operator in this case generates n pairs of uniform pseudo-random deviates (x_j, y_j) in the range of $(0, 1)$, then checks if $x_j{}^2 + y_j{}^2 \leq 1$. If the check passes, the two numbers $X_k = x_j\sqrt{(-2log\ t_j)/t_j}$ $Y_k = y_j\sqrt{(-2log\ t_j)/t_j}$ are used in the sums $S_1 = \sum_k X_k$ and $S_2 = \sum_k Y_k$. The *reduce* operator computes the total sum for S_1 and S_2 and also accumulates the ten counts of deviates in square annuli.

5.2   NAS Integer Sort (IS) Benchmark

In this benchmark N keys are sorted. The keys are uniformly distributed in memory and are generated using a predefined sequential key generator. This benchmark tests both computation speed and communication performance.

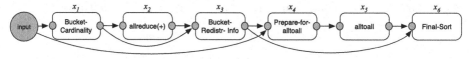

(a) Graphical representation of NAS IS flows.

integer-sort input =
  let
    $x_1 \leftarrow map(Bucket\text{-}Cardinality)\ input$
    $x_2 \leftarrow allreduce(+)\ x_1$
    $x_3 \leftarrow zip_2(Bucket\text{-}Redistr\text{-}Info)\ x_1\ x_2$
    $x_4 \leftarrow zip_2(Prepare\text{-}for\text{-}alltoall)\ x_3\ input$
    $x_5 \leftarrow alltoall\ x_4$
    $x_6 \leftarrow zip_2(Final\text{-}Sort)\ x_3\ x_5$
  in
    x_6

```
compose<flows::nas_is>(
  map(bucket_cardinality<int_t>()),
  allreduce<std::vector<int_t>>(),
  map(bucket_redistr_info()),
  zip<3>(prepare_for_alltoall<int_>(),
  alltoall<int_t>(),
  zip<3>(final_sort())
)
```

(b) The Nas IS composition.

Fig. 5. The NAS Integer Sort Benchmark

The IS benchmark is easily described in terms of skeletons as shown in Fig. 5. Similar to other skeleton compositions presented so far, the IS skeleton composition does not require any global synchronizations between the skeleton invocations and can overlap computation and communication easily. As we show later in the experimental results, avoiding global synchronizations results in better performance on higher core counts.

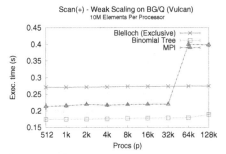

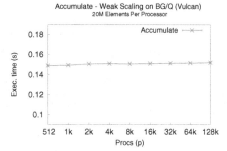

(a) Our inclusive binomial and exclusive *scans* (Section 3) vs. a hand-optimized MPI scan.

(b) Weak scalability of accumulate(+) as an example of the *reduce* skeleton.

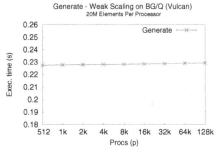

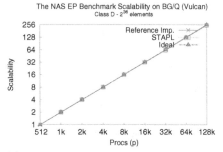

(c) Weak scalability of Generate as an example of the *map* skeleton.

(d) Comparison of the scalability of the NAS EP benchmark with the reference implementation.

Fig. 6. Experimental results for elementary skeletons and the NAS EP benchmarks.

The IS benchmark skeleton composition as presented in Fig. 5 is based on the well-known counting sort. First, the range of possible input values are put into buckets. Each partition then starts counting the number of values in each bucket (*map(Bucket-Cardinality)*). In the second phase, using an *allreduce* skeleton (defined in Fig. 4), the total number of elements in each bucket is computed and is globally known to all partitions. With the knowledge of the key distribution, a partitioning of buckets is devised (*map(Bucket-Redistr)*) and keys are prepared for a global exchange (*zip(Prepare-for-allToall)*). Then with the help of the *alltoall* skeleton (Figs. 4 and 7) the keys are redistributed to partitions. Finally, each partition sorts the keys received from any other partition (*zip(Final-Sort)*).

6 Performance Evaluation

We have evaluated our framework on two massively parallel systems: a 153,216 core Cray XE6 (HOPPER) and a 24,576 node BG/Q system (VULCAN). Each node contains a 16-core IBM PowerPC A2, for a total of 393,216 cores. Our results in Fig. 6 show excellent scalability for the *map*, *reduce*, and *scan* skeletons

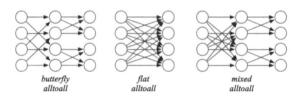

Fig. 7. The three versions of the *alltoall* representations used in the NAS IS benchmark.

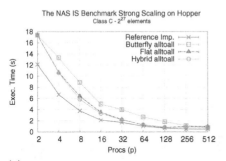 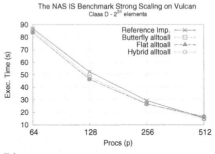

(a) Performance comparison of class C NAS IS benchmark with reference implementation.

(b) Performance comparison of class D NAS IS benchmark with reference implementation.

Fig. 8. The NAS IS benchmarks strong scaling results.

and also the NAS EP benchmark on up to 128k cores. These results show that the ease of programmability in the STAPL Skeleton Framework does not result in performance degradation and our skeleton-based implementation can perform as well as the hand-optimized implementations.

To show a more involved example, we present the result for the NAS IS benchmark. The IS benchmark is a communication intensive application and is composed out of many elementary skeletons such as *map*, *zip*, and *alltoall*. It is therefore a good example for the evaluation of composability in our framework. We compare our implementation of the IS benchmark to the reference implementation in Fig. 8(b).

Having an efficient *alltoall* skeleton is the key to success in the implementation of the IS benchmark. We have implemented *alltoall* in three ways (Fig. 7). Our first implementation uses the *butterfly* skeleton. The second is a flat *alltoall* in which all communication happen at the same level. The third method is a hybrid of *butterfly* and flat *alltoall*s. In both the flat and hybrid implementations, we use a permutation on the dependencies to avoid a node suffering from network congestion.

Our experiments show that the best performance for our skeleton-based implementation of the IS benchmark is achieved using the hybrid version in both C and D classes of the benchmark. Our implementation of the IS benchmark using the hybrid *alltoall* shows comparable performance to the hand-optimized reference implementation (Fig. 8(b)). We have an overhead on lower core counts which is due to the copy-semantics of the STAPL runtime system. The STAPL runtime system at this moment requires one copy between the user-level to the MPI level on both sender and receiver side. These extra copies result in a 30–40 %

overhead on lower core counts. However, this overhead is overlapped with computation on higher core counts. In fact, in the class D of the problem, our implementation is faster than the reference implementation. This improvement is made possible by avoiding global synchronizations and describing skeleton composition as point-to-point dependencies.

7   Conclusions

In this paper, we introduced the STAPL Skeleton Framework, a framework which simplifies parallel programming by allowing programs to be written in terms of algorithmic skeletons and their composition. We showed the coarsening transformation on such skeletons, which enables applications to run efficiently on both shared and distributed memory systems. We showed that the direct mapping of skeletons to data flow graphs and formulating skeleton composition as data flow graph composition can remove the need for global synchronization. Our experimental results demonstrated the performance and scalability of our skeleton framework beyond 100,000 cores.

Acknowledgments. We would like to thank Adam Fidel for his help with the experimental evaluation.

References

1. Aldinucci, M., Campa, S., Danelutto, M., Kilpatrick, P., Torquati, M.: Targeting distributed systems in fastflow. In: Caragiannis, I., et al. (eds.) Euro-Par Workshops 2012. LNCS, vol. 7640, pp. 47–56. Springer, Heidelberg (2013)
2. Aldinucci, M., Danelutto, M., et al.: Fastflow: high-level and efficient streaming on multi-core. (a fastflow short tutorial). Program. Multi-core Many-core Comp. Sys. Par. Dist. Comp. (2007)
3. Bailey, D., Harris, T., et al.: The NAS Parallel Benchmarks 2.0. Report NAS-95-020, Numerical Aerodynamic Simulation Facility, NASA Ames Research Center, Mail Stop T 27 A-1, Moffett Field, CA 94035–1000, USA, December 1995
4. Blelloch, G.E.: Prefix sums and their applications. Technical report CMU-CS-90-190. School of Computer Science, Carnegie Mellon University, November 1990
5. Budimlić, Z., Burke, M., et al.: Concurrent collections. Sci. Prog. **18**(3), 203–217 (2010)
6. Buss, A., et al.: The STAPL pView. In: Cooper, K., Mellor-Crummey, J., Sarkar, V. (eds.) LCPC 2010. LNCS, vol. 6548, pp. 261–275. Springer, Heidelberg (2011)
7. Buss, A., Amato, N.M., Rauchwerger, L.: STAPL: standard template adaptive parallel library. In: Proceedings of the Annual Haifa Experimental Systems Conference (SYSTOR), pp. 1–10. ACM, New York (2010)
8. Buss, A.A., Smith, T.G., Tanase, G., Thomas, N.L., Bianco, M., Amato, N.M., Rauchwerger, L.: Design for interoperability in STAPL: pMatrices and linear algebra algorithms. In: Amaral, J.N. (ed.) LCPC 2008. LNCS, vol. 5335, pp. 304–315. Springer, Heidelberg (2008)
9. Cole, M.I.: Algorithmic Skeletons: Structured Management of Parallel Computation. Pitman, London (1989)

10. Dean, J., Ghemawat, S.: Mapreduce: simplified data processing on large clusters. Commun. ACM **51**(1), 107–113 (2008)
11. Falcou, J., Sérot, J., et al.: Quaff: efficient c++ design for parallel skeletons. Par. Comp. **32**(7), 604–615 (2006)
12. Gamma, E., et al.: Design Patterns: Elements of Reusable Object-Oriented Software. Pearson Education, New York (1994)
13. Gansner, E.R., North, S.C.: An open graph visualization system and its applications to software engineering. Softw. Pract. Experience **30**(11), 1203–1233 (2000)
14. González-Vélez, H., Leyton, M.: A survey of algorithmic skeleton frameworks: high-level structured parallel programming enablers. Softw. Pract. Experience **40**(12), 1135–1160 (2010)
15. Hammond, K., et al.: The PARAPHRASE project: parallel patterns for adaptive heterogeneous multicore systems. In: Beckert, B., Damiani, F., de Boer, F.S., Bonsangue, M.M. (eds.) FMCO 2011. LNCS, vol. 7542, pp. 218–236. Springer, Heidelberg (2013)
16. Harshvardhan, Fidel, A., Amato, N.M., Rauchwerger, L.: The STAPL parallel graph library. In: Kasahara, H., Kimura, K. (eds.) LCPC 2012. LNCS, vol. 7760, pp. 46–60. Springer, Heidelberg (2013)
17. Herrmann, C.A., Lengauer, C.: Transforming rapid prototypes to efficient parallel programs. In: Rabhi, F.A., Gorlatch, S. (eds.) Patterns and Skeletons for Parallel and Distributed Computing, pp. 65–94. Springer, London (2003)
18. Johnston, W.M., Hanna, J., et al.: Advances in dataflow programming languages. ACM Comp. Surv. (CSUR) **36**(1), 1–34 (2004)
19. Kale, L.V., Krishnan, S.: CHARM++: a portable concurrent object oriented system based on C++. SIGPLAN Not. **28**(10), 91–108 (1993)
20. Matsuzaki, K., Iwasaki, H., et al.: A library of constructive skeletons for sequential style of parallel programming. In: Proceedings of the 1st International Conference on Scalable information systems, p. 13. ACM (2006)
21. McCool, M., Reinders, J., et al.: Structured Parallel Programming: Patterns for Efficient Computation. Elsevier, Waltham (2012)
22. Morrison, J.P.: Flow-Based Programming: A New Approach to Application Development. CreateSpace, Paramount (2010)
23. Müller-Funk, U., Thonemann, U., et al.: The Münster Skeleton Library Muesli-A Comprehensive Overview (2009)
24. Musser, D., Derge, G., Saini, A.: STL Tutorial and Reference Guide, 2nd edn. Addison-Wesley, Reading (2001)
25. Newton, P., Browne, J.C.: The code 2.0 graphical parallel programming language. In: Proceedings of the 6th International Conference on Supercomputing, pp. 167–177. ACM (1992)
26. Rabhi, F., Gorlatch, S.: Patterns and Skeletons for Parallel and Distributed Computing. Springer, London (2003)
27. Robison, A.D.: Composable parallel patterns with intel cilk plus. Comp. Sci. Eng. **15**(2), 66–71 (2013)
28. Sanders, P., Träff, J.L.: Parallel prefix (scan) algorithms for MPI. In: Mohr, B., Träff, J.L., Worringen, J., Dongarra, J. (eds.) PVM/MPI 2006. LNCS, vol. 4192, pp. 49–57. Springer, Heidelberg (2006)
29. Tanase, G., Amato, N.M., Rauchwerger, L.: The STAPL parallel container framework. In: Proceedings of the ACM SIGPLAN Symposium on Principles and Practice of Parallel Programming (PPoPP), San Antonio, Texas, USA, pp. 235–246 (2011)

Compilers

Memory Management Techniques for Exploiting RDMA in PGAS Languages

Barnaby Dalton[1], Gabriel Tanase[2], Michail Alvanos[1(✉)], Gheorghe Almási[2], and Ettore Tiotto[1]

[1] IBM Software Group, Toronto, Canada
{bdalton,malvanos,etiotto}@ca.ibm.com
[2] IBM TJ Watson Research Center, Yorktown Heights, NY, USA
{igtanase,gheorghe}@us.ibm.com

Abstract. Partitioned Global Address Space (PGAS) languages are a popular alternative when building applications to run on large scale parallel machines. Unified Parallel C (UPC) is a well known PGAS language that is available on most high performance computing systems. Good performance of UPC applications is often one important requirement for a system acquisition. This paper presents the memory management techniques employed by the IBM XL UPC compiler to achieve optimal performance on systems with Remote Direct Memory Access (RDMA). Additionally we describe a novel technique employed by the UPC runtime for transforming remote memory accesses on a same shared memory node into local memory accesses, to further improve performance. We evaluate the proposed memory allocation policies for various UPC benchmarks and using the IBM® Power® 775 supercomputer [1].

1 Introduction

Partitioned Global Address Space languages (PGAS) [2–6] have been proposed as viable alternatives for improving programmer productivity in distributed memory architectures. A PGAS program executes as one or more processes, distributed across one or more physical computers (*nodes*) connected by a network. Each process has an independent virtual address space called a partition. The collection of all partitions in a program is called the Partitioned Global Address Space or PGAS. A PGAS process can access both data from the local partition as well as remote partitions. Accessing remote data employs the network via a transport Application Interface (API). The network read and write operations, are typically several orders of magnitude slower than local read and write operations to memory.

The global shared array is a data abstraction supported by most PGAS languages that allows users to specify arrays physically distributed across all

---

Researchers are supported by the IBM Center for Advanced Studies, and by the Defense Advanced Research Projects Agency under its Agreement No. HR0011-07-9-0002.

J. Brodman and P. Tu (Eds.): LCPC 2014, LNCS 8967, pp. 193–207, 2015.
DOI: 10.1007/978-3-319-17473-0_13

processes. Compiler and runtime support are subsequently employed to map from the high-level, index-based, access to either local or remote memory accesses. The PGAS runtime or the compiler translates the shared memory addresses to a process identifier and to a virtual address on the remote process. There are three different methods commonly used for computing remote memory addresses:

Sender Side Lookup: For every shared array instantiated the sender maintains a translation table with a list of virtual base addresses, one for each process partition, pointing to the memory block used in that partition. The downside of this approach is the non-scalable memory requirement for every shared array declared. Assuming there are N shared arrays and P processes in a computation, this solution requires $O(N \times P^2)$ storage.

Receiver Side Lookup: In this case, each process only maintains a local translation table with an entry for every shared array instantiated. The table maps from a shared array identifier to the address of the local memory block used for storage. The downside of this approach is the difficulty of exploiting remote direct memory access (RDMA) hardware features where the memory address must be known on the process initiating the communication.

Identical Virtual Address Space on all Processes: A third solution requires all processes to maintain symmetric virtual address spaces and the runtime allocates each shared array at the same virtual address on all processes. This technique is often more complex, but it provides the benefits of the other two methods we already introduced: efficient address inference on the sender side for RDMA exploitation and minimal additional storage for shared arrays tracking.

The XLUPC compiler and its runtime implementation [7] fits into the third category. The performance of accessing a shared array is a function of two main factors: the latency of address translation and the latency of remote accesses. RDMA and the large shared memory nodes present on a modern HPC system are two hardware features that need to be carefully exploited in order to reduce the latency of these operations. This work presents a symmetric memory allocator that allows easy inference of the remote address for shared array data and subsequently low latency access using either RDMA or direct memory access depending on the remote element location. More specifically, the paper makes the following novel contributions:

- Describe the symmetric heap, a memory allocator that guarantees same virtual memory address for shared arrays on all processes of a PGAS computation, enables more efficient address translation and it allows efficient RDMA exploitation. The allocator does not require kernel support for allocating symmetric partitions.
- Describe the symmetric heap mirroring, a novel solution for transforming remote array accesses into local memory accesses, for processes collocated within same shared memory address space.

2 Unified Parallel C Background

The UPC language follows the PGAS programming model. It is an extension of the C programming language designed for high performance computing on large-scale parallel machines. UPC uses a Single Program Multiple Data (SPMD) model of computation in which the amount of parallelism is fixed at program startup time.

Listing 1.1 presents the computation kernel of a parallel vector addition. The benchmark adds the content of three vectors (A, B, and D) to the vector C. The programmer declares all vectors as **shared** arrays. Shared arrays data can be accessed from all UPC threads using an index or shared pointer interface. In this example, the programmer does not specify the layout qualifier (blocking factor). Thus, the compiler assumes that the blocking factor is one. The construct **upc_forall** distributes loop iterations among UPC threads. The fourth expression in the **upc_forall** construct is the affinity expression, that specifies that the owner thread of the specified element will execute the ith loop iteration.

The compiler transforms the upc_forall loop in a simple for loop and the shared accesses to runtime calls to fetch and store data (Listing 1.2). Each runtime call may imply communication, creating fine-grained communication that leads to poor performance. In this example, the

```
1    #define N 16384
2    shared int A[N], B[N], C[N], D[N]
3
4    upc_forall(i=0; i<N-1; i++; i)
5        C[i] = A[i+1] + B[i+1] + D[i];
```

Listing 1.1. A parallel upc_forall loop.

compiler privatizes [8] accesses $C[i]$ and $D[i]$ (Listing 1.2). The compiler does not privatize the $A[i+1]$ and $B[i+1]$ accesses because it is possible that these elements belong to other UPC threads. Before accessing shared pointers, the compiler also creates calls for shared pointer arithmetic (__xlupc_ptr_arithmetic).

```
1    #define N 16384
2    shared int A[N], B[N], C[N], D[N]
3
4    local_ptr_C = __xlupc_local_addr(C); local_ptr_D = __xlupc_local_addr(D);
5    for (i=MYTHREAD; i < N; i+= THREADS){
6        tmp0 = __xlupc_deref( __xlupc_ptr_arithmetic(&A[i+1]) );
7        tmp1 = __xlupc_deref( __xlupc_ptr_arithmetic(&B[i+1]) );
8        *(local_ptr_C + OFFSET(i)) = tmp0 + tmp1 + *(local_ptr_D + OFFSET(i));
9    }
```

Listing 1.2. Transformed upc_forall loop.

In Unified Parallel C Language shared arrays can be allocated either *statically* or *dynamically*. In the *static* scheme, the programmer declares the memory on the heap using the keyword **shared**, as presented in Listing 1.1. Alternatively, the programmer can use the runtime for shared memory allocation:

- **upc_all_alloc(size_t blocks,size_t bytes)**: Allocates *blocks* × *bytes* of shared space with blocking factor *bytes*. This is a collective call and it must be invoked from all UPC threads.
- **upc_global_alloc(size_t blocks,size_t bytes)**: Allocates *blocks* × *bytes* of shared space with blocking factor *bytes*. The call uses one-side communication and it must be invoked from only one UPC thread.

– `upc_alloc(size_t bytes)`: Allocates *nbytes* of shared space with blocking factor bytes with affinity to the calling thread.
– `upc_free(shared void *ptr)`: Frees dynamically allocated shared storage.

3   Symmetric Heap Allocation

Modern 64-bit systems have a virtual address space that is several orders of magnitude larger than available physical memory. In a virtual memory system, physical memory may be mapped to any virtual address. Two independent processes on the same computer may have distinct physical memory with the same virtual address in their respective virtual address spaces. Since most of the virtual address space is unused, and virtual addresses are reserved systemically in well-known regions on a system, a region of memory to reserve for symmetric partition use is typically available.

Figure 1 depicts the main concepts we use throughout this section. Each process has its own heap (memory partition), and the union of all individual partitions is called *global heap*. A section, called the *symmetric partition*, is reserved for storing distributed data structures within each partition. Each symmetric partition is contiguous in virtual memory and begins at the same virtual address. The collection of all symmetric partitions is called the

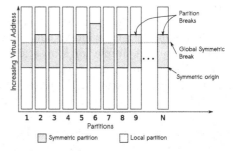

Fig. 1. Layout of the symmetric heap.

symmetric heap. The starting address in each partition is, by design, chosen to be common across all partitions and is called the symmetric origin. The lowest unmapped address greater than the origin is called the *partition break*. Unlike the origin, we do not require the break to be identical across all symmetric partitions.

3.1   Allocation

Allocation is a distinct process from mapping memory in the methodology we propose. One process, labeled the allocating process, maintains all book-keeping information within its partition. All other partitions maintain a mirror of the memory regions as defined by the allocating process. A span of bytes that is unused in one symmetric partition is unused in all symmetric partitions.

The implementation uses the Two-Level Segregated Fit memory allocator (TLSF) [9], adapted to enable symmetric allocation. The symmetric partition of the allocating process is fragmented in one or more contiguous blocks. Two blocks can't overlap and the collection of all blocks covers the entire address space of the symmetric partition. Each block is either free or used. Each block exists isomorphically in every symmetric partition. A block marked as used (resp. free) in one partition is used (resp. free) in every other partition. There is a collection of all unused blocks called the *freelist*.

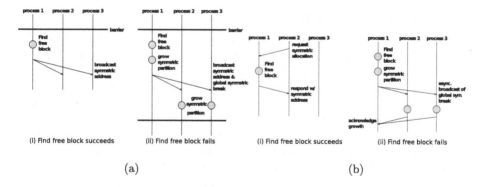

Fig. 2. Operations for collective (left) and independent allocation (right).

3.2 Collective Allocation

An allocation that is executed by all processes concurrently is called collective allocation (e.g., upc_all_alloc). The process receives a pointer to the newly created data structure upon completion. Each process begins the allocation request concurrently for an unambiguous count of bytes per partition and waits at a barrier until all processes have started. The allocator process searches for an unallocated block of memory that is at least as large as the requested size. If a sufficiently large block can not be found, then the allocating process increases the global symmetric break and issues a grow operation on the local symmetric partition. The extended bytes are added to the free store guaranteeing the existence of a block to accommodate the request.

The memory block is then removed from the symmetric free store. If it exceeds the original request it is split and the residue is returned to the free store. The address for the block is broadcasted to all other processes together with the new global symmetric break. The remaining processes issue a grow operation if the global symmetric break exceeds their local partition breaks. At this point, they all agree upon an address that is within the range of their symmetric partition. As a last step, the runtime registers the memory of the shared array with the operating system (memory is pinned, as required by the RDMA protocol).

Figure 2(a) presents two scenarios for the collective allocation. When successful (i), the process issues a Remove-block operation to mark the block as used and remove it from the freelist. The allocation process issues a Split-block operation to create a block and possibly a residue block. It issues an Insert-block operation to return the block to the freelist. Finally, the allocating process sends the virtual address of the block to all processes with a broadcast collective operation. In the second example, Fig. 2(a)(ii), the allocating process is unable to find any free blocks in the freelist. The allocating process increases the global symmetric break by the requested size and issues a Grow operation on its local symmetric partition. The newly mapped memory is inserted into the freelist with a Create-block operation. Allocating process broadcasts the virtual address of the block together with the global symmetric break and the remaining processes issue Grow operations on their local partitions.

3.3   Independent Allocation

If a single process needs to issue a global allocation request without collaboration of other processes, the process of allocation is different from collective allocation. The allocating process maintains all book-keeping information within its partition. If the requesting process is not the allocating process, a request is sent to the allocating process. In either case, all requests for independent allocation are serialized by the allocating process. The allocator process searches for an unallocated block that accommodates the request. If a block is found, it is removed from the free-store and split as necessary. The address is returned to the requester in an acknowledgment message. If no block is found that accommodates the request, then the global symmetric break is increased to guarantee sufficient space in the free store. A local grow operation is executed to map memory into the partition. When all processes acknowledge the updated global symmetric break, the address is returned to the requester in an acknowledgment message.

Figure 2(b) presents two scenarios of independent allocation. In Fig. 2(b)(i), the allocation success and the allocating process returns the address to the requested process. However, if the allocation fails, the allocating process exchanges messages to globally grow the symmetric partitions (Fig. 2(b)(i)). In order to maintain the global symmetric break invariant, process 1 issues interrupting requests to each other process to issue a grow to their local symmetric partitions.

4   Heap Mirroring for Shared Memory Optimizations

In this section we present an extension to the symmetric heap introduced in Sect. 3 we call *heap mirroring*. This extension addresses the need to access quickly the memory which is collocated on the same node, but in a different process. It should be stressed that improving intranode communication will not show improvements in UPC programs that uses both intra and inter-node communication as the later will often dominate the overall communication time.

As with the symmetric heap, each process maintains a local partition at a fixed origin which is common across all processes. In addition, each process maintains a view of every partition from collocated nodes. We call these views, mirrored partitions or mirrored heaps. The mirrored partitions are not memory replicas that need to be maintained; rather they maintain the same physical memory pages mapped into multiple processes virtual address spaces.

At this point we must clarify that symmetric allocation maps distinct memory at identical virtual addresses between distinct processes. In contrast, mirroring maps identical memory at distinct virtual addresses within each process. Both are used for accessing shared memory of a remote process or UPC thread.

4.1   Arrangement of Mirrors

If N UPC threads are collocated on the same node, each thread has a symmetric partition and $N - 1$ mirrored partitions each separated by *sym_gap*. We always place the process's symmetric heap at the symmetric origin.

For each thread i, we introduce a function, $mirror_i(j)$, mapping a UPC thread j, to a value called a mirror-index with the following properties:

- $mirror_i(j) = -1$ if threads i and j are not collocated,
- $mirror_i(i) = 0$,
- $mirror_i(j) \in \{1, \ldots, N-1\}$ if i and j are collocated,

We build this function dynamically into a hash table at startup time. This guarantees fast lookup by checking at most two locations of an array. The function is used to test whether threads are collocated, and if so, the location of the mirrored partition. The mirrored partition of process j within process i is located at $sym\_origin + mirror_i(j) \times sym\_gap$.

4.2   Implementation Challenges Using SystemV Shared Memory

Most common solutions for implementing shared memory across processes are Unix System V, BSD anonymous mapped memory or kernel extensions [10]. Due to portability and availability reasons we selected System V shared memory and next we discuss some key challenges for the implementation.

In System V, for multiple processes to allocate the same physical memory in their address spaces, they need a shared secret called the key. Inside XLUPC memory allocator, the key is a 16-bit integer, alive only during the brief time period when same node processes are mapping the shared memory.

If N collocated processes need to extend the symmetric heap, they each map the new memory in via shmget, and additionally they map the memory of the other $N-1$ processes into their heap. Each of the N memory leases has a shared memory key. They are all valid at the same time, and none of them may collide. To further complicate things, a second instance of the same or other UPC program could be running concurrently also allocating another M segments and they should not collide either. So we need to make collisions impossible between threads in the same program, unlikely between instances of UPC programs running on the same node, but have a resolution scheme that is fast if collisions happen anyway.

The algorithm employed uses the parallel job unique identifier (PID) as a seed from which the keys are inferred. On IBM systems this is the PID of the parallel job launcher (e.g., poe or mpirun) that starts the parallel computation. The algorithm uses the following formula: $keyspace = 0 \times 10000u + atoi(env(PID)) << 14u$. PID's are a 16 bit value and the keyspace is a 32 bit value. This spreads keyspaces with distinct values of PID by at least 16k and avoids the most commonly used first 64k of keys.

Next a scratch space is created in all collocated processes using key $keyspace+0$. This is used for communication and synchronization between collocated processes. If there are N collocated processes, each of them is given an index from $0..N-1$ called their hub_index. Each process will use $keyspace + 1 + hub\_index$ to attempt allocation. In the event of a key collision among the N keys in the scratch pad, detected during allocation of the symmetric heap, we increment the key used by

N (the number of collocated processes) and try again. We record the key used in the scratch space. During mirroring, the runtime looks in the scratch space for the key used by the owner of the symheap. A failure to find the key here is an unrecoverable error.

4.3 Collective and Independent Allocation

The main difference from initial allocation algorithm introduced in Sect. 3.2 is mirroring the collocated heaps. First, while all processes enter the call, only one process will look for a free block. If found its address is broadcasted to all other processes and the function returns. If a block large enough to accommodate this request is not found we calculate the new symmetric heap size that will guarantee a free block large enough and we broadcast the size.

Independent allocation requires the allocator process to asynchronously interrupt all other UPC processes to enter a state where they can collectively work to extend the symmetric and mirrored heaps. When all threads reach the common allocation function than we employ the same mechanism as for collective allocation. Special care is taken to ensure the node-barriers do not deadlock with system-wide barriers.

5 Shared Address Translation

UPC shared objects, such as shared arrays, reside in the shared memory section local to the thread. Shared pointers are actually fat-pointers: a structure that represents the shared address which allows the program to reference shared objects anywhere in the partitioned global address space.

Listing 1.3 presents the structure containing the information. In contrast with the traditional SVD approaches the structure contains all the necessary information for the program to access the data.

```
1   typedef struct xlpgas_ptr2shared_t
2   {
3       xlpgas_thread_t thread; /* Thread index */
4       size_t offset; /* Offset inside thread */
5       xlpgas_local_addr_t base; /* Base address */
6       size_t allocsize; /* Allocated bytes */
7   } xlpgas_ptr2shared_t ;
```

Listing 1.3. Shared pointer structure.

Due to symmetric memory allocator, the base address is the same in all nodes. Thus, the runtime calculates the virtual offset using arithmetic operations. Before accessing shared data, the compiler automatically creates runtime calls to modify the thread and the offset fields. The runtime call (*pointer increment*) calculates the thread containing the data and the relative offset inside it. The runtime updates the shared pointer with the calculated information.

Thus, this approach avoids SVD lookup for local access (less overhead) and the SVD lookup during remote access (guarantees RDMA). Furthermore, this approach increases the possibility of compiler shared pointer arithmetic inlining.

Listing 1.4 presents the naive algorithm for the calculation of the thread and the relative offset. At compile time the compiler linearizes the offset of the shared pointer (idx). The blocking factor (BF) and element size (ES) can be calculated at compile time or runtime. The first step of the runtime is the calculation of the phase and the block. The runtime uses the block information to calculate the thread that contains the shared data and the phase to calculate the local offset. Note that this simplified example ignores the case of using local offsets: when accessing a structure fields from a shared array of structures. Furthermore, during the linearization the compiler also take into calculation the element access size that can be different from the array element size. Unfortunately, this naive approach is computation intensive.

Runtime Optimizations. A first optimization is for the case where the blocking factor is zero, the shared increment is zero, or the increment is the array element size mul-

```
1    phase = (idx % BF);
2    block = (idx / BF);
3    ptr.thread = block % THREADS;
4    ptr.addrfield = ES * (phase + block / THREADS);
5    ptr.base = /* address of A */;
```

Listing 1.4. Naive virtual address calculation.

tiplied by the blocking factor. In this case the runtime makes an addition to the offset and returns to the program. When the number of threads and the blocking factor multiplied by the size of elements are power of two, the runtime uses shifts and masks to calculate the offset and the thread containing the data.

Inlining. The runtime optimizations significantly improve the performance of shared pointer increment. However a large fixed overhead is associated with runtime calls. The PowerPC Application Binary Inerface (ABI) mandates significant cost for a function call due to memory operations. Moreover, the branching code in the runtime is required to check for special cases and inserts additional overhead. To solve this challenge the compiler inlines the shared pointer increment when possible and there is enough information at compile time.

6   Experimental Results

This section analyzes the overhead of memory allocation and presents the performance evaluation of symmetric heap and mirroring optimizations. We first use microbenchmarks to examine the cost of allocation, and six benchmarks to examine the performance of applications with regular and irregular communication patterns. For certain experiments we make a comparison of the latest release with an older version of the compiler employing the Shared Variable Directory (SVD) solution.

The evaluation uses the Power®775 [1] system. Each compute node (*octant-* shared memory address space) has a total of 32 POWER7®cores (3.2 GHz), 128 threads, and up to 512 GB memory. A large P775 system is organized, at a higher level, in *drawers* consisting of 8 octants (256 cores) connected in an all-to-all fashion for a total of 7.86 Tflops/s. The most relevant aspect of the machine for the current paper is the availability of RDMA hardware.

The SVD version uses both active messages and RDMA depending on the data size and available opportunities for symmetric allocation. The active messages use the immediate send mechanism on P775 which allows small packets to be sent by injecting them directly into the network. Thus, the SVD implementation achieves lower latency than the RDMA for small messages. For messages larger than 128 bytes, the SVD implementation uses RDMA if the array happens to be allocated symmetrically. This is an opportunistic optimization whose success depends on the history of previous allocation/deallocations on the system. The main difference relative to the solution we present in this paper is that the symmetric memory implementations always guarantee that shared arrays are allocated symmetrically.

The evaluation uses microbenchmarks and four applications:

Microbenchmarks: A first microbenchmark allocates a large number of small arrays to evaluate the cost of memory allocation. The second microbenchmark contains streaming-like local shared accesses to evaluate the cost of address translation and access latency relative to the SVD solution.

Guppie: The guppie benchmark performs random read/modify/write accesses to a large distributed array. The benchmark uses a temporary buffer to fetch the data, modify it, and write it back. The typical size of this buffer is 512 elements and it is static among different UPC threads.

Sobel: The Sobel benchmark computes an approximation of the gradient of the image intensity function, performing a nine-point stencil operation. In the UPC version [11] the image is represented as a one-dimensional shared array of rows and the outer loop is a parallel *upc_forall* loop.

Bucketsort: The benchmark sorts an array of 16-byte records using bucketsort [12] algorithm. Each node generates its share of the records. Each thread uses a $\frac{17}{16} \times 2\,GB$ buffer to hold records received from other threads, which are destined to be sorted on this thread.

UTS: The Unbalanced Tree Search benchmark [13] belongs in the category of state-space search problems. The Unbalanced Tree Search benchmark measures the rate of traversal of a tree generated on the fly using a splittable random number generator.

GUPS: The GUPS benchmark contains accesses in the form of read-modify-write, distributed across a shared array in random fashion. The compiler optimizes the benchmark using the remote update optimization [8].

6.1 Allocator Performance

To evaluate the overhead of allocating shared memory dynamically we created a simple kernel that repeatedly allocates shared arrays using either the collective `upc_all_alloc()` or the one sided `upc_global_alloc()`. For the one sided case only UPC thread zero is performing the allocation while all other threads are waiting in a barrier. We allocate a total of 100 shared arrays and report the average execution time

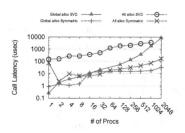

Fig. 3. Performance of global allocation benchmark in average execution time of the call.

per allocation. Figure 3 presents the performance of the global_alloc and all_alloc runtime calls without the mirroring optimization and the performance of the same allocations but using a previous version of the runtime that uses SVD. As expected the all_ alloc runtime call incurs higher overhead than the global_alloc call, due to global synchronization. The all_ alloc has an additional internal barrier in the beginning. The latency of global_alloc increases in two cases: one when the number of UPC increases from 32 to 64 and one when the number of UPC threads increases from 1024 to 2048. These "cliffs" are the result of higher latency communication. Finally, the overhead of using the mirroring optimization is less than 1 %, and for this reason we excluded it from the plot. For reference only, we also include the allocation performance when SVD is used for address translation. However the results can not be compared directly as more optimizations and changes were added it to the latest version of the compiler framework.

6.2   Local Shared Accesses Performance

Many PGAS loops work almost entirely on local data but the compiler is unable to prove this. The SVD implementation has a heavy penalty on these type of loops. Figure 4(a) and (b) presents the results in aggregated MBytes/s. The privatization is a compiler optimization that could interfere with this experiment and for this reason we disable it. The results show that the symmetric implementation is an order of magnitude better than the SVD version. The improvements are mainly due to the fact that symmetric heap solution avoids the SVD table lookup.

6.3   Regular Applications

The Bucketsort and Sobel benchmarks contain regular communication patterns and usually coarse grain messages. The Sobel implementation includes the static coalescing optimization that aggregates the data statically. The mirroring optimizations gives a significant performance improvement on the Bucketsort benchmark, up to +90 %, when running within one node. On the other hand, the Sobel benchmark benefits less than then Bucketsort with the mirroring optimization because most of the shared accesses are local and are privatized by the

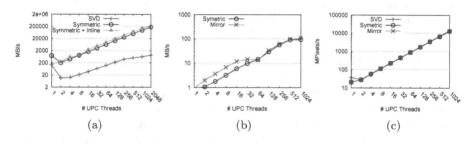

Fig. 4. Performance of local shared read microbenchmark (a), bucketsort (b), and Sobel (c), using weak scaling.

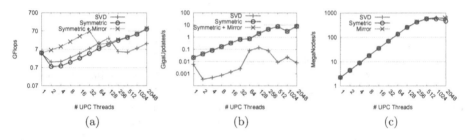

Fig. 5. Performance of Guppie, GUPS, and UTS using strong scaling.

compiler. In regular applications we keep constant the computation per UPC thread.

6.4   Irregular Applications

Figure 5(a) presents the results of the Guppie benchmark. The performance bottleneck is mainly the network latency. The mirroring optimization has the best results for intra node communication. On the other hand, the SVD achieves slightly better performance than the symmetric version for small number of cores. This is because the SVD uses active messages that are optimized to use shared memory within an octant. Symmetric always uses RDMA which is slower than direct shared memory access. The GUPS benchmark uses a different communication mechanism: the remote update packets. In GUPS benchmark, the message creation rate and the address resolution burdens the performance. Thus, the symmetric memory approach is an order of magnitude better than the SVD implementation. There are not any significant differences in the cases of the UTS benchmark. The good shared data locality and in combination with the privatization optimization of the compiler provide good performance, independent from the implementation approach.

6.5   Summary

This benchmark-based performance study shows that he overhead of allocating memory on 2048 UPC thread is less than 35 usec with one side allocation and less than 180 usec for the global allocation. The benchmarks evaluation shows significant improvements in local and shared memory node accesses when using shared pointers due to RDMA exploitation and improved address translation.

7   Related Work

PGAS Allocators. Berkeley UPC compiler [14] uses the GASNet [15] runtime to implement a collective upc_all_alloc call. In high performance machines, the GASNet runtime uses the Firehose [16] technique, an explicit DMA registration. Furthermore, the Berkeley framework supports also collective deallocation. At the program startup, each UPC thread reserves a fixed portion of the address space for shared memory using the `mmap()` system call. This address range is the maximum value on the amount of shared memory per-thread that the program can use. In contrast our implementation does not contain any restriction on dynamic memory allocation. The Berkeley UPC framework also uses fat pointers for accessing shared structures. Michigan UPC runtime (MuPC) [17] and CRAY compilers [18,19] use a symmetric heap way to allocate memory for shared arrays. The main differences compared to our work is the fact that the size of the symmetric heap is fixed and controlled using an environment variable and to the best of our knowledge no in-depth details on how memory is managed are provided.

Cray SHMEM [20] introduces another popular PGAS paradigm that provides the notion of shared arrays. The IBM implementation of SHMEM library employs a symmetric heap allocator similar to the one presented in Sect. 3 to efficiently exploit RDMA. It doesn't however employ the mirroring capability of the allocator presented here.

PGAS Shared Pointer Translation. Researchers also use Memory Model Translation Buffer (MMTB), conceptual similar to the Translation Look Aside Buffers (TLBs). The idea is to use a caching that contains the shared pointer values along with the corresponding virtual addresses [21]. In other approaches, that use a distributed shared variable directory (SVD), an address cache is implemented. The caching of remote addresses reduces the shared access overhead and allows better overlap of communication and computation, by avoiding the SVD remote access [8,22]. Another approach is to simplify the shared pointer arithmetic by removing some fields of the shared pointer structure. Experimental results [23] show that cyclic and indefinite pointers simplification improves the performance of pointer-to-shared arithmetic up to 50 %. Machine specific implementations, such as Cray X1 [18] use this approach. Other researchers focus on techniques for minimized the address translation overhead for multi-dimensional arrays [24]. The authors use an additional space per array to simplify the translation for multi-dimensional arrays. In contrast, our approach does not allocate additional space for the translation of multi-dimensional arrays.

Allocators for Efficient Migration. The techniques presented in this paper are similar with the thread or process data migration used from different runtimes. For example, Charm++ [25] implements "isomalloc" stacks and heaps, which are similar technique with ours. However, they focus on the migration of stack and heap to a different node and not for effectively translating virtual addresses to remote addresses. PM2 runtime system [26] implements a similar technique that guarantees the same virtual address that simplifies the migration. Thus, there is no need to keep pointers in a directory. However, the focus of the runtime is the efficient migration of the working unit rather the exploitation of the RDMA.

Shared Memory with MPI. Shared memory exploitation is also a well know technique for MPI programs that are written for distributed memory systems. For example, MPI-3 interface for RMA can be efficiently implemented on networks supporting RDMA as shown in [10]. The key mechanism the authors of [10] employ for this is a symmetric heap and remote address space mirroring similar to the ones presented in this work. However, this approaches differs in the language targeted, and the protocols used for mirroring. The XPMEM Linux kernel module was not available on the particular machine targeted in our work [1] so we relied on a novel protocol built around the more portable SystemV calls as described in Sect. 4. Other approaches requiring kernel support are addressed in the literature [27] with the drawback that they require a slightly different MPI interface.

8   Conclusion

This paper demonstrates the importance of proper design of memory allocator in PGAS languages. The architecture of the allocator and the remote addresses translation to virtual addresses play an important role on application performance. The evaluation shows that both versions can scale with high number of UPC threads. However, the performance of the symmetric memory allocation is better than the SVD in local shared accesses and guarantees the RDMA usage. Furthermore, the mirroring optimization provides an order of magnitude better performance than the simple symmetric version when running in one node. The current implementation is integrated on the latest version of the XLUPC compiler.

References

1. Rajamony, R., Arimilli, L., Gildea, K.: PERCS: The IBM POWER7-IH high-performance computing system. IBM J. Res. Dev. **55**(3), 1–3 (2011)
2. U. Consortium, UPC Specifications, v1.2, Lawrence Berkeley National Lab LBNL-59208, Technical report (2005)
3. Numwich, R., Reid, J.: Co-array fortran for parallel programming, Technical report (1998)
4. Cray Inc., Chapel Language Specification Version 0.8, April 2011. http://chapel.cray.com/spec/spec-0.8.pdf
5. Charles, P., Grothoff, C., Saraswat, V., Donawa, C., Kielstra, A., Ebcioglu, K., von Praun, C., Sarkar, V.: X10: an Object-oriented Approach to Non-Uniform Cluster Computing. In: Proceedings of the 20th annual ACM SIGPLAN conference on Object-oriented programming, systems, languages, and applications, vol. 40, no. 10. Oct 2005
6. Yelick, K.A., Semenzato, L., Pike, G., Miyamoto, C., Liblit, B., Krishnamurthy, A., Hilfinger, P.N., Graham, S.L., Gay, D., Colella, P., Aiken, A.: Titanium: a high-performance java dialect. Concurrency Pract. Experience **10**(11–13), 825–836 (1998)
7. Tanase, G., Almási, G., Tiotto, E., Alvanos, M., Ly, A., Daltonn, B.: Performance Analysis of the IBM XL UPC on the PERCS Architecture, Technical report (2013). RC25360

8. Barton, C., Cascaval, C., Almasi, G., Zheng, Y., Farreras, M., Chatterje, S., Amaral, J.N.: Shared memory programming for large scale machines. In: Programming Language Design and Implementation (PLDI 2006) (2006)
9. Masmano, M., Ripoll, I., Crespo, A., Real, J.: Tlsf: a new dynamic memory allocator for real-time systems. In: Proceedings of the 16th Euromicro Conference on Real-Time Systems, ECRTS 2004, pp. 79–88. IEEE (2004)
10. Friedley, A., Bronevetsky, G., Hoefler, T., Lumsdaine, A.: Hybrid MPI: efficient message passing for multi-core systems. In: SC, p. 18. ACM (2013)
11. El-Ghazawi, T., Cantonnet, F.: UPC performance and potential: a NPB experimental study. In: Proceedings of the 2002 ACM/IEEE Conference on Supercomputing, Supercomputing 2002, pp. 1–26 (2002)
12. Cormen, T.H., Leiserson, C.E., Rivest, R.L., Stein, C.: Introduction to algorithms. MIT Press, Cambridge (2001)
13. Olivier, S., Huan, J., Liu, J., Prins, J.F., Dinan, J., Sadayappan, P., Tseng, C.-W.: UTS: An unbalanced tree search benchmark. In: Almási, G.S., Caşcaval, C., Wu, P. (eds.) KSEM 2006. LNCS, vol. 4382, pp. 235–250. Springer, Heidelberg (2007)
14. The Berkeley UPC Compiler. http://upc.lbl.gov
15. Bonachea, D.: Gasnet specification, v1.1. Technical report, Berkeley, CA, USA (2002)
16. Bell, C., Bonachea, D.: A New DMA Registration Strategy for Pinning-Based High Performance Networks. In: Proceedings of the International Parallel and Distributed Processing Symposium, pp. 198–208. IEEE (2003)
17. Michigan Technological University, UPC Projects (2011). http://www.upc.mtu.edu
18. Bell, C., Chen, W.-Y., Bonachea, D., Yelick, K.: Evaluating support for global address space languages on the Cray X1. In: Proceedings of the 18th Annual International Conference on Supercomputing, pp. 184–195. ACM (2004)
19. ten Bruggencate, M., Roweth, D.: Dmapp-an api for one-sided program models on baker systems. In: Cray User Group Conference (2010)
20. Barriuso, R., Knies, A.: SHMEM user's guide for C. Technical report (1994)
21. Cantonnet, F., El-Ghazawi, T.A., Lorenz, P., Gaber, J.: Fast address translation techniques for distributed shared memory compilers. In: Proceedings of 19th IEEE International Parallel and Distributed Processing Symposium, p. 52b. IEEE (2005)
22. Farreras, M., Almasi, G., Cascaval, C., Cortes, T.:Scalable RDMA performance in PGAS languages. In: IEEE International Symposium on Parallel & Distributed Processing, IPDPS 2009, pp. 1–12. IEEE (2009)
23. Husbands, P., Iancu, C., Yelick, K.: A performance analysis of the berkeley upc compiler. In: Proceedings of the 17th Annual International Conference on Supercomputing, pp. 63–73. ACM (2003)
24. Serres, O., Anbar, A., Merchant, S.G., Kayi, A., El-Ghazawi, T.: Address translation optimization for unified parallel c multi-dimensional arrays. In: Parallel and Distributed Processing Workshops and Phd Forum (IPDPSW), pp. 1191–1198. IEEE (2011)
25. Huang, C., Lawlor, O.S., Kalé, L.V.: Adaptive MPI. In: Rauchwerger, L. (ed.) LCPC 2003. LNCS, vol. 2958, pp. 306–322. Springer, Heidelberg (2004)
26. Antoniu, G., Bougé, L., Namyst, R.: An efficient and transparent thread migration scheme in the PM2 runtime system. In: Rolim, J.D.P. (ed.) IPPS-WS 1999 and SPDP-WS 1999. LNCS, vol. 1586, pp. 496–510. Springer, Heidelberg (1999)
27. Jin, H.-W., Sur, S., Chai, L., Panda, D.: LiMIC: support for high-performance MPI intra-node communication on Linux cluster. In: International Conference on Parallel Processing: ICPP 2005, pp. 184–191 (2005)

Change Detection Based Parallelism Mapping: Exploiting Offline Models and Online Adaptation

Murali Krishna Emani[✉] and Michael O'Boyle

School of Informatics, The University of Edinburgh, Edinburgh, UK
m.k.emani@sms.ed.ac.uk, mob@inf.ed.ac.uk

Abstract. Parallel programs increasingly execute in highly dynamic environments where mapping program parallelism to dynamically varying system resources is challenging. Traditional offline compiler approaches exploit program knowledge but ignore the runtime environment. Online runtime approaches dynamically adapt to resources but ignore program structure. Furthermore, there is no mechanism to detect and improve the efficiency of these approaches during program execution. This paper develops a new runtime mapping approach based on online change detection. It models runtime scheduling of threads as a Markov Decision Process and exploits an offline trained model to predict the best thread mapping based on both code and environment features. It then develops a novel approach where the accuracy of an environment predictor is used as a measure of the model quality, adjusting thread mapping over time. On evaluating our scheme with varying external workloads and hardware availability, we achieve an average speedup improvement of 2.14x over the default OpenMP policy, 1.58x over an online approach and 1.32x over a state-of-the-art offline trained model.

1 Introduction

Effective exploitation of many-cores is the key challenge for system software designers. They have to best determine how to exploit the parallelism within an application in a dynamic environment. Large-scale data centers are typical of the highly parallel systems where applications have to both co-execute with other parallel workloads to improve system utilization and contend with changes in allocated hardware resources. Minimizing workload interference and effective exploitation of resources is crucial to improve program performance.

Dynamic allocation or mapping of parallel work to hardware is an extensively studied area where we can roughly categorise approaches as *offline* and *online*. Offline compiler approaches try to exploit as much prior knowledge about the system ahead of time and have no runtime information. Thus while they are often program *specific* they are often *fragile* in the presence of change. Online approaches directly tackle this problem. They typically monitor the load of the system and adjust the mapping of the target program to fit the available

© Springer International Publishing Switzerland 2015
J. Brodman and P. Tu (Eds.): LCPC 2014, LNCS 8967, pp. 208–223, 2015.
DOI: 10.1007/978-3-319-17473-0_14

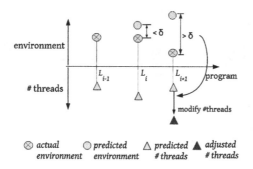

Fig. 1. Using environment predictor to adjust thread mapping at every decision point. If the difference between the actual and predicted environment is small ($<\delta$) the number of threads predicted is unchanged. If the difference is large ($>\delta$) we modify the number of threads used.

resources but they use undifferentiated remapping policies. Thus while they are *robust* approaches they are often *generic*.

Ideally we would like a policy that can exploit prior offline knowledge and discover online when this model needs to be updated. This paper develops such an approach, **CDMapp**, for efficient parallelism mapping based on *online change detection*. Our approach tries to determine the optimal degree of parallelism for every parallel section of a program. We do this by describing runtime scheduling as a *Markov Decision Process* where we aim to find a policy that minimizes overall execution time. First we learn an offline model [6] using predictive modelling. This approach works well when the training set is similar to the online environment. However, if this environment departs significantly from expectations this model has no way of knowing that it is now out-of-date and incorrectly predicting the wrong mapping.

Our novel approach is to build a second model that predicts what the environment should look like if an ideal mapping decision had been made. We then check at the next decision point how accurate this prediction was. If there is a large discrepancy, this means that the assumptions used offline no longer hold true and we should adjust our mapping accordingly. This is shown in Fig. 1 where at every loop L_i, both the best thread number is predicted as well as what the environment should look like if this thread number is optimal. At the next loop, if the difference between the actual and predicted environment is small ($<\delta$, δ is described in further sections) we assume the environment is behaving as expected and we do not change our predicted thread number. If the environment is substantially different from expected ($>\delta$), we assume the environment has changed and adjust the predicted best number of threads accordingly. We first evaluate our approach when a target executes with varying workloads and hardware resources. We further analyze results with *smart* programs in the system each trying to adapt using certain optimization policies.

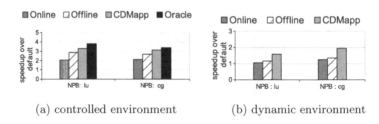

(a) controlled environment   (b) dynamic environment

Fig. 2. Room for improvement in (a) controlled system (b) realistic dynamic system.

This paper makes the following contributions.

– We propose a Markov Decision Process approach for adapting parallel programs to dynamic environment based on online change detection.
– We combine an offline model with online adaptation to determine the best thread number for OpenMP programs.
– We show effectiveness of our approach by achieving significant performance improvement over existing state-of-the-art approaches with no effect on the co-executing workloads.
– We also show that all programs improve when they employ our approach when workloads are adaptive.

2   Motivation

2.1   Scope for Improvement

To show there is scope for performance improvement over existing schemes and determining the best thread number for a target program in a rapid dynamic environment is non-trivial, we ran two experiments on a 12-core system. Here we co-executed lu or cg from NAS as target with just one external workload mg that employs OpenMP default scheme (i.e. set the number of threads equal to number of processors). The first experiment is in a controlled environment with a constant workload and static hardware. The second is in a more realistic dynamic environment with varying workload and hardware. We compared our approach against the OpenMP default scheme, a state-of-the-art online approach [17], an offline trained approach [6] and an idealised oracle.

Since the offline model is trained in a similar execution scenario to the test experiment, it outperforms the default and online approaches. As seen from Fig. 2(a) our approach performs better than all existing techniques, however there is still a scope for an average 13 % improvement to attain the best speedup. In the dynamic system it is not possible to determine the best mapping at runtime. As seen from Fig. 2(b) our approach improves upto 40 % over the offline scheme. This shows that there is a significant room for speedup improvement in a realistic dynamic system and that an offline trained model is limited by its training environment. If the execution environment changes drastically from the one in which it was trained then it is unable to determine best thread number.

Our solution exploits a model that has been learnt offline to dynamically map programs in the presence of external workload. It then improves its quality by detecting any environment change, adjusting its behavior over time.

3   Runtime Scheduling

This section describes current approaches to runtime scheduling of parallel loops and formulates them in terms of Markov Decision Process. A process is Markovian if the next state depends only on the current state and current action.

3.1   Markov Decision Process

A Markov Decision Process (MDP) [16] (S, A, R, P) is a control decision process where decisions have probabilistic outcomes. At each time step t the process is in a state $s \in S$ and must decide an action $a \in A$ that takes it a new state $s' \in S$. The reward for such an action is denoted by $R(a, s, s')$. The goal of a MDP is to choose a sequences of actions that maximise the total reward or value $V = \sum_a R$; this is known as the policy π.

3.2   Scheduling Policies as MDPs

Default: OpenMP default policy assigns a thread number equal to the maximum number of available processors. In this approach the only state modelled is the number of processors available at time t, p^t. There is only one action available, setting the number of threads to the current state.

$$S = \{p^t\}, A = \{n^t = p^t\}$$

The reward of an action R, the total reward V and the state transition probability P are ignored. This gives a simple policy to set the thread number to the maximum number of current processors.

$$\pi_{default}(s^t) = a^t$$

Online: [17] is an online adaptive scheme that changes thread count at runtime based on loop execution time. Here state is modelled as dynamic points in the code where decisions are made.

$$S = \{(s_i^t)\}, A = \{n_i^t = 1, \ldots, p_i^t\}$$

where i refers to the parallel code section and t refers to the of its dynamic instance. The actions are setting the thread number up to the maximum number of current processors. The reward of an action is explicitly recorded as $R(s_i^t)$. This is the time taken for a particular code section i at dynamic instance t. The state transition probability P is ignored.

$$\pi_{online}(s_i^t) : n_i^t = \begin{cases} j, t\%3 = 0 \\ n_i^{t-1} + 1, t\%3 = 1 \\ n_i^{t-2} - 2, t\%3 = 2 \end{cases}$$

where $j = argmax_{j=0,1,2} R(s_{i-j}^t)$.

In other words, set the number of threads to the best time seen in the last 2 dynamic instances of this parallel section every 3 instances. Otherwise vary the number of threads by $+1/-2$.

Offline: [6] predicts a thread number at runtime based on an offline-trained model to map programs in the presence of external workloads. The offline approach explicitly considers the state of the program and the environment in terms of features.

$$S = \{(f_i^t = [c_i^t, e_i^t]\}, A = \{n_i^t = 1, \dots, p_i^t\}$$

where at time t, c_i^t are the static code features of the loop i to be scheduled, e_i^t are the dynamic environment features, which are combined to given f_i^t. The actions are the same as the online approach, setting the thread number up to the maximum number of current processors. The reward R for a particular action a is the time taken for a parallel loop and is explicitly recorded during offline training as is the total reward R. Instead of using value iteration to determine a policy, a model x is learnt that given an action a and a state $s = f$ returns an approximation of eventual value

$$x(a, f) = \hat{V}(a)$$

where ˆ is used to denote an approximation. The policy then simply selects the action that maximizes this value:

$$\pi_{offline}(f) : n = (argmax_a(x(a, f)))$$

Note that this policy is learnt offline and applied dynamically at runtime. There is no change or re-learning of policy at runtime.

Change Detection: Our approach has the same state description S as offline approach and also builds a function $w(a, f)$ to predict the reward of a particular action. It differs in that it explicitly considers the state transition function $P(s, s', a)$ and modifies its policy online based on the transition It builds a *state predictor 'm'* offline

$$m(f_t) = \hat{e_{t+1}}$$

that predicts the environment at the next time stamp. If this prediction is incorrect then $P(s, s', a)$ has changed and the offline policy $\pi_{offline}(a)$ is out-of-date. This is known as change detection [3]. We modify our policy based on this change:

$$\pi_{CDMapp}(s) = \begin{cases} \pi_{offline} & \text{if } \|e_t - \hat{e_t}\| \leq \delta \\ \pi_{offline} +/- k\|e_t - \hat{e_t}\| & \text{otherwise} \end{cases}$$

Table 1. List of features, regression coefficients

Static features	w	m	Dynamic features	w	m
f^1: Load/Store count	0.104	0.213	f^4: Number of workload threads	−1.198	−0.124
f^2: Branch count	0.612	−0.420	f^5: Number of available processors	0.956	0.872
f^3: Instruction count	−1.323	1.091	f^6: Load (ldavg1)	−0.166	−0.049
			f^7: Load (ldavg5)	0.158	0.313
			f^8: Runtime queue length	0.351	1.190
error	−1.443	0.69			

i.e. if the environment is nearly as predicted, use the offline model to select number of threads else adjust predicted thread number proportional to the amount of change in the environment.

4   Our Approach

4.1   Predictive Models

Our approach relies on *two* models: 'w' predicts the optimal thread number based on the program characteristics and runtime environment and 'm' predicts the ensuing runtime environment after selecting the optimal number of threads based on the current features. We train and build our models offline based on the widely used three step supervised learning: generate training data; train and build a model; deploy this learnt model in an unseen setting. No further additional training is required for new programs.

Programs from NAS benchmark suite are chosen for training. The training data is obtained by running each training program in the presence of external load with varying number of threads as described in [6]. We capture static program structure c and environment behaviour e in a set of *features* f. We record the best number of threads which gave best overall performance retaining the environment features that resulted from selecting this best thread number.

4.2   Features

We characterize a program by a set of static code features and the environment by a set of dynamic runtime features. During the training phase 134 features, f, were collected, comprising of many code (c) and environment (e) parameters available within our LLVM based compiler and Linux. From these, 8 features were chosen based on the quality of information gain and are listed in Table 1. At loop i, the feature vector $f_i = (f^1{}_i, .., f^8{}_i)$ is formed by these 8 features. The code features at every loop were normalized to the total number of instructions in the program. Figure 3 shows the importance of selected features across both models. We define *impact* of a feature as the drop in prediction accuracy of the model when this feature alone was removed from the feature set. It can be observed that static and dynamic features are equally important for the predictive models.

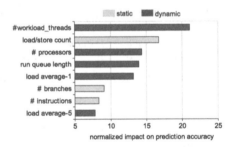

Fig. 3. Impact of selected features on our models.

4.3   Building the Model

We use standard linear regression technique employing standard least squares method to automatically generate the heuristic that can be ported to any platform. We build two models, $n_i = \underline{wf}_i$ and $\|e_{i+1}\| = \underline{mf}_i$ where the first is used to predict thread number, the second is used to determine a future environment (L_2 norm of features). The regression coefficients for these models are listed in Table 1 against each selected feature.

4.4   Deployment: Combining Action and Reward

Once the compiler has extracted static code features, it links this compiled version to a runtime library. At execution time, the runtime system features are collected and fed as input to the two models w and m. The parallel section executes with the predicted thread number $\hat{n}_i$ and the predicted environment $\hat{e_{i+1}}$ is used to detect change. The absolute difference between actual and predicted environment normalized to number of available processors is computed. If this is below a predetermined threshold δ, it implies that prediction of our model w was accurate and the decision was good. The value of threshold δ is determined to be 0.5 obtained from a sensitivity analysis study as shown in Fig. 11(c). If there is a large difference, then these models are inaccurate and need updating. In the prediction function w we adjust the numeric error component with the addition of the difference between observed and predicted environment, $\|e_i - \hat{e}_i\|$, (here $k = 1$).

5   Experimental Methodology

5.1   Hardware and Software Configurations

We ran our experiments on a dual socket 4-core Intel Xeon E5530 2.40 GHz system with hyperthreading enabled (total 16 threads) running kernel 2.6.18. All programs were compiled using *gcc* 4.6 with -O3 optimization level. We evaluated our approach on 14 OpenMP-based C programs from NAS, SpecOMP and Parsec benchmarks all with largest input datasets.

Table 2. Workload configuration

Workload type	Benchmarks
Light	(i) `is`,`cg`
	(ii) `ammp`,`fft`
	(iii) `ep`,`art`
Moderate	(i) `ft`,`lu`,`ammp`
	(ii) `bscholes`, `cg`, `equake`, `ep`
	(iii) `is`,`mg`,`ep`,`art`,`btrack`
Massive	(i) `bt`,`sp`,`equake`,`is`,`cg`,`art`
	(ii) `bscholes`,`lu`,`bt`,`sp`,`fmine`,`art`,`mg`
	(iii) `lu`,`sp`,`btrack`,`mg`,`ep`,`equake`,`ft`

5.2 Experimental Scenarios

In a dynamic execution environment, each target program co-executes with varying workload programs and potentially changing number of processors where other external system issues are inherent in the collected features.

External Workload: We vary the number of workload programs chosen from above programs classified as *light, moderate* and *massive* and their number of threads. We also dynamically change the workload every 2 s. For each workload type, we consider three different sets of benchmarks as shown in Table 2. All results are averaged over the three different benchmark sets. Each run was repeated 10 times for noise minimization. In all cases we reproduce the same external workload for each of the evaluated schemes to ensure fair comparison.

Changing Hardware Resources: We implement two settings to change hardware resources at runtime. (a) ***proc_drop***: We start with maximum number of available processors, 16 and drop to 4 to reflect a sudden drop in hardware resources due to any failures. (b) ***proc_inc***: We increase processor count from 4 to 16 to reflect an expansion in computing resources. We modify the processor count by switching '*online*' values (1 = enable, 0 = disable) for each CPU in */proc* filesystem.

5.3 Evaluation

We evaluated our model using standard leave-one-out cross-validation technique. From the training set we remove the program to be evaluated and build the heuristic based on remaining programs. Thus we ensure that the model always predicts on an unseen program. We compare our approach against the OpenMP *default* policy, an *Online* [17] and an *Offline* [6] schemes.

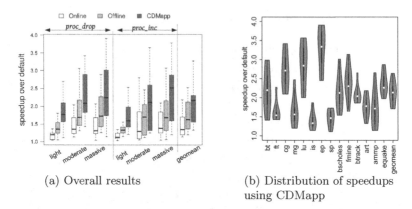

(a) Overall results

(b) Distribution of speedups using CDMapp

Fig. 4. (a) Speedup comparison of each scheme per workload and hardware resource scenario, averaged across target benchmarks. On average online improves performance by 1.35x, offline by 1.62x while CDMapp achieves 2.14x improvement (b) Distribution of achieved speedups for all benchmarks across all experimental scenarios

6   Results

In this section we first evaluate our approach against other schemes in a dynamic setting. We then consider the impact of each scheme on the workload and analyze what happens if the workload starts to adapt too. Finally, we consider a controlled experiment where the best or "oracle" schedule can be determined. This provides a limit study of our approach.

6.1   Dynamic Environment Evaluation

Figure 4(a) shows the performance of each scheme relative to the OpenMP default. These summary results are averaged across all benchmark programs and shown for different workload and hardware settings. Overall, online scheme improves performance by 1.35x, offline technique achieves a speedup of 1.62x while our approach CDMapp achieves 2.14x improvement over OpenMP default. The default policy results in significant contention due to resource overprovision. The adaptive online technique improves on this by changing the thread number based on the execution time but wastes time trying to find the best thread number. The offline model does better still frequently predicting a good thread number initially but when the hardware changes at runtime, it is unable to adapt. Our technique adjusts the optimal thread number whenever there is a misprediction or change in hardware. All approaches give a slightly better average performance in *proc_drop* yet as the workload environment becomes more intense, only our approach continues to improve. Both the online and offline approaches however do not further improve from moderate to massive workload.

Figure 4(b) shows the distribution of speedups obtained for each target programs across different experiment settings. For memory intensive programs, such

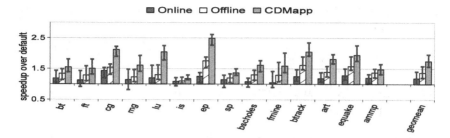

Fig. 5. For light workloads we improve performance 1.74x over OpenMP default, 1.4x over online approach and 1.21x over offline model.

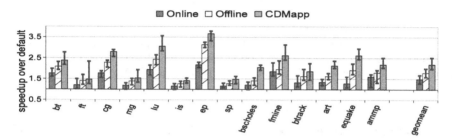

Fig. 6. For moderate-workloads we outperform by 2.2x over OpenMP default, 1.47x over online approach and 1.22x over offline model.

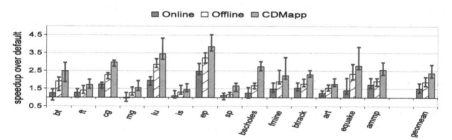

Fig. 7. With massive workloads we improve performance 2.37x over OpenMP default, 1.57x over online approach and 1.27x over offline model.

as mg and sp this improvement factor is relatively low as they spend most of the time in data-access and related memory operations. Compute-intensive programs such as ep achieve much greater speedup. Program is is uniformally poor achieving an average speedup of 1.3x due to lack of parallelism, while other benchmarks such as bt have great variation in performance depending on the workload.

Now we examine these results in detail on a per benchmark basis, averaged over the 3 workloads per workload setting and the two changing hardware scenarios.

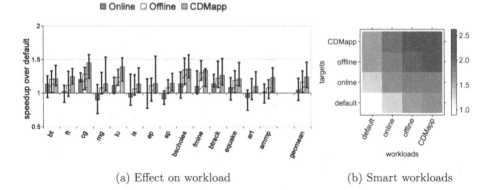

(a) Effect on workload (b) Smart workloads

Fig. 8. (a) Impact of various approaches on the co-executing workload. Speedup greater than 1 implies no impact on the workload (b) Throughput evaluation of competitive approaches with *smart* workloads on x-axis and targets on y-axis. On average we improve 2.5x times when both target and workloads use CDMapp compared to the default.

Light Workload: Here the resource contention is initially minimal as shown in Fig. 5. For certain programs e.g., cg the online approach is competitive with the offline scheme while in other cases it occasionally slows the program down relative to the default scheme on mg,is,sp,bscholes and fmine. The offline scheme approaches the performance of CDMapp on ammp and achieves significant improvement on ep, btrack, equake but in each case it is outperformed by CDMapp which improves programs performance by 1.73x on average.

Moderate Workload: On average, all the schemes increase their performance relative to the default as they were able to reduce the degree of contention. The online and offline schemes were able to find significant improvement on bt,ep and ftime, but not on equake. On average CDMapp achieves speedup improvement of 2.22x over the default outperforming the other schemes as shown in Fig. 6.

Massive Workload: Once again the online and offline schemes provide good performance improvement on ep and the offline approach is also able to show significant improvement on lu. However, in certain cases the online scheme has slowdowns relative to the default for bt, mg, is, sp. The offline scheme is significantly poorer than CDMapp on bscholes, ammp which increases its overall improvement to a 2.37x speedup over the default as observed from Fig. 7.

6.2   Impact on Workload

Here we examine the impact on the external workload and what happens if the workload starts to adapt as well.

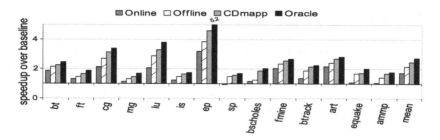

Fig. 9. In a controlled static environment. Our model improves speedup of 11.7 % over offline model and is within 12 % of oracle.

Comparison by Scheme: In Fig. 8(a) we evaluate the impact of various approaches on external co-executing programs. In our approach we actually reduce system-wide contention which leads to a marginal speedup improvement for external programs. The online approach critically affects the external programs. By contrast, both the offline model and our approach improve workload performance by 1.20x and 1.25x respectively.

Smart Workloads: Here we consider the case where we execute one target with one workload program where *both* can use each of the dynamic mapping schemes evaluated in this paper. Here we measure the total execution time of the target and the workload; the results are averaged across all program-pairs from the selected benchmarks and summarized in Fig. 8(b) as a heatmap diagram. The first column represents the setting explored so far in this section: a workload with the default policy and different policies applied to the target program. As expected CDMapp is better than the offline technique which in turn is better than the online and default schemes. What is interesting is that as the workload starts to use the same policies, the overall performance increases. When the target and the workload both employ our technique, the combined speedup is increased by 2.5x on average compared to both using default policy. This improvement is due to the reduction in the overall system contention.

6.3   Oracle Study

Here we describe a limited study to compare our technique with the known best '*oracle*' in a controlled environment. To determine the best oracle schedule, in a replicated experimental setup as [6], we evaluated all possible thread numbers assigned to each parallel loop and recorded the best execution time.

The results are shown in Fig. 9 where on average we are within 12 % of the oracle proving that our model is near-accurate. In more dynamic settings, such learning breaks down and our approach is more powerful.

7   Analysis

This section analyses the performance of our approach. It first investigates how often each mapping approach changes the thread number in both controlled and dynamic environments. It then evaluates the accuracy of the environment and thread number predictor in the controlled environment. This is followed by an evaluation of the threshold used by our scheme to modify thread prediction.

7.1   Thread Number Change: How Often, How Much

Figure 10 show the distribution of changes in thread number selected by each of the schemes in static and dynamic environments. In the controlled static environment we can compare this result with the known oracle. In both environments, the online approach has same behaviour changing the number of threads significantly but by a small amount and is therefore slow to react to change.

As expected the offline scheme performs well in the controlled environment as it is similar to its training set. As the ideal number of thread changes increases,

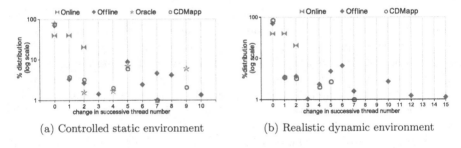

(a) Controlled static environment   (b) Realistic dynamic environment

Fig. 10. (a) In a controlled static environment with known oracle, our approach closely follows the oracle scheme. (b) In a dynamic environment with unknown oracle, our approach changes to the optimal thread number only as and when required.

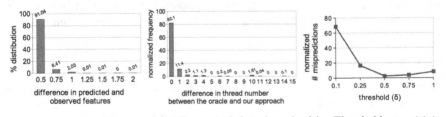

(a) Efficiency of environment predictor   (b) Efficiency of thread predictor   (c)   Threshold   sensitivity analysis

Fig. 11. (a) Difference between predicted and actual environment. We achieve near-accurate (91 %) environment prediction within the threshold. (b) Difference in thread numbers between the oracle and our approach. We predict same thread number as oracle in 80 % cases.(c) Sensitivity of threshold value (δ) to the number of mispredictions, $\delta = 0.5$ has least mispredictions.

however, the offline approach diverges from the oracle mispredicting change in the 5 to 10 threads region. This large change in thread number is more apparent in the dynamic environment resulting in reduced relative performance. Our approach follows the oracle in the controlled environment changing infrequently. Unlike the offline scheme, it follows the oracle more closely when larger changes are needed. In the dynamic environment, compared to the offline approach, it is much less aggressive in selecting large changes leading to significant performance improvement.

7.2   Environment Prediction Accuracy

The accuracy in predicting near accurate future environment is crucial as it determines the efficiency of thread number prediction. In Fig. 11(a) we plot a frequency distribution of the difference between predicted and actual environment in the limited controlled study. This difference when confined within the threshold of 0.5 is around 91 % of the cases. This shows that our approach yields accurate environment prediction based on current information and hence the thread number that was predicted by our model is useful.

7.3   Thread Prediction Accuracy

The oracle study, while limited allows us to evaluate how accurate our thread predictor is. In Fig. 11(b), we plot the difference in thread numbers between the oracle and our model. Over 80 % of the time there is no difference in thread numbers showing the accuracy of our approach.

7.4   Sensitivity Analysis

Figure 11(c) provides a sensitivity analysis of the threshold parameter used to decide mispredictions. The threshold value that has least percent of mispredictions is chosen to judge the quality of prediction. It is clear that a threshold of 0.5 is the sweet-spot for determining mispredictions.

8   Related Work

Online Adaptation: Petabricks [1,2] determines the best runtime algorithm for a program that requires priori offline implementations. Self-optimizing memory controllers are proposed in [10]. Sambamba [19], CAER [14] adapt programs online but they are slow to respond to changes in the environment.

Markov Decision Processes: MDPs are widely used in resource allocation problems [9]. Approach in [12] uses MDP to describe monitoring in a sensor network using an offline predictive model.

Dynamic Resource Allocation: ReSense [5] uses resource sensitivity to map dynamic workloads of co-located applications. ParallelismDial [18] proposes a model for runtime parallelism management. Approaches in [4,8] provide optimal resource allocation adapting to phase changes. FACT [15] co-schedules programs to reduce contention but affects external workloads. The work in [11] describes dynamic resource management for hybrid programming.

Compiler based mapping: A predictive model for thread number prediction in presence of static workload is proposed in [7]. Compiler-based techniques have also been applied to assist runtime scheduling in [13,20].

9   Conclusion

In this paper we presented an approach that determines best thread mapping for any parallel program that is adaptive to change in hardware resources and co-executing external programs. We introduced a novel technique based on *online change detection* to improve predictions of offline trained models that have limited knowledge of best scheme at runtime by predicting future environment that acts as feedback to improve mapping policy. We evaluated our approach in presence of varying loads and hardware resources. Our technique achieves speedup improvement of 2.14x over OpenMP default, 1.58x over an online approach and 1.32x over an offline trained model. We aim to extend this work to optimize programs to a wide range of dynamic execution environments ranging from mobile devices to cloud and datacenters.

Acknowledgments. We thank Charles Sutton for helping formulate runtime loop scheduling as a Markov Decision Process.

References

1. Ansel, J., Pacula, M., Wong, Y.L., Chan, C., Olszewski, M., O'Reilly, U.M., Amarasinghe, S.: Siblingrivalry: online autotuning through local competitions. In: CASES 2012 (2012)
2. Ansel, J., Wong, Y.L., Chan, C., Olszewski, M., Edelman, A., Amarasinghe, S.: Language and compiler support for auto-tuning variable-accuracy algorithms. In: CGO 2011 (2011)
3. Basseville, M., Nikiforov, I.V.: Detection of Abrupt Changes: Theory and Application. Prentice-Hall Inc., Upper Saddle River (1993)
4. Bitirgen, R., Ipek, E., Martinez, J.F.: Coordinated management of multiple interacting resources in chip multiprocessors: a machine learning approach. In: MICRO 2008 (2008)
5. Dey, T., Wang, W., Davidson, J.W., Soffa, M.L.: Resense: mapping dynamic workloads of colocated multithreaded applications using resource sensitivity. ACM TACO 10(4), 41 (2013)
6. Emani, M.K., Wang, Z., O'Boyle, M.F.P.: Smart, adaptive mapping of parallelism in the presence of external workload. In: CGO 2013 (2013)
7. Grewe, D., Wang, Z., O'Boyle, M.F.P.: A workload-aware mapping approach for data-parallel programs. In: HiPEAC 2011 (2011)

8. Hoffmann, H., Maggio, M., Santambrogio, M., Leva, A., Agarwal, A.: A generalized software framework for accurate and efficient management of performance goals. In: Embedded Software (EMSOFT) (2013)

9. Huh, W.T., Liu, N., Truong, V.A.: Multiresource allocation scheduling in dynamic environments. Manufact. Serv. Oper. Manage. **15**, 280–291 (2013)

10. Ipek, E., Mutlu, O., Martínez, J.F., Caruana, R.: Self-optimizing memory controllers: a reinforcement learning approach. SIGARCH Comput. Arch. News **36**, 39–50 (2008)

11. Li, D., de Supinski, B.R., Schulz, M., Nikolopoulos, D.S., Cameron, K.W.: Strategies for energy-efficient resource management of hybrid programming models. IEEE Trans. Parallel Distrib. Syst. **24**, 144–157 (2013)

12. Liu, N., Ulukus, S.: Optimal distortion-power tradeoffs in sensor networks: Gauss-markov random processes. CoRR abs/cs/0604040 (2006)

13. Luk, C.K., Hong, S., Kim, H.: Qilin: exploiting parallelism on heterogeneous multiprocessors with adaptive mapping. In: MICRO 42 (2009)

14. Mars, J., Vachharajani, N., Hundt, R., Soffa, M.L.: Contention aware execution: online contention detection and response. In: CGO 2010 (2010)

15. Pusukuri, K.K., Vengerov, D., Fedorova, A., Kalogeraki, V.: Fact: a framework for adaptive contention-aware thread migrations. In: CF 2011 (2011)

16. Puterman, M.L.: Markov Decision Processes: Discrete Stochastic Dynamic Programming. Wiley, New York (1994)

17. Raman, A., Zaks, A., Lee, J.W., August, D.I.: Parcae: a system for flexible parallel execution. In: PLDI 2012 (2012)

18. Sridharan, S., Gupta, G., Sohi, G.S.: Holistic runtime parallelism management for time and energy efficiency. In: ICS 2013 (2013)

19. Streit, K., Hammacher, C., Zeller, A., Hack, S.: *Sambamba*: a runtime system for online adaptive parallelization. In: O'Boyle, M. (ed.) CC 2012. LNCS, vol. 7210, pp. 240–243. Springer, Heidelberg (2012)

20. Voss, M.J., Eigenmann, R.: Adapt: automated de-coupled adaptive program transformation. In: ICPP 2000 (2000)

Automatic Streamization of Image Processing Applications

Pierre Guillou[✉], Fabien Coelho, and François Irigoin

MINES ParisTech, PSL Research University, Paris, France
{pierre.guillou,fabien.coelho,francois.irigoin}@mines-paristech.fr

Abstract. New many-core architectures such as the Kalray MPPA-256 provide energy-efficiency and high performance for embedded systems. However, to take advantage of these opportunities, careful manual optimizations are required. We investigate the automatic streamization of image processing applications, implemented in C on top of a dedicated API, onto this target accessed through the ΣC dataflow language. We discuss compiler and runtime design choices and their impact on performance. Our compilation techniques are implemented as source-to-source transformations in the PIPS open-source compilation framework. Experiments show lowest energy consumption on the Kalray MPPA target compared to other hardware targets for a range of 8 test applications.

1 Introduction

As predicted by Moore's law, billions of transistors can be integrated today into a single chip, enabling multi-core or even many-core architectures, with hundreds of cores on a chip. The low energy consumption Kalray MPPA-256 processor [17], released in 2013, offers 256 computing VLIW-cores for 10 W. Task and/or data parallel approaches can be used to take advantage of such parallel processing power for a given application domain.

We show how to use this innovative hardware to run image processing applications in embedded systems such as video cameras. In order to enable fast time-to-market developments of new products, applications must be ported quickly and run efficiently on these targets, a daunting task when done manually. To alleviate this issue, we have built a compiler chain to automatically map an image processing application developed on top of a dedicated software interface, FREIA [14], considered as a domain specific language, onto the MPPA processor using the ΣC dataflow language and runtime. Images are streamed line-by-line into a task graph whose vertices are image operators.

Streaming languages [31] have been studied for a long time, and have recently received more attention [28] for exposing pipelining, data parallelism and task paralellism, as well as hiding memory management. The Kahn Process Networks [22] are one of the first streaming model, relying on FIFOs for interprocess communication. As subclasses of this model, Synchronous DataFlow [25,26] languages are statically determined in order to avoid deadlocks and to ensure safety.

© Springer International Publishing Switzerland 2015
J. Brodman and P. Tu (Eds.): LCPC 2014, LNCS 8967, pp. 224–238, 2015.
DOI: 10.1007/978-3-319-17473-0_15

Common SDF languages include LUSTRE [20], Signal [24] and StreamIt [1]. The latter shares some ground concepts with the ΣC dataflow language such as decomposing programs in a graph of basic interconnected units which consume and produce data or focusing on easing programming onto multi-core and many-core targets. In particular, some optimizations of StreamIt applications (operator replication to enable data parallelism, operator fusion to reduce communication overheads [18]) are close to those presented in this paper. Other projects such as DAGuE [9] or FlumeJava [10] propose frameworks for managing and optimizing tasks targetting current multi-core architectures.

Optimization of image processing applications on massively parallel architectures have been the subject of multiple studies. Ragan-Kelley [29] proposes an image processing Domain Specific Language and an associated compiler for optimizing parallelism onto standard CPUs or GPUs. Clienti [12] presents several dataflow architectures for specific image analysis applications. Stencil operators are the most limitating operators in our implementation. Several alternative techniques for optimizing this class of operators have been proposed [6,16].

This paper focusses on the design of a compiler and a runtime using the MPPA chip as an accelerator, including: (1) domain specific transformations on the input code to expose larger image expressions; (2) code generation for a dataflow language; (3) automatic operator aggregation to achieve a better task balance; (4) a small runtime to provide streaming image operators; (5) data-parallel agents for slower operators. We also demonstrate the effectiveness of our approach with a source-to-source implementation in PIPS [15,21] by reporting the time and energy consumption on a sample of image applications.

We first describe the overall compilation chain in Sect. 2, then in Sect. 3 we focus on our hardware and software targets. Section 4 presents our key contributions about the compiler and runtime designs. Section 5 reports our time and energy performance results.

2   Compilation Chain Overview

The starting point of our compilation chain (Fig. 1) is an image processing application, built on top of the FREIA C language API. This provides a 2D image type, I/Os abstractions and dozens of functions to perform basic image operations (arithmetics, logical, morphological, reductions), as well as composed operators which combine several basic ones. Typical applications locate text in an image, smooth visible blocks from JPEG decoding, or detect movements in an infra-red surveillance video. An example of FREIA code is shown in Fig. 2. Our test case applications typically include up to hundreds of basic image operations, with 42 as a median. These operations are grouped in few (1–3, up to 8) independent static image expressions that can be accelerated, stuck together with control code.

The ANR FREIA [7] project developed a source-to-source compilation chain [14] from such inputs to various hardware and software targets: the SPoC image processing FPGA accelerator [13], the TERAPIX 128 processing elements SIMD array FPGA accelerator [8], and multi-cores and GPUs using

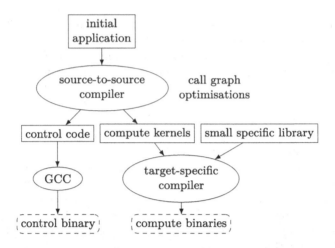

Fig. 1. Overview of our compilation chain

```
1  freia_aipo_erode_8c(im1, im0, kernel);    // morphological
2  freia_aipo_dilate_8c(im2, im1, kernel);   // morphological
3  freia_aipo_and(im3, im2, im0);            // arithmetic
```

Fig. 2. Example FREIA code with a sequence of 3 operations

OpenCL [23]. This new development adds Kalray's MPPA-256 chip as a target hardware by providing a new code generation phase and its corresponding runtime.

The FREIA compiler chain is made of three phases. The first two phases are generic, and the last one is the target specific code generation. Phase 1 builds sequences of basic image operations, out of which large image expressions can be extracted. For this purpose, inlining of composed and user operators, partial evaluation, loop unrolling, code simplifications and dead code suppression are performed. An important preliminary transformation for a dataflow hardware target such as SPoC and MPPA is while-loop unrolling as detailed below in Sect. 4. Phase 2 extracts and optimizes image expressions, as directed acyclic graphs (DAG) of basic image operations. Optimizations include detecting common subexpressions, removing unused image computations, and propagating copies forwards and backwards.

The target execution model depicted in Fig. 3 uses the parallel hardware as an accelerator for heavy image computation, while the host processor runs the control code and I/Os. The runtime environment includes functions for manipulating images such as allocate, receive, emit, and the various operators. The accelerated version has to manage the transfers between the host and the device used for operator computations. For our MPPA target, this is achieved by using named pipes to send images to agents on the host. Theses images are first streamed to the device for computation, then streamed back on a host agent, then back to the main program.

Control code   Host binary   I/O cluster   Compute clusters

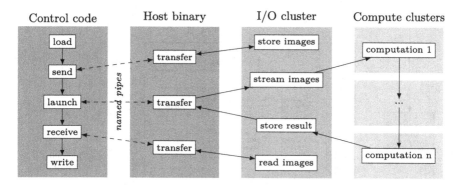

Fig. 3. Summary of our runtime environment

3   Hardware and Software Target

We are targetting the Kalray MPPA-256 many-core architecture through the
ΣC dataflow language, compiler and runtime, which allows us to build a runtime
for streaming image operators that can be connected to process large expressions.

3.1   MPPA-256 Architecture

Kalray MPPA-256 [17] is a high-efficiency 28 nm *System-on-Chip* featuring 256
compute cores providing 500 GOPs with a typical power consumption of 10 W.
Competing MPPA architectures include the Tilera TILE*Pro*64 [3], the Adapteva
Epiphany [4], or the TSAR Project [2]. This massively parallel processor aims
at a wide range of embedded applications and boasts a fast time-to-market for
complex systems.

Figure 4 shows MPPA-256's computes cores divided into sixteen compute
clusters. Each of these clusters includes a 2 MB non-coherent shared L2 cache.
The compute cores offer instruction parallelism as 32 bits multithreaded *Very
Long Instruction Word* cores. SIMD instructions operating on pairs of fixed-
point and floating-point instructions are also supported. Every compute cluster
also runs a minimalistic real-time Operating System (*NodeOS*) on a separate
and dedicated core. This OS manages the 16 compute cores of one cluster by
executing multithreaded binary programs onto them. The compute clusters communicate with each other through a high-speed toroidal *Network-on-Chip*.

The MPPA-256 chip also includes four additional clusters for managing external communications. These input/output clusters provide several interfaces, such
as PCI-Express for connecting to a host machine, DDR interface to access local
RAM, Ethernet or Interlaken for directly connecting several chips together.

We used the MPPA-256 as a hardware accelerator. The chip is placed aside
a 4 GB dedicated RAM onto a PCI-Express extension card. This card is then
accessed through the PCI-Express bus of a typical computer workstation.

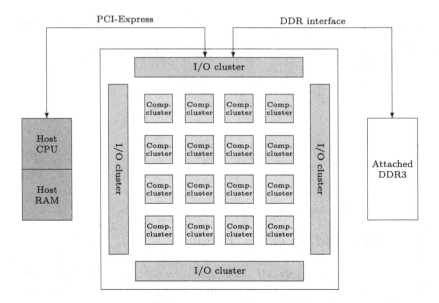

Fig. 4. The MPPA-256 chip and its environment

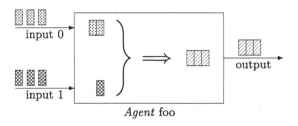

Fig. 5. A ΣC agent with two inputs and one output (see code in Fig. 6)

3.2 The ΣC Programming Language

To ease the programming on their manycore chip [5], Kalray offers the classic parallel libraries PThread and OpenMP [27] as well as a specific dataflow programming language called ΣC [19]. ΣC is a superset of C which provides a dataflow programming model and relies on the concept of *agents*, which are basic compute blocks similar to Kahn Processes [22]. These blocks receive and consume a fixed amount of data from input channels, and produce data on their output channels. The agent represented in Fig. 5 has two input channels and one output channel. When two pieces of data are available on the first input channel and one on the second, the agent produces three pieces of data on its sole output. The corresponding ΣC code is shown in Fig. 6.

This model has two consequences. First, the scheduling of agents on available cores and the inter-agent buffer allocation requires the ΣC compiler to know the number of input/output channels of an agent, and the number of data items processed. This implies that image sizes must be known at compile time.

```
1   agent foo() {
2     interface {              // define I/O channels
3       in<int> in0, in1;      // 2 input integer channels
4       out<int> out0;         // 1 output integer channel
5       spec{in0[2],in1,       // define flow scheduling
6            out0[3]};
7     }
8     void start() exchange    // DO SOMETHING!
9       (in0 i0[2], in1 i1, out0 o[3]) {
10      o[0] = i0[0], o[1] = i1, o[2] = i0[1];
11    }
12  }
```

Fig. 6. ΣC example: a basic agent merging two integer streams (see Fig. 5)

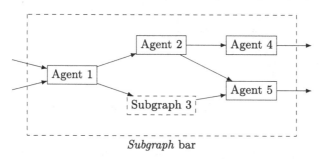

Subgraph bar

Fig. 7. A ΣC subgraph composed of 4 agents and one subgraph (see code in Fig. 8)

Then, when several independent graphs are mapped, the compiler assumes that these graphs may be active at the same time, thus the mapping reserves non-overlapping memory and cores for the tasks. If only one graph at a time is really active, resources can be under-used.

The performance model implies that tasks must provide significant computations in order to amortize communication costs. In particular, communication times include a constant overhead, which must be amortized with significant data volumes. However, as memory is scarse, it is best to require small inter-task buffers: a trade-off must be made. Another key point of the static dataflow model is that the slowest task in the graph determines the overall performance. Therefore, elementary tasks must be as fast and as balanced as possible.

Agents can be connected to each other in order to compose a ΣC *subgraph* which can recursively compose upper-level subgraphs. A subgraph representation and the corresponding ΣC code are respectively showed in Figs. 7 and 8. The top-level subgraph is called **root** and corresponds to the classic C **main** function. A ΣC agent can be executed either by one of MPPA-256's compute cores or by a core of an input/output cluster. Agents can also be executed by the processor of the host machine, therefore providing access to files. Kalray provides also a ΣC compiler for MPPA-256, which handles the mapping of ΣC agents on the compute cores of their chip.

```
1   subgraph bar() {
2     interface {                          // define I/O channels
3       in<int> in0[2];
4       out<int> out0, out1;
5       spec{ { in0[][3]; out0 }; { out1[2] } };
6     }
7     map {
8       agent a1 = new Agent1();            // instantiate agents
9       agent a2 = new Agent2();
10      agent a3 = new Subgraph3();
11      agent a4 = new Agent2();
12      agent a5 = new Agent4();
13      connect (in0[0], a1.input0);        // I/O connections
14      connect (in0[1], a1.input1);
15      connect (a4.output, out0);
16      connect (a5.output, out1);
17      connect (a1.output0, a2.input);     // internal connections
18      connect (a1.output1, a3.input);
19      connect (a2.output0, a4.input);
20      connect (a2.output1, a5.input0);
21      connect (a3.output, a5.input1);
22    }
23  }
```

Fig. 8. ΣC example: a basic subgraph (see graph in Fig. 7)

The ΣC programming language provides an effective way to take advantage of the MPPA-256, and serves as the main target language for demonstrating our automatic streamization compiler and runtime.

4   Compiler and Runtime Design

A DAG produced by our compilation chain has a structure similar to streaming programs. Indeed, image analysis operators can be directly transposed as ΣC agents, and DAGs as ΣC subgraphs.

4.1 ΣC Image Processing Library

Aside from our compilation chain, we developed a ΣC library of elementary image analysis operators. Each operator is implemented as one ΣC agent, such as: (1) arithmetic operators performing elementary operations onto pixels of input images; (2) morphological operators [30], which are the more compute intensive operators; (3) reduction operators returning a scalar value.

The 2 MB per compute cluster memory limit implies that our ΣC agents cannot operate on a whole image. Since the transition between two states of an agent is rather slow, we cannot afford to operate on one pixel at a time. Thus our agents process images line by line. Measuring per pixel execution time of several applications for several input image sizes (see Fig. 9) reveals that larger lines are computed more efficiently than shorter ones, as communication times are better amortized. This also simplifies the implementation of stencil operators by easing the access to neighboring pixels.

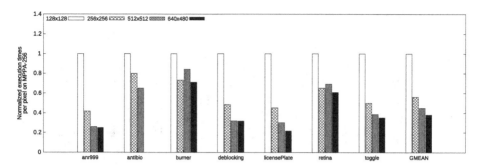

Fig. 9. Impact of the image size on the average execution time per pixel

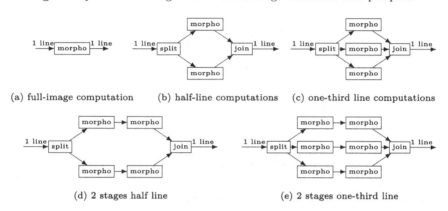

(a) full-image computation   (b) half-line computations   (c) one-third line computations

(d) 2 stages half line   (e) 2 stages one-third line

Fig. 10. Analysed cases of data parallelism for morphological operators

The morphological agents, the most complex operators, have a direct impact on the performance of our applications. Consisting of an aggregate function (min, max, average) on the value of a subset of the neighbor pixels, they are often used in large pipelines in image analysis applications. We used several optimizations during their implementation. Firstly, as stencil operators, they need to access not only the current processed line, but also the previous and the next lines. As a consequence, each agent has a 3-line internal buffer to store the input lines needed for computation. Also, the incoming input lines are stored into this 3-lines buffer and processed in a round-robin manner, avoiding time-consuming copies. Finally, these agents benefitted from an optimized assembly kernel to use guarded instructions not automatically generated by the compiler.

We also investigated data parallelism by splitting input lines and computing each portion with several morphologic agents. This approach allows us to take advantage of the MPPA-256 unused compute cores, since application DAGs are usually much smaller than the number of available cores. Because morphological operators are stencils, we use overlapping lines when splitting and joining. Our measures showed that having several stages of computing agents in the (d) and (e) cases of Fig. 10 slows down the whole process, so we focused on comparing

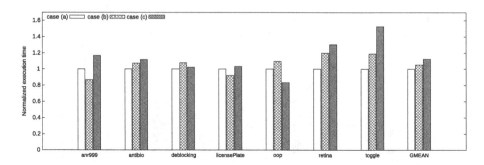

Fig. 11. Execution times with parallel morphological operators

```
1   subgraph foo() {
2       int16_t kernel[9] = {0,1,0, 0,1,0, 0,1,0};
3       ...
4       agent ero = new img_erode(kernel);
5       agent dil = new img_dilate(kernel);
6       agent and = new img_and_img();
7       ...
8       connect(ero.output, dil.input);
9       connect(dil.output, and.input);
10      ...
11  }
```

Fig. 12. Corresponding ΣC code to FREIA code in Fig. 2

the (a), (b) and (c) 1-stage cases represented in Fig. 10. As shown in Fig. 11, the results are quite mixed and application-dependent. Replacing one morphological agent by four or more agents induces more inter-cluster communications, leading to a loss in performance, even if computed data is reduced by half.

4.2 ΣC Code Generation

As stated in Sect. 2, our compilation chain produces DAGs of elementary image analysis operators from which we generate ΣC subgraphs using our image analysis agents. For example, Fig. 12 shows an extract of the generated ΣC code from the FREIA source code in Fig. 2.

In order to be correctly transposed into a running dataflow program, we must ensure that there is no scalar dependency between two agents of the same subgraph. Indeed, since images are processed on a per line basis, a scalar produced from a whole image cannot be applied on the lines of the same image by an other agent on the same subgraph without causing lines accumulation in inter-agent buffers, and thus major performance loss. A split-on-scalar-dependencies pass is used ahead of our ΣC generator to provide scalar-independent DAGs, which can then be transposed directly to ΣC subgraphs.

Some complex image analysis operators involve a convergence loop over an image-dependent parameter. Such operators, being idempotents, can be unrolled with no consequences on the final result. However, this unrolling pass leads to a greater number of generated ΣC agents, and thus an increase occupation of the MPPA compute cores. We measured the influence of the unrolling factor of these particular loops on the execution times of the relevant applications (see Fig. 13). Our results show that unrolling dramatically increases the performance of our applications. For these applications, an unrolling factor of 8 leads to a fair speedup while mobilizing a reasonable amount of compute cores.

Split and unrolled image expression DAGs are then encoded as ΣC subgraphs. Our implementation of the generation of ΣC subgraphs is pretty straighforward: for each vertex of one image expression DAG, our compiler PIPS generates a ΣC instantiation statement for the corresponding ΣC agent first, then connection statements between the agent instance and its predecessors or successors in the DAG. Small differences between the input DAGs structure and the ΣC dataflow model have been addressed during this implementation: (1) since the number of inputs and outputs of our ΣC agents are predetermined, we have to insert replication agents when required; (2) DAG inputs and outputs are specific cases and must be dealt with separately; (3) scalar dependencies must be provided to the correct agents by a dedicated path. Similarly, scalar results must be sent back to the host.

In the dataflow model, the slowest task has the greatest impact on the global execution. Since arithmetic operators do little computation compared to morphologic ones, we investigated the fusion of connected arithmetic operators into compound ΣC agents, thus freeing some under-used compute cores. We implemented this pass on top of our ΣC generator. We tested our optimization pass onto several applications with a variable number of merged operators. Execution time results (Fig. 14) show little to no difference in performance compared to the reference one agent/operator application. These measures confirm that aggregated operators are not limiting the global execution while freeing computing power, therefore validating our approach.

4.3   Runtime Environment

ΣC code generated by our compilation chain often includes several independant and non-connected subgraphs that are all mapped on the MPPA cores. In order to launch the adequate subgraphs at the right time and to control the I/Os, we developed a small runtime in C. It runs on top of the generated ΣC applications

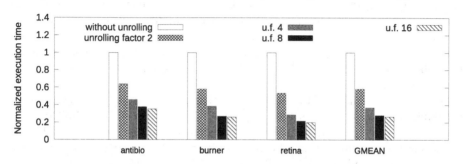

Fig. 13. Relative execution time as a function of unrolling factor

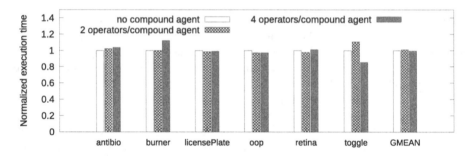

Fig. 14. Influence of the fusion of connected arithmetic operators on execution times

and communicates with them through Unix named pipes, as depicted in Fig. 3. For each function of this runtime, we added a dedicated ΣC subgraph with agents mapped on the host CPU and the I/O clusters cores to handle the task. This runtime is also used for loading and saving images from the host hard drive. To this end, we use a software implementation of FREIA, called Fulguro [11].

The other dedicated control functions allow us to allocate and free the accelerator embedded RAM, to send or receive images to or from the MPPA, and to launch a compute subgraph onto one or more images. On the ΣC side of the application, several independant subgraphs manage control signals sent through named pipes and transfer them to the chip.

The general design of our compilation chain, based on a source code generator, an elementary library and a small runtime environment, allowed us to quickly get functionnal applications on the MPPA-256. With the implementation of a set of specific optimizations (loop unrolling, fusion of fast tasks, splitting of slow tasks, bypassing of the MPPA RAM), we were able to take better advantage of the compute power of this processor. Once this was done, we compared the MPPA-256 to a set of hardware accelerators running the same applications generated by the same compiler.

5   Performance Results

We have evaluated our compilation chain with eight real image analysis applications covering a wide range of cases. Table 1 shows that our applications contain from 15 elementary operators (*toggle*) to more than 400 (*burner*), most of them morphological operators. Table 1 also illustrates the number of ΣC subgraphs generated by our compilation chain, and the number of occupied compute clusters when running on the MPPA-256. These applications generally include less than three independent image expression DAGs.

Our compilation chain targets several software and hardware accelerators: a reference software implementation, Fulguro [11], on an Intel Core i7-3820 quad-core CPU running at 3.6 GHz with an average power consumption of 130 W; ΣC code running directly on the same CPU (iΣC); the MPPA-256 processor (10 W) using ΣC; SPoC [13] and Terapix (TPX) [8], two image processing accelerators implemented on a FPGA (26 W); two CPUs using OpenCL [23]: an

Table 1. Characteristics of used image analysis applications

Apps.	#operators				#subgraphs	#clusters	image size
	arith	morph	reduc	total			
anr999	0	20	3	23	1	2	224×288
antibio	8	41	25	74	8	6	256×256
burner	18	410	3	431	3	16	256×256
deblocking	23	9	2	34	2	10	512×512
licensePlate	4	65	0	69	1	5	640×383
oop	7	10	0	17	1	2	350×288
retina	15	38	3	56	3	4	256×256
toggle	8	6	1	15	1	1	512×512

Intel dual-core (i2c - 65 W) and an AMD quad-core CPU (a4c - 60 W); and three NVIDIA GPUs again with OpenCL [23]: a GeForce 8800 GTX (120 W), a Quadro 600 (40 W) and a Tesla C 2050 (240 W).

We compared the output of our compilation chain from the previously described applications onto these 8 hardware targets, both in terms of execution times and energy consumption. For the MPPA-256 chip, time and energy measures were obtained using Kalray's `k1-power` utility software, ignoring transfers and control CPU consumption. Time figures for the FPGAs, CPUs and GPUs were taken from [14]. Energy figures were derived from target power consumption. Results are shown in Tables 2 and 3, with best performances in bold. Compared to the Fulguro monothreaded sofware implementation, ΣC on CPU is relatively slow, due to the numerous threads communicating with each other. To take individual MPPA-256 compute cluster power supply into account, we added in Table 3 a column "MPPA ideal" representing the energy of clusters

Table 2. Execution times (ms) of our applications on the different hardware targets

Apps	Software		Hardware							
				FPGA		OpenCL				
	Flgr	iΣC	MPPA	SPoC	TPX	i2c	a4c	GTX	Quadro	Tesla
anr999	4.3	36.5	8.3	**0.9**	3.5	12.2	7.2	9.8	1.5	**0.9**
antibio	80.2	1026	670	**41.9**	88.5	254.1	135.3	204.3	57.4	93.4
burner	795.3	814.4	113	**17.2**	83.8	162.2	124.4	321.0	576.2	142.0
deblocking	141.4	121.0	84	30.7	11	25.1	16.7	11.1	3.5	**1.3**
licensePlate	483.9	152.7	20.2	13.3	36.8	32.2	21.9	36.6	7.3	**2.3**
oop	4.0	39.3	11.3	124.6	63.3	12.3	8.3	5.8	1.8	**1.0**
retina	149.0	222.5	95	**7.4**	32.4	93.5	55.4	75.5	60.8	33.9
toggle	6.2	69.8	22.6	12.6	4.3	15.0	9.0	6.3	1.4	**0.7**
AVG/MPPA	1.13	3.28	1.00	0.32	0.49	0.85	0.54	0.64	0.23	0.12

Table 3. Energy (mJ) used by our test cases on different targets

Apps.	Software		Hardware								
			MPPA		FPGA		OpenCL				
	Flgr	iΣC	real	ideal	SPoC	TPX	i2c	a4c	GTX	Quadro	Tesla
anr999	559	4745	50	*6*	**23**	91	793	432	1176	60	221
antibio	10425	133380	3500	*1313*	**1089**	2301	16517	8118	24516	2296	22883
burner	103390	105900	**388**	*388*	447	2179	10543	7464	38520	23048	34790
deblocking	18382	15730	431	*269*	798	286	1632	1002	1332	**140**	319
licensePlate	62907	24284	**120**	*38*	354	957	2093	1314	4392	292	564
oop	520	5110	**59**	*7*	3240	1646	800	498	696	72	245
retina	19370	28925	487	*122*	**192**	842	6078	3324	9060	2432	8306
toggle	806	9074	119	*7*	328	112	975	540	756	**56**	172
AVG/MPPA	28.78	83.38	**1.00**	*0.25*	1.65	2.52	10.81	6.33	15.01	1.79	5.45

actually used for the computations, according to Table 1. Disconnecting unused compute cores would provide us an extra reduction in energy consumption.

These results show that although MPPA/ΣC is not faster than dedicated hardware targets, it provides the lowest average energy consumption for tested applications. The high degree of task parallelism induced by the use of the ΣC dataflow language on the 256 cores of the MPPA-256 processor is thus a strength facing dedicated hardware in low energy and embedded applications.

6   Conclusion and Future Work

We added a new hardware target to the FREIA ANR project: a 256 cores processor with a power consumption of 10 W through the use of the ΣC dataflow programming language. Using the PIPS source-to-source compiler, we generated ΣC dataflow code based upon a small image analysis library written in ΣC. The execution of the generated applications relies on a small runtime environment controlling the execution of the different ΣC subgraphs mapped on the cores of the MPPA-256 processor. We implemented a set of specific optimizations from automatic fast operator aggregation to data-parallel slow operators to achieve better performance. The performance of our approach is shown by comparing the MPPA-256 results to other hardware accelerators using the same compilation chain. MPPA/ΣC proves to be the most energy-efficient programmable target, which competes in performance with specific image-processing dedicated hardware such as the SPoC FPGA processor.

In the current approach, several subgraphs are mapped onto different compute cores, meaning only a fraction of the chip is used at a given time. Future work includes the investigation of dynamically mapping distinct ΣC subgraphs on the same cores when they do not need to be run concurrently. Another way to save energy, especially for small applications, would be the ability to disconnect unused clusters within the chip, as shown in column "MPPA ideal" in Table 3. More performance improvements could also be obtained on some applications by generating automatically kernel-specific convolutions, which would reduce execution time by skipping altogether null-weighted pixels.

Aknowledgements. Thanks to Danielle Bolan and Pierre Jouvelot for proof-reading, Antoniu Pop for his advises and bibliography pointers, Kalray engineers Frédéric Blanc, Jérôme Bussery and Stéphane Gailhard for their support and to anonymous reviewers whose comments greatly helped to improve this paper.

References

1. The streamit language (2002). http://www.cag.lcs.mit.edu/streamit/
2. Tera-scale architecture (2008). https://www-asim.lip6.fr/trac/tsar/wiki
3. The TilePro64 many-core architecture (2008). http://www.tilera.com/
4. The Epiphany many-core architecture (2012). http://www.adapteva.com/
5. Aubry, P., Beaucamps, P.E., Blanc, F., Bodin, B., Carpov, S., Cudennec, L., David, V., Dore, P., Dubrulle, P., Dupont de Dinechin, B., Galea, F., Goubier, T., Harrand, M., Jones, S., Lesage, J.D., Louise, S., Chaisemartin, N.M., Nguyen, T.H., Raynaud, X., Sirdey, R.: Extended cyclostatic dataflow program compilation and execution for an integrated manycore processor. In: Alexandrov, V.N., Lees, M., Krzhizhanovskaya, V.V., Dongarra, J., Sloot, P.M.A. (eds.) ICCS. Procedia Computer Science, pp. 1624–1633. Elsevier, Amsterdam (2013)
6. Bandishti, V., Pananilath, I., Bondhugula, U.: Tiling stencil computations to maximize parallelism, November 2012
7. Bilodeau, M., Clienti, C., Coelho, F., Guelton, S., Irigoin, F., Keryell, R., Lemonnier, F.: FREIA: Framework for Embedded Image Applications (2008–2011). freia.enstb.org, French ANR-funded project with ARMINES (CMM, CRI), THALES (TRT) and Télécom Bretagne
8. Bonnot, P., Lemonnier, F., Edelin, G., Gaillat, G., Ruch, O., Gauget, P.: Definition and SIMD implementation of a multi-processing architecture approach on FPGA. In: Design Automation and Test in Europe, pp. 610–615. IEEE, December 2008
9. Bosilca, G., Bouteiller, A., Danalis, A., Herault, T., Lemarinier, P., Dongarra, J.: DAGuE: a generic distributed DAG engine for high performance computing. Parallel Comput. **38**(1–2), 37–51 (2012). http://linkinghub.elsevier.com/retrieve/pii/S0167819111001347
10. Chambers, C., Raniwala, A., Perry, F., Adams, S., Henry, R.R., Bradshaw, R., Weizenbaum, N.: FlumeJava: easy, efficient data-parallel pipelines, p. 363. ACM Press (2010). http://portal.acm.org/citation.cfm?doid=1806596.1806638
11. Clienti, C.: Fulguro image processing library. Source Forge (2008)
12. Clienti, C.: Architectures flots de données dédiées autraitement d'images par la Morphologie MATHÉMATIQUE. Ph.D. thesis, MINES ParisTech, September 2009
13. Clienti, C., Beucher, S., Bilodeau, M.: A system on chip dedicated to pipeline neighborhood processing for mathematical morphology. In: EUSIPCO: European Signal Processing Conference, August 2008
14. Coelho, F., Irigoin, F.: API compilation for image hardware accelerators. ACM Trans. Archit. Code Optim. **9**(4), 1–25 (2013)
15. CRI, MINES ParisTech: PIPS (1989–2012). pips4u.org, open source research compiler, under GPLv3

16. Datta, K., Murphy, M., Volkov, V., Williams, S., Carter, J., Oliker, L., Patterson, D., Shalf, J., Yelick, K.: Stencil computation optimization and auto-tuning on state-of-the-art multicore architectures. In: SC 2008: Conference on Supercomputing, pp. 1–12. IEEE Press (2008)

17. Dupont de Dinechin, B., Sirdey, R., Goubier, T.: Extended cyclostatic dataflow program compilation and execution for an integrated manycore processor. In: Procedia Computer Science, vol. 18 (2013)

18. Gordon, M.I., Thies, W., Amarasinghe, S.: Exploiting coarse-grained task, data, and pipeline parallelism in stream programs. ACM SIGPLAN Not. **41**(11), 151 (2006). http://portal.acm.org/citation.cfm?doid=1168918.1168877

19. Goubier, T., Sirdey, R., Louise, S., David, V.: ΣC: a programming model and language for embedded manycores. In: Xiang, Y., Cuzzocrea, A., Hobbs, M., Zhou, W. (eds.) ICA3PP 2011, Part I. LNCS, vol. 7016, pp. 385–394. Springer, Heidelberg (2011)

20. Halbwachs, N., Caspi, P., Raymond, P., Pilaud, D.: The synchronous dataflow programming language LUSTRE. Proc. IEEE **79**(9), 1305–1320 (1991)

21. Irigoin, F., Jouvelot, P., Triolet, R.: Semantical interprocedural parallelization: an overview of the PIPS project. In: Proceedings of ICS 1991, pp. 244–251. ACM Press (1991)

22. Kahn, G.: The semantics of a simple language for parallel programming. p. 5 (1974)

23. KHRONOS group: OpenCL computing language v1.0, December 2008

24. Le Guernic, P., Benveniste, A., Bournai, P., Gautier, T.: Signal-a data flow-oriented language for signal processing. IEEE Trans. Acoust. Speech Signal Process. **34**(2), 362–374 (1986)

25. Lee, E.A., Messerschmitt, D.G.: Static scheduling of synchronous data flow programs for digital signal processing. IEEE Trans. Comput. **36**(1), 24–35 (1987)

26. Murthy, P.K., Lee, E.A.: Multidimensional synchronous dataflow. IEEE Trans. Signal Process. **50**, 3306–3309 (2002)

27. OpenMP architecture review board: OpenMP application program interface, Version 3.0, May 2008

28. Pop, A.: Leveraging streaming for deterministic parallelization - an integrated language, compiler and runtime approach. Ph.D. thesis, MINES ParisTech, September 2011

29. Ragan-Kelley, J., Barnes, C., Adams, A., Paris, S., Durand, F., Amarasinghe, S.: Halide: a language and compiler for optimizing parallelism, locality, and recomputation in image processing pipelines. In: PLDI 2013, p. 12, June 2013

30. Soile, P.: Morphological Image Analysis. Springer, Heidelberg (2003)

31. Stephens, R.: A Survey Of Stream Processing. Springer, Heidelberg (1995)

Evaluation of Automatic Power Reduction with OSCAR Compiler on Intel Haswell and ARM Cortex-A9 Multicores

Tomohiro Hirano[1]([⊠]), Hideo Yamamoto[1], Shuhei Iizuka[1], Kohei Muto[1], Takashi Goto[1], Tamami Wake[1], Hiroki Mikami[1], Moriyuki Takamura[1,2], Keiji Kimura[1], and Hironori Kasahara[1]

[1] Green Computing Systems Research Center, Waseda University, Tokyo, Japan
{hirano,shuhei,kmuto,tgoto,waketama,mikami,
takamura.moriyu}@kasahara.cs.waseda.ac.jp,
magoroku15@gmail.com, {keiji,kasahara}@waseda.jp
http://www.kasahara.cs.waseda.ac.jp/
[2] Fujitsu Laboratories Ltd., Kanagawa, Japan

Abstract. Reducing power dissipation without performance degradation is one of the most important issues for all computing systems, such as supercomputers, cloud servers, desktop PCs, medical systems, smartphones and wearable devices. Exploiting parallelism, careful frequency-and-voltage control and clock-and-power-gating control for multicore/manycore systems are promising to attain performance improvements and reducing power dissipation. However, the hand parallelization and power reduction of application programs are very difficult and time-consuming. The OSCAR automatic parallelization compiler has been developed to overcome these problems by realizing automatic low-power control in addition to the parallelization. This paper evaluates performance of the low-power control technology of the OSCAR compiler on Intel Haswell and ARM multicore platforms. The evaluations show that the power consumption is reduced to 2/5 using 3 cores on the Intel Haswell multicore for the H.264 decoder and 1/3 for Optical Flow on 3 cores with the power control compared with 3 cores without power control. On the ARM Cortex-A9 using 3 cores, the power control reduces power consumption to 1/2 with the H.264 decoder and 1/3 with Optical Flow. These show that the OSCAR multi-platform compiler allows us to reduce the power consumption on Intel and ARM multicores.

Keywords: Automatic parallelization · Power control · Power reduction · Multicore processor · Multiple platforms

1 Introduction

Multicore processors have been used for various computing systems from smartphones and tablets, PCs to cloud servers and super computers [1]. The multicore processors have been adapted to obtain higher performance with relatively low

© Springer International Publishing Switzerland 2015
J. Brodman and P. Tu (Eds.): LCPC 2014, LNCS 8967, pp. 239–252, 2015.
DOI: 10.1007/978-3-319-17473-0_16

power. However, the issue of power consumption is getting more serious because the use of more processor cores to obtain higher performance gives us large power increase.

To reduce the power consumption on multicore for smart devices, the Samsung Exynos 5 Octa uses the big.LITTLE architecture [2]. This approach uses low-power cores in addition to the standard processor cores when processor workloads are low. In addition, Intel implemented an integrated on-chip voltage regulator in Haswell processors to realize more fine-grained power control [3].

Recent software development environments for multicores support parallel application program interface (API) such as OpenMP [4] and CUDA [5] while they require manual parallelization. Also, these development environments do not provide interfaces for power control supported by current multicore hardware.

The combination of the Optimally SCheduled Advanced multiprocessoR (OSCAR) automatic parallelizing compiler and the OSCAR API allow the automatic parallelization of an application program for various platforms [6–8]. In addition to parallelization, the OSCAR compiler allows us to reduce power consumption by inserting power control codes for dynamic voltage and frequency scaling (DVFS), clock gating, and power gating, into the parallelized program. Especially for the case of power control, each architecture has its own control interface. In order to utilize these architecture dependent power control interfaces, the OSCAR compiler generates a parallelized and power optimized program annotated with the OSCAR API directives, which work as interfaces between the OSCAR compiler and various multicores. Then, these directives are translated into runtime library calls for a target architecture. Thus, the OSCAR compiler can provide generate power reduced parallel code for various multicore architectures.

This paper evaluates power reduction performance of the OSCAR compiler on an Intel Haswell processor for servers and desktop computers, and an ARM Cortex-A9 multicore for smart-phones using real-time applications. It also shows the OSCAR compiler and the OSCAR API can utilize the different power control mechanisms in both processors.

The remainder of this paper is organized as follows. Section 2 provides an overview of the OSCAR compiler and API. Section 3 explains the runtime platform in a current Linux system and the interface used to call clock gating from applications. Section 4 presents the results of the performance evaluation using two different platforms. Finally, conclusions are described in Sect. 5.

2   OSCAR Compiler and OSCAR API

This section presents an overview of the power reduction scheme implemented in the OSCAR automatic parallelizing compiler with the OSCAR API.

2.1   Multigrain Parallel Processing with the OSCAR Compiler

The OSCAR compiler exploits multigrain parallelism, which comprises coarse grain task parallelism, loop iteration level parallelism, and statement level near-fine grain parallelism.

To exploit multigrain parallelism, the OSCAR compiler decomposes a sequential C or Fortran program into coarse-grained tasks called macro-tasks(MTs), such as basic blocks, loops, and subroutine calls. The OSCAR compiler analyzes the control flow and the data dependencies among MTs, thereby generating a macro-flow-graph (MFG). Next, the compiler analyzes the earliest executable condition [9] by exploiting the parallelism among MTs by analyzing both the control dependencies and the data dependencies together. The results of the analysis are represented as a macro-task-graph (MTG) for an MFG.

If an MT is a subroutine call or a loop that includes coarse grain task parallelism, the OSCAR compiler hierarchically generates MTs inside the MT. In addition, loop iteration level parallelism is translated into coarse-grained task parallelism by decomposing a loop into multiple loops.

These MTs are assigned to the processor cores using static scheduling or dynamic scheduling, where a dynamic scheduling routine is generated for each source program by the OSCAR compiler [9].

2.2   Low-Power Optimization by the OSCAR Compiler

When the OSCAR compiler applies static scheduling to real-time application programs with deadlines, such as those considered in this work, the compiler tries to apply frequency reduction with voltage scaling to the critical path of the schedule-result to satisfy the deadline [10]. Next, the compiler applies frequency reduction, clock gating, or power gating to the MTs, as well as to the busy wait loops used for synchronization that are not present on the critical path, while considering the overhead of the power state transitions [11].

2.3   OSCAR API

The OSCAR API comprises a set of directives that support power control, DMA transfer, group barriers, and local and distributed shared memory management on various shared memory multiprocessor and multicores for servers, desktop computers, and embedded systems [8].

The OSCAR API uses **section**, **flush** and **threadprivate** directives in OpenMP. In addition to these directives, **distributedshared** and **onchipshared** are added to utilize distributed shared memory and on-chip shared memory while **threadprivate** is used for local data memory. Furthermore, the OSCAR API employs user-level power control in addition to thread control and memory allocation. The OSCAR compiler generates a parallelized program by inserting these compiler directives.

The API translator translates the directives of the OSCAR API into runtime library calls. The translator was developed specifically for embedded systems that have no OpenMP compilers. In this case, an ordinary sequential compiler such as gcc finally generates the parallelized executable binary.

The OSCAR API provides the `fvcontrol` and `get_fv_status` directives for power control. These `fvcontrol` directives set the power status of a hardware module in a target system to a specified value. `get_fv_status` acquires the current power status from a specified hardware module.

The API translator translates the `fvcontrol` and `get_fv_status` directives into `oscar_fvcontrol()` and `oscar_get_fv_status()` function calls, respectively. These functions wrap the operations for the power control interface of a target system.

3   Runtime Support for Power Control

Power consumption of applications can be optimized by the OSCAR compiler by power control mechanisms like DVFS, clock gating, and power gating through the `oscar_fvcontrol()` function.

To fully utilize the power control by the OSCAR compiler, `oscar_fvcontrol()` must be appropriately implemented to support power control mechanisms provided in each target multicore with low overhead. This section provides an overview of the target architectures, the power control frameworks that are available for these architectures, and the interfaces implemented for DVFS and clock gating.

3.1   Power Control Frameworks Available in Linux

This section describes the power control frameworks that are currently available in Linux platforms.

An ordinary execution state, such as P-state in Intel platforms, controls the processor frequency with corresponding the workload. The processor frequency is controlled by the driver: cpufreq [13]. The power of the target device is reduced by controlling the frequency and its corresponding voltage.

In an ordinary Linux system, dynamic frequency scaling is achieved using an on-demand governor, which monitors the utilization rate of each core. This governor sets the higher or lower frequencies dynamically when the load exceeds or falls below the thresholds. In addition, the userspace governor described in this paper allows a user-program to specify the clock frequency via the cpufreq.

3.2   Intel-Specific Power Control Interface

This section describes the `MWAIT` interface which is implemented in OSCAR runtime.

`MWAIT` is an instruction to transit to the C-states [12], where the C-states are low-power idle states. For example, the C1 state is an auto-halt mode and the C3 state is a deep sleep mode, where numerically higher C-states comprise greater power saving actions, but with higher latency.

In the current Linux implementation for Haswell, an MWAIT instruction changes the processor power state into a C-state as well as returning to the P-state when there is a change in content of a specific address checked by a MONITOR instruction.

MONITOR and MWAIT instructions are available at "Ring 0" and applications cannot use these instructions. Thus, the kernel module is developed to access MWAIT and MONITOR instructions from user applications via "ioctl" system call.

Figure 1 shows the method for realizing clock gating, or a transition to a C-state, as well as a transition to the P-state from a C-state using the OSCAR API fvcontrol directive. If the processor core-0 is clock gated by a directive fvcontrol(0,CPU,0), fvcontrol calls a function slave_to_master(*flag). The slave_to_master(*flag) function executes an MWAIT instruction in the kernel module via "ioctl". The MWAIT instruction makes the MONITOR to watch a specific address pointed by "flag". Next, the MWAIT changes the state of the core-0 into a C-state.

When the core-1 changes the state of the core-0 from a C-state into the P-state via a directive fvcontrol(0,CPU,100), the core-1 calls the master_to_slave(flag) function. The master_to_slave(flag) function changes the content of flag. Next, the MONITOR on the core-0 detects that the content pointed by flag has changed and it changes the power state of the core-0 from the C-state to the previous P-state. Finally, the core-1 sets the frequency of the core-0 into 100 %, or 3.5[GHz], by the cpufreq driver.

Figure 2 shows the effect of clock gating using the MWAIT instruction. Figure 2-(a) shows the power for a busy wait loop at 3.5[GHz] in the P-state without clock gating. The average power consumption is 40[W]. Figure 2-(b) shows the same busy wait loop applying clock gating, or the C-state using the

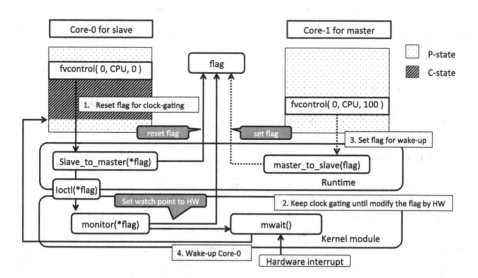

Fig. 1. Procedure for calling the MWAIT flow

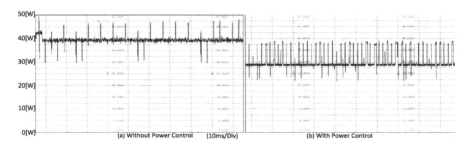

Fig. 2. Performance of clock gating using `MWAIT` at 3.5 GHz

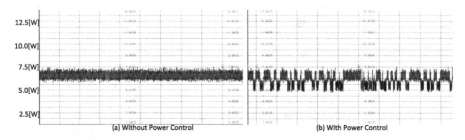

Fig. 3. Performance of clock gating using `MWAIT` at 800 MHz

MWAIT. During this busy wait loop, 10,000-cycle clock gating and state check-ing at the P-state driven at 3.5[GHz] are repeated. In this case, the average power consumption is reduced to 28[W].

This result shows that the OSCAR API `fvcontrol` implemented using the MWAIT successfully reduces the power with low overheads.

Figure 3 shows the result of the same experiment when the frequency was 800[MHz]. Figure 3-(a) shows that the average power consumption was 7[W] when the frequency is the lowest (800[MHz]) without clock gating. Figure 3-(b) shows the power when the C-state is applied. The average power consumption is reduced to 6[W].

This result shows that clock gating is still effective even at the lowest fre-quency and the lowest voltage.

3.3 ARM-Specific Power Control Interface

This section describes the wait-for-interrupt (`WFI`) instruction in ARM cores for clock-gating used in an optimized program by the OSCAR compiler.

The `WFI` instruction suspends the execution on the processor core and stops the clock. Specifically, the `WFI` instruction shuts down any process until an interrupt or a debug event occurs [14]. To utilize the characteristics of `WFI` as a low power optimization in the runtime library, modifications were made in the Android [15] Linux kernel to allow `WFI` to stop the clock at an interval of 500[μs] [16].

3.4   Examples of Target Architectures

Intel and ARM platforms are prepared to investigate the differences in power consumption between a server system and an embedded system. Table 1 shows the detailed configurations of the both platforms. The power reduction control parameters for each platform, which are comprised transitions in the frequency time, the power consumption of each frequency, and the other elements, are set in the OSCAR compiler.

Intel(Haswell). The H81M-A ASUS motherboard with an Intel processor Core i7 4770k is used as an example of a server environment, where the DVFS could be controlled independently for each core.

   On the Intel platform, three frequency levels are tested in this experiment: full (3500[MHz]), medium (1800[MHz]), and low (800[MHz]), respectively. The clock cycles for frequency transition are about 10,000. Moreover, each core of the `cpufreq` governor is set to ondemand when the power control is not applied. When the power control is applied, the core 0 is set to ondemand. On the other hand, the core-1 to the core-3 are set to the userspace for benchmark applications.

ARM(ODROID-X2). The ODROID-X2 is an evaluation board [17] for the Samsung Exynos4412 Prime chip [18,19], which comprises the 4-core ARM Cortex-A9. Frequency and voltage of all cores are changed together in this platform. In this evaluation, the frequencies are tested at three levels: full (1700[MHz]), medium (900[MHz]), and low (400[MHz]), respectively. As same as in the Intel platform, each core of the `cpufreq` governor is set to the ondemand when the power control is not applied whereas the userspace is set when the power control is applied.

4   Performance Evaluation with Intel 4-Cores and ARM Cortex-A9 4-Cores

This section describes the analysis of the power consumption by the Intel 4-cores and the ARM cortex-A9 4-cores. In this evaluation, the benchmark applications described in Sect. 4.2 were parallelized and the power was controlled by the OSCAR compiler and the OSCAR API.

4.1   Modification of the Evaluation Boards to Measure the Chip Power Consumption

In this evaluation, the boards were modified to measure the power of the processor chips directly. In particular, a 5[mΩ] shunt resistor was attached between the power source circuit of the cores and the Power Management IC [20] on H81M-A, and a 40[mΩ] shunt resistor on ODROID-X2. Moreover, general purpose IO pins [16,21] were used to measure the power consumption of a specific program section.

Table 1. Evaluation environment

Platform	Intel platform	ARM platform
Platform board	H81M-A	ODROID-X2
CPU	Intel Core i7 4770k	Samsung Exynos4412 Prime
Number of cores	4	4
Maximum clock frequency	3.5 [GHz]	1.7 [GHz]
L1 Cache	I/D cache 32/32[KB/core]	I/D cache 32/32[KB/core]
L2 Cache	unified 256[KB/core]	1[MB/chip]
L3 Cache	8 [MB/chip]	N/A
DDR	16[GB]	2[GB]

4.2 Application Programs Used in the Evaluation

This section describes the specifications of the two real-time applications used in the power evaluations.

H.264. H.264 is a video compression format. The JM version module was originally developed as ISO/IEC 14496-10 for reference purposes [22,23]. On the Intel platform, the deadline for H.264 was set to 30[fps] (33[ms] per frame) and the input file was HD720p (1280 × 720 pixels). On the ARM platform, the deadline for H.264 was set to 30[fps] (33[ms] per frame) and the input size was 360p (640 × 360 pixels).

Optical Flow. The Optical Flow is a benchmark application, which is used as a reference in OpenCV [24]. This real-time application tracks 16 × 16 blocks between two images by calculating the velocity fields. On the Intel platform, the deadline for Optical Flow was set to 15[fps] (66[ms] per frame) and the Input file was HD720p. On the ARM platform, the deadline for Optical Flow was set to 30[fps] (33[ms] per frame) and input frame size was 256 × 128 pixels.

4.3 Power Consumption on the Intel Haswell Multicore Platform

This section describes the power consumption by the Intel Haswell Multicore platform when Optical Flow and H.264 are executed.

Figure 4 shows the power consumption of Optical Flow and H.264 with different numbers of processor cores. In Fig. 4, the consumed power for H.264 decoding without power control increases from 29.67[W] for one core to 37.11 [W] for two cores and 41.81 [W] for three cores, respectively. By the power control, the consumed power are reduced to 17.37[W] for one core, 16.15[W] for two cores and 12.50[W] for three cores, respectively.

The results show the OSCAR compiler's power reduction method reduces the power for three cores about 2/5 against ordinary one core execution without power control, and about 1/3 against the same three cores without power control.

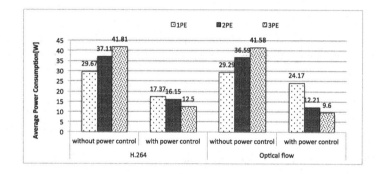

Fig. 4. The power consumption on the Intel Haswell multicore

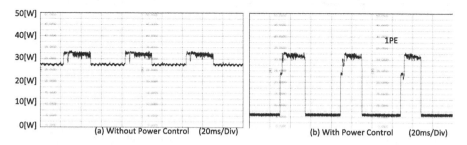

Fig. 5. Power waves of H.264 with one-core on Intel Haswell

Similarly, the consumed power of the Optical Flow without power control increases from 2.29[W] for one core to 36.59[W] for two cores and 41.58[W] for three cores, respectively. On the contrary, the power consumption with the power control decreases to 24.17[W] for one core, 12.21[W] for two cores and 9.60[W] for three cores, respectively.

The power reduction method successfully reduces the power to about 1/3 against ordinary one core execution without power control and 1/4 against three cores without power control.

Figure 5-(a) and (b) show the power waves for H.264 using one-core on the Intel platform without and with power control, respectively. Similarly, Fig. 6-(a) and (b) show those for Optical Flow.

Comparing these figures, the peak power with the power control and that of not using the power control are almost same, which indicates both cases are driven at the highest frequency and voltage. However, the bottom power of using the power control is about 5[W] while the power without the power control is 30–33[W]. This shows the power control by the OSCAR compiler efficiently uses clock gating using the MWAIT instruction.

Next, Fig. 7-(a) and (b) show the power waves for H.264 using three-cores on the Intel platform with and without the power control, and Fig. 8-(a) and (b) show those for Optical Flow, respectively.

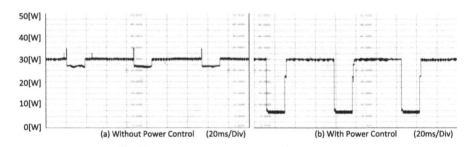

Fig. 6. Power waves of Optical Flow with one-core on Intel Haswell

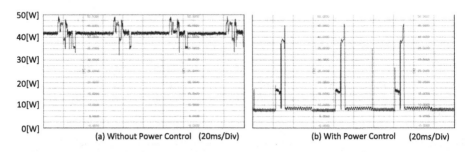

Fig. 7. Power waves of H.264 with three-cores on Intel Haswell

Figures 7-(b) and 8-(b) show the compiler tries to set the lowest clock frequency as long as possible at the calculation phase of the application, then applies clock-gating until a deadline. On the other hand, as shown in Figs. 7-(a) and 8-(a), the clock frequency is always high even at the waiting time for a deadline as shown at the flat line in the wave form.

These results show, in addition to parallelization, DVFS and clock gating can sufficiently reduce the average power consumption by utilizing the MWAIT instructions inserted by the OSCAR compiler.

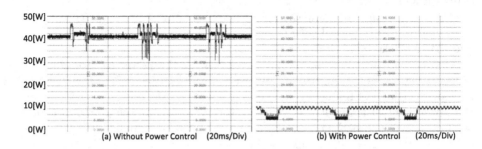

Fig. 8. Power waves of Optical Flow with three-cores on Intel Haswell

4.4   Power Consumption on the ARM Cortex-A9 Multicore

This section describes the power consumption when Optical Flow and H.264 are executed on the ARM Crotex-A9 multicore.

Figure 9 shows the power consumption for Optical Flow and H.264 with different numbers of cores. This Figure shows the almost same characteristics as in the Intel Haswell platform: When the power control by the OSCAR compiler is applied, the power consumption of three-cores is lower than that of one-core for both applications. Also, without the power control, the power consumption is increased along with the increasing number of cores.

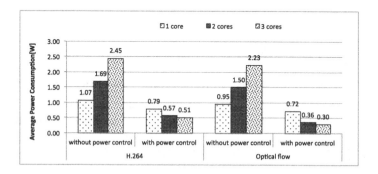

Fig. 9. The power consumption on the ARM Cortex-A9 multicores

The power for H.264 without power control increases 1.07[W] for one core to 1.69[W] for two cores and 2.45[W] for three cores, respectively. On the other hand, the powers with power control are reduced to 0.79[W] for one core, 0.57[W] for two cores and 0.51[W] for three cores, respectively.

Therefore, the power consumption is reduced to about 1/2 compared with one core without power control and about 1/5 compared with same three cores without power control.

Similarly, the power for Optical Flow are increased from 0.95[W] for one core to 1.50[W] for two cores and 2.23[W] for three cores, respectively. The powers with the power control are reduced to 0.72[W] for one core, 0.36[W] for two cores and 0.30[W] for three cores, respectively.

Namely, the power for three cores is reduced to about 1/3 compared with one core without power control and about 1/7 compared with three cores without power control.

Figure 10-(a) and (b) show the power waves for H.264 using one-core on the ARM platform with and without power control, respectively. Similarly, Fig. 11-(a) and (b) show those for Optical Flow. Also, Fig. 12-(a) and (b) show the power waves for H.264 using three-cores with and without power control, and Fig. 13-(a) and (b) show those for Optical Flow, respectively. These figures also show the almost same characteristics as in the Intel platform.

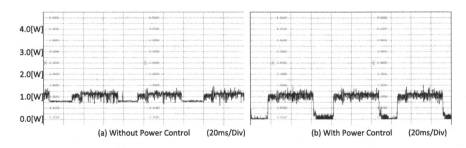

Fig. 10. Power waves of H.264 with one-core on ARM Cortex-A9

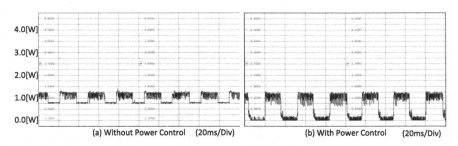

Fig. 11. Power wave of Optical Flow with one-core on ARM Cortex-A9

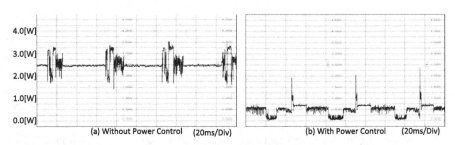

Fig. 12. Power wave of H.264 with three-cores on ARM Cortex-A9

For example, comparing Fig. 10-(a) and (b), the peak power with the power control and that of not using the power control are still almost same. However, the bottom power of using the power control is almost 0.0[W] while that without the power control is 0.8[W]. The clock gating the WFI instruction in the ARM core efficiently reduces the power consumption. Figures 12-(b) and 13-(b) also show the compiler tried to set the lowest clock frequency as long as possible and applied clock-gating until a deadline.

In summary, the automatic parallelization and power optimization can efficiently reduce the power consumption on both of the Intel platform and the ARM Cortex-A9 platform. The appropriately implemented runtime systems using the MWAIT for the Intel platform and the WFI for the ARM platform collaborated with the OSCAR compiler and the OSCAR API realize the power efficient parallel processing on different multicores.

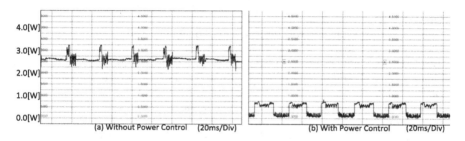

Fig. 13. Power wave of Optical Flow with three-cores on ARM Cortex-A9

5 Conclusion

This paper has evaluated the power reduction capability of the OSCAR compiler on the Intel Haswell multicore with clock gating implemented using the `MONITOR` and the `MWAIT` instructions, as well as on the ARM Cortex-A9 multicore with clock gating implemented using the `WFI` instruction.

The evaluation result showed the power used by Optical Flow without power control increased from 29.3[W] with one core to 36.6[W] with two cores and 41.6[W] with three cores on the Haswell multicore. By contrast, with the power control, the power decreased to 24.2[W] with one core, 12.2[W] with two cores and 9.6[W] with three cores, respectively. In particular, the power control reduced the power for three cores to 1/3 against ordinary one core execution without the power control and to 1/4 against three cores without the power control

On three cores of the ARM Cortex-A9 multicore, the power consumption of Optical Flow without power control increased from 1.0[W] with one core to 1.5[W] with two cores and 2.2[W] with three cores. By contrast, with power control, the power decreased to 0.7[W] with one core, 0.4[W] with two cores and 0.3[W] with three cores, respectively. In particular, the power for three cores with the power control is less than 1/3 of the one core execution without the power control and 1/7 of the three cores without the power control.

The results of the power reduction clearly show that the OSCAR compiler significantly reduced the power consumption of real-time applications such as H.264 and Optical Flow both on Intel Haswell and ARM Cortex-A9 multicores.

References

1. NVIDIA Corporation: White paper NVIDIA Tegra: Multi-processor Architecture. (2010)
2. ARM:Jeff, B.: Advances in big.LITTLE Technology for Power and Energy Savings. Write paper, 1–11 (2012)
3. Kurd, N., Chowdhury, M., Burton, E., Thomas, T.P., Mozak, C., Boswell, B., Lal, M., Deval, A., Douglas, J., Elassal, M., Nalamalpu, A., Wilson, T.M., Merten, M., Chennupaty, S., Gomes, W., Kumar, R.: Haswell: A family of IA 22nm processors. In: Solid-State Circuits Conference Digest of Technical Papers, pp. 112–113 (2014)

4. OpenMP. http://openmp.org/
5. Cuda. http://www.nvidia.com/object/cuda_home_new.html
6. Kasahara, H., Obata, M., Ishizaka, K.: Automatic coarse grain task parallel processing on SMP using openMP. In: Midkiff, S.P., Moreira, J.E., Gupta, M., Chatterjee, S., Ferrante, J., Prins, J.F., Pugh, B., Tseng, C.-W. (eds.) LCPC 2000. LNCS, vol. 2017, pp. 189–207. Springer, Heidelberg (2001)
7. Obata, M., Shirako, J., Kaminaga, H., Ishizaka, K., Kasahara, H.: Hierarchical parallelism control for multigrain parallel processing. In: Pugh, B., Tseng, C.-W. (eds.) LCPC 2002. LNCS, vol. 2481, pp. 31–44. Springer, Heidelberg (2005)
8. Kimura, K., Mase, M., Mikami, H., Miyamoto, T., Shirako, J., Kasahara, H.: OSCAR API for real-time low-power multicores and its performance on multicores and SMP servers. In: Gao, G.R., Pollock, L.L., Cavazos, J., Li, X. (eds.) LCPC 2009. LNCS, vol. 5898, pp. 188–202. Springer, Heidelberg (2010)
9. Honda, H., Kasahara, H.: Coarse grain parallelism detection scheme of a fortran program. Syst. Comput. Jpn. **22**, 24–36 (1991)
10. Shirako, J., Oshiyama, N., Wada, Y., Shikano, H., Kimura, K., Kasahara, H.: Compiler control power saving scheme for multi core processors. In: Ayguadé, E., Baumgartner, G., Ramanujam, J., Sadayappan, P. (eds.) LCPC 2005. LNCS, vol. 4339, pp. 362–376. Springer, Heidelberg (2006)
11. Shirako, J., Yoshida, M., Oshiyama, N., Wada, Y., Nakano, H., Shikano, H., Kimura, K., Kasahara, H.: Performance evaluation of compiler controlled power saving scheme. In: Labarta, J., Joe, K., Sato, T. (eds.) ISHPC 2006 and ALPS 2006. LNCS, vol. 4759, pp. 480–493. Springer, Heidelberg (2008)
12. Intel: Mobile 4th Generation Intel Core Processor Family, Mobile Intel Pentium Processor Family, and Mobile Intel Celeron Processor Family. Datasheet - vol. 1 of 2 (2014)
13. CPU hotplug Support in Linux(tm) Kernel. https://www.kernel.org/doc/Documentation/cpu-hotplug.txt
14. ARM Corporation: Cortex-A9 Technical Reference Manual. http://infocenter.arm.com/help/topic/com.arm.doc.ddi0388i/DDI0388I_cortex_a9_r4p1_trm.pdf
15. Google: Android Developers. http://developer.android.com/index.html
16. Yamamoto, H., et al.: OSCAR compiler controlled multicore power reduction on android platform. In: Caşcaval, C., Montesinos-Ortego, P. (eds.) LCPC 2013 - Testing. LNCS, vol. 8664, pp. 155–168. Springer, Heidelberg (2014)
17. ODROID-X2. http://www.hardkernel.com/renewal2011/products/prdtinfo.php?gcode=G135235611947
18. Samsung Electronics: White Paper of Exynos 5 (2011)
19. Samsung Electronics: Samsung Exynos 4 Quad (Exynos 4412) RISC Microprocessor User's Manual (2012)
20. Samsung Semiconductors Global Site. https://www.samsung.com/global/business/semiconductor/product/poweric/overview
21. GPIO Interfaces. https://www.kernel.org/doc/Documentation/gpio.txt
22. H.264. http://iphome.hhi.de/suehring/tml/
23. Lee, C., Potkonjak, M., Mangione-Smith, W.: MediaBench: a tool for evaluating and synthesizing multimedia and communications systems. In: Proceedings of the 30th Annual ACM/IEEE International Symposium on Microarchitecture, pp. 330–335 (1997)
24. Opencv. http://www.opencv.org

π Abstraction: Parallelism-Aware Array Data Flow Analysis for OpenMP

Fahed Jubair[1], Okwan Kwon[2], Rudolf Eigenmann[1],
and Samuel Midkiff[1(✉)]

[1] Purdue University, West Lafayette, USA
[2] Nvidia Corporation, Santa Clara, USA
{fjubair,eigenman,smidkiff}@purdue.edu, okwank@nvidia.com

Abstract. Array data flow analysis (ADFA) is a classical method for collecting array section information in sequential programs. When applying ADFA to parallel OpenMP programs, array access information needs to be analyzed in loops whose iteration spaces are partitioned across threads. The analysis involves symbolic expressions that are functions of the original loop iteration spaces, subscript expressions and thread numbers. Adequate representations of, and operations on, these expressions can be critical for the accuracy of the analysis. This paper presents a new ADFA compiler framework for OpenMP programs. We introduce the π *operator* to abstractly represent the parallelism effects in array section expressions and improve the accuracy of the cross-thread analysis during data flow computation. We also present a novel *delayed symbolic evaluation* technique that enables all array section operations in the data flow computation to be performed fully accurately. Using four NAS OpenMP benchmarks, we show that the π operator improves array section operations' accuracy (i.e., reduces conservative operations) during data flow computation by 66 %, on average, compared to the best alternative. In addition, it reduces the number of terms, and thus the complexity of computed array sections by 33 %, on average. We also show that delayed symbolic evaluation eliminates conservative operations and does so without significant increase in complexity when combined with π operators.

1 Introduction

OpenMP [2] is a popular, directive-based programming model targeting shared memory architectures. OpenMP users annotate regions of code that can be executed in parallel, with the compiler handling details of scheduling regions marked as parallel onto different threads and enforcing the OpenMP memory model. Researchers have developed optimizations for OpenMP compilers that go beyond simply handling the details necessary for correct execution. The optimizations include automatic array privatization [11], barrier elimination [14] and compilers that extend OpenMP beyond shared memory (e.g., OpenMP-to-MPI

This work was supported, in part, by the National Science Foundation under grants No. 0720471-CNS, 0707931-CNS, 0833115-CCF, 0916817-CCF and 1346896-CCF.

© Springer International Publishing Switzerland 2015
J. Brodman and P. Tu (Eds.): LCPC 2014, LNCS 8967, pp. 253–267, 2015.
DOI: 10.1007/978-3-319-17473-0_17

translation [9]). These optimizations rely on information about array elements accessed by the OpenMP program's statements, information that traditionally has been provided by *Array Data Flow Analysis* (ADFA).

Traditional ADFAs target sequential programs. For OpenMP programs, ADFAs need to collect array section information across multiple threads. Insufficient symbolic information while analyzing cross-thread relationships of array section expressions and limitations in internal representations often forces ADFAs to perform array section operations (intersection, union and subtraction) conservatively, reducing accuracy.

In order to use ADFAs with OpenMP programs, previous approaches [8,9] proposed expressing the bounds of partitioned parallel loops as symbolic functions of the thread number. This allows the compiler to view a multi-threaded program as a serial program with a parameterized thread number. We refer to this method as *explicit static partitioning*.

Explicit static partitioning is reasonably accurate for representing array sections collected within a parallel loop; however, when analyzing array sections collected across multiple parallel loops, data flow computation tend to introduce inaccuracy for the aforementioned reasons.

We introduce the π *operator*, an abstract representation of partitioned iteration spaces that captures the partitioning semantics implied by OpenMP directives. The π operator retains the knowledge of original iteration spaces and the partitioning scheme across threads; this information is lost by explicit partitioning, but is useful for accurate array section operations.

Using the π operator, we present the producer-consumer array data flow analysis (PCDFA) that collects prior produced and upwardly exposed consumed array sections for an OpenMP program's statements. PCDFA is essentially a classical ADFA that takes the memory model semantics of OpenMP into consideration.

In addition, this paper introduces the concept of *delayed symbolic evaluation*: If a dataflow step would yield a conservative result for an operation, the algorithm postpones evaluating the operation by representing it as an unevaluated expression. Later in the analysis, postponed unevaluated expressions are either simplified or evaluated as further symbolic information becomes available. Should a full compile-time evaluation of some operations not be possible, delayed symbolic analysis simplifies and retains them as unevaluated expressions, allowing them to be accurately evaluated at runtime.

We evaluate the performance of PCDFA by measuring (i) *operation accuracy*, which measures the difference between the precise evaluation of PCDFA array section operations and the actual evaluation (which may be approximate and conservative); and (ii) *array section complexity*, which measures the number of terms in array sections' expressions. Array section complexity is a direct indication of the runtime work (i.e., overhead) needed to evaluate the symbolic expressions of generated array sections.

When performing PCDFA on four NAS OpenMP benchmarks [1], the π operator, on average, improves operation accuracy by 66 % and reduces array section complexity by 33 %, compared to explicit static partitioning (the best alternative). When applying delayed symbolic evaluation, both representations have 100 % operation accuracy (i.e., no conservative operations). However, this is achieved while increasing array section complexity by 1.96x, on average, for explicit static partitioning. In contrast, using delayed symbolic evaluation with the π operator reduces overall array section complexity for two benchmarks and increases array section complexity by no more than 1.1x with other benchmarks.

The remainder of the paper is organized as follows: Sect. 2 describes the π operator. Section 3 presents PCDFA. Section 4 describes delayed symbolic evaluation. Section 5 evaluates the performance. Section 6 discusses related work and Sect. 7 concludes the paper.

2   The π Operator

The π operator is an abstract representation that captures the high level semantics of partitioning while hiding its implementation. We describe how to use the π operator for both iteration and data spaces.

2.1   Iteration Space Representation

Consider the iteration space $(l{:}u{:}s)$, where l, u, and s are, respectively, the lower bound, upper bound and stride expressions. The π operator represents partitioning on this iteration space using the abstract form $\pi_x(l{:}u{:}s)$, where x is the type of partitioning applied to this iteration space as stated or implied by OpenMP directives (see Table 1). π operators encapsulate high-level knowledge of partitioning schemes and hide implementation details about how these schemes are actually computed.

The compiler parses OpenMP *schedule* directives of parallel loops and represents their iteration spaces with the appropriate π operator from Table 1. π_s and π_m operators represent iteration spaces of loops that are within OpenMP *single* and OpenMP *master* regions, respectively. The π_m operator also represents the iteration space of a sequential loop, since loops that do not correspond to a parallel region execute on the master thread.

Figure 1 shows an example of the internal representation by the π operator and state-of-the-art explicit static partitioning.

2.2   Data Space Representation

In OpenMP, the mapping of array elements onto threads depends on the partitioning scheme in iteration spaces and the array subscript functions. Hence, a partitioned data space of an array access can be represented using an algebra that applies array subscript functions to π operators.

We first describe the *regular section descriptor (RSD)* [7], an array section representation that is accurate for array accesses with linear subscripts. Let $A[f_1][f_2]\ldots[f_m]$ be an m-dimensional array access, where f_j is the subscript

Table 1. List of π operators. Block-cyclic partitioning currently is supported conservatively as dynamic partitioning.

$\pi_b(l:u:s)$	Divide into chunks of approximately equal size and map to threads in monotonic order (block partitioning)
$\pi_c(l:u:s)$	Map elements to threads in round-robin fashion (cyclic partitioning)
$\pi_m(l:u:s)$	Map all elements to the master thread
$\pi_s(l:u:s)$	Map all elements to a single thread
$\pi_d(l:u:s)$	Mapping is unknown (dynamic partitioning)
$(l:u:s)$	A non-partitioned space (all elements are mapped to every thread)

expression for dimension $j, 1 \leq j \leq m$. Let A be contained in a loop nest with depth n, where the outer-most loop has the index variable i_1 and the innermost loop has the index variable i_n. Let array subscript f_j be a linear function of 0 or 1 indices in $i_1, \ldots, i_n$, i.e., subscripts are not coupled. The same index can appear in more than one dimension. Using RSDs, the array section of A is $(l_1{:}u_1{:}s_1)\ldots(l_m{:}u_m{:}s_m)$, where the bounds in $(l_j{:}u_j{:}s_j)$ are computed from applying array subscript f_j to the bounds of corresponding iteration spaces.

We build on the RSD and introduce the πRSD representation, a simple extension of the RSD representation such that π operators can represent dimensions that have partitioned data spaces. For example, $\pi_b(l_1{:}u_1{:}s_1)(l_2{:}u_2{:}s_2)$ has a block-partitioned data space in the first dimension and a non-partitioned data space in the second dimension.

A partitioned data space for an array access with a linear subscript function is computed by the following algebraic property: $a + b \times \pi(l:u:s) = \pi(a + b \times l : a + b \times u : b \times s)$. For example, consider the read array access $A[i+1][j]$ of statement $S2$ in Fig. 1b. The iteration spaces corresponding to the first and

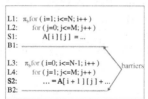 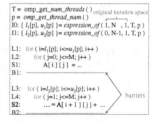

(a) OpenMP input.   (b) The π operator.   (c) Explicit static partitioning.

Fig. 1. The internal representation of an OpenMP program. π operators are annotations that provide partitioning information to parallel loops while keeping original iteration spaces intact (see Table 1). By contrast, the explicit static partitioning method explicitly expresses loop partitions; it introduces new complex loop bounds that are parameterized by the thread number.

second dimensions are $\pi_b(0:N-1:1)$ and $(1:M:1)$, respectively. Therefore, the read array section of this access is $\pi_b(1:N:1)(1:M:1)$.

A partitioned data space for an array access with a non-linear subscript function (e.g., $A\,[B\,[j]]$) is conservatively approximated (using overestimation or underestimation). Note that there are no accuracy constraints for linear subscript functions that have non-linear bounds. For example, if $A[1+i]$ is being accessed inside a parallel loop with the partitioned iteration space $\pi_b(1:B(j):1)$, then the partitioned data space of this array access is $\pi_b(2:1+B(j):1)$.

2.3 The π Operator versus Explicit Static Partitioning

Compared to explicit static partitioning, the abstract representation provided by π operators is more concise and enables improved cross-thread analysis of array section expressions. This is because: (i) it hides the complexity of partitioning and keeps expressions simple (functions of original data spaces), and (ii) it provides high-level knowledge about the partitioning semantics.

Consider the written array section in Statement $S1$ and the read array section in statement $S2$ in the OpenMP code of Fig. 1a. With explicit static partitioning, the written and the read sections are $(l_1[p]:u_1[p]:1)(0:M:1)$ and $(l_2[p]+1:u_2[p]+1:1)(1:M:1)$, respectively (see Fig. 1c). Because the number of threads and the thread number are unknown at compile time, the cross-thread relationships of the parameterized bounds are also unknown. For example, the result of an intersection operation is unknown. With the π operator, the written and the read sections are $\pi_b(1:N:1)(0:M:1)$ and $\pi_b(1:N:1)(1:M:1)$, respectively (see Fig. 1b). Partitioned dimensions in both sections are shown to be the same. For example, the result of an intersection operation is $\pi_b(1:N:1)(1:M:1)$. We discuss array section operations in Sect. 3.

In general, explicit static partitioning explicitly represents the complex loop partitions, which tends to lead to inaccurate cross-thread analysis of array section expressions and therefore inaccurate array section operations. The π operator improves this accuracy.

3   Producer-Consumer Array Data Flow Analysis

The producer-consumer array data flow analysis (PCDFA) collects prior produced and future consumed array section information by each thread for the statements in an OpenMP program.

We first describe the *Producer-Consumer Flow Graph (PCFG)* [4]. PCFG is a *Control Flow Graph* that represents both the control flow and the relevant memory model semantics of an OpenMP program. In particular, *barrier* nodes, which denote points where memory is to be made coherent across threads, are placed at the end of parallel loops that do not have an OpenMP *nowait* directive. Each node in the PCFG corresponds to a program statement or an OpenMP directive.

$$DEF_{in}(e) = \bigcup_{x \in Pred(e)} DEF_{out}(x)$$

$$DEF_{out}(e) = \begin{cases} \phi & , \ e \ is \ barrier \ node \\ \Big(DEF_{in}(e) - KILL_{all}(e)\Big) \bigcup wGEN(e) & , \ otherwise \end{cases}$$

Fig. 2. Reaching Definitions analysis. Note that $KILL_{all}$ is across all threads, all other sets are for the current thread.

$$USE_{out}(e) = \bigcup_{x \in Succ(e)} USE_{in}(x)$$

$$USE_{in}(e) = \Big(USE_{out}(e) - KILL_{all}(e)\Big) \bigcup rGEN(e)$$

Fig. 3. Liveness analysis. Note that $KILL_{all}$ is across all threads, all other sets are for the current thread.

For a node e in PCFG: (i) $Succ(e)$ and $Pred(e)$ are the sets of successor and predecessor statements, respectively; (ii) $wGEN(e)$ and $rGEN(e)$ contain the shared array elements that are written and read, respectively, by a thread in e; and (iii) $KILL_{all}(e)$ contains the aggregated shared array elements that are written by *all threads* in e.

The PCDFA consists of Reaching Definition analysis (Fig. 2) and Liveness analysis (Fig. 3). For every node e in PCFG: (i) Reaching Definition analysis computes $DEF_{in}(e)$ and $DEF_{out}(e)$, which are the reaching definitions of shared array elements at the entry and the exit of e, receptively, for a thread; and (ii) Liveness analysis computes $USE_{in}(e)$ and $USE_{out}(e)$, which are the upwardly exposed uses of shared array elements at the entry and the exit of e, respectively, for a thread.

The PCDFA is similar to classical Liveness and Reaching Definition analyses, but takes the coherence semantics of OpenMP's memory model into consideration, as follows: (i) The definitions $DEF_{in}(e)$ and $DEF_{out}(e)$ are the result of writes that have occurred since the *last barrier* (i.e., the most recent produced data since the last global coherent point), and (ii) $KILL_{all}(e)$ contains the aggregated kills across *all* threads. This is because an element killed in a thread is killed in every thread (their copy of this element becomes invalid).

We now describe the compiler framework that performs PCDFA while using the π operator for representing partitioned iteration and data spaces. The compiler uses a set of array sections (represented with πRSDs) to represent Gen, Kill, use and definition sets.

First, the compiler computes Gen ($wGEN$ and $rGEN$) and Kill ($KILL_{all}$) sets for each node in PCFG. Then, the compiler performs PCDFA. During

PCDFA's computation, the analysis needs to perform array section operations (as shown in Figs. 2 and 3). We classify operations into two types: *tractable* or *intractable* operations. An operation is tractable if the partitioning semantics of its result can be described using a known partitioning scheme in Table 1. Otherwise, the operation is *intractable*.

For example, the intersection operation of $\pi_b(1:N:1)$ and $(0:N:1)$ is tractable (can be statically computed) and the result is $\pi_b(1:N:1)$. This is because all partitions before the intersection operation are the same after performing the operation and therefore can be described using the π_b operator with the same original data space. On the other hand, the intersection operation of $\pi_b(1:N:1)$ and $(2:N:1)$ is intractable. This is because there is at least one partition (which has the element 1) that is changed while performing the intersection operation.

The algorithms for performing union, intersection and subtraction operations for πRSD sections are as described for RSD sections [7]. However, their results are kept only if they are tractable. Intractable operations would lead to approximation. Section 4 provides an accurate solution for intractable operations.

As discussed earlier, we build on RSDs to represent partitioned data spaces. π operators require no alteration to RSDs' expressions or operations. In the implementation, π operators are notations that are attached to array section expressions to abstractly describe partitioning semantics.

4 Delayed Symbolic Evaluation

We introduce delayed symbolic evaluation to improve the accuracy of PCDFA's computation in the presence of intractable operations. At a dataflow step that has an intractable operation, the analysis delays this operation to later dataflow steps by representing it as an unevaluated expression. The key observation is that the unevaluated expressions at later dataflow steps can be simplified (i.e., do not grow in complexity) because additional symbolic information becomes available.

Subtraction operations are most critical in this context. To represent the unevaluated expression of a subtraction operation, we extend the πRSD representation and introduce the ERSD representation, as follows: ERSD = $\pi RSD_1 - \pi RSD_2 - \cdots - \pi RSD_n$, where n is the number of terms. During PCDFA's computation, operations with ERSD sections get performed or simplified using the mathematical rules of set theory.

The unevaluated expression of an intractable union operation is a set of two sections. In PCDFA, unevaluated intersections operations are not needed. However, in general, the unevaluated expression of an intersection operation can also be represented as a set of sections, i.e., a set can have an implicit union or intersection operation based on the dataflow equations of the ADFA.

The ERSD representation retains subtracted sections that would otherwise be lost by conservative approximation. In doing so, ERSDs (i) provide additional symbolic information at later computation steps, which allow simplification, and (ii) allow PCDFA to terminate with simplified and unevaluated but accurate

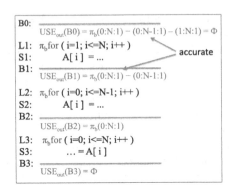

(a) Without delayed symbolic evalua-   (b) With delayed symbolic evaluation.
tion.

Fig. 4. The result of PCDFA at barrier nodes. Delayed Symbolic evaluation avoids conservative approximation of the intractable subtract operation at barrier $B1$.

expressions of intractable operations. Expressions that remain unevaluated when PCDFA terminates will be evaluated at runtime with minimal cost.

Consider PCDFA's computation result for the OpenMP example code in Fig. 4. Without delayed symblic evaluation, intractable subtract operations get approximated. This yields inaccurate array sections at barriers $B0$ and $B1$, as shown in Fig. 4a. In Fig. 4b, delayed symbolic evaluation yields accurate array sections because: (i) the intractable subtract operation at barrier $B1$ is postponed, and (ii) the symbolic information at barrier $B0$ is sufficient to perform the postponed subtraction operation from $B1$ accurately.

An important property of PCDFA is that subtracted terms ($\pi\mathrm{RSD}_2$, ..., $\pi\mathrm{RSD}_n$) in ERSD expressions are $KILL_{\mathrm{all}}$ sets (see Figs. 3 and 2). These sets contain non-partitioned RSD sections that the analysis, in practice, can merge (i.e., minimize) into a small number of terms (no more than 3 terms in tested benchmarks).

As a concept, delayed symbolic evaluation is orthogonal to the π operator and can be applied with other representations such as explicit static partitioning. However, the additional complexity of doing so is significantly higher than the case with π operators, as will be shown in our performance evaluation.

5   Performance Evaluation

We evaluate the performance of PCDFA using both representations, the π operator and state-of-the-art explicit static partitioning. We also evaluate the impact of using delayed symbolic evaluation on each representation.

5.1   Performance Metrics

We evaluate using two metrics: *operation accuracy* and *array section complexity*. Operation accuracy describes the difference between precise evaluation of PCDFA array section operations and the actual evaluation (which may be approximate and conservative). Array section complexity measures the number of terms in array sections' expressions, as well as the number of delayed subtract operations.

To measure PCDFA's operation accuracy, we compute the volume of the overlap between prior produced and future consumed (DEF_{in} and USE_{out}) at barriers (i.e., communication volume). The operation accuracy is then given as a percentage of the ideal volume to this volume. The ideal volume is obtained by a separate runtime computation of PCDFA, where all operations are kept precise due to available full knowledge about cross-thread relationships at runtime. We choose communication volume because its accuracy directly impacts the performance of several optimizations such as barrier elimination [14] and OpenMP-to-MPI translation [9].

A 100 % operation accuracy means that no conservative PCDFA operations were performed. Note that operation accuracy does not account for the inaccuracy that results from approximating indirect memory accesses or other nonlinear subscripts that cannot be represented accurately by RSDs.

We measure array section complexity by counting the number of array section terms and delayed subtraction operations. This metric represents the work (i.e., the overhead) needed to evaluate array section expressions at runtime.

5.2 Experimental Setup

We implemented the PCDFA compiler framework, including π operators and explicit static partitioning, in the Cetus Compiler Infrastructure [3]. We also implemented a runtime tool that receives produced and consumed array sections from the compiler and determines operation accuracy and array section complexity. Figure 5 shows an example of the function calls used by the compiler to pass produced and consumed array sections to the runtime tool.

We evaluate using four OpenMP benchmarks taken from the NAS Parallel Benchmarks suite [13]: FT, SP, BT and SP. All functions were automatically inlined by the Cetus Compiler. The FT benchmark was optimized using the *owner alignment* technique presented in [8], which was applied before performing PCDFA with all FT experiments.

5.3 Evaluation of the Producer-Consumer Array Data Flow Analysis

Figure 6 shows the operation accuracy and the array section complexity for BT, SP, CG and FT. Without delayed symbolic evaluation, on average, the π operator and explicit static partitioning have operation accuracy of 76 % and 46 %, respectively. In addition, the π operator reduces array section complexity by 33 %, compared to explicit static partitioning. When applying delayed symbolic evaluation, both representations have 100 % operation accuracy, while increasing array section complexity by 1.96x with explicit static partitioning and by no more than 1.1x with the π operator.

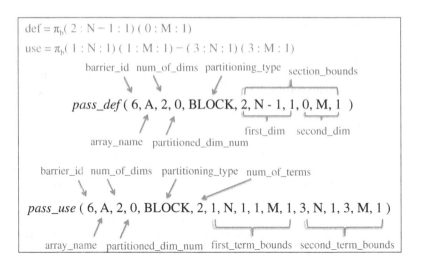

Fig. 5. An example of the function calls used by the π operator's compiler to pass produced and consumed array sections to the runtime tool for a particular barrier. Function calls only specify one partitioned dimension because all tested benchmarks have one-dimensional parallelism (no nested parallelism). In the case of explicit static partitioning, the same function calls are used except that there are no *partitioned_dim_num* or *partitioning_type* fields. The total number of function calls is equal to the total number of array sections.

Explicit static partitioning has insufficient knowledge of cross-thread relationships during PCDFA's computation. Without delayed symbolic evaluation, this causes a large number of conservative subtraction operations and explains the inferior operation accuracy of explicit static partitioning compared to the π operator. This holds for all benchmarks except for CG. CG is a case where subtract operations are less frequent and can be performed accurately with explicit static partitioning. Our solution obtains the same accuracy for CG but reduces array section complexity to 70 %.

Figure 7 shows the number of generated array sections by PCDFA for the π operator and explicit static partitioning. It also shows the impact of delayed symbolic evaluation on both representations. For two benchmarks (FT and SP), using delayed symbolic evaluation with the π operator reduced the total number of array sections. This is due to the additional symbolic knowledge provided by delayed symbolic evaluation during PCDFA's computation, which increases accuracy and reduces the number of array sections. With explicit static partitioning, delayed symbolic evaluation has high complexity because of the insufficient symbolic information during PCDFA's computation (i.e., a large number of conservative subtract operations were delayed).

In general, the π operator is a better representation than explicit static partitioning. In addition to being more concise, the π operator improves operation accuracy and reduces the complexity of computed array sections. Delayed symbolic evaluation is a useful technique for both representations that can eliminate conservative operations. Its complexity, however, is dependent on the representation.

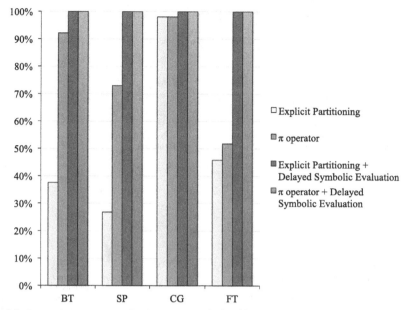

(a) Operation accuracy (higher is better). 100% means all operations are performed accurately.

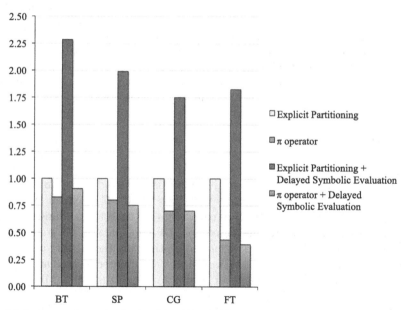

(b) Array section complexity (number of terms and delayed operations) normalized to array section complexity obtained with explicit static partitioning (lower is better).

Fig. 6. Operation accuracy and array section complexity of PCDFA averaged over 8, 16, 32 and 64 threads.

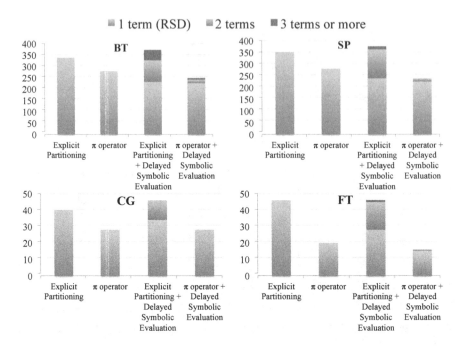

Fig. 7. The number of array sections generated by PCDFA, categorized into RSDs (which have 1 term) and ERSDs (which can have 2 terms or more). Without delayed symbolic evaluation, π operators lead to 33 % fewer array sections, on average, than explicit static partitioning. When applying delayed symbolic evaluation, the ratio of generated ERSDs (delayed subtract operations) is below 8 % with the π operator and is 26–39 % with explicit static partitioning. The largest number of terms in an ERSD section is 3 with π operators and 5 with explicit static partitioning.

6   Related Work

Several compiler analyses in the literature rely on information about accessed array elements, information that traditionally is collected using an array data flow analysis (ADFA). For example, Granston et al. [6] used an ADFA and targeted parallel programs with *doall* constructs for detecting redundant shared array references. Li et al. [10] presented an ADFA for parallel programs written with *POSIX* threads [5] with the purpose of optimizing the locality of core-data allocation on multi-core platforms. Kwon et al. [9] presented a translation scheme of OpenMP to MPI that included an ADFA for analyzing OpenMP programs and used its result for communication generation.

In this paper, we present concepts that allow traditional ADFAs to be extended to OpenMP programs while accounting for the partitioning semantics using the π operator. By contrast, prior ADFAs use explicit static partitioning as the internal representation of iteration and data spaces. As shown by our experiments, this representation causes conservative approximations of array section operations due to its limited symbolic information. An OpenMP-to-MPI translation

```
L0:  for( i=0; i <= N-1; i++) {

         #pragma omp parallel for
L1:      for ( k=i+1; k <= N; k++ ) {
S1:          ratio = A[k][i] / A[i][i] ;
L2:          for ( j=i+1; j <= N; j++ )
S3:              A[k][j] −= ratio * A[i][j];
S4:          B[k] −= ratio * B[i];
         }
     }
```

(a) Gausian Elimination (GE) [12], a non-repetitive OpenMP program.

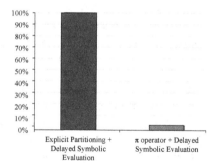

(b) The communication volume in the translated GE normalized to explicit static partitioning (lower is better).

Fig. 8. The internal representation impacts the performance of ongoing work on automatic translation of non-repetitive OpenMP programs into MPI.

scheme [8] was proposed to perform ADFA for OpenMP programs at runtime (where all cross-thread relationships are known). However, this runtime solution introduces substantial overhead and therefore is not scalable beyond programs where this overhead cannot be amortized.

In addition, this paper has presented delayed symbolic evaluation. While the general concept of delaying inaccurate compiler analysis to runtime is not new, to the best of our knowledge, this concept has not been incorporated in prior ADFA frameworks. Doing so may be assumed to lead to unbounded growth of the involved expressions. We have shown concepts and an implementation that avoids such growth.

7   Conclusions and Future Work

Previous compilers used explicit static partitioning to represent partitioned iteration and data spaces in OpenMP programs. This representation loses information about partitioning schemes and original bounds of partitioned spaces, information that this paper showed is needed for accurate array section operations in array data flow analyses. To improve accuracy, we introduced the π operator, which represents the effects of partitioning on iteration and data spaces in an abstract form, without loss of information.

Using the π operator, we extended classical Reaching Definitions and Liveness analyses for OpenMP. Using four NAS OpenMP benchmarks, we evaluated the accuracy of array section operations for these analyses and showed that the π operator, on average, improves the accuracy by 66 % and reduces the number of terms (i.e., the complexity) of array sections by 33 %, compared to state-of-the-art explicit static partitioning.

In addition, we presented the concept of delayed symbolic evaluation, which postpones the evaluation of conservative data flow operations to later steps in the analysis. During the dataflow computation, expressions of delayed operations are either simplified or evaluated as further symbolic information becomes available. For all benchmarks, delayed symbolic evaluation achieves full accuracy (no conservative operations) while increasing complexity (number of terms and postponed operations) by 1.96x, on average, with explicit static partitioning and by less than 1.1x with the π operator. For two benchmarks, combining delayed symbolic evalution with the π operator caused overall complexity to be reduced. Our results show the feasibility of delayed symbolic evaluation when combined with the π operator to obtain a fully accurate array data flow analysis with minimal runtime overhead to perform delayed operations.

The work presented in this paper is part of an ongoing project to build an OpenMP-to-MPI translation system for *non-repetitive* OpenMP programs: a class of applications that was not considered in prior translation systems [8,9]. In a non-repetitive program, communicated array elements at statements needing communication (e.g., barriers) vary for different execution instances of the same statements. For example, in Gaussian Elimination (GE) (shown in Fig. 8a), shared array elements written or read by a given thread in the inner loop $L1$ vary for different iteration of the outer serial loop L0. As a result, communicated array elements at the exit of the parallel loop L1 (where an implicit barrier exists) vary for different iterations of L0.

For an ADFA to compute accurate array section information for non-repetitive programs, it needs to reason about individual *instances* of statements with variant written or read shared array elements. To this end, we use the π operator as an abstract representation that enables the analysis to view array sections as parameterized expressions with the indices of outer serial loops. Therefore, the analysis can now reason about different instances of these expressions. By contrast, explicit static partitioning introduces complex expressions into array sections that often force ADFAs to make conservative approximation.

Figure 8b shows an early result for the impact of using the π operator for reducing communication when translating GE. In ongoing work, we are studying and evaluating this translation on a set of OpenMP benchmarks.

The π operator and delayed symbolic evaluation provide general concepts that can be extended to other parallel programs, beyond OpenMP. To use the π operator, user directives or compiler analyses are needed to retrieve high-level information about the partitioning applied to parallel loops. To use delayed symbolic evaluation, the compiler needs to represent unevaluated expressions of delayed operations such that they get simplified along the dataflow computation.

References

1. NAS Parallel Benchmarks 3.3. http://www.nas.nasa.gov/publications/npb.html
2. OpenMP Application Programming Interface 4.0. http://openmp.org
3. Bae, H., Mustafa, D., Lee, J.W., Lin, A.H., Eigenmann, C.D.R., Midkiff, S.: The cetus source-to-source compiler infrastructure. Int. J. Parallel Program. **41**(6), 1–15 (2012)

4. Basumallik, A., Eigenmann, R.: Incorporation of OpenMP memory consistency into conventional dataflow analysis. In: Eigenmann, R., de Supinski, B.R. (eds.) IWOMP 2008. LNCS, vol. 5004, pp. 71–82. Springer, Heidelberg (2008)
5. Butenhof, D.R.: Programming with POSIX Threads. Addison-Wesley Longman Publishing Co. Inc., Boston (1997)
6. Granston, E.D., Veidenbaum, A.V.: Combining flow and dependence analyses to expose redundant array accesses. Int. J. Parallel Prog. **23**(5), 423–470 (1995)
7. Havlak, P., Kennedy, K.: An implementation of interprocedural bounded regular section analysis. IEEE Trans. Parallel Distrib. Syst. **2**(3), 350–360 (1991)
8. Kwon, O., Jubair, F., Eigenmann, R., Midkiff, S.: A hybrid approach of OpenMP for clusters. In: Proceedings of the 17th ACM SIGPLAN Symposium on Principles and Practice of Parallel Programming (PPoPP), New Orleans, Louisiana, pp. 75–84 (2012)
9. Kwon, O., Jubair, F., Min, S.-J., Bae, H., Eigenmann, R., Midkiff, S.P.: Automatic scaling of OpenMP beyond shared memory. In: Rajopadhye, S., Mills Strout, M. (eds.) LCPC 2011. LNCS, vol. 7146, pp. 1–15. Springer, Heidelberg (2013)
10. Li, Y., Abousamra, A., Melhem, R., Jones, A.K.: Compiler-assisted data distribution for chip multiprocessors. In: Proceedings of the 19th International Conference on Parallel Architectures and Compilation Techniques (PACT), Vienna, Austria, pp. 501–512 (2010)
11. Liu, Z., Chapman, B.M., Weng, T.-H., Hernandez, O.: Improving the performance of OpenMP by array privatization. In: Voss, M.J. (ed.) WOMPAT 2003. LNCS, vol. 2716, pp. 244–259. Springer, Heidelberg (2003)
12. McGinn, S.F., Shaw, R.E.: Parallel gaussian elimination using OpenMP and MPI. In: Proceedings of the 16th Annual International Symposium on High Performance Computing Systems and Applications (HPCS), Washington, DC, pp. 169–173 (2002)
13. NAS Parallel Benchmarks version 3.3. http://www.nas.nasa.gov/publications/npb.html
14. Satoh, S., Kusano, K., Sato, M.: Compiler optimization techniques for OpenMP programs. Sci. Program. **9**(203), 131–142 (2001)

Static Approximation of MPI Communication Graphs for Optimized Process Placement

Andrew J. McPherson[1]([⊠]), Vijay Nagarajan[1], and Marcelo Cintra[2]

[1] School of Informatics, University of Edinburgh, Edinburgh, Scotland
{ajmcpherson,vijay.nagarajan}@ed.ac.uk
[2] Intel, Intel, Germany
marcelo.cintra@intel.com

Abstract. Message Passing Interface (MPI) is the de facto standard for programming large scale parallel programs. Static understanding of MPI programs informs optimizations including process placement and communication/computation overlap, and debugging. In this paper, we present a fully context and flow sensitive, interprocedural, best-effort analysis framework to *statically* analyze MPI programs. We instantiate this to determine an approximation of the point-to-point communication graph of an MPI program. Our analysis is the first pragmatic approach to realizing the full point-to-point communication graph without profiling – indeed our experiments show that we are able to resolve and understand 100 % of the relevant MPI call sites across the NAS Parallel Benchmarks. In all but one case, this only requires specifying the number of processes.

To demonstrate an application, we use the analysis to determine process placement on a Chip MultiProcessor (CMP) based cluster. The use of a CMP-based cluster creates a two-tier system, where inter-node communication can be subject to greater latencies than intra-node communication. Intelligent process placement can therefore have a significant impact on the execution time. Using the 64 process versions of the benchmarks, and our analysis, we see an average of 28 % (7 %) improvement in communication localization over *by-rank* scheduling for 8-core (12-core) CMP-based clusters, representing the maximum possible improvement.

1 Introduction

Message Passing Interface (MPI) is the de facto standard for programming large scale parallel programs. Paradigm-aware static analysis can inform optimizations including process placement and communication/computation overlap [8], and debugging [27]. Fortunately, message-passing lends itself effectively to static analysis, due to the explicit nature of the communication.

Previous work in MPI static analysis produced several techniques for characterizing communication [5,24,25]. Common to these techniques is the matching of send and receive statements, which while potentially enabling interprocess

© Springer International Publishing Switzerland 2015
J. Brodman and P. Tu (Eds.): LCPC 2014, LNCS 8967, pp. 268–283, 2015.
DOI: 10.1007/978-3-319-17473-0_18

dataflow analyses, can limit coverage. More importantly, the techniques are limited in their context sensitivity, from being limited to a single procedure [5,24], to only offering partial context sensitivity [25]. Therefore, the existing techniques do not provide tools applicable to determining the full communication graph.

In comparison to static approaches, profiling can be effective [7], but is more intrusive to workflow. As Zhai et al. [28] note, existing tools such as KOJAK [20], VAMPIR [21], and TAU [23] involve expensive trace collection, though lightweight alternatives e.g., mpiP [26] do exist. *The main question we address is whether a static analysis can provide comparable insight into the MPI communication graph, without requiring the program to be executed.*

Tools for understanding MPI communication have several applications. For example, one can consider the running of an MPI program on a cluster of Chip Multiprocessors (CMP). Here, there exists a spatial scheduling problem in the assignment of processes to processor cores. In MPI, each process is assigned a *rank*, used to determine its behavior and spatial scheduling. For example, OpenMPI [10] supports two schedules, **by-rank** – where processes fill every CMP slot before moving onto the next CMP, and **round-robin** – where a process is allocated on each CMP in a round-robin fashion. Without intervention, there is no guarantee that the communication is conducive to either schedule. This may lead to pairs of heavily communicating processes scheduled on different nodes. Communication between nodes, using ethernet or even Infiniband, can be subject to latencies significantly larger than in intra-node communication. This inefficient scheduling can cause significant performance degradation [2,19,29]. Prior analysis allows intelligent placement to alleviate this issue.

In this work, we propose a fully context and flow sensitive, interprocedural analysis framework to statically analyze MPI programs. Our framework is essentially a forward traversal examining variable definitions; but to avoid per-process evaluation, we propose a data-structure to maintain context and flow sensitive partially evaluated definitions. This allows process sensitive, on-demand evaluation at required points. Our analysis is best-effort, prioritizing coverage over soundness; for instance we assume global variables are only modified by compile-time visible functions. Underpinning our analysis is the observation that for a significant class of MPI programs, the communication pattern is broadly input independent and therefore amenable to static analysis [5,6,11,22].

We instantiate our framework to determine an approximation of the point-to-point communication graph of an MPI program. Applying this to programs from the NAS Parallel Benchmark Suite [4], we are able to resolve and understand 100 % of the relevant MPI call sites, i.e., we are able to determine the sending processes, destinations, and volumes for all contexts in which the calls are found. In all but one case, this only requires specifying the number of processes.

To demonstrate an application, the graph is used to optimize spatial scheduling. An approximation is permissible here, as spatial scheduling does not impact correctness in MPI programs. We use the extracted graph and a partitioning algorithm to determine process placement on a CMP-based cluster. Using the 64 process versions of the benchmarks, we see an average of 28 % (7 %) improvement in communication localization over *by-rank* scheduling for 8-core (12-core) CMP-based clusters, representing the maximum possible improvement.

The main contributions of this work are:

- A novel framework for the interprocedural, fully context and flow sensitive, best-effort analysis of MPI programs.
- A new data structure for maintaining partially evaluated, context and flow sensitive variable representations for on-demand process sensitive evaluation.
- An instantiation of the framework, determining optimized process placement for MPI programs running on CMP-based clusters.

2   Related Work

2.1   Static Analysis of MPI Programs

Several techniques have been proposed to statically analyze MPI programs. However, they have limitations that prevent their application to the problem described. Noted by multiple sources are the SPMD semantics of MPI [5,18,25]. The SPMD semantics are important as they largely define the methods that can be, and are, used to perform communication analysis.

MPI-CFG [24] and later MPI-ICFG [18,25] annotate control-flow graphs (CFGs) with process sensitive traversals and communication edges between matched send and receive statements. Backward slicing is performed on the pure CFG to simplify expressions that indirectly reference process rank in the call parameter. *The lack of full context sensitivity prevents these works being applied to the problem described.* However, they do highlight the need to use slicing to determine process sensitive values and the need for an interprocedural approach.

Bronevetsky [5] introduces the parallel CFG (pCFG). It represents process sensitivity by creating multiple states for each CFG node as determined by conditional statements. Progress is made by each component until they reach a communication, where they block until matched to a corresponding statement. Communication is then modeled between sets, providing a scalable view of communication. The complex matching process is limited to modeling communication across Cartesian topologies. Due to their proof requirements, wildcards cannot be handled [5]. pCFG tuples are comparable with the data structure proposed in this work, but as detailed in Sect. 3 we dispense with sets, and with matching, achieving the data representation by different means. *Most importantly, pCFG is intraprocedural and therefore ineffective with real programs.*

2.2   Profiling and Dynamic Analysis of MPI Programs

Profiling and dynamic analysis techniques have also been applied to MPI programs [20,21,23,26]. Targeting the same optimization as this work, MPIPP [7]

uses the communication graph, extracted via profiling, to optimize process placement. *This approach would compare unfavorably to a static approach achieving similar coverage, given the cost of repeated executions on potentially scarce
resources.*

Recognizing the burden of profiling, FACT [28] seeks to understand communication by only profiling a statically determined program slice. *While reducing
the cost of profiling, the authors of FACT note that the slicing may alter the
communication pattern in non-deterministic applications.*

Dynamic approaches include Adaptive MPI [15,16], which provides a runtime system, capable of automatic communication/computation overlap, load
balancing, and process migration. These techniques allow it to take advantage
of communication phases in the program. *Given the cost of migration and need
for a runtime system, the methods described are required to overcome further
overhead to achieve better speedup.* For programs that lack distinct temporal
phases of communication, this may not be possible.

3 Our Approach

In this section we explain the key elements of our approach in terms of design
decisions, data structures, and present an overall analysis algorithm. To motivate
our approach we examine a sample MPI program, presented as Fig. 1.

3.1 General Principles

The basic aim of a static approach to approximating the point-to-point communication graph is to understand *MPI_Send* calls (as in line 22 of our example).
There are four elements to this, the **source** - which processes make the call, the
destination - to which processes do they send data, the **send count** and the
datatype - from which the volume of bytes can be calculated.

```
#include <mpi.h>                                            1
int my_rank, comm_size, indata, outdata;                    2
MPI_Status stat;                                            3
                                                            4
int main (int argc, char **argv) {                          5
  MPI_Init (&argc, &argv);                                  6
  MPI_Comm_rank (MPI_COMM_WORLD, &my_rank);                 7
  MPI_Comm_size (MPI_COMM_WORLD, &comm_size);               8
  indata = comm_size + 4;                                   9
  if (my_rank < 5)                                          10
    communicate ();                                         11
  if (my_rank < 6)                                          12
    indata = indata + my_rank;                              13
  if (my_rank > 7)                                          14
    communicate ();                                         15
  MPI_Finalize ();                                          16
  return 0;                                                 17
}                                                           18
```

```
void communicate () {                                       20
  if (my_rank % 2 == 0 && my_rank < comm_size - 1)          21
    MPI_Send (&indata, 1, MPI_INT, my_rank + 1, 0,          22
      MPI_COMM_WORLD);                                      23
  else                                                      24
    MPI_Recv (&outdata, 1, MPI_INT, MPI_ANY_SOURCE,         25
      0, MPI_COMM_WORLD, &stat);                            26
  indata = 0;                                               27
}                                                           28
```

Fig. 1. Example of a simple MPI program

As we can see from line 10, the call to *communicate*, which contains the
MPI_Send can be conditional. On this basis we can say that an interprocedural
approach is essential, as an intraprocedural approach fails to capture the fact

that any process with a *rank* greater than 4 would not make the first call to *communicate* and therefore not reach the *MPI_Send* in this instance.

Accepting the need for full context sensitivity, there are two basic approaches that could be employed. One could use some form of interprocedural constant propagation [12], within a full interprocedural dataflow analysis [14], to determine the relevant parameter values (*destination, send count* and *datatype*). However, such an approach is not without issue. Significantly, the SPMD nature of MPI programs means the path through the program may be process sensitive (as seen in our example). Therefore, a constant propagation approach would require complete evaluation of the program for each intended process to determine the processes communicating (*source*) at each call site. Also, even with flow sensitivity, the coverage achieved by such a rigorous approach may not be enough to provide an approximation of the communication graph.

The alternative basic approach is a static slicing, based on a partial data flow analysis [13], that identifies the *MPI_Send* and then evaluates at the program point before the call, for each of the contexts in which the call is found. While such a technique is possible and requires potentially less computation than the previous approach [9], it suffers from the same weaknesses, with regard to strictness and full reevaluation to determine the *source*.

Due to these issues, we choose to follow a composite approach based largely on a forward traversal to establish interprocedural context without backtracking. This traversal walks through the CFG of a function, descending into a child function when discovered. This is analogous to an ad-hoc forward traversal of the Super CFG [3], but with cloned procedures. To avoid full reevaluation, we do not treat process sensitive values as constants and instead leave them partially evaluated in a data structure introduced in Sect. 3.3. Therefore, we progress in a process insensitive manner, only performing process sensitive evaluation for calls and MPI statements, using our data structure to perform on-demand slicing. To enable broader coverage, we make the approach best-effort, applying the assumption that global variables are only modified by functions visible to the compiler. While this renders our evaluations strictly unsound, this is required to achieve even fractional coverage.

3.2   Context, Flow, and Process Sensitivity

Focusing on the *MPI_Send* in our example, we see that establishing definitions with our approach requires understanding two elements; which processes enter the parent *communicate* function (context sensitivity) and of those processes, which reach the call (flow sensitivity). Due to the SPMD semantics, process sensitivity (which processes reach a certain program point), is derived from the context and flow sensitivities. These are handled using two related techniques.

To understand which processes call the parent function and therefore potentially make the *MPI_Send*, we introduce the "live vector", a boolean vector to track which processes are live in each function as we perform the serial walk. The length of the vector is the number of processes for which we are compiling, initialized at the main function as all true. Requiring the number of processes to be defined entails compiling for a specific scale of problem. However we do not believe this is a significant imposition, given the typical workflow of scientific and high-performance computing. Notably, this requirement also applies to profiling, where a new run is needed for each change in the number of processes.

The live vector is a simplification of the context of the call for each process. This allows for, at a subsequent assignment or call, evaluation using the live vector and flow information, rather than repeated reevaluations within the context of the entire program. When a call is found, we generate a live vector for that function before descending into it. This "child live vector" is generated from the live vector of the parent function of the call and is logically a subset of those processes that executed the parent function. The evaluation of which processes are live in the child live vector uses the flow sensitivity technique, described next.

Within a function, which processes make a call depends on the relevant conditions. We examine the CFG in a Static Single Assignment form where the only back edges are for loop backs, all other edges make forward progress. A relevant condition is defined as one meeting three requirements. Firstly, the basic block containing the condition is not post-dominated by the block containing the call. Secondly, there are no blocks between the condition block and the call block that post-dominate the condition block. Thirdly, there exists a path of forward edges between the condition block and the call block.

The evaluation of relevant conditions is done with regard to their position in the CFG and the paths that exist between them. This ensures that calls subject to interdependent conditions, as seen in line 21 of our example, can be evaluated correctly. The definitions for the condition and its outcome can be process sensitive, so the evaluation of the relevant conditions must be performed separately for each process. The method by which this and the evaluation of MPI arguments is achieved is introduced in the next section.

3.3   On-Demand Evaluation

To evaluate the conditions and the arguments of the *MPI_Send* as detailed above, we implement a tree-based representation to hold the partially evaluated variables as our approach requires. Our representation provides the ability to perform on-demand static slicing, sensitive to a particular process, without repeated analysis of the program. In fact, since only a fraction of the variables influence the communication graph, most will not need evaluation.

For each assignment or ϕ-node encountered, a new node of our representation is created, or if the variable already exists, its node is modified. These nodes are stored in either the global or the local hash tables allowing efficient lookup and discarding of out of scope definitions that are unreferenced by any in scope.

Each node is of one of eight types, representing all the cases that arise. **Constant** - representing a number. **SPMD** - for definitions generated by operations with process sensitive results, e.g., a call to *MPI_Comm_rank*. **Expression** - represents an arithmetic expression and contains an operator and pointers to nodes upon which to apply it. **Many** - handles repeated definitions to the same variable, allowing context, flow, and process sensitive resolution. **Builtin** - required for built in functions (e.g., square root), contains an operator and pointer to the node upon which it is to be applied. **Iterator** - identical to Constant, but specially controlled for loop operations. **Array** - for handling array definitions, see Sect. 3.4. **Unknown** - for when a definition is unresolvable.

The node type used is defined by the node types of the operands of the defining statement and whether a definition already exists. ϕ-nodes are treated as multiple definitions to a variable, resulting in a **many** node.

To better convey the operation of this data structure we present Fig. 2, which shows the state of *indata* by the end of the program described in Fig. 1 (line 16). By the end of the program, *indata* has been defined multiple times, but not all definitions apply to all processes. For this example, we assume the program has been compiled for 12 processes.

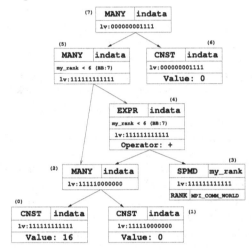

Fig. 2. The representation of *indata* at line 16 in Fig. 1. **lv** represents live vector

The first definition (line 9), is to add *comm_size* to the constant 4. While *comm_size* is an SPMD value, because it is the same for all processes this expression can be reduced to a **constant** (marked (0) in Fig. 2). Then after descending into *communicate* for the first time, *indata* is redefined in line 27. Since *indata* has already been defined, as well as creating a new **constant** definition (marked (1)), a **many** (marked (2)), copying the live vector of the new definition is also created, as the new definition does not apply to all processes. Definition (2) is now the current definition stored in the hashtable. Were *indata* to be evaluated at this point, processes with a rank of less than 5 would take the right branch (to the newer definition) and evaluate *indata* as 0, whereas all others would use the previous definition.

Upon returning to the parent function, *indata* is redefined again (line 13). This time as its previous definition plus the rank of the process. Since the components are not both of type **constant**, an **expression** is created (marked (4)). This **expression** will combine the evaluation of the child **many** (marked (2)) with the rank for *MPI_COMM_WORLD* for the particular process (an **SPMD** marked (3)). Again because this variable has been defined before, a **many** (marked (5)) is created, linking the old and new definitions. Note that we do not need to copy the old definition, merely including it in the new definition with appropriate pointers is sufficient. Note also that this new definition is subject to a condition, the details of which are also associated with both the **expression** and the **many**. The association of conditional information allows for differentiation between multiple definitions where the live vector is the same, i.e., the difference is intraprocedural. Finally, the program descends again into *communicate*, creating another definition (marked (6)) and **many** (marked (7)).

3.4 Special Cases

There are a few special cases that merit further explanation:

Arrays - Viewing elements as individual variables, there is a complication where the index of an array lookup or definition is process sensitive. Operating on the assumption that only a small fraction of elements will actually be required, efficiency demands avoiding process sensitive evaluation unless necessary. Therefore, an array is given a single entry in the hash table (type **array**), that maintains a storage order vector of definitions to that array. A lookup with an index that is process sensitive returns an **array** with a pointer to this vector, its length at the time of lookup, and the unevaluated index. Evaluating an element then requires evaluating the index and progressing back through the vector from the length at time of lookup, comparing (and potentially evaluating) indices until a match is found. If the matched node doesn't evaluate for this process, then taking a best effort approach, the process continues. This ensures that the latest usable definition is found first and elides the issue of definitions applying to different elements for different processes.

Loops - Again we take a best effort approach, assuming that every loop executes at least once, unless previous forward jumps prove this assumption false. At the end of analyzing a basic block, the successor edges are checked and if one is a back edge (i.e., the block is a loop latch or unconditional loop), then the relevant conditions are resolved without respect to a specific process. This determines whether the conditions have been met or whether we should loop. This means that when an iterator cannot be resolved as the same for all processes, the contents of the loop will have been seen to execute once, with further iterations left unknown. These loops are marked so that calls inside them are known to be subject to a multiplier. For more complex loops with additional exits, these are marked during an initial scan and evaluated as they are reached.

The choice to only resolve loops with a process insensitive number of iterations does potentially limit the power of the analysis. However, it is in keeping with our decision to analyze serially. Parallelizing for the analysis of basic blocks and functions inside a loop would complicate the analysis to the point where it would be equivalent to analyzing the program for each process individually. As we see in Sect. 4, this decision does not have a negative impact on our results with the programs tested.

Parameters - Both pass-by-value and pass-by-reference parameters are handled. In the case of pass-by-value, a copy of the relevant definition is created to prevent modifications affecting the existing definition.

3.5 Overall Algorithm

Combining the elements described, we produce an algorithm for the analysis of MPI programs, presented as Listing 1.1. The only specialization of this framework required to create an analysis of point-to-point communication, is the generation of graph edges based on the evaluation of *MPI_Send* statements. This is achieved by evaluating the *MPI_Send*, in the same manner as other functions, to determine for which processes graph edges need to be generated. Then for each of these processes, the relevant parameters (**send count, datatype**, and **destination**), are subjected to process sensitive evaluation.

```
1   global_defs = ∅
2
3   walker (function, live_vector, param_defs) {
4     local_defs = ∅
5     for basic block in function
6       for statement in basic block
7         if is_assignment (statement)
8           [ record to global_defs or local_defs as appropriate
9         else if is_call (statement)
10          child_live_vector = live_vector
11          for live_process in live_vector
12            [ evaluate relevant conditions to this call, in the context of each process, marking false in the
13            [ child_live_vector if the process won't make the call or the conditions are unresolvable
14          if is_mpi (call)
15            [ evaluate as appropriate
16          else if has_visible_body (call)
17            [ Generate parameter definitions based on the variables passed to the child function
18            walker (call, child_live_vector, child_param_defs)
19        [ If loop back block or additional exit, analyze conditions and adjust current basic block as
20          appropriate
21  }
```

Listing 1.1. Algorithm for process and context sensitive traversal

3.6 Scalability

Scaling the number of processes results in a worst case $O(n)$ growth in the number of evaluations. This is due to the worst case being where all evaluations are process sensitive, with the number of evaluations increasing in line with the number of processes. A caveat to this is if the length of the execution path changes with the number of processes. Specifically, if the length of the execution path is broadly determined by the number of processes then the scalability would be program specific and unquantifiable in a general sense. However, in such a situation one would often expect to see better scalability than the stated worst case, as a fixed problem size is divided between more processes, reducing the length of the execution path.

To improve upon the worst case, process sensitive and insensitive evaluation results are stored for each node. This includes all nodes evaluated in the process of evaluating the requested node. These results are then attached to the relevant nodes. This means that reevaluation simply returns the stored result. While storage of these results requires additional memory, it prevents reevaluation of potentially deep and complex trees. Since we find only a fraction of nodes need evaluating, this does not pose a great memory issue. As we will show in Sect. 4.4, we achieve far better than the worst case for all the benchmarks.

3.7   Limitations

There are a few limitations to the technique, some are fundamental to the static analysis of MPI, others particular to our design.

Pointers - The use of pointers in a statically unprovable way, with particular reference to function pointers, can lead the analysis to miss certain definitions. Again we prioritize coverage over soundness, neglecting the potential impact of statically unresolved pointer usage.

Recursive Functions - We take no account of recursive functions, which could lead to non-termination of the algorithm. Subject to the previous caveat, recursiveness can be determined by an analysis of the call graph or as the algorithm runs. The simple solution would be to not pursue placement if recursion is detected, but it is perhaps possible to allow some limited forms.

Incomplete Communication Graphs - If the complete communication graph cannot be resolved, it could produce performance degradation if placement or other optimizations are pursued. However, as we see in Sect. 4.2, certain forms of incompleteness can be successfully overcome. Automatically dealing with incompleteness in the general case remains an open problem.

4   Results

The primary goal of our experiments is to evaluate the efficacy of our framework in understanding communication in MPI programs. To this end, we evaluate our coverage – in terms of the percentage of sends we are able to fully understand. Next we investigate the improvements in communication localization that are available from better process placement, guided by our analysis. This is followed by an evaluation of the performance improvements available from improved process placement. Finally, we explore the scalability of the technique.

We implemented our framework in GCC 4.7.0 [1], to leverage the new interprocedural analysis framework, particularly Link Time Optimization. Experiments were performed using the 64 process versions of the NAS Parallel Benchmarks 3.3 [4], compiling for the *Class A* problem size. We tested all NAS programs that use point-to-point communication (BT, CG, IS, LU, MG and SP).

Spatial scheduling is considered as a graph partitioning problem. To this end we applied the k-way variant of the Kernighan-Lin algorithm [17]. It aims to assign vertices (processes) to buckets (CMPs) as to minimize the total weight of non-local edges. As the algorithm is hill-climbing, it is applied to 1,000 random starting positions, and the naive schedules, to avoid local maxima.

Table 1. Coverage results and comparison with profiling for NAS Class A problems using 64 MPI processes

	Profiling		Analysis	
	No. Call Sites	No. Bytes	No. Call Sites Correct	No. Bytes
BT	12	8906903040	12	$58007040 + n(44244480)$
CG	10	1492271104	10	1492271104
IS	1	252	1	252
LU	12	3411115904	12	$41035904 + n(13480320)$
MG	12	315818496	12[a]	$104700416 + n(52779520)$[a]
SP	12	13819352064	12	$48190464 + n(34427904)$

[a] Requires partial input specification, see Sect. 4.1.

4.1   Coverage Results

We quantify coverage by two metrics: the number of *MPI_(I)Send* call sites that we can *correctly* understand, and the the total *number of bytes* communicated. An *MPI_(I)Send* is said to be understood correctly if we can identify the calling process, the destination process, and the volume of data communicated *in all the circumstances under which the call is encountered* – as seen in Fig. 1, the same call site can be encountered in multiple contexts. In addition to this, each of the sends can repeat an arbitrary number of times, necessitating that the analysis resolves relevant loop iterators. To quantify this, we measure the total number of bytes communicated.

The coverage our analysis provides is shown in Table 1, with profiling results for comparison. With the exception of MG, each *MPI_(I)Send* call site is being automatically and correctly evaluated in all contexts for all processes. This means that our analysis is correctly identifying the calling processes, the destination and the volume of data for every *MPI_(I)Send*.

In CG and IS the number of bytes communicated also matches the profile run. For these programs, the relevant loops could be statically resolved by our framework. However, in BT, LU, MG and SP an unknown multiplier n exists. This occurs when the iteration count of a loop containing send calls cannot be statically determined; in the case of the four benchmarks affected, the iteration count is input dependent. As will be seen in the following section, this has no impact on the schedule, and hence the communication localization.

In contrast, simple analysis of MG fails to determine the point-to-point communication graph. Our analysis correctly determines the sending processes (**source**) and the **datatype**, for each call site. However, the **destination**, **send count**, and number of iterations are input dependent. In the case of MG, the **destination** and **send count** depend on four input variables (nx, ny, nz, and lt). If these variables, which determine the problem scale, are specified, then our analysis is able to correctly evaluate each call site. With programs such as MG where the input is partially specified, one could specify the whole input (including the number of iterations), but this is not necessary.

The case of MG highlights the issue of input dependency and how it can blunt the blind application of static analysis. For programs where the communication pattern is input dependent, analyses of the form proposed in this work will never be able to successfully operate in an automatic manner. However, by supplying input characteristics (as would be required for profiling), it is possible to determine the same communication graph that profiling tools such as mpiP observe. Crucially, unlike profiling, this is without requiring execution of the program. For the following sections, we will assume that the four required input variables have been specified for MG, with results as shown in Table 1.

4.2 Communication Localization

In this section, we evaluate the communication localized by applying the partitioning algorithm to the communication graph generated by our analysis. We compare our localization with four other policies. *Round-robin* and *by-rank*, the two default scheduling policies; *random* which shows the arithmetic mean of 10,000 random partitionings; and *profiling* in which the same partitioning algorithm is applied to the communication graph generated by profiling.

As described in the previous section, four of the programs (BT, LU, MG and SP) have an unknown multiplier in the approximation extracted by analysis. To see the impact of this, communication graphs for each of these benchmarks were generated using values of n from 0 to 1,000. Partitioning these graphs yielded the same (benchmark specific) spatial schedules for all non-negative values of n. Therefore we can say that the optimal spatial schedules for these programs are insensitive to n (the only difference in coverage between profiling and analysis).

Figure 3 shows partitioning results for the NAS benchmarks on 8-core and 12-core per node machines. One can see from these results that of the naive partitioning options *by-rank* is the most consistently effective at localizing communication, better than *round-robin* as has previously been used as a baseline [7]. In fact we see that *random* is more effective than *round-robin* for these programs. Confirming our coverage results from the previous section, and our assertion of the null impact of the unknown multipliers, we see that our *analysis* localization results match the *profiling* localization results for each of the programs tested, as the same schedules are generated.

At 8-core per node we see improvement in 4 out of the 6 benchmarks. On average[1] we see 28 % improvement over *by-rank*. We also see that *round-robin* performs equivalently to *by-rank* in 3 cases (BT, LU and SP), in the others it performs worse. For 12-core per node systems we see improvement in 5 out of the 6 benchmarks. On average we see 7 % improvement over *by-rank*. Again *round-robin* significantly underperforms other strategies. In fact in 4 cases it fails to localize any communication.

As Fig. 3 shows, it is not always possible to improve upon the best naive scheduling (*by-rank*). This occurs when the program is written with this scheduling in mind and the underlying parallel algorithm being implemented is conducive to it.

---

[1] Geometric mean is used for all normalized results.

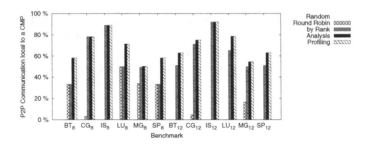

Fig. 3. Percentage of point-to-point communication localized to a CMP

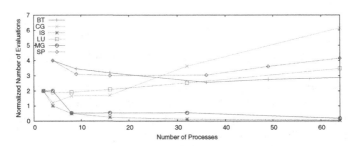

Fig. 4. Normalized total number of evaluations at each usable number of processes. BT and SP are normalized to 4 processes as they only support square numbers

However as the results show, analysis of the communication graph and intelligent scheduling can increase the localization of communication.

4.3 Performance Results

While our main focus is on developing an accurate static analysis that matches the results of profiling, we performed a number of experiments to confirm the impact of improved spatial scheduling observed by others [7]. We used a gigabit ethernet linked shared use cluster which has both 8-core and 12-core nodes available. We found that the impact of improved spatial scheduling was greater on the 12-core nodes. In this configuration, the best result was with CG, where the improved spatial scheduling resulted in 18 % (8 %) execution time reduction over *round-robin* (*by-rank*). On average, across all benchmarks, the improved schedule resulted in 5 % (2 %) execution time reduction over *round-robin* (*by-rank*).

4.4 Scalability Results

To confirm our assertions in Sect. 3.6, we compiled the benchmarks for different numbers of processes. Figure 4 presents the results by comparing the total number of nodes of the data structure evaluated during each compilation. Note that a reevaluation returning a stored result still adds 1 to total count.

As Fig. 4 shows, we achieve notably better than the $O(n)$ worst case. This demonstrates the effectiveness of the optimizations described in Sect. 3.6. With particular reference to IS and MG, we can also see the impact of the reduction in work per process, manifesting as a reduction in the number of evaluations, as the process specific program simplifies. Overall the scalability results are positive for all programs, with significant improvement over the worst case.

5 Conclusions

In this work we proposed a novel framework for the interprocedural, fully context and flow sensitive, best-effort analysis of MPI programs. This framework leverages a new data structure for maintaining partially evaluated, context sensitive variable representations for on-demand process sensitive evaluation. We instantiated this framework to provide a static method for determining optimal process placement for MPI programs running on CMP-based clusters.

Our analysis is able to resolve and understand 100 % of the relevant MPI call sites across the benchmarks considered. In all but one case, this only requires specifying the number of processes. Using the 64 process versions of the benchmarks we see an average of 28 % (7 %) improvement in communication localization over *by-rank* scheduling for 8-core (12-core) CMP-based clusters, which represents the maximum possible improvement.

Acknowledgements. We thank Rajiv Gupta, Michael O'Boyle and the anonymous reviewers for their helpful comments for improving the paper. This research is supported by EPSRC grant EP/L000725/1 and an Intel early career faculty award to the University of Edinburgh.

References

1. GCC: GNU compiler collection. http://gcc.gnu.org
2. Agarwal, T., Sharma, A., Laxmikant, A., Kalé, L.V.: Topology-aware task mapping for reducing communication contention on large parallel machines. In: IPDPS (2006)
3. Aho, A.V., Lam, M.S., Sethi, R., Ullman, J.D.: Compilers: Principles, Techniques, and Tools, 2nd edn, pp. 906–908. Addison-Wesley Longman Publishing Co., Inc, Boston (2006)
4. Bailey, D.H., Barszcz, E., Barton, J.T., Browning, D.S., Carter, R.L., Dagum, L., Fatoohi, R.A., Frederickson, P.O., Lasinski, T.A., Schreiber, R., Simon, H.D., Venkatakrishnan, V., Weeratunga, S.: The NAS parallel benchmarks. IJHPCA 5(3), 63–73 (1991). doi:10.1177/109434209100500306
5. Bronevetsky, G.: Communication-sensitive static dataflow for parallel message passing applications. In: CGO, pp. 1–12 (2009)
6. Cappello, F., Guermouche, A., Snir, M.: On communication determinism in parallel HPC applications. In: ICCCN, pp. 1–8 (2010)
7. Chen, H., Chen, W., Huang, J., Robert, B., Kuhn, H.: MPIPP: an automatic profile-guided parallel process placement toolset for SMP clusters and multiclusters. In: ICS, pp. 353–360 (2006)

8. Danalis, A., Pollock, L.L., Swany, D.M., Cavazos, J.: MPI-aware compiler optimizations for improving communication-computation overlap. In: ICS, pp. 316–325 (2009)
9. Duesterwald, E., Gupta, R., Soffa, M.L.: Demand-driven computation of interprocedural data flow. In: POPL, pp. 37–48 (1995)
10. Gabriel, E., et al.: Open MPI: goals, concept, and design of a next generation MPI implementation. In: Dongarra, J., Kacsuk, P., Kranzlmüller, D. (eds.) EuroPVM/MPI 2004. LNCS, vol. 3241, pp. 97–104. Springer, Heidelberg (2004)
11. Faraj, A., Yuan, X.,: Communication characteristics in the NAS parallel benchmarks. In: IASTED PDCS, pp. 724–729 (2002)
12. Grove, D., Torczon, L.: Interprocedural constant propagation: a study of jump function implementations. In: PLDI, pp. 90–99 (1993)
13. Gupta, R., Soffa, M.L.: A framework for partial data flow analysis. In: ICSM, pp. 4–13 (1994)
14. Hall, M.W., Mellor-Crummey, J.M., Carle, A., Rodríguez, R.G.: FIAT: a framework for interprocedural analysis and transformation. In: Banerjee, U., Gelernter, D., Nicolau, Alexandru, Padua, David A. (eds.) LCPC 1993. LNCS, vol. 768, pp. 522–545. Springer, Heidelberg (1994)
15. Huang, C., Lawlor, O.S., Kalé, L.V.: Adaptive MPI. In: Rauchwerger, Lawrence (ed.) LCPC 2003. LNCS, vol. 2958, pp. 306–322. Springer, Heidelberg (2004)
16. Huang, C., Zheng, G., Kalé, L.V., Kumar, S.: Performance evaluation of adaptive MPI. In: PPOPP, pp. 12–21 (2006)
17. Kernighan, B.W., Lin, S.: An efficient heuristic procedure for partitioning graphs. Bell Syst. Tech. J. **49**(1), 291–307 (1970)
18. Kreaseck, B., Strout, M.M., Hovland, P.: Depth analysis of MPI programs. In: AMP (2010)
19. Mercier, G., Jeannot, E.: Improving MPI applications performance on multicore clusters with rank reordering. In: Cotronis, Y., Danalis, A., Dongarra, J., Nikolopoulos, D.S. (eds.) EuroMPI 2011. LNCS, vol. 6960, pp. 39–49. Springer, Heidelberg (2011)
20. Mohr, B., Wolf, F.: KOJAK – a tool set for automatic performance analysis of parallel programs. In: Böszörményi, L., Hellwagner, H., Kosch, H. (eds.) Euro-Par 2003. LNCS, vol. 2790, pp. 1301–1304. Springer, Heidelberg (2003)
21. Nagel, W.E., Arnold, A., Weber, M., Hoppe, H.-C., Solchenbach, K.: VAMPIR: visualization and analysis of MPI resources. Supercomputer **12**, 69–80 (1996)
22. Preissl, R., Schulz, M., Kranzlmüller, D., de Supinski, B.R., Quinlan, D.J.: Using MPI communication patterns to guide source code transformations. In: Bubak, M., van Albada, G.D., Dongarra, J., Sloot, P.M.A. (eds.) ICCS 2008, Part III. LNCS, vol. 5103, pp. 253–260. Springer, Heidelberg (2008)
23. Sameer, S.S., Malony, A.D.: The TAU parallel performance system. Int. J. High Perform. Comput. Appl. **20**(2), 287–311 (2006)
24. Shires, D.R., Pollock, L.L., Sprenkle, S.: Program flow graph construction for static analysis of MPI programs. In: PDPTA, pp. 1847–1853 (1999)
25. Strout, M.M., Kreaseck, B., Hovland, P.D.: Data-flow analysis for MPI programs. In: ICPP, pp. 175–184 (2006)
26. Vetter, J.S., McCracken, M.O.: Statistical scalability analysis of communication operations in distributed applications. In: PPOPP, pp. 123–132 (2001)
27. Xue, R., Liu, X., Wu, M., Guo, Z., Chen, W., Zheng, W., Zhang, Z., Voelker, G.M.: MPIWiz: subgroup reproducible replay of MPI applications. In: PPOPP, pp. 251–260 (2009)

28. Zhai, J., Sheng, T., He, J., Chen, W., Zheng, W.: FACT: fast communication trace collection for parallel applications through program slicing. In: SC (2009)
29. Zhang, J., Zhai, J., Chen, W., Zheng, W.: Process mapping for MPI collective communications. In: Sips, H., Epema, D., Lin, H. (eds.) Euro-Par 2009. LNCS, vol. 5704, pp. 81–92. Springer, Heidelberg (2009)

Automatic Parallelism Through Macro Dataflow in MATLAB

Pushkar Ratnalikar$^{(\boxtimes)}$ and Arun Chauhan

Indiana University, Bloomington, IN 47405, USA
{pratnali,achauhan}@cs.indiana.edu

Abstract. Dataflow computation model is a powerful paradigm that exploits the inherent parallelism in a program. It is especially relevant on modern machines that offer multiple avenues for parallelizing code. However, adopting this model has been challenging as neither hardware- nor language-based approaches have had much success in the past outside specialized contexts. We argue that macro dataflow, where each dataflow operation is computationally non-trivial, can be implemented effectively on contemporary general-purpose hardware with the help of a runtime system employing a modern task-oriented library, such as Intel Threading Building Blocks (TBB). In order to make this approach attractive to community of scientific programmers, a strategy that enables programs written in popular programming languages to execute as dataflow computations is required.

We present a fully automatic compilation technique to translate MATLAB programs to *dynamic* dataflow graphs that are capable of handling unbounded structured control flow. These graphs are executed on multicore machines in an event driven fashion with the help of a runtime system built on top of Intel TBB. Array statements in MATLAB naturally lead to coarse-grained tasks that are translated to C++ code and executed in task-parallel fashion using TBB. By letting each task itself be data parallel, we are able to leverage existing data parallel libraries and utilize parallelism at multiple levels. We use type inference to aid in the creation of *macro* tasks with sufficient granularity. Our experiments on a set of benchmarks show speedups of up to 18x using our approach, over the original code on a machine with two 16-core processors.

1 Introduction

Dataflow computing presents a compelling model for exploiting parallelism at multiple levels afforded by modern computers [1]. Unfortunately, specialized dataflow programming languages have not gained much popularity. On the other hand, MATLAB provides a natural syntax for writing matrix and vector operations that correspond closely to the mathematical formulations that often underlie the algorithms encoded in these languages thus, providing an attractive syntax for scientific computing. Array syntax in MATLAB exposes fine-grained data

---

A. Chauhan—Currently with Google Inc.

© Springer International Publishing Switzerland 2015
J. Brodman and P. Tu (Eds.): LCPC 2014, LNCS 8967, pp. 284–299, 2015.
DOI: 10.1007/978-3-319-17473-0_19

parallelism in the program, which is exploited in MATLAB's multi-threaded libraries. While being easy to use, this library-based approach is restricted to data parallelism that may not be efficient for many array operations or may not be worthwhile for smaller arrays. MATLAB's Parallel Computing Toolbox does provide a limited form of task-parallelism, but fails to fully leverage the available parallelism across statements [2].

Broadening parallelism within MATLAB-like imperative languages that operate in the realm of Von Neumann model involves imposing a minimal (partial) ordering constraint determined by *data* and *control* dependencies on program execution. The challenge is to implement this efficiently on contemporary mainstream hardware, without requiring any special effort from the programmers. This translates to two main problems:

(1) Partitioning the program into *macro* operations, or tasks, that maximize parallelism while minimizing the overhead per task; and
(2) Scheduling the tasks so that all the control- and data-dependencies in the original program are satisfied.

This paper explores a strategy involving compiler algorithms, aided by a task-oriented runtime system, to bring dataflow execution to MATLAB. We present a heuristic solution to the first problem, where using the type inference engine we identify array statements and create a task using each one of them. Scalar statements are folded into these tasks to satisfy data dependencies. This ensures that each task is coarse (hence *macro*) and does not consist of only simple scalar computations. The second problem is addressed by carefully orchestrating the execution of these tasks, which dynamically spawn new tasks as needed, to ensure adherence to data and control dependencies in the original program. This lets us handle loops with unbounded iteration count (while-loops).

We have prototyped our strategy in a MATLAB compiler to automatically translate MATLAB to task-parallel C++ code that uses a runtime system built on top of Intel Threading Building Blocks (TBB) [3] for dataflow-style execution and Armadillo [4], a data-parallel linear algebra library. Armadillo C++ has a syntax very similar to MATLAB and provides C++ implementation for a large number of MATLAB functions. Unlike the MATLAB libraries, Armadillo is reentrant and thread-safe, which lets us make concurrent calls to the library from multiple tasks.

The main contributions of the paper include:

(1) A compiler strategy to automatically build independent tasks for a MATLAB program such that their execution respects the *data* and *control* dependencies, without introducing additional control tasks;
(2) Design and implementation of a runtime system that leverages Intel TBB for efficient dataflow-style execution of MATLAB code translated by our compiler; and
(3) Performance evaluation of our implementation on benchmarks from a variety of domains, comparing to the highly optimized data-parallel MATLAB libraries.

2   Approach

The compiler and runtime system cooperate to manage the creation, execution and destruction of tasks such that the control and data-dependencies of the MATLAB programs are honored. In this section, we discuss the design of each major component.

2.1   Control Flow and Control Dependencies

Even though the analysis of MATLAB code is simplified due to the absence of aliasing and pointers, the interplay of data and control dependencies complicate the problem of translating for dataflow-style execution. In the past, approaches such as PDW [5] and gated SSA [6], have been proposed to handle data flow through control constructs, which introduce extra synchronization and additional tasks to route the data correctly. We have designed a translation scheme that avoids these costs. It involves solving two main problems:

(1) Handling loops with unknown iteration counts (i.e., while-loops).
(2) Handing data dependencies crossing iteration boundaries, including loop-carried dependencies and dependencies flowing into or out of loop bodies.

Figure 1 shows a hypothetical example with a while-loop. Boxes represent tasks. The graph in the middle is the standard data dependence graph. On the right hand side is the equivalent static dataflow graph showing the flow of data between the static representations of the tasks. Brown colored edges indicate flows that cross the loop boundary and are conditional, based upon the labeled expressions. Two additional tasks have been added, which are described later. There are three cases of data flow that can occur with loops:

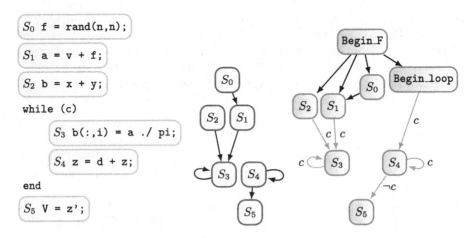

Fig. 1. A hypothetical example (left), its data dependence graph (middle), and static dataflow (right) graph in which some of the edges (labeled) are conditional.

(1) Data flowing from outside the loop into the loop body. In Fig. 1 dependencies from S_1 to S_3 is an example of such data flow. We consider partial array updates as a *use* as well as a *def*. Hence, the dependency S_2 to S_3 on account of b is also such a case.

(2) Data flowing from within the loop to a statement outside the loop. This always flows from the last iteration of the loop. The dependency from S_4 to S_5 is always caused by the last instance of S_4 that produces the data.

(3) Data flowing from an iteration to subsequent iteration to the same or another statement, caused by loop-carried dependencies. Data flow from S_4 to S_4 is an example of that.

The dependencies can be arbitrarily complex with varying dependence distances, or even unknown dependence distances. Similarly, it may not be known a priori which statement instance produces the final data element that is consumed by a task outside the loop. We use two key techniques to handle loops:

(1) We use the *loop iteration vector* to *version* each task. Every time a new instance of S_3 or S_4 is created it gets a new iteration vector, uniquely identifying it at run-time. Indexing using iteration vectors clearly separates loop-independent dependencies from loop-carried dependencies.

(2) We assume that each loop-carried dependency has dependence distance of one. Thus, if a dependency is carried by a loop, it is assumed to cause a dataflow from the source task to the target task in the next iteration of the surrounding loop nest. While conservative, this assumption never results in incorrect code.

It is important to note that iteration vectors associated with tasks are computed at run-time. As a result, we do not need to know loop bounds statically (even symbolically). Dependencies entering the loop body from outside the loop (S_1 to S_3 in the example) are always to the first version of the tasks inside the loop. For loop-carried dependencies, we assume that the data generated by an instance of source (S_4) are always consumed by the next higher version of the sink (S_4). This is equivalent to assuming a data dependence distance of one for all loop-carried dependencies. Notice that this assumption does not affect the correctness of the program, although it may create some additional constraints on parallelism in some cases. In general, dependencies crossing loop boundaries need to be predicated on loop termination or loop continuation conditions, as shown in Fig. 1 and discussed in Sect. 3.1.

New tasks are dynamically created by the tasks that generate data for them. In our example, the first instance of S_3 is created by S_1. Subsequent versions of S_3 are created by the prior versions. If multiple tasks generate inputs for a task then the first task generating an input creates the task, and the subsequent tasks simply add to the new task's inputs. As soon as all the inputs to a task are ready it is scheduled for execution.

An interesting scenario arises when there are no loop-carried dependencies in a loop. In this case, all versions of the tasks within a loop body could run concurrently. Thus, they should all be created as early as possible. Suppose that the dependency from S_4 to S_4 did not exist in Fig. 1. Since there would be no incoming dependency for S_4, no task would be responsible for creating the first version of S_4. To get around this issue we create a special task, Begin_loop, that is responsible for creating the version of any task within the loop body that has no incoming dependency. In order to create subsequent revisions we allow a task within a loop to create the next revision of itself, as soon as it can.

Finally, the task labeled Begin_F is the task that kick-starts the computation within a function and passes on the input arguments. In this example we are assuming that the free variables in the statements are input arguments.

2.2   Automatic Task Generation

Algorithm 1 outlines the overall algorithm for generating task-parallel code for a MATLAB function. The algorithm assumes that an earlier pass has identified and abstracted (lambda-converted) a computationally intensive portion of the original function. The abstracted function is passed to the algorithm as F.

---

1 **Algorithm:** GenerateTasks

2 **Input**: Function, F

3 **Output**: TBB code equivalent to F

4 $F \leftarrow$ Convert-for-to-while(F) ;

5 $F \leftarrow$ Convert-to-SSA(F) ;

6 $I \leftarrow$ Infer-types(F) ;

7 $D_F \leftarrow$ Compute-data-dependence-graph(F, I) ;

8 $T \leftarrow$ Identify-tasks(F, I, D_F) ;

9 $D_T \leftarrow$ Compute-reduced-dependence-graph(D_F, T) ;

10 **for** *each task type, t, in T* **do**

11 $\quad \lfloor$ Generate-computation-task-class(task-t, p, T, D_T);

12 Generate-begin-task-class(task-begin-F, T, D_T) ;

13 **for** *each loop, L, in F that is not within a task in T* **do**

14 $\quad \lfloor$ Generate-begin-loop-task-class(task-begin-loop-L, T, L, D_T);

15 $\quad \lfloor$ Generate-end-loop-task-class(task-end-loop-L, T, L, D_T);

16 Generate-wrapper(F, task-begin-F, T) ;

Algorithm 1. Generating TBB tasks from a given MATLAB program.

Steps 4 and 5 canonicalize the input by changing all for-loops to while-loops and converting it into the SSA form. The first step is not as drastic as it seems, because our target language is C++, which really only has while-loops[1]. Step 6 performs type inference based on the strategy of making type inference code explicit and partially evaluating it [7,8].

---

[1] The for-loop in C/C++ (excluding C++11) is not a true for-loop, just a convenient form of while. In contrast, MATLAB supports Fortran-style true for-loops.

Step 8, uses the type information to identify candidate array statements to be treated as individual tasks. This could be configured based on a threshold array size and the specific operation. All the scalar computations required by that task are replicated to satisfy the data dependencies. Step 9 creates the reduced data-dependence graph, D_T, between tasks by merging statement nodes of D_F belonging to one task. The reduced graph is used to create task dependencies in the subsequent steps. The bulk of task-creation work happens in the loop at line number 10. The task identification step creates the static description of each type of task. One or more statements of the original function, F, might be combined into one task. Note that this is a static description because if those statements happen to be inside a loop, multiple instances of those tasks will need to be created to complete the execution. The step at line 12 and the loop at line 13 generate classes for tasks that are needed to account for certain dependencies and to kick-start loops, as explained below. Finally a wrapper function to initialize the task queue is generated at line number 16.

Figure 2 shows the high-level overview of the translation. The code in Fig. 2(a) is decomposed into four tasks as shown in (b) and the final generated C++ code for Task 3 is shown in (c). It is important to note that the code for Tasks in (b) is in SSA form and C++ code is generated directly from the SSA form. In (c), DoubleMat is the array data type defined in our runtime system. It is a wrapper over the Armadillo mat type and amongst other things has support for *reference count* based garbage collection. Lines 4—5 initialize the local matrix object with

Task 1

```
k$1  = 500;
H$1=zeros(k$1,k$1);
j$1  = 2;
tmp4$1=j$1<=k$1;
```

```
n = length(v);
k = 500;
H = zeros(k,k);
V = zeros(n,k);
...

...
j = 2;
tmp4  = j <= k;
while(tmp4),
    ...

    V(:,j) = v;
    H(1:j,j) = h;
    j = j + 1;
    tmp4 = j <= k;
end
```

a) Example code

Task 2

```
n$1 = length(v$0);
k$1  = 500;
V$1  = zeros(n$1,k$1);
j$1  = 2;
tmp4$1=j$1<=k$1;
```

Task 3

```
V$1(:,j$2) = v$1;
j$3  = j$2+1;
tmp4$3=j$3<=k$1;
```

Task 4

```
H$1(1:j$2,j$2)=h$1;
j$3  = j$2+1;
tmp4$3=j$3<=k$1;
```

b) Breakup into Tasks

```
 1 task* CT6::execute(){
 2  i_vec tv;
 3  task_map.erase(task_id);
 4  DoubleMat v$1(v$1_data);
 5  DoubleMat V$1(V$1_data);
 6  V$1()(span(),j$2-1) = v$1();
 7  j$3 = j$2 + 1;
 8  tmp4$3 = j$3 <= k$1;
 9  if(tmp4$3){
10    tv = {0,0,0,j$3};
11    t1 = GetTask<CT6>(6,tv);
12    t1->Add_V$1(V$1);
13    t1->Add_j$2(j$3);
14    t1->Add_k$1(k$1);
15  }
16  root_dec_ref_count();
17  return NULL;
18 }
```

c) Generated Code

Fig. 2. High-Level overview of translation.

the reference of inputs. Line 6 does the core computation. Lines 7—15 check the loop condition and accordingly pass data to next iteration task.

2.3 Dataflow Computation with Mutable Arrays

Adherence to *single assignment* semantics of the dataflow model removes all but true dependencies. However, this incurs prohibitively high data-copying costs for array variables. We use a hybrid approach by using mutable arrays. Figure 3 illustrates the trade-offs. In the first case we can get increased parallelism if we created a new copy in the third statement, but at a high copying cost. In the second case, mutability incurs no penalty. In the third case, the trade-off is trickier, since additional dependencies might restrict parallelism across iterations.

```
Fx(:,k) = ...
...
... = Fx(:,k)
...
Fx(:,k) = ...
```
Straight-line code

```
for k = 1: n
  Fx(:,k) = Fx(:,k)*
              G;
  ...
end
```
No loop-carried dependence

```
for k = 1: n
  Fx(:,k)=Fx(:,k-1)*
              G;
  ...
end
```
Loop-carried dependence

Fig. 3. Passing arrays by reference.

2.4 Scalar Computations

Scalar statements, which involve inputs and outputs that are scalars with "simple" scalar computations do not form separate tasks. Instead, we piggyback these statements on array statements that require the results of those computations. Scalar statements in loop bodies, which control iterations, are exceptions as they are replicated unconditionally across all tasks in the loop body. They also help in identifying the target tasks where these outputs can be consumed and the runtime conditions to be satisfied for the data to be passed.

3 Implementation

Our compiler translates MATLAB code to C++. The compiler is implemented in a Ruby-embedded DSL called RubyWrite. GNU octave is used to parse MATLAB source and convert it to an AST. Preliminary transformations like **flattening** are applied to simplify complex expressions in the code, which ultimately benefit subsequent optimization passes. SSA translation is done using standard dominance frontier-based algorithm [9]. Translation to SSA simplifies type inference which is critical for the implementation of our heuristic for task creation. Details of the type inference can be found in [8]. SSA form also helps in the dependency analysis used for implementing dataflow style computation and is described next.

```
2  Fx$1 = zeros(n$0, a$0);
3  drx$1 = zeros(n$0, n$0);
4  x$1 = Fx$1(:, n$0);
5  G$1 = 1e-11;
6  t$1 = 1;
7  tmp1$1 = t$1<=T$0;
8  while(tmp1$2)
10    k$2 = 1;
11    tmp2$2 = k$2 <= n$0;
12    while(tmp2$3)
14      j$3 = 1;
15      tmp3$3 = j$3 <= n$0;
16      while(tmp3$4)
18        Fx$5(:,k$3) = G$1;
19        j$5 = j$4 + 1;
20        tmp3$5 = j$5<=n$0;
      end
21      k$4 = k$3 + 1;
22      tmp2$4 = k$4 <= n$0;
    end
23    tmp4$2 = t$2 == 2;
24    if(tmp4$2);
26      continue;
    end
28    Fx$6(:, t) = G$1 * drx$1;
29    f$1 = Fx$6(:, k$3);
30    t$3 = t$2 + dT$0;
31    tmp1$3 = t$3 <= T$0;
   end
```

Fig. 4. Sample program.   Fig. 5. Control dependence graph(CDG).

```
 1  Algorithm: ComputeDepConditions
 2  Input: CDG G, Source src, Destination dst, CFG cfg
 3  Output: Predicate Expression L
 4  S ← {c_1, ..., c_k, s_1, ...s_k}  /* seq. of all cond. exprs enclosing src   */
 5  D ← {c_1, ..., c_k, d_1, ...d_k}  /* seq. of all cond. exprs enclosing dst   */
 6  L ← ¬(s_1∧, ..., ∧s_k) ∧ (d_1∧, ..., ∧d_k)
 7  for each n in {c_1, ...c_k} do
 8    │  if (c ← ClearPath(src, n, dst, cfg)) then
 9    │  │   L ← L ∧ c
10    │  else
11    │  └   break;
```

Algorithm 2. Compute the predicate expression

3.1   Dependence Analysis

In dataflow style computation, as soon as a node in the dataflow graph finishes computation, its output data has to be passed to the node which consumes that data. It means possibly passing data from one basic block to another bypassing intermediate computation. The consumer node may be embedded in a loop and for the semantics of the program to hold, the *predicates* resulting in control-flow from *producer* node (task) to *consumer* node (task) must be asserted before data is sent. Once the control predicates are computed, statements computing them can be folded in with the producer tasks enabling them to send data only when the predicates are asserted. We use control dependence to compute the predicates. Statement A is *control-dependent* on statement B in a program, iff B controls the execution of A. Control dependence graph ($\mathcal{CDG}$) encodes this information and we use it to determine the predicates. Figure 4 shows a sample program and Fig. 5 shows its $\mathcal{CDG}$. In the program, the statement numbers are non-sequential as our compiler labels statements that way. The *green* nodes in $\mathcal{CDG}$ represent compound statements and the *pink* nodes represent statements that are control-dependent on the *geeen* nodes. Nodes 0 and 32 are the dummy *start* and *end* node generated during conversion to CFG.

Algorithm 2 finds paths $src \rightarrow dst$ such that given the predicates, no reaching definition other than src reaches dst. In Step 4, we get all the conditional expressions controlling src and in Step 5, we get all the conditional expressions controlling dst. Both steps could be achieved by doing DFS on the $\mathcal{CDG}$ starting at the *start* node. In step 6, we compute the initial value of L by negating the expressions *exclusively* controlling src ($s_1, .., s_k$) in the $\mathcal{CDG}$ and enabling the expressions *exclusively* controlling dst in the $\mathcal{CDG}$. For src, it means exiting the loop if s_i represents a loop. If s_i is an If-Else or a switch statement, no action is required. For dst, it means entering the loop if d_i is a loop node and if d_i is an If-Else or a switch statement, using the predicate that would lead to the dst in the CFG. In Step 7, we use the control-expressions that are common to both src and dst and try and find *ClearPath*, for those expressions. The idea is to find a path $src \rightarrow n \rightarrow dst$, such that no other definition lies on the path $src \rightarrow n \rightarrow dst$ that would kill src. *ClearPath* works by performing a depth-first search (DFS) on the CFG starting at node src until n is reached, not following through any node that contains a killing definition. It returns false if n cannot be reached. Next, starting at n it tries to reach dst, returning an expression if dst can be reached and false, otherwise.

3.2   Runtime System

The runtime systems is responsible for task management and garbage collection. Every program has a root task that passes all input arguments to their consumers. In general, a producer task passes data to consumers in two steps:

(1) Check if a consumer task t uniquely identified by $\langle S_{id}, I_{vec} \rangle$, exists in the TaskMap. If not, create a new one and add it to TaskMap.
(2) If task t is found in TaskMap, call the appropriate Add_* method on t to pass the particular variable to task t.

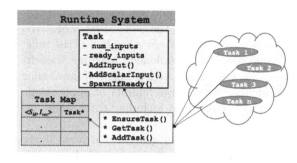

Fig. 6. Runtime system.

Figure 6 shows a high-level overview of the runtime system. All tasks in the system interact with the runtime using the three methods EnsureTask, GetTask and AddTask. Within the Task class, which is an extension of the tbb::task class, some fields are used for bookkeeping. The num_inputs member, is initialized to the number of *rvals* of all the program statements in the task. On task creation, ready_inputs is initialized to 0. For every input added to the task using AddScalarInput or AddInput, it is atomically incremented, a check (ready_inputs == num_inputs) performed and the task spawned if true. As mentioned in Sect. 2.3, we pass non-scalar data as references. For garbage collection reference count is used and the wrapper classes around Armadillo matrix and vector classes help manage the reference count of non-scalar data objects. This is done by incrementing the count when data is passed using AddInput method to the consumer task and decrementing when task execution finishes.

The TaskMap is a TBB concurrent HashMap container. The key is the pair $\langle S_{id}, I_{vec} \rangle$ and the value is task object reference. S_{id} is the static identifier for a task and I_{vec} is the iteration vector which differentiates between task instances with same S_{id}. Thus, $\langle S_{id}, I_{vec} \rangle$ uniquely identifies tasks in the system.

3.3   TBB Code Generation

Once tasks have been identified, each task is translated into a corresponding TBB task class in C++. The class consists of local data members and a setter method for each input to the task. For scalar inputs, the data is received by value. For array and matrix objects, the data is received by reference in the setter method and in addition to the steps for scalar values, the reference count of the data is incremented. The **execute** method consists of core computation part and a set of statements that send the outputs of the computations to the consumer tasks. These include the conditional sends, based on the identification of the target tasks and the associated conditions based on the description in Sect. 3.1. Figure 2(c) shows the example of generated C++ code.

4   Experimental Evaluation

We ran several benchmarks to evaluate our approach. MATLAB version 2013a was used on a dual 16-core AMD Opteron 6380 (2.5 GHz, 64 GB DDR3 memory, 16 MB L3 cache) machine running Cray Linux Environment 4.1.UP01. GCC 4.8.1 was used for compiling generated C++ code. Armadillo C++ library version 4.000 was used along with Intel MKL 11.0 and for consistency, MAT-LAB was configured to use the same version and not the older version of MKL it is shipped with. Results presented for benchmarks are a median of 10 runs, distributed over a wide range of input sizes on an unloaded machine. Benchmarks were specifically selected such that they had a high number of non-scalar statements compared to scalar statements. Of the large number of applications that we studied, we present results for 11 applications including three where we observe slowdown.

Arnoldi is an algorithm to find the eigenvalues of general matrices. NBody 3D an NBody 1D perform a three-dimensional and one-dimensional N-body simulations respectively. HeatedPlate solves the steady state heat equation. Wav1 and WaveCrossCov are DSP kernels which compute the wavelet transform and wavelet cross covariances respectively. ComputeNew is a kernel from the molecular dynamics simulation code and has *irregular* computation. Tasks in it operate on varying number of matrix elements based on runtime conditions. Adi is a method to solve heat diffusion equations using alternating direction implicit (ADI) scheme. BurgPR is the Burg spectral analysis method and part of the CREWES seismology toolbox [10]. QR performs QR factorization of the input matrix. Gaussr does the Gauss elimination on the input matrix.

In Fig. 7 "(Task+Data)-Parallel" indicates the speedup achieved using our strategy of creating tasks out of a single array statement along with the required scalar statements over baseline MATLAB code run in multi-threaded data-parallel mode, for increasing input sizes. In order to isolate the gains from translating to C++, we ran the code with a single task, represented by "Data-Parallel", so that only intra-task data-parallelism is utilized, as in the original MATLAB code.

In 8 out of 11 cases there is a significant performance improvement with our strategy. For Arnoldi, the task-parallel code shows a slowdown compared to its MATLAB version, because the inter-statement dependencies do not allow any concurrent execution of statements and the slowdown is primarily because of task management overhead in the runtime system.

For two other cases, Adi and HeatedPlate, the task-parallel code performs better than the baseline MATLAB implementation but slows down compared to the data-parallel version. The primary reason is that while statements within loop bodies execute in parallel, some dependencies act as barriers and limit task-parallelism across loops.

For Gaussr, we were able to easily change the granularity of tasks in the generated task-parallel version. The resulting code performs far better than the original task-parallel version and only reiterates the findings on the effect of task-granularity on performance [11]. Finally, using MATLAB parfor construct for HeatedPlate (it is the only benchmark that presented us with this opportunity), does not result in improved performance.

To evaluate the concurrency that we actually achieve, we measure the number of concurrently running tasks. We get the snapshot of the running application by using a global counter, which is atomically incremented when a task enters its *execute* method and decremented when the task exits it. This lets us visualize the

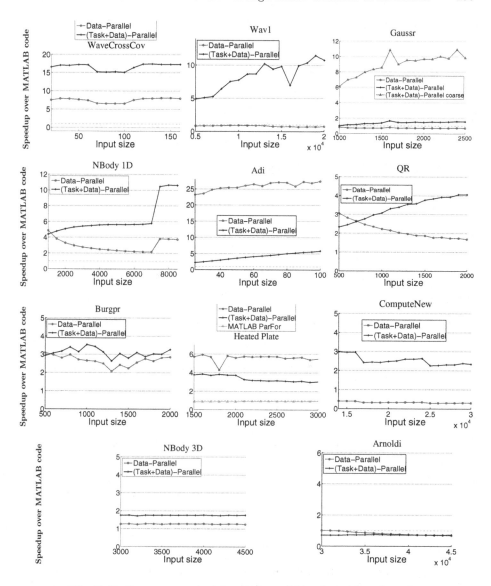

Fig. 7. Performance against input sizes of 11 selected benchmarks.

number of concurrently executing tasks at each logical time-step throughout the lifetime of the application. Figure 8 presents the results. The zoomed-in section underneath plots the numbers for the time-span highlighted by the red rectangle. For Adi, the number of concurrently executing tasks never exceeds 8 which underutilizes the 32-core machine. Moreover, this number falls to 1 frequently. While a similar behavior is seen for NBody 3D, because the program statements in the code operate on 3D-arrays and hence coarser tasks, the resulting greater

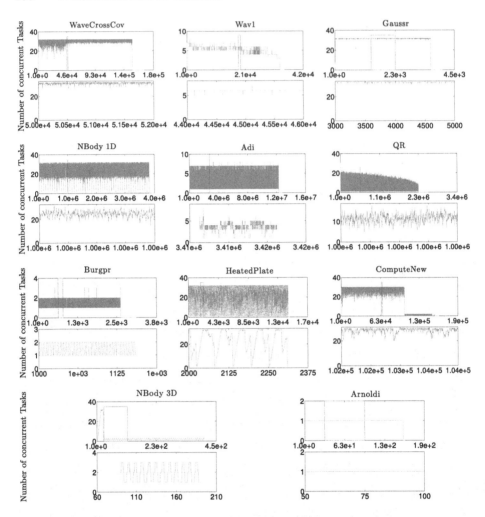

Fig. 8. Concurrently executing tasks.

data-parallelism in each task, compensates for limited task-parallelism and we still see speedup. In Adi and HeatedPlate, tasks are usually operating on single matrix columns at a time, which means limited data-parallelism.

In Fig. 9 we plot the percentage of the total running time of the application that is spent doing the computation within tasks on each core of the machine. For this we time only the computational portion of each task's execute method and store the accumulated times in per-core counters. We call this number *task efficiency*. We see that Gaussr has the highest task efficiency, even though the overall applications speedup is lower compared to WaveCrossCov and Wav1. The reason is that for Gaussr a high level of concurrency is sustained throughout the execution of programs as seen in Fig. 8.

On the other hand, there is some fluctuation in the number of concurrently executing tasks for both `Wave CrossCov` and `Wav1`. For some applications not all cores are used for computation (e.g., `Arnoldi`) and for some there is unequal distribution of work across the

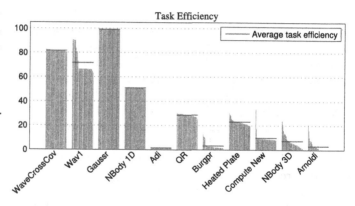

Fig. 9. Percentage time spent in computation.

cores. This is primarily the result of differences in the complexity of computation in each task. Note that task efficiency does not capture the data-parallelism within tasks. This is the reason why `NBody 3D`, which has lower task-efficiency but coarser tasks leveraging data-parallelism, performs better than its data-parallel version as against `HeatedPlate`, which has better task efficiency but inherently fine-grained tasks with poorer data parallelism.

Overall, the results demonstrate that our strategy of creating *macro* tasks where single array statement is grouped with required scalar statements result in good performance improvements for MATLAB code in which vector operations are common. In some cases, performance can be improved by coarsening the task granularity, which is a possible direction to explore for future research.

5   Related Work

Emergence of platforms and libraries, such as, Intel Cilk [12] and Intel TBB [3], has revived the interest in exploiting task-parallelism in algorithms. Leveraging these approaches require programming in C/C++ and no solutions for automatically converting MATLAB code to leverage these libraries have been proposed.

MathWorks's Parallel Computing Toolbox [2] provides parallel programming constructs like `parfor` and an explicit job- and task-control API. There have also been compiler efforts for parallelizing MATLAB. A source-level approach [13] enables conversion of intrinsic MATLAB functions and operators to ScaLAPACK and other routines to exploit available task and data parallelism. The authors convert MATLAB code to a macro dataflow graph and translate some of functions to ScaLAPACK calls. While similar in style, their approach depends primarily on ScaLAPACK for performance. It is also not clear how they handle arbitrary control dependencies. Several library-based efforts also exist for running MATLAB code on clusters, including, Star-P [14], MATLAB*G [15], and pMATLAB [16]. These solutions rely on overloading MATLAB operators to invoke specialized libraries for matrix operations.

Dataflow execution model has been around since the early 1970's. There have been specialized architectures as well as languages for dataflow computation. There have been attempts at compiling imperative languages for dataflow architectures like Monsoon [17] as well as compiling dataflow languages for conventional computers [18]. Use of dataflow graph as an executable intermediate representation and its ability to extract both coarse-grain and fine-grain parallelism has been proposed in the past [17]. The program dependence web [5] is another intermediate representation based on gated-SSA [6] that can be directly interpreted using control-, data-, or demand-driven execution model. The main motivation behind these efforts has been to compile FORTRAN onto dynamic dataflow architecture.

Recently there has been renewed interest in dataflow execution model. The Open Community Runtime (OCR) and ETI SWARM parallel computing framework are such efforts, which are aimed mainly at fine-granularity tasks.

6   Conclusion and Future Work

We have described a fully automatic method of translating MATLAB to utilize the latent task-parallelism within the applications, in addition to the data parallelism that is obvious in the array statements. We have shown that this approach can be implemented with dataflow-style execution using existing task libraries for scheduling *macro* dataflow operations. We have implemented our approach in a MATLAB-to-C++ compiler and demonstrated that a simple heuristic for generating tasks containing a single array statement with required scalar statements is effective and delivers good performance on a variety of benchmarks.

Possible future work includes more sophisticated algorithms to identify tasks; extending the execution model to heterogeneous environments such as GPUs; and studying the impact of locality on task scheduling.

References

1. Johnston, W.M., Hanna, J.R.P., Millar, R.J.: Advances in dataflow programming languages. ACM Comput. Surv. **36**(1), 1–34 (2004)
2. MathWorks Inc.: Parallel Computing Toolbox (2014). http://www.mathworks.com/help/distcomp/index.html
3. Willhalm, T., Popovici, N.: Putting intel® threading building blocks to work. In: Proceedings of the 1st International Workshop on Multicore Software Engineering, IWMSE 2008, pp. 3–4. ACM, New York (2008)
4. Sanderson, C.: Armadillo: an open source C++ linear algebra library for fast prototyping and computationally intensive experiments. Technical report (2010)
5. Ottenstein, K.J., Ballance, R.A., MacCabe, A.B.: The program dependence web: a representation supporting control-, data-, and demand-driven interpretation of imperative languages. SIGPLAN Not. **25**(6), 257–271 (1990)
6. Tu, P., Padua, D.: Gated SSA-based demand-driven symbolic analysis for parallelizing compilers. In: Proceedings of the 9th International Conference on Supercomputing, ICS 1995, pp. 414–423. ACM, New York (1995)

7. Chauhan, A., Kennedy, K.: Slice-hoisting for array-size inference in MATLAB. In: Rauchwerger, L. (ed.) LCPC 2003. LNCS, vol. 2958, pp. 495–508. Springer, Heidelberg (2004)
8. Shei, C.Y., Chauhan, A., Shaw, S.: Compile-time disambiguation of MATLAB types through concrete interpretation with automatic run-time fallback. In: HiPC, pp. 264–273. IEEE (2009)
9. Cytron, R., Ferrante, J., Rosen, B.K., Wegman, M.N., Zadeck, F.K.: Efficiently computing static single assignment form and the control dependence graph. ACM Trans. Program. Lang. Syst. **13**(4), 451–490 (1991)
10. Margrave, D.G.: CREWES. http://www.crewes.org
11. Sterling, T., Keuhn, J., Thistle, M., Anastasio, T.: Studies on optimal task granularity and random mapping. In: Gao, G.R., Bic, L., Gaudiot, J.L. (eds.) Advanced Topics in Dataflow Computing and Multithreading. Wiley-IEEE Computer Society Press, Los Alamitos (1995)
12. Frigo, M., Leiserson, C.E., Randall, K.H.: The implementation of the Cilk-5 multithreaded language. In: Proceedings of the ACM SIGPLAN 1998 Conference on Programming Language Design and Implementation, PLDI 1998, pp. 212–223. ACM, New York (1998)
13. Ramaswamy, S., Hodges IV., E.W., Banerjee, P.: Compiling MATLAB programs to ScaLAPACK: exploiting task and data parallelism. In: Proceedings of the 10th International Parallel Processing Symposium, IPPS 1996, pp. 613–619. IEEE Computer Society, Washington, DC (1996)
14. Choy, R., Edelman, A., Gilbert, J.R., Shah, V., Cheng, D.: Star-P: high productivity parallel computing. In: 8th Annual Workshop on High-Performance Embedded Computing (HPEC 2004) (2004)
15. Teo, Y.-M., Chen, Y., Wang, X.: On grid programming and MATLAB*G. In: Jin, H., Pan, Y., Xiao, N., Sun, J. (eds.) GCC 2004. LNCS, vol. 3251, pp. 761–768. Springer, Heidelberg (2004)
16. Travinin Bliss, N., Kepner, J.: pMatlab parallel MATLAB library. Int. J. High Perform. Comput. Appl. **21**(3), 336–359 (2007)
17. Beck, M., Johnson, R., Pingali, K.: From control flow to dataflow. J. Parallel Distrib. Comput. **12**, 118–129 (1989)
18. Jagannathan, R.: Coarse-grain dataflow programming of conventional parallel computers. In: Gao, G.R., Bic, L., Gaudiot, J.L. (eds.) Advanced Topics in Dataflow Computing and Multithreading. Wiley-IEEE Computer Society Press, Los Alamitos (1995)

Re-Engineering Compiler Transformations to Outperform Database Query Optimizers

Kristian F.D. Rietveld[(✉)] and Harry A.G. Wijshoff

LIACS, Leiden University, Leiden, The Netherlands
{krietvel,harryw}@liacs.nl

Abstract. Traditionally, Query Optimization and Compiler Optimizations have been developed independently. Whereas Query Optimization aims at optimizing database queries to minimize the number of disk operations, Compiler Optimizations target to maximize performance of generic executable codes. While query optimizers were originally designed for systems that needed to process large volumes of data with little main memory, the size of computer main memory has increased significantly. As a result, techniques are now being considered in the database community that have been developed in the field of compiler optimization. In this paper, we demonstrate that the converse is much more lucrative: extend compiler transformations to also target query optimization. By doing so, advanced compiler optimizations are employed as the driving force in query optimization and database systems can be on par with future complex computer architectures.

1 Introduction

The fields of Query Optimization and Compiler Optimizations have been developed by different communities since these form the solutions for two different problems. In Query Optimization, requests for the retrieval of a specific set of data from a database formulated in the form of queries need to be translated to an execution plan. This execution plan consists of the steps that are to be taken to produce the requested data set. These steps are encoded with relational operators, such as selection, projection and join. The goal of Query Optimization is to optimize these execution plans. Because the size of databases were traditionally significantly larger than main memories of computers, the optimization objective is typically to reduce the number of disk I/O operations that need to be carried out. On the other hand the objective of Compiler Optimization is to maximize the performance of generic executable codes. Essentially, the objective is to minimize the execution time of a given program by making best use of the characteristics of the targeted hardware platform. The main characteristic is the size and structure of the cache and memory hierarchy. By properly exploiting this hierarchy significant performance improvements can be attained for loop nests in which the majority of the execution time is spent.

There is no reason why these two fields of optimization should be separate and independent. Furthermore, disruptive changes in computer architectures also

© Springer International Publishing Switzerland 2015
J. Brodman and P. Tu (Eds.): LCPC 2014, LNCS 8967, pp. 300–314, 2015.
DOI: 10.1007/978-3-319-17473-0_20

warrant the separation of these two fields to be reconsidered. These disruptive changes are caused by the fact that computer architectures are starting to diversify more than they are currently doing due to the stagnation of the improvement of single-core performance. Therefore, it comes to no surprise that in the database community techniques are being considered that have been developed in the field of compiler optimizations. Recent research includes translating query execution plans to C++ code, which is subsequently optimized by an optimizing compiler [12] and translating query execution plans to machine code using a strategy that keeps data in CPU registers as long as possible [18]. These developments have been initiated by the fact that the size of computer main memories has increased significantly, resulting in an interest in the exploitation of intrinsic internal features of computer systems in addition to a focus on optimizing disk I/O. For query optimizers to continue to be successful, compiler techniques must be incorporated in order to maximize performance. The question arises: whether query optimization should be taken as a starting point to be improved with compiler optimizations or whether compiler transformations should be extended (re-engineered) to also target query optimization.

In this paper, we demonstrate that by re-engineering existing compiler transformations and by adding a few simple new transformations, optimizing compilers can be made capable of optimizing codes that represent database queries and outperform state-of-the-art database query optimizers. All relational operators are essentially loops over data sets. Our methodology translates a database query to a set of loops, on which these compiler techniques are applied. We show that using these transformations, key implementations of the relational join operator, such as Hash Join, can be derived automatically, resulting in significantly better performance results than state-of-the-art query optimizers.

This paper is organized as follows. Section 2 introduces the *forelem* intermediate representation. Section 3 describes how compiler transformations are re-engineered so that they can be used with *forelem* loops. Section 4 discusses how queries are optimized through the use of existing compiler transformations. Section 5 discusses a strategy for the application of the transformations to optimize queries. Section 6 describes how the *forelem* framework is implemented. Section 7 presents an experimental evaluation using the TPC-H benchmark. Section 8 discusses related work. Section 9 presents our conclusions.

2   The Forelem Intermediate Representation

In this section the basics of the *forelem* intermediate representation are described. The intermediate representation is centered around the *forelem* loop construct. Each *forelem* loop iterates over a specific array of structures. The subscripts of this array that are accessed are fetched from an "index set" that is associated with the array.

The arrays of structures that are iterated by *forelem* loops are modeled after database tables which are defined as multisets. The structure reflects the format of a database tuple. The tuples are stored either row-wise or column-wise. In the latter case, a structure of arrays is iterated. Conversion between these two layouts is a trivial transformation within the *forelem* framework. In an array of structures A a tuple at index i is accessed with A[i] and a specific field *field1* in that tuple is accessed with A[i].field1.

The body of a *forelem* loop often outputs tuples to a temporary or result array. Temporary arrays are generally named $\mathcal{T}_1, \mathcal{T}_2, \ldots, \mathcal{T}_n$ and result sets $\mathcal{R}_1, \mathcal{R}_2, \ldots, \mathcal{R}_n$.

An *index set*[1] is a set containing subscripts i $\in \mathbb{N}$ into an array. Since each array subscript is typically processed once per iteration of the array, these subscripts are stored in a regular set. Index sets are named after the array they refer to, prefixed with "p". For example, pA is the index set of all subscripts into an array A: $\forall s \in$ A : $\exists$i $\in$ pA : A[i] $= s$. Random access of an index set by subscript is not possible, instead all accesses are done using the $\in$ operator. i $\in$ pA stores the current subscript into i and advances pA to the next entry in the index set.

Considering an array A with fields *field1* and *field2*, a *forelem* loop that iterates all entries of A, outputting the value of *field1* of each row, is written as follows:

```
forelem (i; i ∈ pA)
    R = R ∪ (A[i].field1)
```

Although the *forelem* loop appears to be very similar to a *foreach* loop that exists in many common programming languages, *forelem* loops distinguish themselves with the use of the index sets. Every *forelem* loop iterates a single array, using subscripts from an index set that is associated with that array. A *forelem* loop does not have an explicit looping structure and the exact semantics of the iteration of the array are determined in the course of the optimization process. Index sets are the essence of *forelem* loop nests as they encapsulate iteration and simplify the loop control so that aggressive compiler optimizations can be successfully applied.

Using conditions on index sets it is possible to narrow down the range of the array that is iterated. For example, the index set denoted by pA.field2[k] contains only those subscripts into A for which *field2* has value k. This is expressed mathematically as follows:

$$\texttt{pA.field2[k]} \equiv \{\texttt{i} \mid \texttt{i} \in \texttt{pA} \land \texttt{A[i].field2} = \texttt{k}\}$$

So, to only iterate entries of A in which the value of *field2* is 10, the following *forelem* loop is used:

```
forelem (i; i ∈ pA.field2[10])
    R = R ∪ (A[i].field1)
```

Note that pA.field2[10] is not expressed more explicitly as the exact execution of the loop will be determined by the optimization process, see Sect. 4.2.

---

[1] Index sets should not be confused with database indexes and serve a different purpose. An index set is used to specify iteration in the *forelem* framework. Many index sets are only used in the intermediate representation and are not materialized.

More sophisticated index sets are possible, such as having conditions on multiple fields, in this case on *field1* and *field2*:

$$\texttt{pA.(field1,field2)}[(k_1, k_2)] \equiv$$
$$\{i \mid i \in \texttt{pA} \wedge \texttt{A[i].field1} = k_1 \wedge \texttt{A[i].field2} = k_2\}$$

Instead of a constant value, the values k_n can also be a reference to a value from another array. To use such a reference, the array, subscript into the array and field name must be specified, e.g.: `A[i].field`. To select values `field1` > 10 an interval is used: $(10, \infty)$.

Note: *forelem* loop nests should not be considered as a new programming methodology, but rather as a compiler intermediate representation, invisible to the programmer. So, SQL queries are being parsed into the *forelem* intermediate[2]. See also Sect. 6.

3   Transformations for *forelem* Loops

Existing compiler transformations can be re-engineered so that these can be applied to *forelem* loop nests. This re-engineering is necessary because *forelem* loops do not have a pre-defined iteration order. As a first transformation, consider Loop Interchange. The standard Loop Interchange transformation changes the order in which the statements in the loop are executed. This transformation is only valid if the new execution order preserves all dependencies of the original execution order [24]. Commonly, data-dependence analysis [2,3,13] is employed to formally verify whether the data-dependence relations are preserved across loop transformations. In general, only certain loop-carried dependencies can prevent application of Loop Interchange.

A *forelem* loop does not specify a particular execution order and therefore loop-carried dependencies cannot exist[3]. As a consequence, interchanges of loops in a perfect loop nest are always valid. Loop-carried dependencies are therefore only caused by dependencies of the loop bounds of inner loops on outer loop iteration counters. In this case, Loop Invariant Code Motion is first used to move the conditions to the inner loop before the loop nest is reordered and back to the outermost loop after the reordering. This way, Loop Interchange is applied to a perfectly nested loop nest. To demonstrate this, consider the loop:

```
forelem (j; j ∈ pY)
  forelem (i; i ∈ pX.(field1,field2)[(Y[j].field2,val)])
    ℛ = ℛ ∪ (Y[j].field1)
```

First, the conditions are moved to the inner loop and made explicit as if-conditions:

---

[2] A description of how to translate SQL queries to *forelem* will be part of a forthcoming publication.

[3] Note that the update operation $\mathbb{R} = \mathbb{R} \cup \ldots$ could be interpreted as an output dependency. However, the fact that $\mathbb{R}$ is a multiset does not impose a strict order on the execution, therefore we do not consider this as a dependency.

```
forelem (j; j ∈ pY)
  forelem (i; i ∈ pX)
    if (X[i].field1 == Y[j].field2 && X[i].field2 == val)
      ℛ = ℛ ∪ (Y[j].field1)
```

Now that the loop nest is in a perfectly nested form, the Loop Interchange transformation can be applied, resulting in:

```
forelem (i; i ∈ pX)
  forelem (j; j ∈ pY)
    if (X[i].field1 == Y[j].field2 && X[i].field2 == val)
      ℛ = ℛ ∪ (Y[j].field1)
```

Another traditional compiler optimization that can be readily applied to *forelem* loops is Loop Fusion [10]. The transformation can, under certain conditions, merge two loops (at the same level if contained in a larger loop nest) into a single loop. Application of Loop Fusion is only prohibited by certain loop-carried dependencies. Such loop-carried dependencies do not exist in *forelem* loops. Therefore, Loop Fusion can be applied on two adjacent *forelem* loops if the iteration spaces of the two loops are equal. This is the case if the index sets for both loops refer to the same table and contain the same set of subscripts into these tables. After Loop Fusion has been applied, the bodies of both loops are executed for the same set of subscripts into the same array. For example:

```
forelem (i; i ∈ pTable1)
  ℛ₁ = ℛ₁ ∪ (Table1[i].field1)
forelem (i; i ∈ pTable1)
  ℛ₂ = ℛ₂ ∪ (Table1[i].field2)
```

can be rewritten into the following, because of the equal iteration bounds:

```
forelem (i; i ∈ pTable1)
{
  ℛ₁ = ℛ₁ ∪ (Table1[i].field1)
  ℛ₂ = ℛ₂ ∪ (Table1[i].field2)
}
```

Note that *forelem* loops generally only access the array being iterated using the subscript of the current iteration. E.g., an access into an array always has the form i and not $i + 2$ or similar. As a consequence, a condition preventing Loop Fusion from being applied will in general not occur.

Other existing compiler transformations that can be re-engineered in a similar way are Loop Blocking, Inlining and Dead Code Elimination. Figure 1 presents a number of code examples of these transformations. Within the *forelem* framework also extensive use is made of Def-Use analysis [1,9]. In this analysis statements are analyzed to see whether they are a definition (an assignment) or a use of a value. This analysis is used to find unused variables, or to infer the current value of a variable by looking at preceding definitions of the variable in the Def-Use chain.

Finally, a number of extensions have been devised that are used in the optimization of query codes. The Table Propagation transformation is similar to

Loop Invariant Code Motion

Before:

```
forelem (i; i ∈ pX)
  forelem (j; j ∈ pY)
    if (X[i].field2 == value &&
        Y[j].field2 == X[i].field1)
      ℛ = ℛ ∪ (Y[j].field1)
```

After:

```
forelem (i; i ∈ pX)
  if (X[i].field2 == value)
    forelem (j; j ∈ pY)
      if ([j].field2 == X[i].field1)
        ℛ = ℛ ∪ (Y[j].field1)
```

Loop Fusion

Before:

```
forelem (i; i ∈ pTable1)
  ℛ₁ = ℛ₁ ∪ (Table1[i].field1)
forelem (i; i ∈ pTable1)
  ℛ₂ = ℛ₂ ∪ (Table1[i].field2)
```

After:

```
forelem (i; i ∈ pTable1)
{
  ℛ₁ = ℛ₁ ∪ (Table1[i].field1)
  ℛ₂ = ℛ₂ ∪ (Table1[i].field2)
}
```

Iteration Space Expansion

Before:

```
count = 0;
forelem (i; i ∈ pA.field[X])
    count++;
tmp = count;
```

After:

```
count[] = 0;
forelem (i; i ∈ pA)
  count[A[i].field]++;
tmp = count[X];
```

Table Propagation

Before:

```
forelem (i; i ∈ pX.field2[value])
    𝒯 = 𝒯 ∪ (X[i].field3)

forelem (i; i ∈ p𝒯)
    ℛ = ℛ ∪ (𝒯[i].field3)
```

After:

```
forelem (i; i ∈ pX.field2[value])
    𝒯 = 𝒯 ∪ (X[i].field3)

forelem (i; i ∈ pX.field2[value])
    ℛ = ℛ ∪ (X[i].field3)
```

Fig. 1. A number of common *forelem* transformations. For an explanation and further details the reader is referred to [20].

Scalar Propagation that substitutes the use of variables whose value is known at compile-time with that value. Table Propagation is an extension of Scalar Propagation that replaces the use of a temporary table of which the contents are known with a loop nest that generates the same contents as this temporary table. This eliminates unnecessary copying of data to create the temporary table, but also enables further transformations because the loop nest that generates the contents of the temporary table can now be considered together with the loop nest that iterates the temporary table. Another extension is the Iteration Space Expansion transformation. This transformation is based on Scalar Expansion. With Iteration Space Expansion the iteration space of a *forelem* loop is expanded by removing conditions on its index set. By doing so, a loop is executed once for all tuples, instead of repeatedly executing the loop for different arguments to be tested against the conditions. An example of both of these transformations can again be found in Fig. 1.

4   Performing Query Optimization with Compiler Transformations

In this section, we discuss the optimization of queries through the use of existing compiler transformations, rather than the use of query planning techniques used by traditional query optimizers. For instance, through the application of Inline and Loop Invariant Code Motion, multi-block queries can be rewritten as single-block queries and uncorrelated subqueries can be moved out of the loop nest such that it is only executed once. We will now demonstrate how two important problems of query optimization, join reordering and join operator evaluation, are solved using solely existing compiler techniques.

4.1   Join Reordering

The most important task of a traditional query optimizer is to determine in which order the joins in a query should be processed. Selecting an appropriate order is crucial for keeping the execution time of the query under control. To determine such an order, a query optimizer considers the search space consisting of equivalent query plans and for each plan computes the cost of executing this plan. This cost depends on the number of disk I/Os that have to be performed and the estimated cost of executing every relational operator that is present in the query tree.

In the *forelem* framework a query performing multiple joins is represented as a nested loop. At each nesting level a different table is accessed. Using the Loop Interchange transformation, the order of loops in the loop nest is reordered. This is essentially the same operation as join reordering. The two outermost loops of a loop nest represent the join condition that is tested for every tuple of the corresponding table. The two innermost loops represent the join that is only executed for tuples that satisfied the join conditions of all outer loops.

Loop Interchange sets up a search space of all possible orderings of the loops in a loop nest. A compiler can select an appropriate order at compile-time through the use of heuristics, such as putting loops imposing most conditions as the outermost loops, and by incorporating run-time information in an iterative compilation [7,11] process. By exploiting the collected run-time information, the compiler will select better performing loop orders each time the code is executed and the compiler is also enabled to adapt to changes in the data set.

4.2   Execution of Join Operator

After an order in which joins are to be processed is selected, a query optimizer needs to select for each join operator in the query tree with which algorithm to evaluate that join. Common algorithms are Nested Loops, Block Nested Loops, Index Nested Loops and Hash Join. The selection of algorithm is based on properties of the join (whether it is an equijoin or not), cardinality of involved database relations and the availability of suitable indexes on disk.

Within the *forelem* framework, no fixed implementations of join operators are implemented. Rather, the loops in the loop nest are executed as usual with the support of an *forelem* index set. This *forelem* index set may either be present on disk (like a usual database index on a relation), is generated at run-time (for instance, like a hash table in Hash Join) or none is generated and all tuples of a table are visited (like in Nested Loops join execution). Crucial for good performance is the selection of what *forelem* index sets are to be used in the execution of the loop nest and whether (and how) these need to be generated at run-time.

This selection process is carried out using a mix of compiler techniques: explicating an index set as if-conditions, multi-version code generation [5] and data copying. By explicating an index set as if-conditions, the index set that is iterated by a *forelem* loop is written as an if-statement explicitly testing all conditions in the body of the loop. This is an important preparation for other compiler optimizations to be applied (such as Loop Interchange).

In multi-version code generation [5], all possible paths through multiple basic blocks (traces) are generated, and code is generated for each of these paths. In this particular context, this technique is used to find out what conditions the tuples are tested for and what data is retrieved from each table in case a condition is satisfied. For conditions that are tested most frequently or multiple times, according to the traces, an index set can be generated at run-time before the execution of the *forelem* loop. Even more powerful is the capability of collecting traces at run-time and using these in subsequent recompilations of the query. With this run-time information, better selections can be made for what index sets to generate at run-time, or to decide to keep persistent copies of certain index sets updated on disk to avoid recreating the index set at run-time every time it is needed by a query.

The actual generation of the index set is similar to a compiler technique known as data copying [14, 21]. In data copying, a partial copy is made of a block of data that is processed by a loop. Although there is a cost involved in making this copy, the copy results in a much better utilization of the cache and thus in a significant increase in performance. The initial cost of making the copy is redeemed.

To generate an index set a partial copy is made of a database table. A common index set is one in which the tuple subscript can be looked up for a particular field value. This index set is generated by copying field and subscript values from the original table to a temporary table that represents the index set. Another example consists of a *forelem* loop, in which an index set is used to obtain a tuple subscript i for a field value ($A.field$) and subsequently this subscript is used to access a single field in another table ($B[i].field$). The latter table access will often cause very irregular memory traffic. The code generation process that has been described will detect that only a single field is used. The compiler can therefore decide to make a data copy consisting of values *A.field, B[i].field* instead of *A.field, i*.

So far, we have considered the content of an index set in terms of tuples. The final component of this process is to determine *how* to store these tuples. Different orders of tuples and access methods (i.e. direct access or hashing) are possible. The Materialization techniques that are defined within the *forelem* framework [20] are used to devise a data storage format for each index set. From the definition of this storage format, code can be generated that instantiates the index set at run-time and code to access this index set. Note that this definition may be changed in subsequent steps of an iterative compilation process, for instance due to the influence of collected run-time traces.

5   Optimization and Code Generation Strategies

In order to successfully optimize *forelem* loop nests using the transformations described in Sect. 3, a strategy is needed that determines in which order to perform the transformations on the *forelem* loop nests. The *forelem* framework uses the following strategy to decide in which order to apply the transformations:

- Firstly, subqueries are inlined, so that these can be considered in combination with the calling context.
- As a second step loops are reordered such that as many conditions as possible are tested in the outermost loops. Priority is given to move conditions that test against a constant value to the outermost loop. This step is a combination of the application of Loop Interchange with Loop Invariant Code Motion.
- Thirdly, opportunities for the application of Iteration Space Expansion are looked for. An example of such an opportunity is a loop iterating an index set with a condition on a field, of which the body computes an aggregate function. Iteration Space Expansion is followed by Loop Invariant Code Motion, because the loop computing the aggregate function is often made loop invariant by the Iteration Space Expansion transformation. Iteration Space Expansion is not applied on loops iterating temporary tables.
- The fourth step is to apply Table Propagation to prepare for the elimination of unnecessary temporary tables.
- Fifth, Dead Code Elimination is performed to remove any loop that computes unused results.
- Finally, code is inserted which implements the run-time generation of index sets that are needed to speed up query execution.

Another optimization strategy is to perform a brute-force exploration of the entire optimization space. This is useful, for example, for queries that are run many times on changing data so that the costly optimization effort is worth it. We plan to study brute-force exploration of the optimization search space in future work.

Next to strategies for the application of transformations on the *forelem* intermediate representation, there are also strategies for the generation of efficient code from the *forelem* intermediate representation. These strategies are for a large part concerned with the selection of *forelem* loops for which index sets should be generated at run-time and the selection of efficient data structures for such index sets.

Different data structures are used as index set, such as flat arrays, hash tables or tree structures, depending on the properties of the index set. For example, if it is known that the field an index set is created for has a unique value for each row in the array, a one-to-one-mapping is set up using a flat array or hash table. This property can be known to the code generator because the field was specified as primary key in the table schema, or the generated code detects at run-time that the table data satisfies this condition. For index sets that yield multiple subscripts that are iterated in a loop nest, a balanced tree is used.

Additionally, the code generator can easily generate both row-wise and column-wise data access code. Within the *forelem* framework, a change from row-wise to column-wise layout is a trivial transformation. Which layout should be used is determined by the amount of fields in an array that are accessed.

6   Implementation of the Forelem Framework

The *forelem* framework has been developed as a generic library, *libforelem*, to be able to support different programming languages and data access frameworks. This library is capable of creating and manipulating *forelem* loop nests, by representing these using an internal Abstract Syntax Tree (AST).

Different applications can make use of *libforelem* to create and manipulate *forelem* ASTs. For example, to support the vertical integration of database applications, the *libforelem* library is capable of parsing a given SQL statement into a *forelem* AST. On the AST, various analyses and transformations can be applied, many of which are implementations of traditional compiler (loop) transformations that function on the *forelem* AST. An abstract code generation interface is present in the library to generate code from any *forelem* AST. Currently, the output of C/C++ code and algebraic *forelem* is supported. However, the use of *forelem* loops is not restricted to C/C++ and other languages can be supported by implementing the abstract code generation interface.

Typically in the optimization process, the code generator is called when optimization on the *forelem*-loop level has completed. In the case C/C++ code is to be generated from the optimized *forelem* AST, the *forelem* loops are translated to C *for* loops that iterate index sets and access subscripts of plain C arrays. In the C code, an index set is a generic interface and the exact data structure of the index set is opaque. As has been described in Sect. 4.2, the optimization process will generate a data storage format for each index set as part of the optimization process. Since materialization of index sets is not obligatory, the optimization process might also decide to not generate an index set, but rather to test the conditions during iteration of the table.

Note that *forelem* loops are only used by the compiler tooling and are never visible to the end user. The general nature of the *forelem* frameworks allows for its usage with other problems. Other parsers that take a certain language as input and produce *forelem* loops can be developed next to the SQL parser, so that other problem domains can be supported.

7   Experimental Results

Experiments have been conducted using the queries from the TPC-H benchmark [22], which is the de facto benchmark for the evaluation of query optimizers. The TPC-H queries were parsed into the *forelem* intermediate representation, optimized using the transformations described in this paper and C/C++ code has been generated from the optimized AST. These executables access the database data through memory-mapped I/O. The execution time of the queries is compared to the execution time of the same queries as executed by PostgreSQL [19], which is a robust DBMS that is in use in many deployments, and MonetDB [17], a contemporary state-of-the-art database system. Two different scale factors were used to perform tests with in-memory and out-of-memory data sets.

All experiments have been carried out on an Intel Core 2 Quad CPU (Q9450) clocked at 2.66 GHz with 4 GB of RAM. The software installation consists out of Ubuntu 10.04.3 LTS (64-bit), which comes with PostgreSQL 8.4.9. The version of MonetDB used is 11.11.11 (Jul2012-SP2), which is the latest version that could be obtained from the MonetDB website [17] for use with this operating system.

Table 1 shows the speedup of the different queries run against a TPC-H data set of scale factor 1.0. For three queries the PostgreSQL measurements have not been completed because these queries showed exorbitant run times. In all cases,

Table 1. Speedup of the execution time of TPC-H queries optimized with the *forelem* framework compared to PostgreSQL (left) and MonetDB (right) on a data set of scale factor 1.0. The PostgreSQL measurements for Q17, Q20, Q21 were not completed due to exorbitant run times.

Query	Speedup	Query	Speedup	Query	Speedup	Query	Speedup
Q1	118.35	Q12	21.00	Q1	2.84	Q12	2.67
Q2	5004.24	Q13	1.37	Q2	1.65	Q13	1.94
Q3	25.76	Q14	44.82	Q3	1.21	Q14	2.08
Q4	19.16	Q15	102.17	Q4	1.39	Q15	4.09
Q5	25.66	Q16	30.11	Q5	1.33	Q16	1.37
Q6	55.32	Q17	-	Q6	3.64	Q17	3.22
Q7	8.07	Q18	35.90	Q7	2.79	Q18	2.68
Q8	74.07	Q19	6.79	Q8	1.63	Q19	1.71
Q9	17.45	Q20	-	Q9	1.28	Q20	1.38
Q10	17.60	Q21	-	Q10	1.62	Q21	1.55
Q11	16.03	Q22	8.86	Q11	1.98	Q22	1.39

Table 2. Speedup of the execution time of TPC-H queries optimized with the *forelem* framework compared to MonetDB on a data set of scale factor 10.0.

Query	Speedup	Query	Speedup	Query	Speedup	Query	Speedup
Q1	8.81	Q7	3.00	Q13	1.34	Q19	3.56
Q2	3.06	Q8	1.03	Q14	1.74	Q20	1.11
Q3	5.00	Q9	2.81	Q15	1.38	Q21	3.40
Q4	5.19	Q10	4.54	Q16	1.16	Q22	3.21
Q5	1.41	Q11	2.27	Q17	1.47		
Q6	4.00	Q12	6.33	Q18	15.61		

the *forelem*-optimized queries outperform PostgreSQL. The speedups achieved by the *forelem*-optimized queries range from a factor of 1.37 (Q13) to 5004.24 (Q2). This is also the case when compared to MonetDB and speedups are seen from a factor of 1.21 (Q3) to 4.09 (Q15).

We have also conducted experiments with an out-of-memory data set with a scale factor of 10.0. This data set is approximately 10 GB in size, which is 2.5 times as large as the main memory available in the machine on which the experiments were conducted. Already for SF 1.0, PostgreSQL needed significantly more than 31 s to execute 5 of the queries. For SF 10.0 the run times were impractical for many of the queries. Therefore, we have only performed the experiments for SF 10.0 with MonetDB and *forelem*.

The results with the out-of-memory data set are summarized in Table 2. For all cases, the *forelem*-optimized codes outperform MonetDB, resulting in speeds from a factor of 1.03 (Q8) to 15.6 (Q18).

The results presented in this section show that by re-engineering existing compiler transformations and by adding a few simple new transformations, a level of performance can be attained that goes beyond that of state-of-the-art database systems such as MonetDB.

8   Related Work

In the database community, techniques are being considered that have been developed in the field of compiler optimizations. A branch of recent research has focused on the translation of query execution plans to C, C++ or LLVM intermediate, from which efficient machine codes are generated using code generation techniques. Krikellas et al. describe a technology called "holistic query evaluation" by which a query execution plan is transformed into C++ source code [12]. Thereupon, this source code is compiled into a shared library using an aggressively optimizing compiler. The shared library is then linked into the database server for processing. The UltraLite system, described in [23], follows a similar approach and compiles queries found in an embedded SQL code to C code. This is achieved by sending a query to a host database server, which parses and optimizes the query using traditional techniques. An execution plan is returned which is used to generate the C code, which is linked together with the application.

Cloudera's Impala [6] is a SQL query engine which relies on LLVM for the generation of efficient machine codes. Queries are parsed and planned using traditional techniques and subsequently from the query plan runtime code, specific to that query, is generated using LLVM. During this code generation process various optimizations are carried out such as inlining function calls and user-defined functions, dead code elimination and minimization of branching. Separate from this work, also code generation techniques have been developed specifically for making runtime codes for queries more efficient. For instance, Neumann et al. present a strategy for the generation of efficient machine code from query plans by keeping data in CPU registers as long as possible [18].

The major difference of these approaches with the work presented in this paper is that in these approaches optimizing compiler technology is used to generate efficient machine code given a query execution plan that is already optimized using traditional query planning techniques, whereas our work enables compiler technology to replace the traditional query planning. So, instead of using traditional query planning techniques, in our work compiler technology itself is used to optimize ("plan") queries. Instead of manipulating a query execution plan data structure, compiler transformations are applied directly on the code.

Andrade et al. describe an approach for multi-query optimization [4] by writing queries as imperative loops and applying compiler transformations such as loop fusion, common subexpression elimination and dead code elimination. Their work is however specific to a certain specific class of analysis queries. Kang et al. describe a different approach to multi-query optimization [8], where optimization techniques are applied to the "algorithm-level" of a database program. In the algorithm-level, a query is represented as a sequence of algorithms, e.g. selection, join, that should be performed to compute the query results. The exact implementation of the algorithms is not made explicit at this level. As a consequence, knowledge is required about the implementation of algorithms that can appear in the representation by the optimizer in order to be able to carry out optimizations. Contrary, within our approach strategies for efficient selection and joins are generated automatically through the application of compiler transformations.

Database Programming Languages (DBPLs) are a specific class of programming languages that include the ability to iterate through sets and were popular for the implementation of database applications in the early '90s. For such languages, compile-time optimizations similar to relational transformations like join reordering have been described [16]. These transformations make standard transformation-based compilers capable of optimizing iterations over sets that correspond to joins. This was later extended to include transformations that enable the parallelization of loops in DBPLs [15].

There are a number of important differences with the *forelem* framework. DBPLs were meant as programming languages to be used by an end user, whereas *forelem* loops are only an intermediate representation to be used by code optimization backends. This way, the *forelem* framework is capable of handling different combinations of application programming languages and database statement expressions. Additionally, DBPLs, such as O++ which is discussed in [15,16], use a run-time system for the iteration and manipulation of sets. *forelem* loops can be immediately lowered to low-level C codes that iterate over arrays, or another data structure as generated automatically using materialization techniques, that enable further low-level compiler optimizations. Despite that, several of the techniques presented in these papers could be implemented in the *forelem* framework in the future.

9 Conclusions

In this paper the optimization of database queries using compiler transformations has been described. This optimization process is carried out in the *forelem* framework. The *forelem* framework provides an intermediate representation to which queries can be naturally transformed and on which compiler transformations can be applied to optimize the loop nest, contrary to the traditional optimization of queries by the generation of an efficient query execution plan. The compiler transformations that are used in this process are a combination of existing transformations that have been re-engineered for use with *forelem* loops and a few simple extensions. Strategies for the application of these transformations in order to successfully optimize queries were discussed.

Experiments using the queries from the TPC-H benchmark show that using compiler transformations implemented within the *forelem* framework the queries could be optimized to perform significantly better than contemporary database systems. Compared to MonetDB, an average improvement was shown of a factor of 3 and in certain cases a speedup was achieved of up to a factor of 15.

References

1. Allen, F.E., Cocke, J.: A program data flow analysis procedure. Commun. ACM **19**(3), 137–147 (1976)
2. Allen, J.R.: Dependence Analysis for Subscripted Variables and its Applications to Program Transformations. Ph.D. Dissertation, Rice University (1983)
3. Allen, R., Kennedy, K.: Automatic translation of fortran programs to vector form. ACM Trans. Program. Lang. Syst. **9**, 491–542 (1987)
4. Andrade, H., Aryangat, S., Kurç, T.M., Saltz, J.H., Sussman, A.: Efficient execution of multi-query data analysis batches using compiler optimization strategies. In: LCPC, pp. 509–524 (2003)
5. Byler, M., Wolfe, M., Davies, J.R.B., Huson, C., Leasure, B.: Multiple version loops. In: ICPP, pp. 312–318 (1987)
6. Cloudera: Impala, August 2014. http://impala.io/
7. Fursin, G.G., O'Boyle, M., Knijnenburg, P.M.W.: Evaluating iterative compilation. In: Pugh, B., Tseng, C.-W. (eds.) LCPC 2002. LNCS, vol. 2481, pp. 362–376. Springer, Heidelberg (2005)
8. Kang, M.H., Dietz, H.G., Bhargava, B.K.: Multiple-query optimization at algorithm-level. Data Knowl. Eng. **14**(1), 57–75 (1994)

9. Kennedy, K.: A survey of data flow analysis techniques, Muchnik, S.S., and Jones, N.D. (eds.), Program Flow Analysis: Theory and Applications, pp. 5–54. Prentice-Hall, Englewood Cliffs (1981)

10. Kennedy, K., McKinley, K.: Maximizing loop parallelism and improving data locality via loop fusion and distribution. In: Banerjee, U., Gelernter, D., Nicolau, Alexandru, Padua, David A. (eds.) LCPC 1993. LNCS, vol. 768. Springer, Heidelberg (1994)

11. Knijnenburg, P., Kisuki, T., O'Boyle, M.: Combined selection of tile sizes and unroll factors using iterative compilation. J. Supercomput. **24**(1), 43–67 (2003)

12. Krikellas, K., Viglas, S., Cintra, M.: Generating code for holistic query evaluation. In: ICDE, pp. 613–624 (2010)

13. Kuck, D.J., Kuhn, R.H., Padua, D.A., Leasure, B., Wolfe, M.: Dependence graphs and compiler optimizations. In: Proceedings of the 8th ACM SIGPLAN-SIGACT Symposium on Principles of Programming Languages, POPL 1981, pp. 207–218. ACM, New York (1981)

14. Lam, M.D., Rothberg, E.E., Wolf, M.E.: The cache performance and optimizations of blocked algorithms. SIGARCH Comput. Archit. News **19**(2), 63–74 (1991)

15. Lieuwen, D.F.: Parallelizing loops in database programming languages. In: ICDE, pp. 86–93 (1998)

16. Lieuwen, D.F., DeWitt, D.J.: A transformation-based approach to optimizing loops in database programming languages. In: SIGMOD Conference, pp. 91–100 (1992)

17. MonetDB Project: MonetDB, February 2013. http://www.monetdb.org/

18. Neumann, T.: Efficiently compiling efficient query plans for modern hardware. Proc. VLDB Endow. **4**, 539–550 (2011)

19. PostgreSQL Project: PostgreSQL: The world's most advanced open source database, February 2013. http://www.postgresql.org/

20. Rietveld, K.F.D., Wijshoff, H.A.G.: Forelem: A versatile optimization framework for tuple-based computations. In: CPC 2013: 17th Workshop on Compilers for Parallel Computing, July 2013

21. Temam, O., Granston, E., Jalby, W.: To copy or not to copy: A compile-time technique for assessing when data copying should be used to eliminate cache conflicts. In: Proceedings of the Supercomputing 1993, pp. 410–419 (1993)

22. Transaction Processing Performance Council: TPC-H, May 2009. http://tpc.org/tpch/default.asp

23. Yach, D.P., Graham, J.D., Scian, A.F.: Database system with methodology for accessing a database from portable devices. US Patent #6341288, Jan 2002

24. Zima, H., Chapman, B.: Supercompilers for Parallel and Vector Computers. ACM, New York (1991)

Debugging

Systematic Debugging of Concurrent Systems Using Coalesced Stack Trace Graphs

Diego Caminha B. de Oliveira[1], Zvonimir Rakamarić[1(✉)],
Ganesh Gopalakrishnan[1], Alan Humphrey[1,2], Qingyu Meng[1,2],
and Martin Berzins[1,2]

[1] School of Computing, University of Utah, Salt Lake City, USA
[2] School of Computing and SCI Institute, University of Utah, Salt Lake City, USA
{caminha,zvonimir,ganesh,ahumphre,qymeng,mb}@cs.utah.edu

Abstract. A central need during software development of large-scale parallel systems is tools that help to quickly identify the root causes of bugs. Given the massive scale of these systems, tools that highlight changes—say introduced across software versions or their operating conditions (e.g., inputs, schedules)—can prove to be highly effective in practice. Conventional debuggers, while good at presenting details at the problem-site (e.g., crash), often omit contextual information to identify the root causes of the bug. We present a new approach to collect and coalesce stack traces, leading to an efficient summary display of salient system control flow differences in a graphical form called Coalesced Stack Trace Graphs (CSTG). CSTGs have helped us debug situations within a computational framework called Uintah that has been deployed at very large scale. In this paper, we detail CSTGs through case studies in the context of Uintah where unexpected behaviors caused by different versions of software or occurring across different time-steps of a system (e.g., due to non-determinism) are debugged. We show that CSTG also gives conventional debuggers a far more productive and guided role to play.

1 Introduction

There is widespread agreement that software engineering principles, including systematic debugging methods, must be brought to bear on high-performance computing (HPC) software development [1,11]. HPC frameworks form the backbone of all science and engineering research, and any savings in the effort to locate and fix bugs in the short term, and maintain their integrity over the decades of their lifetime maximizes the "science per dollar" achieved. Formal analysis methods such as model-checking, symbolic analysis, and dynamic formal analysis [14] are among the plethora of recent efforts addressing this need. Yet, with the growing scale and complexity of systems, most of these techniques are not applicable on real deployed software, and hence of no direct value to people in the debugging trenches of advanced HPC software.

Large-scale concurrent HPC systems—for instance, computational frameworks for solving massive and complex problems—are in a state of continuous

Supported in part by NSF awards CCF-1241849 and ACI-1148127.

J. Brodman and P. Tu (Eds.): LCPC 2014, LNCS 8967, pp. 317–331, 2015.
DOI: 10.1007/978-3-319-17473-0_21

development, in response to new user applications, larger problem scales, as well as new hardware platforms and software libraries. Tools that help expediently in the root-cause analysis of bugs are crucially important during the software development of such systems. Conventional HPC-oriented debuggers have made impressive strides in recent years (e.g., DDT [10] and RogueWave [20]), allowing large programs to be examined in interesting ways (e.g., memory views, forward and backward executions, innovative stepping and breakpoint facilities). Unfortunately, debugging is never a linear story: the actual bug manifestation (e.g., a crash) may often have very little to do with the instructions present at the crash site. A designer, in general, needs far more contextual information before a bug is identified and corrected. Unfortunately, research on such error localization tools has made inadequate progress compared to the growing needs of this area. As a result, advanced developers are often forced to roll-up their own `printf`-based solutions in a fairly ad hoc and inefficient manner.

This paper makes a contribution in this area by proposing a simple, yet versatile methodology for locating bugs with a useful amount of contextual information. Called *Coalesced Stack Trace Graphs (CSTG)*, our mechanism offers a succinct graphical display of a system execution focused on call paths to a set of target functions chosen by a user. This is a three-step process: (1) a user chooses target functions where stack trace collectors are inserted, (2) our CSTG tool records the system behavior executing the inserted collectors in these functions, and (3) succinctly displays the differences between two such recordings over two scenarios. Typically, the target functions g_i are chosen based on the scenario/bug under investigation (e.g., the g_i could be an MPI messaging call or a hash-table insert call). Stack traces are then recorded over a user-chosen period of the system run. Each such stack trace is a nest of function calls $f_1, f_2, \ldots, g_k$ for some target function g_k. These call chains are merged whenever we have the situation of f_i calling f_{i+1} from the same calling context (i.e., program counter location). Figures 3 and 4 show CSTGs and their usages, which we explain in much greater detail in the coming sections. In particular, we illustrate how CSTGs have helped during the development and analysis of Uintah [13], an extensible software framework for solving complex multiscale multi-physics problems on cutting-edge HPC systems. We present the following real bug case studies: (1) a hash-table lookup error we localized to a scheduler error, (2) a non-deterministic crash which revealed no issues at the crash site, (3) another crash we explored using two different inputs applied to the same system version, (4) an issue caused by mismatching MPI sends and receives, and (5) a *GNU Flex* example where CSTGs could easily identify the source of output mismatches in two different versions. These case studies show in detail how CSTGs have been used so far to better understand (and in many cases identify the root-cause of) these bugs.

2   Related Work

A stack trace is a sequence of function calls active at a certain point in the execution of a program. Stack traces are commonly used to observe crashes and identify likely causes. There are empirical evidences that show that they help developers to fix bugs faster [22]. They are also often leveraged in parallel debugging. For instance, STAT [3] uses stack traces to present a summary view of the state of a distributed program at a point of interest (often around hangs). It works by building equivalence classes of processes using stack traces, showing the split of these equivalence classes into divergent flows using a *prefix tree*. STAT corresponds well to the needs of MPI program debugging due to the SPMD (single program, multiple data) nature of MPI programs resulting in a prefix tree stem that remains coalesced for the most part. Debugging is accomplished by users noticing how process equivalence classes split off, and then understanding why some of the processes went with a different equivalence class.

Spectroscope [21] is another tool based on stack trace collection, where the emphasis is on performance anomaly detection. It works by comparing request flows (i.e., paths taken by the requests and time separations) across two executions. There are also efforts around the Windows Error Reporting system which helps analyze crash logs [4,9,15,16]. More recent anomaly detection methods involve clustering and machine learning, and have located errors by identifying the *least progressed* of threads [8].

Synoptic [6] and Dynoptic [7] are tools that mine a model of the system from system execution logs. Synoptic mines a finite state machine (FSM) model representations of a sequential system from its logs capturing event orderings as invariants. Dynoptic mines a communicating FSM model from a distributed system. These systems have not been applied to large-scale code bases such as Uintah, and have not been demonstrated with respect to various modalities of differential exploration that we have investigated.

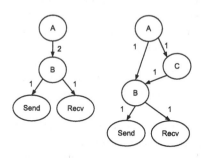

Fig. 1. CSTGs of a simple working (left) and crashing (right) program runs.

CSTGs are effectively used on anomaly detection based on the general approach of comparing two different executions or program versions, also known as *delta debugging* [25]. There are tools that spot behavioral differences such as RADAR [18]. However, they use different data and visualization methods. One novelty of our proposed method is using stack traces as the main source of information in the delta debugging process. Imagine a simple scenario where a program is run twice, the first time successfully, but the second time crashing just after making MPI **Send** and **Recv** calls. Figure 1 summarizes these executions in terms of a CSTG. The differences between the call paths leading to the **Send** and **Recv** are highly likely to play a significant role in identifying the root-cause of the bug, as our case studies show later.

2.1 Stack Trace Structures

One can roughly classify previous stack trace structures [2] into three classes as illustrated in Fig. 2. In Dynamic Call Trees (DCT), each node represents

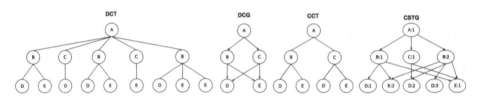

Fig. 2. Different stack trace viewing methods.

a single function activation. Edges represent calls between individual function activations. The size of a DCT is proportional to the number of calls in an execution. In Dynamic Call Graphs (DCG), each node represents all function activations. Edges represent calls between functions. The size of a DCG grows with the number of unique functions invoked in an execution. In Calling Context Trees (CCT), each node represents a function activation in a unique call chain. Edges represent calls between function activations from different call chains. CCT is a projection of a dynamic call tree that discards redundant contextual information while preserving unique contexts.

3   Coalesced Stack Trace Graphs (CSTG)

Different from the previously described structures, CSTGs do not record every function activation, but only the ones in stack traces leading to the user-chosen function(s) of interest (see Fig. 2). Each CSTG node represents all the activations of a particular function invocation. Hence, in addition to function names, CSTG nodes are also labeled with unique invocation IDs. Edges represent calls between functions. The size of a CSTG is determined by the number of nodes (function call sites) encountered across the paths reaching the observation points of interest. In our experience, this size has been modest.

The feature of not recording every function activation is crucial to reduce the overhead and improve scalability. Many stack-trace-based methods, especially those used for performance measurement, employ sampling and record only a small percentage of all function activations. However, given that debugging is our end goal, doing sampling and not recording every call can potentially result in crucial information being missed. Hence, we choose to record every stack trace leading to the few user-chosen functions of interest. We also found such user input to be crucial in taming CSTG size since typically tracking only a small portion of program functions suffices to understand and identify the root-cause of a bug. Tracking all function invocations from a large program in a CSTG graph would significantly increase the effort necessary to understand the collected graphs, not to mention the difficulty of root-cause analysis.

There are many scenarios where CSTGs can be used, some of which are illustrated in this paper. Here we list some of these scenarios. Using CSTGs, one can make comparisons across different:

- versions of a system (Sect. 5.1, Case Study 1);
- runs of the same system to understand the effects of nondeterminism (Sect. 5.1, Case Study 2);
- inputs (Sect. 5.1, Case Study 3), outputs (Sect. 5.2, Scenario 2);
- matching events such as allocate/free, open/close, lock/unlock, send/receive (Sect. 5.2, Scenario 1);
- time-steps, loop iterations, or cycling events;
- processes and threads.

3.1 Formal Definition

Consider an execution of an arbitrary sequential or concurrent program with a set of instructions $\{p_1, p_2, \ldots, p_N\}$ that collect stack traces. Executing an instruction p_j returns a snapshot s_k of the currently active call stack, i.e., it returns a stack trace. Each s_k is a stack of function names paired with their calling context[1]: $s_k = \langle f_1 : c_1 \rangle, \langle f_2 : c_2 \rangle, \ldots, \langle f_{Top-1} : c_{Top-1} \rangle, \langle f_{Top} : c_{Top} \rangle$. Here, for every $\langle f_i : c_i \rangle$ in s_k, where $i \neq Top$, c_i is the context (i.e., line number) within function f_i from which f_{i+1} is invoked. f_{Top} is the function within which an instruction p_j occurs and c_{Top} is context within function f_{Top} from which the instrumentation p_j is executed. Now, given the stack traces $s_1, s_2, \ldots, s_M$, we define a coalesced stack trace graph (CSTG) over these traces as follows:

- For each $\langle f_i : c_i \rangle$ present in some stack trace s_k, introduce the node $\langle f_i : c_i \rangle$. This node represents all the $\langle f_i : c_i \rangle$ instances present across the stack traces.
- Whenever a stack trace has two adjacent entries $\langle f_{i-1} : c_{i-1} \rangle$ and $\langle f_i : c_i \rangle$, introduce a directed edge from the latter to the former, weighted by the number of times such edge occurs across all stack traces.

As an illustration, in Fig. 3 there were 76 (left CSTG) and 77 (right CSTG) stack traces collected during the respective executions. The stack trace collection instructions were injected into functions DW::put(), DW::reduceMPI(), and DW::override(). Each ⟨*function* : *context*⟩ pair appears only once in the CSTG (some contexts were omitted for simplicity); functions appear more than once when they have different contexts (e.g., AMRSim::run()). Edge weights give the number of times a consecutive pair of elements occurred across all stack traces.

4   Driving Example: Uintah HPC Framework

Uintah serves as a non-trivial test-bed for our work, given its complexity and continuing development both in terms of applications and in terms of parallel scalability. Uintah is an open-source, extensible software framework for solving complex multiscale multi-physics problems on cutting edge HPC systems [23].

---

[1] Say, the line number where the call to the next function in the stack is made or the instrumentation code is found.

The class of problems solved by Uintah includes fluid, structure, and fluid-structure interaction problems, both with and without adaptive mesh refinement [5]. The framework has been in constant development and improvement over the past 10 years and now has about 1M lines of code and comments, and runs in a scalable manner on machines such as DOEs Titan at Oak Ridge National Laboratory and Mira at Argonne National Laboratory [17].

To promote reuse, easier maintenance, and extensibility, the developers of Uintah adopted component-based software engineering approach early on. A component-based design of Uintah enforces separation between large entities of software that can be swapped in and out, allowing them to be independently developed and tested within the entire framework. In addition, such modular software architecture promotes a clear separation of domain expert and infrastructure developer concerns.

Uintah employs a task-graph-based specification of the (sequential) user application code that is executed via a highly parallel task-based runtime system. Such an approach enables domain expert users to focus on what they know best, which is implementing sequential simulations components. At the same time, the runtime system can be independently improved without changing the user code as it relies only on the task abstraction and not on the details of what the tasks actually do. This distinction is important as it allows the parallel infrastructure components to be improved by computer scientists, who do not have to understand the simulation components in detail.

5 Case Studies

5.1 Root Cause Analysis of Uintah Bugs

The case studies we detail in this section focus on root-causing real bugs present in previous versions of Uintah. We leveraged traditional techniques, such as the use of `printfs` and a debugger (Allinea DDT [10]), in conjunction with CSTGs during the debugging process. All the debugging was carried out by a non-developer of the Uintah code-base who only had very limited knowledge of the overall Uintah code. The source code of Uintah and our CSTG-based tool, as well as the full graphs of our case studies are available online.[2]

Case Study 1: Mini Coal Boiler. The *Mini Coal Boiler* problem is a real-world example modeling a smaller-scale version of the PSAAP [19] target problem that simulates coal combustion under oxy-coal conditions. This case study illustrates a typical scenario of a system under constant development where a new component replacing an existing one causes a bug. We identified the root-cause of this bug using CSTGs to compare different versions of this Uintah simulation.

Uintah simulation variables are stored in a data warehouse. The data warehouse is a dictionary-based hash-map which maps a variable name and simulation patch id to the memory address of a variable. When running Uintah on the

---

[2] www.cs.utah.edu/fv/CSTG/. For the ease of presentation, we simplify many of the function and variable names involved.

```
void DW::get(ReductionVariableBase& var,
             const VarLabel* label,
             const Level* level,
             int matlIndex /*= -1*/) {
  ...
  if(!d_levelDB.exists(label, matlIndex, level)) {
    THROW(UnknownVariable(label->getName(),
          getID(), level, matlIndex,"on_reduction",
          __FILE__, __LINE__));
  }
  ...
}
```

Listing 1.1. Uintah Code Excerpt where the Mini Coal Boiler Exception is Thrown.

Mini Coal Boiler problem, an exception is thrown in the data warehouse function DW::get(). After studying the code (see Listing 1.1), we discovered that the problem is caused by the triple (label, matlIndex, level) not being found in the hash table d_levelDB. However, the same error does not occur when using a different Uintah scheduler component.

At such a juncture, it is quite likely that an HPC developer equipped with a debugger such as DDT or RogueWave would derive no benefit from the power and sophistication of the debugger. They would likely have to fall back to using printfs. We show that CSTGs offer a better path.

One can think of two possible reasons why this element was not found in the data warehouse: either it was never inserted, or it was prematurely removed from it. With this line of investigation in mind, we proceed by inserting our CSTG stack trace collectors before every put() and remove() call of the hash table d_levelDB. Whenever one of these locations is reached during an execution, a stack trace is collected to create a CSTG. The leaves of the generated CSTGs are unique places where the collectors were added. We run Uintah twice, each time with a different version of the scheduler (i.e., buggy and correct), and collect stack traces visualized as CSTGs. Figure 3 shows the CSTGs of the working and crashing executions.

It is not necessary to see all the details[3] in these CSTGs: it is apparent that there is a path to reduceMPI() in the working execution that does not appear in the crashing one. Figure 4 focuses on that difference—the extra green path does not occur in the crashing execution. (The other difference is related to the different names of the schedulers.) By examining the path leading to reduceMPI(), we observe in the source code that the new, buggy scheduler never calls function initiateReduction() that would eventually add the missing data warehouse element causing the crash. Since the root cause of this bug is distant from the actual crash location, traditional debugging methods would not have been able to offer such useful contextual information that CSTGs provided.

Case Study 2: Poisson2. The *Poisson2* problem is the second of four Uintah examples that solve Poisson's equation on a grid using Jacobi iteration,

---

[3] The zoomed out region of the CSTGs contains no information relevant for this study.

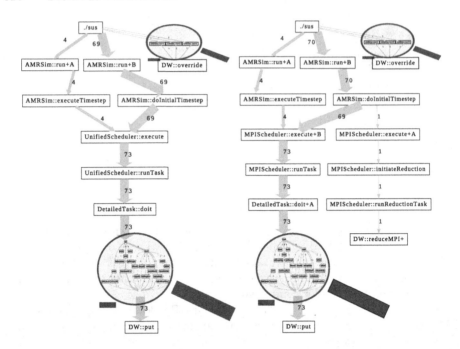

Fig. 3. Mini coal boiler case study CSTGs. Crashing execution is on the left and working execution is on the right. CSTGs contain all the paths leading to the instrumentations added before the `put()` and `remove()` calls of the hash table `d_levelDB`.

and each example exercises specific portions of the infrastructure. In this example, Poisson's equation is discretized and solved using an iterative method. The *Poisson2* problem employs the Uintah's sub-scheduler feature that enables finer iteration within a given simulation timestep of the top-level scheduler. It exercises a bug causing nondeterministic crashes during Uintah runs—a segmentation error occurs in the scheduler component of Uintah, more precisely in function `resetWaittime()`. In this scenario, we leveraged CSTGs to compare different, nondeterministic runs of the same version of the system.

Our root-cause exploration proceeded as follows. First, we investigated function `resetWaittime(double)`, where we noticed nothing out of the ordinary—there is only a simple assignment to the variable `d_waitstart`, as in Listing 1.2. Then, after running Uintah a few times on the same input, we noticed that the crash is nondeterministic: it typically occurs (in time-steps 1 or 2), but not always. Next, we decided to leverage our CSTGs to investigate this problem further. We added stack trace collectors to observe the execution history and paths leading to the crashing function `resetWaitTime()`. In this case study, we observe executions of the same system version where the crash does and does not happen.

Figure 5 shows the CSTG delta resulting from these collections. We immediately learn that the crashing run contains the user-provided function `Poisson2::`

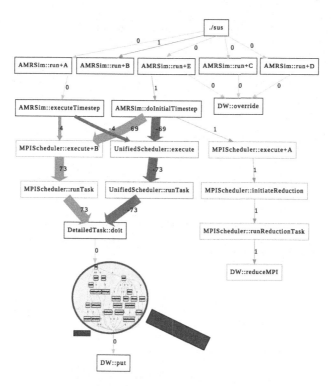

Fig. 4. Mini coal boiler case study CSTG delta. It highlights the differences between the CSTGs in Fig. 3.

timeAdvance() that is executed every time-step; however, only once does time-Advance() invoke the observed function resetWaittime(). (It is worth remembering that functions are not recorded when invoked, but only when/if a collection point is reached.) Armed with much better understanding of when exactly the crash occurs, we switched to using a debugger to step through the code. We observed that the value of the variable numThreads_ is abnormally high in the function execute() on the crashing path. There are two common reasons why this happens: either the variable is uninitialized or it suffers memory corruption.

Further exploration of the source code reveals that numThreads_ is indeed never initialized before being used for the first time. While an initial value of an uninitialized variable is often zero, that is not guaranteed by the compiler—hence the nondeterministic behavior we observed. When the initial value of numThreads_ happens to be zero, resetWaittime() is not invoked. Occasionally, when the initial value is not zero, resetWaittime() is invoked and the crash happens soon thereafter. Note that resetWaittime() gets invoked several times from different parts of the code, but only once through the problematic path leading to the crash, as clearly shown in Fig. 5. As it turns out, the variable d_waitstart is only allocated and numThreads_ initialized in the function problemSetup() that never gets invoked.

```
void UnifiedSchedulerWorker::resetWaittime(double start) {
    d_waitstart = start;  // crashing point
    d_waittime = 0.0;
}
```

Listing 1.2. Uintah Code Excerpt where the *Poisson2* Crash Occurs.

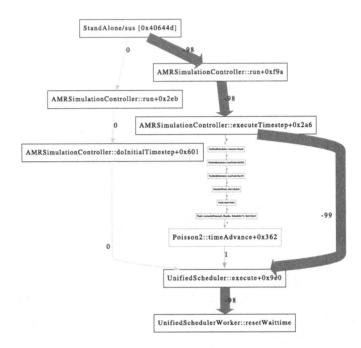

Fig. 5. Poisson2 case study CSTG delta. There are 3 paths leading to the observed function in the crashing run, but only 2 paths in the non-crashing run. The extra path is highlighted in green.

As an additional exercise, we used Valgrind [24] to expose this problematic usage of an uninitialized variable. And while Valgrind was successful in locating the problem, it took us several days to reach that point due to the large performance overhead of using Valgrind—each Uintah run took several hours to finish, while a Uintah run without Valgrind would take a couple of minutes. Collecting CSTGs, on the other hand, incurs almost no performance overhead (see Sect. 7) and provides us with more contextual information than Valgrind.

To summarize, this is a user-introduced bug related to incorrect usage of the Uintah system. It is nondeterministic in nature, and hence could have stayed dormant for a long time. The use of CSTGs, and especially the ability to compare across two different executions, helped us to identify the root-cause of this bug. The synergistic role of a traditional debugger is also apparent, and such versatile solutions in root-cause analysis are paramount to improving the productivity of HPC developers.

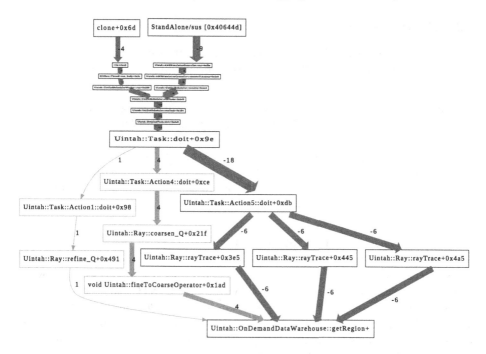

Fig. 6. Arches case study CSTG delta comparing runs on different input files.

Case Study 3: Arches. Our third case study examines a radiative heat transfer benchmark simulation using the *Arches* component, which was designed for the simulation of turbulent reacting flows with participating media radiation. During this Uintah simulation, an exception is thrown in the data warehouse function `getRegion()`. After we performed the initial inspection of the source code, we observed that the problem is related to simulation patches and grid regions. However, the exact details were unclear. Here, we leveraged CSTGs to compare runs on slightly different inputs. In particular, we managed to only slightly modify the input to obtain a run that finishes without a crash.

A typical input file of Uintah contains many parameters defining grid values, variables, algorithms, and components used in setting up simulations. In this case study, we changed the problematic input file, modifying several parameters that we suspected were related to the crash, until we were able to obtain an input that finishes normally. We then generated CSTGs using the two different input file versions to compare the executions. Figure 6 shows the CSTG delta. The paths traversing the green nodes only happen in the crashing run. Hence, our hypothesis was that there was something wrong in one of the functions belonging to these paths. Reporting back to the Uintah developers, we were able to confirm that the function `Uintah::Ray::refine_Q()` was calling `getRegion()` with wrong parameters, which resulted in this crash.

5.2 Other Usage Scenarios

We listed many envisioned CSTG usage scenarios in Sect. 3, some of which we covered in the previous section. We now only briefly present two more.

Scenario 1: Matching Events. In this scenario, we are leveraging CSTGs to observe call paths leading to MPI_Isend and MPI_Irecv in Uintah. In a typical message passage application, the number of message sends and receives should match. But in this case, we can notice from CSTGs that they do not match by looking at the incoming edges and their degrees (denoted with numbers on the edges). Similar CSTGs can be used as initial points of investigations of mismatches in the number of matching events.

Scenario 2: Same Inputs, Different Outputs. In this scenario, we obtained two different versions of the GNU lexical analyzer *Flex* from the Software-artifact Infrastructure Repository [12]. For a particular input, these two versions were unexpectedly printing different outputs. We leveraged CSTGs to observe the call paths leading to the print character function in *Flex* called outc(). The CSTG delta clearly marks a path that occurs three times less in the execution of one version of *Flex* versus the other. We confirmed that this call path contains the modified code that generated the different output.

6 Implementation Details

In our current implementation of CSTGs in the context of Uintah running MPI on several nodes, we collect stack traces separately at every process. We achieve this by invoking the backtrace() function (from *execinfo.h*) each time a stack trace collection instruction is executed. An example of a stack trace collected is:

```
stack_trace:
MPIScheduler::postMPISends(DetailedTask*, int)+0xa15
MPIScheduler::runTask(DetailedTask*, int)+0x3b7
MPIScheduler::execute(int, int)+0x78f
AMRSimulationController::executeTimestep(double)+0x2a6
AMRSimulationController::run()+0x103b
StandAlone/sus() [0x4064d2]
__libc_start_main()+0xed
StandAlone/sus() [0x403469]
```

Each line in the stack trace is comprised of a complete function signature and a hexadecimal address indicating the calling context of the next called function.

We collect such stack traces to create a CSTG in memory at each process. After processing each stack trace, the current CSTG is updated with new nodes and/or edge-weights; the stack trace is then discarded. The cost of creating a CSTG is equal to maintaining a hash table, so the complexity is $\mathcal{O}(N)$ on average for N stack traces collected. Hence, CSTGs are memory efficient. At the end of

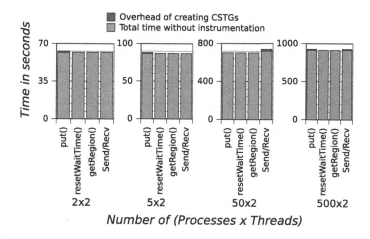

Fig. 7. Scaling experiments showing overhead of CSTG creation.

an execution, per-process CSTGs are merged into one global graph. The merge operation itself is simple: if an edge already exists, its weight is incremented, and otherwise a new edge is added. Finally, we compare CSTGs by creating a graph diff, showing weight deficits as negative numbers (on red edges) and excesses as positive numbers (on green edges).

7   Scaling Experiments

In this section, we present preliminary scaling studies of the viability of using CSTGs at larger scale, approaching 1,000 nodes. In the scaling studies, we used the same stack trace collection points as before (namely put() as in *Mini Coal Boiler*, resetWaitTime() as in *Poisson2*, getRegion() as in *Arches*, and Send/Recv as in *Mathing Events*), albeit a different Uintah input file that was easy to scale. We compare pure Uintah runtimes with runtimes when the code was instrumented, stack traces collected, CSTGs created in memory, and graph files written to disk. The used input files do not produce crashes so that we can run the simulations to completion and build the full CSTGs. The experiments were performed on a cluster with 66 nodes, each node with 4 AMD Opteron Magny-Cours 6164HE 12-core 1.7 GHz CPUs, 64 GB RAM, 7200 RPM SATA2 hard drives, and 10 Gigabit Ethernet.

Figure 7 shows that the overhead of collecting stack traces and creating CSTGs in memory for various collection points. The overhead is very small (less than 1 % in average) in all the scenarios tested, and clearly our solution scales well in practice. The time to collect a stack trace depends of the number of stack frames to be transversed. However, the time to collect the same stack trace is constant throughout the execution of the program. The complexity of creating a CSTG with N stack traces is $N \cdot \Theta(1)$, or $\mathcal{O}(N)$ on average, which is related to maintaining a hash table. In addition, there is no communication between processes involved (each process creates its own CSTG merged in the end), and the final files written are quite small (negligible I/O demand). Hence, the total overhead of creating CSTGs primarily depends on the number of stack traces collected, which changes depending on the simulated problem and inserted collection points. In our experiments, the number of stack traces collected per run ranges from 150 to 322,000. To conclude, our preliminary scaling studies show the feasibility of employing CSTGs without significant overhead in parallel HPC computational frameworks such as Uintah.

8   Conclusions

Finding the root-causes of bugs in the context of large-scale HPC projects is resource-intensive: it takes lead developers away from doing useful science, and engages them in a "fire-fighting" frenzy. Often, the actual bug manifestation (e.g., a crash site) has scanty information pertaining to its root-cause. We propose a facility for expeditiously debugging sequential and parallel programs called Coalesced Stack Trace Graphs (CSTG). Our approach relies on finding salient differences in executions using CSTGs, and possible scenarios include comparing: different versions of a system, runs of the same system to understand the effects of nondeterminism, runs on different inputs, matching events such as message sends/receives, and different time-steps, loop iterations, or processes.

In the traditional debugging process, as a user gains knowledge about the problem at hand, he/she can use CSTGs to provide the necessary contextual information and greatly accelerate the identification of the root-cause. We demonstrated the applicability of CSTGs in several real bug case studies, primarily in the context of Uintah, an open-source software framework for solving complex multiscale multi-physics problems on cutting edge HPC systems. Our implementation of CSTGs is simple, has low overhead, and scales well in practice. It can be used in many scenarios to help in the debugging process of concurrent or sequential software, and despite most of our case studies were applied to Uintah, it does not depend on it as we illustrated with our *Flex* case study.

References

1. Ahn, D.H., Lee, G.L., Gopalakrishnan, G., Rakamarić, Z., Schulz, M., Laguna, I.: Overcoming extreme-scale reproducibility challenges through a unified, targeted, and multilevel toolset. In: International Workshop on Software Engineering for High Performance Computing in Computational Science and Engineering (SE-HPCCSE) (2013)
2. Ammons, G., Ball, T., Larus, J.R.: Exploiting hardware performance counters with flow and context sensitive profiling. In: PLDI, pp. 85–96 (1997)
3. Arnold, D.C., Ahn, D.H., de Supinski, B.R., Lee, G.L., Miller, B.P., Schulz, M.: Stack trace analysis for large scale debugging. In: IPDPS, pp. 1–10 (2007)
4. Bartz, K., Stokes, J.W., Platt, J.C., Kivett, R., Grant, D., Calinoiu, S., Loihle, G.: Finding similar failures using callstack similarity. In: Workshop on Tackling Computer Systems Problems with Machine Learning Techniques (SysML) (2008)

5. Berzins, M.: Status of release of the Uintah computational framework. SCI Technical report UUSCI-2012-001, SCI Institute, Utah (2012)
6. Beschastnikh, I., Brun, Y., Ernst, M.D., Krishnamurthy, A., Anderson, T.E.: Mining temporal invariants from partially ordered logs. In: SLAML (2011)
7. Beschastnikh, I., Brun, Y., Schneider, S., Sloan, M., Ernst, M.D.: Leveraging existing instrumentation to automatically infer invariant-constrained models. In: Symposium on the Foundations of Software Engineering (FSE), pp. 267–277 (2011)
8. Bronevetsky, G., Laguna, I., Bagchi, S., de Supinski, B., Ahn, D., Schulz, M.: AutomaDeD: Automata-based debugging for dissimilar parallel tasks. In: IEEE/ IFIP International Conference on Dependable Systems and Networks (DSN), pp. 231–240 (2010)
9. Dang, Y., Wu, R., Zhang, H., Zhang, D., Nobel, P.: Rebucket: A method for clustering duplicate crash reports based on call stack similarity. In: International Conference on Software Engineering (ICSE), pp. 1084–1093 (2012)
10. Allinea DDT. http://www.allinea.com/products/ddt
11. de Oliveira, D.C.B., Rakamarić, Z., Gopalakrishnan, G., Humphrey, A., Meng, Q., Berzins, M.: Practical formal correctness checking of million-core problem solving environments for HPC. In: International Workshop on Software Engineering for Computational Science and Engineering (SE-CSE 2013) (2013)
12. Do, H., Elbaum, S.G., Rothermel, G.: Supporting controlled experimentation with testing techniques: An infrastructure and its potential impact. Empirical Softw. Eng. Int. J. **10**(4), 405–435 (2005)
13. Germain, J.D.D.S., McCorquodale, J., Parker, S.G., Johnson, C.R.: Uintah: A massively parallel problem solving environment. In: IEEE International Symposium on High Performance Distributed Computing (HPDC), pp. 33–41 (2000)
14. Gopalakrishnan, G., Kirby, R.M., Siegel, S., Thakur, R., Gropp, W., Lusk, E., De Supinski, B.R., Schulz, M., Bronevetsky, G.: Formal analysis of MPI-based parallel programs. Commun. ACM **54**(12), 82–91 (2011)
15. Han, S., Dang, Y., Ge, S., Zhang, D., Xie, T.: Performance debugging in the large via mining millions of stack traces. In: ICSE, pp. 145–155 (2012)
16. Kim, S., Zimmermann, T., Nagappan, N.: Crash graphs: An aggregated view of multiple crashes to improve crash triage. In: DSN, pp. 486–493 (2011)
17. Meng, Q., Humphrey, A., Schmidt, J., Berzins, M.: Investigating applications portability with the Uintah DAG-based runtime system on petascale supercomputers. Technical report UUSCI-2013-003, SCI Institute, Utah (2013)
18. Pastore, F., Mariani, L., Goffi, A.: Radar: A tool for debugging regression problems in C/C++ software. In: ICSE, pp. 1335–1338 (2013)
19. Cleaner, Cheaper Energy is Goal of Supercomputer Research. http://unews.utah.edu/news_releases/16m-for-coal-energy-research/
20. Rogue Wave Software. http://www.totalviewtech.com
21. Sambasivan, R.R., Zheng, A.X., De Rosa, M., Krevat, E., Whitman, S., Stroucken, M., Wang, W., Xu, L., Ganger, G.R.: Diagnosing performance changes by comparing request flows. In: NSDI, pp. 4–4 (2011)
22. Schroter, A., Bettenburg, N., Premraj, R.: Do stack traces help developers fix bugs? In: Conference on Mining Software Repositories (MSR), pp. 118–121 (2010)
23. Uintah. http://www.uintah.utah.edu/
24. Valgrind. http://valgrind.org
25. Zeller, A.: Yesterday, my program worked. Today, it does not. Why? In: Symposium on the Foundations of Software Engineering (FSE), pp. 253–267 (1999)

LightPlay: Efficient Replay with GPUs

Min Feng[1]([envelope]), Farzad Khorasani[2], Rajiv Gupta[2], and Laxmi N. Bhuyan[2]

[1] NEC Laboratories America, Princeton, NJ, USA
mfeng@nec-labs.com
[2] University of California, Riverside, CA, USA

Abstract. Previous deterministic replay systems reduce the runtime overhead by either relying on hardware support or by relaxing the determinism requirements for replay. We propose LightPlay that fulfills stricter determinism requirements with low overhead without requiring hardware or OS support. LightPlay guarantees that the memory state after each instruction instance in a replay run is the same as in original run. It reduces logging overhead using a lightweight thread local technique that avoids synchronization between threads during the recording run. GPUs are used to efficiently identify the memory ordering constraints that produce the same memory states before the replay run. LightPlay incurs low space overhead for logging as it only stores the part of log where data races occur. During the logging run LightPlay is 20x–100x faster than logging the total order and requires only 1 % space overhead.

1 Introduction

The ability to replay a program's execution plays an important role in developing software. Software often fails due to bugs that are difficult to locate. To find the root cause of the bug, developers need to reproduce the bug and observe its manifestation. Replay systems record and reproduce program execution and this capability has proven to be useful in debugging [8,17,18] and fault tolerance [4].

Many traditional replay systems [5,9] record a multi-threaded program's input and the order of shared-memory accesses to achieve deterministic replay on a multiprocessor system. However, logging the shared-memory accesses incurs huge overhead since the execution of these memory accesses needs to be serialized. Many techniques have been proposed to reduce the overhead of logging and replaying shared-memory accesses on multiprocessors. Most of them require hardware modifications to record cache coherence events [6,13–15,20,22]. LEAP [7] is a software replay system that uses JAVA source code information to reduce the locking overhead used for serializing memory accesses. To make replay more accessible, other efforts have been directed towards reducing the logging overhead using purely software techniques. These techniques relax the determinism requirements so that less information needs to be recorded during the logging phase. Many of the software replay systems [1,12,16,19,21,23] guarantee *external determinism* or *output determinism*. *External determinism* only

This work is supported by NSF grants CNS-1157377 and CCF-0905509 to UCR.

© Springer International Publishing Switzerland 2015
J. Brodman and P. Tu (Eds.): LCPC 2014, LNCS 8967, pp. 332–347, 2015.
DOI: 10.1007/978-3-319-17473-0_22

ensures reproducing identical program state at certain execution points in the replay run while *output determinism* just promises that the same values are sent to output devices such as screens, networks, and disks. There are also software replay systems [10, 11] that target even more relaxed determinism requirements, e.g., *failure determinism*. With failure determinism, they only guarantee that the same error states are produced in replay runs. *For these software replay systems, while the output replay may reproduce the same results, the root cause of the error may not be preserved or even reproduced. Therefore, if we use a replay run for debugging, we may not be able to find the original root cause of the bug.*

Figure 1 shows a code example where the failure may not be reproduced. In the example, thread 2 collects values from all threads, calculates the summation, and prints the result. Consider a program run that has the following execution order: T1:1, T2:1, T2:2, T1:3, and T2:3, but the output is 5 due to a bug inside function add(). To replay this execution, an output

Thread 1		Thread 2
1 A = 2;	1	B = 2;
2 ...	2	C = add(A,B);
3 A = 3;	3	print(C);

Fig. 1. Example: failures may not be reproduced under relaxed determinism.

deterministic replay system may produce an execution in which the output is still 5, but the execution order is T1:1, T1:3, T2:1, T2:2, and T2:3. 3 plus 2, however, is 5 and thus the replay run does not show any fault. Developers cannot find the bug using this replay run.

In this paper, we propose LightPlay, which is a deterministic replay system designed to log and replay multithreaded programs that are executed in parallel on multiprocessors. The system does not require any modification to the hardware or the OS. LightPlay delivers a stricter determinism requirement - *internal determinism*. We guarantee that the internal memory state after each instruction instance in a replay run is the same as in the original run. By keeping the internal states the same, we can ensure that the root cause of the bug is unchanged in the replay run. However, achieving *internal determinism* using prior software techniques is costly. Recording either total orders [9] or load values [2] requires serializing shared memory accesses, atomic execution of instrumented code, and/or data privatization. We have developed a set of techniques to make LightPlay efficient. In LightPlay, the logging overhead is reduced via use of lightweight thread local technique which is designed to avoid additional synchronization between threads in the recording runs. Since the thread interactions are not recorded, it is necessary to search for an equivalent multi-threaded execution before the replay run. To enable searching, execution is divided into timeslices and values read and written by shared-memory accesses during each interval are roughly recorded at runtime without serializing the accesses. In this way, we reduce the logging time by migrate the runtime overhead from the recording run to the replay run. To further improve the search performance, we use GPUs to perform the search in parallel. The GPU uses recorded values for a slice to search for an ordering of shared-memory accesses that produces the same memory state. The ordering recovered by the GPU is then saved and used during deterministic replay. Our experiments show that LightPlay is 20x–100x faster than logging the total order in the logging run and requires only 1 % space overhead. The search procedure on the GPU is also shown to be efficient, causing less than 30x slowdown for most PARSEC benchmarks.

2   The LightPlay System

LightPlay is a deterministic replay system that records and reproduces execution of multithreaded applications. It uses a purely software logging mechanism which, unlike other software solutions that introduce high runtime overhead, is very light-weight. The recorded trace is composed of a set of incremental checkpoints. Therefore, the replay can be begun from any point in the execution. However, the trace captured via logging cannot be directly used to reproduce the execution as thread interactions are not recorded in order to achieve light-weight logging. This issue is addressed by searching for an execution that has no observable difference from the original execution. To perform the search efficiently, we propose to exploit the massive parallelism offered by GPUs. After finding the desired execution, it is replayed using a uniprocessor.

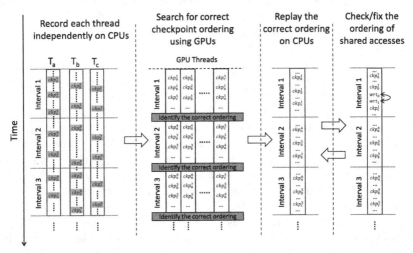

Fig. 2. System overview.

Figure 2 shows the four steps of LightPlay. First, the logging of each thread in the multithreaded application is performed independently via incremental checkpoints. The program's execution is divided into intervals referred to as time slices such that they contain *nearly equal* numbers of checkpoints. In the second step, the system uses GPUs to search for a correct checkpoint ordering before replaying the execution. The search can be done offline or it can be done online (i.e., as the program executes on the CPUs, the GPU can search for the ordering). In step three, the system infers the thread schedule on a uniprocessor that reproduces the execution. Checkpoint ordering sometimes does not lead to a correct replay. If this happens, in step four, the system uses the error information to adjust the thread schedule. The third and fourth steps are repeated until a correct replay is achieved.

2.1 Logging

Our logging mechanism is designed to be both lightweight (i.e., it introduces little execution time overhead) and entirely implemented in software. Traditionally, to record a multithreaded execution without hardware support, synchronization points are injected for collecting: (1) ordering of shared memory accesses (i.e., thread schedule); and/or (2) input and output values of shared memory accesses. This additional synchronization introduces huge runtime overhead. Our logging mechanism collects neither the ordering nor the accurate input/output values of shared memory accesses. Instead it records each thread independently and only inserts lightweight incremental checkpoint sites to record the program state before and after (although not necessarily immediately before/after) shared memory accesses. We then search for an equivalent execution that produces exactly the same values at the checkpoints when performing replay.

Thread 1	Thread 2
A = B = 0;	
	...
record B;	record A;
A = B + 1;	C = A + 1;
record A;	record C;
	...
	record A, C;

Fig. 3. Example showing checkpoints.

```
ss = ++slice_size; // get the current slice size
if ( ss == T+1 ) { // first thread reaching a new slice
    wait_current_slice_finish();
    checkpointing();
    slice_size -= T;
    notify_other_threads();
}
if ( ss > T+1 ) // other threads wait if the slice is full
    wait();
// shared memory access here;
```

Fig. 4. Timeslicing code.

Inserting Optimistic Checkpoints. LightPlay introduces lightweight checkpoints using PIN for quick prototyping (static insertion can also be used). The checkpoints are inserted at: (1) before/after each shared memory accesses; and (2) after each time slice. Checkpoints are added before (after) each shared memory access to record the state of the read (written) memory location. We treat all memory accesses other than accesses to the stacks or thread local storage as potentially shared memory accesses. In the example given in Fig. 3, we record B & A before the two memory accesses and A & C after the accesses. The recorded values may not equal the input and output values of the shared memory accesses since we do not perform the original memory access and their recording *atomically*. This *optimistic* approach is used for reducing overhead. In vast majority of the cases the values will be correctly recorded and in the few cases where they are not, step four of our approach will account for them. Checkpoints are also inserted to record the program state at the end of each time slice to enable

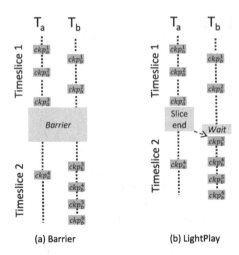

Fig. 5. Barrier vs. our slicing implementation.

ordering of the writes before the end of each time slice. We only record the state of memory locations that have been updated. For example, in Fig. 3, A & C are recorded at the end of the time slice since they have been updated.

Timeslicing. All threads need to be synchronized at the end of each time slice. This synchronization can be done with the use of barriers, as shown in Fig. 5(a). However, barriers may greatly slowdown the execution due to resulting stalls. In addition, using hand coded barriers may cause imbalance in time slices, that is, different time slices may have different number of shared memory accesses, making checkpoint ordering costly for large time slices. Our timeslicing scheme avoids using barriers and creates timeslices of equal size. At the end of each timeslice, we use one thread to finish the timeslice and allow the other threads to continue until encountering new shared memory accesses (see Fig. 5(b)). Figure 4 shows the pseudo-code of our timeslicing implementation. Code is inserted before each shared memory access to divide the execution into time slices that contain equal number (i.e., T) of shared memory accesses. The increment (i.e., ++) and compound assignment (i.e., -=) operators in the example are made to be atomic using the *atomic fetch-and-add instructions* provided in the x86 instruction set. This ensures if a thread grows the slice size beyond T, it waits until the current slice is completed. This improves performance over using barriers since a thread can continue to perform local memory accesses even when another thread is finishing the current time slice.

Reducing Overhead of Logging Values. Value logging can incur huge space overhead. For example, logging the `streamcluster` benchmark [3] will produce over 10 GB of trace per minute. If the trace is constantly dumped onto a disk, logging performance suffers. Therefore, instead of keeping value logs for all slices, we only keep logs for the time slices that have data races. If there is no data race in the slice, the slice can be replayed with any thread schedule. We only need to store two numbers in the log file, each number indicating the number of shared accesses performed by a thread. This optimization does not cause any information loss since all memory accesses in the rest of the time slices can be viewed as local memory accesses which do not require logging. This optimization greatly reduces the trace size since most time slices usually do not have any data race. To further improve performance, we create separate threads to check the existence of data race in parallel with the program execution. Thus, the overhead of data race checking is removed from the critical path of the program execution,

2.2   Checkpoint Ordering

Finding the checkpoint ordering not only reproduces the execution, but it can also help users debug their programs because it helps in understanding of cross-thread interactions, i.e., shared-memory dependencies. We propose to use GPUs to accelerate the search for the correct ordering. The search is performed one timeslice at a time. During the search, we optimistically assume that each shared memory access and the checkpoints around it were executed atomically. In other words, we treat the checkpoints before and after each shared memory access as one memory instruction, which reads the memory locations recorded before the access and writes the locations recorded after the access. The GPU searches for an ordering of such memory instructions that correctly produces the program state at the end of the slice, which is recorded by the checkpoints. The resultant ordering should satisfy the ordering in each thread in the original execution. The detail of using GPUs for searching will be elaborated in Sect. 3. The search for the ordering can be done online and offline.

During the above search we optimistically assume that shared memory access and the checkpoints around it were executed atomically. However, this is not the case because we do not enforce atomicity during the logging phase. As a result, we might not be able to find a correct ordering in some cases or the ordering found may not lead to a correct replay. However, this situation is rare and when it does arise, it is handled by fixing the replay as described later in Sect. 2.4.

2.3   Replay

Once we obtain the checkpoint ordering, we can reproduce the execution of the time slice on a uniprocessor (see Fig. 6). Recall that we treat the checkpoints before and after each shared memory access as one memory instruction in the searching. Therefore, each element of sorted_checkpoint_list is a checkpoint pair. During replay, we enumerate the checkpoint pairs according to the ordering and execute the memory instructions associated with the checkpoint pairs. If the output values match the recorded program state after the instruction, we have successfully replayed the instruction and go to the next pair of checkpoints. Otherwise, the replay has failed and our system will try to fix the replay as described in the next section. If all instructions are replayed successfully, then we have correctly reproduced program behavior via an equivalent execution. The original and equivalent executions produce the same program state at the end of

```
foreach checkpoint_pair (x, y) in sorted_checkpoint_list {
    i = the memory instruction associated (x, y);
    perform i;
    if the output values match y {
        // succeed
        update the memory;
    } else {
        // replay fails
        return error;
    }
}
```

Fig. 6. Pseudo-code for replaying.

each time slice. In each thread, the two executions reach the checkpoints in the same order and produce the same values. Compared to previous software-based replay systems such as DoublePlay [19], the determinism we achieve is more strict since they achieve external determinism (i.e., the orders of system calls and program states at the end of each timeslice are identical).

2.4 Fixing the Ordering

Since we do not enforce the atomic execution of each shared memory access and its checkpoints, we may not be able to correctly reproduce the execution in the previous steps. There are two types of errors that might occur: (1) a checkpoint ordering can be found but the output values of a replayed instruction do not match the values stored in the subsequent checkpoint; and (2) no checkpoint ordering can be found. Next we describe how to fix the replay in each case.

Figure 7 shows the algorithm for fixing the memory access ordering when the first case described above arises. There could be two reason behind this: (1) another thread updates the input memory locations immediately before the misreplayed instruction; and/or (2) another thread overwrites the output memory locations immediately after the misplayed instruction. In the first case, we examine all subsequent memory instructions to see if they write to the input memory location. If another instruction does and can be moved before the misreplayed instruction without breaking the existing def-use chain, we try moving it before the misreplayed instruction. If the new output values matches, we then get the correct ordering. Similarly for the second case, we can try moving another instruction immediately after the misreplayed instruction. If the ordering cannot be fixed, the method presented next handles the situation in which no checkpoint ordering can be found.

When no checkpoint ordering can be found, we relax the condition for ordering searching by treating each checkpoint as an independent memory instruction. If the checkpoint is set before a memory access, it is considered a read. Otherwise it is considered a write. We then send the new set of memory instructions to the GPU for searching ordering. Because in the new search we give up the

```
func fix_ordering(checkpoint_pair(x, y)){
    i = the associated mem instruction;
    foreach checkpoint_pair(s, t) after (x, y)
    {
        j = instrn associated with (s, t);
        if ( t updates the location in x and
        j can be moved before i ) {
            perform i using the values in t;
            if output values matches {
                move (s, j, t) before i;
                return Succ;
            }
        }
    }
    foreach checkpoint_pair (s, t) {
        j= instruction associated with (s, t);
        if ( t matches y and
        j can be moved after i ) {
            move (s, j, t) after i;
            return;
        }
    }
    return Fail; }
```

```
foreach ordering in ordering_list {
    i = first memory instrn in instr_list;
    while (i in instr_list) {
        do {
            if i not in ordering {
                find checkpoint_pair (x, y)
                associated with i;
                insert i after x in ordering;
            } else {
                move i to the next position
                in ordering;
            }
        } while (i break the def-use chain
        in ordering and
        i is before y);
        if (i inserted successfully)
            i = next instrn in instr_list;
        else
            i = previous instrn in instr_list;
    }
    if (all instrns inserted successfully)
        return ordering;
}
```

Fig. 7. Fixing the instruction ordering in the presence of mismatched output values.

Fig. 8. Searching instruction ordering when no checkpoint ordering is found.

assumption that a memory access and its associated checkpoints are executed atomically, the position of each memory access in the resultant ordering may not be inferred directly. Figure 8 shows the algorithm to search the ordering of all shared memory accesses given the ordering of checkpoints. The algorithm tries to insert each memory access into positions between the two associated checkpoints until a correct ordering of the shared memory accesses is found.

2.5   Minimal Constraints Construction

Our search algorithm on the GPU is designed to find all correct orders of shared memory accesses. With the information, we are able to identify a minimal set of memory ordering constraints, which can help programmers understand the bug and enable fast parallel replay. We use a simple efficient method to extract minimal constraints between memory instructions by knowing all correct possible orderings for them in a timeslice. Instruction ordering within each thread applies the first set of constraints to the memory instructions. We also consider one of all correct permutations as the reference correct ordering. The sufficient condition for two memory instructions from different threads to be dependent upon each other is that they access the same memory region and at least one of them writes. For pairs of memory instructions that satisfy this condition, if in all the correct orderings the same pattern is observed, we introduce this pattern as the constraint. Otherwise, we introduce the constraint between two instructions using the reference correct ordering.

3   Searching for Ordering via GPUs

We use GPUs for searching the correct checkpoint ordering since the massive parallelism of GPUs is a good fit for searching. The step in Sect. 2.2 requires that we find the ordering of checkpoint pairs. We begin by treating the checkpoints before and after each shared memory access as one memory instruction. We need to find an ordering of such memory instructions that correctly produces the program state at the end of the slice. Besides, the resultant ordering should satisfy the ordering in each thread during the original execution. The step in Sect. 2.4 requires that we find the ordering of individual checkpoints but all the rest remains the same. Therefore the problem we need to solve on the GPU is, how to identify the correct ordering of a set of memory instructions given: (1) the input/output values; (2) the final program state; and (3) the instruction ordering within each thread. To perform searching, we first transfer the data regarding the time slice to the device memory and then each GPU thread works on a different ordering to see if that ordering works for the slice. Because of the massive parallelism available on the GPU, this step is done more efficiently on the GPU. Finally the correct ordering found is transferred to the host.

3.1   Ordering Search

The following three-step procedure is performed on each GPU thread to find correct ordering of memory instructions. Given a time slice, we first generate all permutations of the memory instructions on the GPU and each GPU thread is assigned one permutation. Second, the thread emulates the memory instructions using the ordering indicated by the permutation. Finally, we verify the program state with recorded state. The details of this procedure are given next.

Generating the Permutation. A unique permutation of the memory instructions in a given slice is created according to the GPU thread ID. When the algorithm creates the unique permutation, it respects the instruction ordering within each thread. In other words, our algorithm guarantees that the instruction orderings in the generated permutations match the recorded local instruction orderings. In this way, we eliminate most incorrect permutations of instructions in the generation step, which increases available GPU resources for each permutation, allowing handling of bigger slices with more instructions.

The slice information is stored in three arrays: *instr_list*, *cpu_tid_list*, and *thread_size*. Array *instr_list* stores the instruction IDs. In a time slice, instructions are sorted by their thread IDs and numbered from 1 (as shown in Fig. 9(a)). Array *cpu_tid_list* contains the thread ID of each instruction and *thread_size* keeps the number of instructions in each thread. The number of possible permutations is

CPU Thread 1	CPU Thread 2
I1→I2→I3	I4→I5

(a) A recorded slice with two CPU threads.

GPU Thread ID	Permutation
0	I1→I2→I3→I4→I5
1	I1→I2→I4→I3→I5
2	I1→I2→I4→I5→I3
3	I1→I4→I2→I3→I5
4	I1→I4→I2→I5→I3
5	I1→I4→I5→I2→I3
6	I4→I1→I2→I3→I5
7	I4→I1→I2→I5→I3
8	I4→I1→I5→I2→I3
9	I4→I5→I1→I2→I3

(b) Generated permutation on each GPU thread.

Fig. 9. Example of generated permutations.

Iteration	Thread 0	Thread 1	rank	perm_cnt	instr_list	cpu_tid_list	my_perm
Init.	I1→I2→I3	I4→I5	4	10	{1,2,3,4,5}	{0,0,0,1,1}	{}
#0	I2→I3	I4→I5	4	6	{2,3,4,5}	{0,0,1,1}	{I1}
#1	I2→I3	I5	1	3	{2,3,5}	{0,0,1}	{I1,I4}
#2	I3	I5	1	2	{3,5}	{0,1}	{I1,I4,I2}
#3	I3	φ	0	1	{3}	{0}	{I1,I4,I2,I5}
#4	φ	φ	0	0	{}	{}	{I1,I4,I2,I5,I3}

Fig. 10. Permutation generation on GPU thread 4.

stored in *perm_count*, which is initially set by the following equation where T is the number of threads and *slice_size* is the number of instructions in the slice.

$$perm\_count = \frac{slice\_size!}{\prod_{i=0}^{T}(thread\_size_i!)}$$

Figure 9(a) shows a recorded slice with two threads. In the example, thread 1 contains three instructions numbered from 1 to 3 and thread 2 contains two instructions numbered 4 and 5. Figure 10 gives all the permutations generated by our algorithm. We can see that all permutations match the recorded local instruction orders. Figure 10 shows the step-by-step procedure of generating a permutation on GPU thread 4 using our algorithm. Each step removes an instruction from thread 1 or 2 and assigns it to *my_perm*. The procedure ends when all instructions are assigned to *my_perm*.

One possible way to create all permutations is to create them on the CPU once and then transfer them to the GPU. In this way, aside from the initial workload for moving the permutation table, the number of memory accesses on the GPU increases enormously, degrading the performance. In our approach, each thread creates its own permutation by using its own registers and shared memory and therefore no time is wasted on memory accesses.

Emulating the Instructions. The given memory instructions are emulated in the GPU memory. Figure 11 shows how the instructions are emulated. Execution of each instruction is emulated on an array of registers assigned to the thread. Memory instructions are verified one by one. If the instruction is a write, the emulation array (EmuMeM) will be updated using the recorded value. If the instruction is a read, the emulation array is searched for the corresponding value. For each read, we check if the values gotten from the emulation array matches the recorded values. If not, this permutation is wrong and the thread will be killed. At the end, a final memory state is created based on the ordering corresponding to the permutation.

Verifying the Final State. Finally the contents of emulation array are compared with the recorded final state of the time slice. If they do not match, the permutation does not work and the thread is killed. If there is a match, the permutation indicates a correct order of shared memory accesses is transferred back to the CPU.

3.2 Optimizations

Slice Refinement. To reduce the search space, we apply two levels of refinements to a slice. In the first level of refinement, we remove the local memory accesses from the slice. The second level of refinement splits a big slice into smaller ones to further reduce the searching overhead.

Data Transfer. To improve the data transfer performance, multiple CUDA streams should be used. Instead of one, multiple time slices of instructions are processed in parallel with multiple streams. By enqueueing operations of multiple streams in a breadth-first manner, data transfer and searching (i.e., kernel) are performed concurrently. Overlapping of host-device data transfer and kernel execution accelerates the GPU algorithm by improving the throughput. For fast copying of results back to the CPU, we use the host zero-copy memory to hold them. Since the result is accessed just once during the kernel call, using zero-copy method instead of copying the data from the GPU global memory to the CPU memory greatly improves the performance. Since each GPU thread ID indicates a specific ordering, we only need to store the thread IDs in the zero-copy memory, which further reduces the data transfer overhead.

4   Evaluation

To evaluate our LightPlay we conducted experiments by running PARSEC benchmark suite [3] on a machine with twelve Intel i7 processors (3.20 GHz) and two NVIDIA GeForce GTX 780 cards. Most PARSEC benchmarks (except Blackscholes) have data races between threads. We used the large input set provided with the PARSEC benchmarks for evaluation. All PARSEC benchmarks were

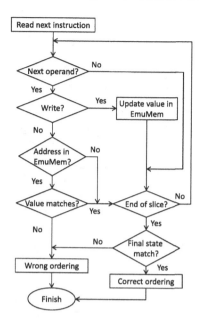

Fig. 11. Flowchart of verifying an ordering.

run using 4 threads unless specified otherwise. We used two GeForce GTX 780 graphic cards for the experiments with CUDA driver version 5. We used the constant memory on the GPU to store the slices. Accesses to constant memory, unlike regular global memory, are cached. During GPU kernel launches, we used shared memory and registers to improve performance as much as possible. Considering the fact that GeForce GTX 780 has around 48 KBytes of shared memory, we had to choose maximum possible size of a slice so that block size be a multiple of warp size and also each thread block can have a suitable quota of shared memory for operations. We selected 32 as the block size of each GPU kernel call and it confined maximum possible slice size to 18. In the experiments, each GPU uses at least two streams to maximize overlapping between data transfer and kernel execution.

4.1 Logging Performance

Figure 12 shows the logging performance of LightPlay compared to total order recording. Total order recording is implemented by atomically executing an memory instruction with the corresponding recording instructions. We can see that LightPlay is faster than total order recording by at least a factor of 20x.

Table 1 lists the log size of LightPlay and total order recording. Compared to total order recording, LightPlay does not need to record the trace for all memory instructions. We only record values for slices which contain data races. As shown in Table 2, all benchmarks contain less than 0.002 % slices that have data races.

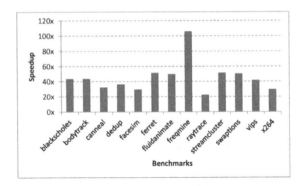

Fig. 12. Logging performance over total order recording.

Table 1. Log size (KB) of LightPlay and total order recording.

Benchmark	LightPlay	Total order recording
blackscholes	2,624	649,343
bodytrack	10,749	2,577,869
canneal	16,002	3,948,534
dedup	39,729	9,817,656
facesim	315,683	78,124,661
ferret	22,609	5,584,933
fluidanimate	18,311	4,458,619
freqmine	51,016	12,621,886
raytrace	363,978	89,987,985
streamcluster	193,901	5,535,742
swaptions	11,523	2,850,757
vips	34,882	8,632,856
x264	8,155	2,005,157

Table 2. Percentage of slices with data races.

Benchmark	Percentage
blackscholes	0.0000 %
bodytrack	0.0062 %
canneal	0.0019 %
dedup	0.0015 %
facesim	0.0000 %
ferret	0.0011 %
fluidanimate	0.0024 %
freqmine	0.0002 %
raytrace	0.0007 %
streamcluster	0.1460 %
swaptions	0.0006 %
vips	0.0004 %
x264	0.0010 %

Thus, our log size is significantly smaller than that of total order recording. We observed reduction in the log size of over two orders of magnitude.

4.2 Search Performance

Figure 13 shows the search performance for most PARSEC benchmarks (except `blackscholes` and `streamcluster`) using GPUs. In the experiment, we run the benchmarks using 2, 4, and 8 CPU threads. The slowdowns were measured over the original execution time of the same benchmarks. We can see that for most benchmarks, the slowdown caused by the search is below 30x. We do not show `blackscholes` in the figure since it has no slice with data races. The search performance for `streamcluster` is 1000x 2000x because its trace contains 673 K slices. The performance for `streamcluster` is still acceptable compared to other search-based replay systems.

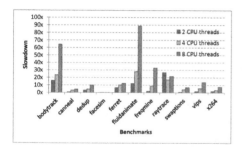

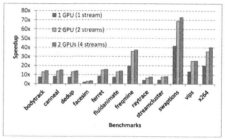

Fig. 13. Search performance using GPU.

Fig. 14. Search performance compared to a CPU implementation.

In Fig. 14, we compare our search performance with a CPU implementation, which runs a similar algorithm. The GPU performance was measured by using 2 GPUs, each with 4 streams. The host-pinned memory was used to help transfer data to the GPUs. We used 8 threads for the CPU implementation. Compared to the CPU implementation, our GPU implementation is on average 28x faster, which demonstrates GPU is a good platform for performing the search. Figure 15 shows a breakdown of the execution time of the GPU kernel. For all benchmarks, over 96 % of time is spent on computation. Therefore, our GPU implementaiton has very high computation to data transfer ratio.

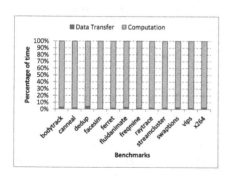

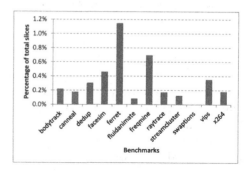

Fig. 15. Breakdown of GPU kernel execution time.

Fig. 16. Percentage of slices that need to be fixed.

4.3   Fixing the Order Performance

Figure 16 shows the percentage of slices that need to be fixed after the search. For all benchmarks, only less than 1.5 % of slices require the fixing procedure. The swaptions benchmark shows an empty bar since it does not have any slices requiring order fixing.

Figure 17 shows the performance of the fixing procedure. The slowdowns were measured over the original execution time of the same benchmarks. The fixing procedure causes less than 2x slowdown for most benchmarks except streamcluster. It takes much less time than the search. For streamcluster,

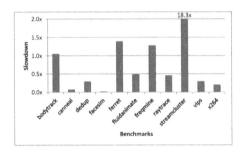
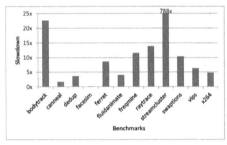

Fig. 17. Performance of order fixing.

Fig. 18. Performance of constructing the minimal ordering constraints.

the fixing procedure causes around 18x slowdown since it has more than 800 slices that need to be fixed.

4.4 Constructing Minimal Ordering Constraints

Figure 18 shows the performance of constructing the minimal ordering constraints. The minimal ordering constraints were constructed on the CPU. We can see that for most benchmarks, the slowdown caused by the construction is below 25x, which costs less than the search procedure. The constraint construction for `streamcluster` takes longest time, causing 788x slowdown. This is because its trace contains 673 K slices. The step of constructing minimal ordering constraints is optional since the constraints are not necessary for replay.

5   Conclusion

We presented a software solution to record and replay multithreaded programs. Our solution does not require recording shared-memory dependences. Each thread only records its own memory instructions locally. In the replay run, GPUs are used to quickly identify the correct total order of shared memory accesses. In the recording phase, memory accesses are organized in time slices to reduce the search space. To reduce the logging overhead, the traces for time slices are selectively saved and the checkpointing at the end of a time slice is done using a parallel thread. The experiments show that logging overhead is very low and GPUs are much faster than CPUs in building correct ordering of shared accesses.

References

1. Altekar, G., Stoica, I.: Odr: output-deterministic replay for multicore debugging. In: SOSP, pp: 193–206 (2009)
2. Bhansali, S., Chen, W.-K., de Jong, S., Edwards, A., Murray, R., Drinić, M., Mihočka, D., Chau, J.: Framework for instruction-level tracing and analysis of program executions. In: VEE, pp. 154–163 (2006)
3. Bienia, C., Kumar, S., Singh, J.P., Li, K.: The parsec benchmark suite: characterization and architectural implications. In: PACT (2008)

4. Bressoud, T.C., Schneider, F.B.: Hypervisor-based fault tolerance. ACM Trans. Comput. Syst. **14**(1), 80–107 (1996)

5. Dunlap, G,W., Lucchetti, D.G., Fetterman, M.A., Chen P.M.: Execution replay of multiprocessor virtual machines. In: VEE (2008)

6. Hower, D.R., Hill, M.D.: Rerun: exploiting episodes for lightweight memory race recording. In: ISCA, pp. 265–276 (2008)

7. Huang, J., Liu, P., Zhang, C.: Leap: lightweight deterministic multi-processor replay of concurrent java programs. In: FSE, pp. 207–216 (2010)

8. King, S.T., Dunlap, G.W., Chen, P.M.: Debugging operating systems with time-traveling virtual machines. In: USENIX (2005)

9. LeBlanc, T.J., Mellor-Crummey, J.M.: Debugging parallel programs with instant replay. IEEE Trans. Comput. **36**(4), 471–482 (1987)

10. Lee, D., Said, M., Narayanasamy, S., Yang, Z.: Offline symbolic analysis to infer total store order. In: HPCA. IEEE (2011)

11. Lee, D., Said, M., Narayanasamy, S., Yang, Z.: Pereira. Offline symbolic analysis for multi-processor execution replay. In: MICRO, pp. 564–575 (2009)

12. Lee, D., Wester, B., Veeraraghavan, K., Narayanasamy, S., Chen, P.M., Flinn, J.: Respec: efficient online multiprocessor replayvia speculation and external determinism. In: ASPLOS, pp. 77–90 (2010)

13. Montesinos, P., Ceze, L., Torrellas, J.: Delorean: recording and deterministically replaying shared-memory multiprocessor execution efficiently. In: ISCA, pp. 289–300 (2008)

14. Nagarajan, V., Gupta, R.: Ecmon: exposing cache events for monitoring. In: ISCA, pp. 34–360 (2009)

15. Narayanasamy, S., Pereira, C., Calder, B.: Recording shared memory dependencies using strata. In: ASPLOS, pp. 229–240 (2006)

16. Park, S., Zhou, Y., Xiong, W., Yin, Z., Kaushik, R., Lee, K.H., Lu, S.: Pres: probabilistic replay with execution sketching on multiprocessors. In: SOSP, pp. 177–192 (2009)

17. Srinivasan, S.M., Kandula, S., Andrews, C.R., Zhou, Y.: Flashback: a lightweight extension for rollback and deterministic replay for software debugging. In: USENIX (2004)

18. Tucek, J., Lu, S., Huang, C., Xanthos, S., Zhou, Y.: Triage: diagnosing production run failures at the user's site. In: SOSP (2007)

19. Veeraraghavan, K., Lee, D., Wester, B., Ouyang, J., Chen, P.M., Flinn, J., Narayanasamy, S.: Doubleplay: parallelizing sequential logging and replay. In: ASPLOS, pp. 15–26 (2011)

20. Vlachos, E., Goodstein, M.L., Kozuch, M.A., Chen, S., Falsafi, B., Gibbons, P.B., Mowry, T.C.: Paralog: enabling and accelerating online parallel monitoring of multithreaded applications. In: ASPLOS, pp. 271–284 (2010)

21. Weeratunge, D., Zhang, X., Jagannathan, S.: Analyzing multicore dumps to facilitate concurrency bug reproduction. In: ASPLOS (2010)

22. Xu, M., Bodik, R., Hill, M.D.: A "flight data recorder" for enabling full-system multiprocessor deterministic replay. In: ISCA, pp. 122–135 (2003)

23. Zamfir, C., Candea, G.: Execution synthesis: a technique for automated software debugging. In: EuroSys, pp. 321–334 (2010)

Vectorization

Exploring and Evaluating Array Layout Restructuring for SIMDization

Christopher Haine, Olivier Aumage[✉], Enguerrand Petit,
and Denis Barthou

LaBRI/INRIA, University of Bordeaux, Bordeaux, France
{christopher.haine,olivier.aumage,enguerrand.petit,
denis.barthou}@labri.fr

Abstract. SIMD processor units have become ubiquitous. Using SIMD instructions is the key for performance for many applications. Modern compilers have made immense progress in generating efficient SIMD code. However, they still may fail or SIMDize poorly, due to conservativeness, source complexity or missing capabilities. When SIMDization fails, programmers are left with little clues about the root causes and actions to be taken.

Our proposed guided SIMDization framework builds on the assembly-code quality assessment toolkit MAQAO to analyzes binaries for possible SIMDization hindrances. It proposes improvement strategies and readily quantifies their impact, using *in vivo* evaluations of suggested transformation. Thanks to our framework, the programmer gets clear directions and quantified expectations on how to improve his/her code SIMDizability. We show results of our technique on TSVC benchmark.

Keywords: SIMDization · Performance tuning · Performance model

1 Introduction

Nowadays microprocessors feature SIMD vector units, potentially providing substantial performance improvement by concurrently applying the same instruction to all the elements of a vector. A rich and complex API of SIMD instructions has been developed on multiple architectures (such as AVX for Intel or NEON for ARM). Thus, the performance of a code is highly dependent on the use of the SIMD instructions, and compilers are virtually unavoidable for performing SIMDization in an efficient and portable manner. However, the performance of an SIMD code is itself highly dependent on data structure layouts. Unfortunately, although commercial compilers (e.g. IBM xlc, Intel icc, PGI pgcc) have made significant advances in auto-SIMDization, a lot of source codes remain too complicated for a compiler to SIMDize, especially when complex data structures or memory access patterns are involved.

Optimizing for SIMDization may require transformations on code and data structure. A lot of research work has been devoted to improve the capability of

© Springer International Publishing Switzerland 2015
J. Brodman and P. Tu (Eds.): LCPC 2014, LNCS 8967, pp. 351–366, 2015.
DOI: 10.1007/978-3-319-17473-0_23

compilers to perform appropriate transformations on the code structure [1–5]. On the data structure side instead, compilers usually do not override the data layout chosen by the programmer. Several works have studied data layout restructuring for specific applications (e.g. stencils [6]). For general purpose compilers, the impact of such transformations on the whole application is difficult to assess at compile-time, even with inter-procedural optimization enabled. It is also difficult for a compiler to determine whether the layout of a data structure should be changed for the whole application or for a limited scope (inducing extra copies), such as a performance critical kernel. The consequence is that the choice of the right data structure still largely depends on the programmer. And, when SIMDization fails due to sub-optimal data layouts, the compilers leave the user with little clue about what may be the cause of performance inefficiency, let alone about how the source code and data structures could be transformed in order to improve SIMDization. This is unfortunate, as in certain cases only a moderate amount of modifications would be required from the programmer to enable SIMDization by the compiler.

Tools such as Intel VTune [7] may suggest that the user hand-SIMDizes his code using intrinsics on the x86 architecture. However, resorting to intrinsics may hinder the portability of the code. More elaborate works focus on specific code optimization [8,9], other works [6] suggest data restructuring, but are limited to very specific cases such as stencils here. In a recent work [10] we proposed a framework built on the MAQAO toolkit, to analyze binary codes and to formulate user-targeted hints about SIMDization potentials and hindrances. These hints provide the user with possible strategies to remove SIMDization hurdles, such as code transformations or data restructuring. However, this preliminary work conducted a qualitative analysis only, thus lacking worthiness quantification in applying advised transformations.

We propose a new integrated qualitative and quantitative approach to guided SIMDization. Our approach reports possible code improvement strategies involving data layout restructuring. Moreover, it offers a fast assessment of the performance improvement (or lack thereof) to be expected from applying each such strategy respectively using the concept of *in vivo* transformation evaluation.

This paper is organized as follows. Section 2 gives the context and motivating example for this work. Section 3 presents the big picture of our proposal. Section 4 exposes the binary analysis stage of our proposal identifying SIMDization issues related to data layout and memory access patterns. Section 5 exposes the assessment stage of our proposal. Section 6 presents evaluation results on kernels from the TSVC benchmark suite. Section 7 discusses positioning of our contribution with respect to related works. Section 8 concludes this paper.

2   Motivating Example

The listing on Fig. 1 shows a kernel extracted from the TSVC benchmark suite [11,12], a suite of codes for the evaluation of SIMDization capabilities of compilers. This kernel is part of the function s1115.

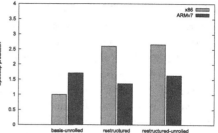

```
1  for ( i = 0;  i < N; i++) {
2    for ( j = 0;  j < N; j++) {
3      a[ i ][ j ] = a[ i ][ j ]*c[ j ][ i ]
4              + b[ i ][ j ];
5    }
6  }
```

Fig. 1. Kernel "s1115" from TSVC suite, showing the need for quantified optimization strategy assessment.

Array c is stored row-major, but accessed column-major, which hinders SIMDization. A possible strategy is to transpose the c array. Another classical strategy is to perform partial loop unrolling. A third strategy is to combine both data transpose and loop unrolling.

The barplot on Fig. 1 shows the relative speed-ups of these strategies compared to the original version. Comparisons are made both for an x86 architecture, the Intel Sandy Bridge E5–2650 @2GHz using icc 13.0.1, and an ARM architecture, the ST-Ericsson Snowball (ARMv7 Cortex-A9 @800MHz) using gcc 4.6.3. Both architectures clearly show very dissimilar behaviors on this example, to the point that the two strategies showing good results on x86 perform poorly on the ARM architecture. To address such situations, we propose a framework enabling the fast assessment of SIMDization strategies.

3   Principle of Fast Data Layout Exploration

Our framework reports possible code improvement strategies involving data layout restructuring using a binary-level static and dynamic analysis. It then enables the programmer to explore the value of these strategies before actually engaging into expensive source code modifications. It offers a fast assessment of the performance improvement (or lack thereof) to be expected from applying these strategies. For that, it uses the concept of *in vivo* transformation evaluation.

The benefit of strategies is evaluated as shown on Fig. 2 through the following steps: (1) The original application binary is instrumented with MAQAO [13] in order to trace the targeted hotspot region (a key application function for instance).

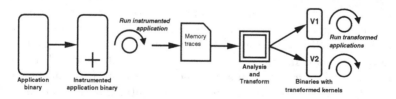

Fig. 2. Overview

(2) The instrumented binary is then run to generate a trace of memory references. This trace consists of the sequence of addresses accessed for each read/write operation and for each thread. (3) The application binary together with the generated memory traces are analyzed in order to propose possible transformation strategies to improve SIMDizability. The analysis determines which arrays are accessed and how they are accessed, then the transformation changes this data layout in order to enhance spatial locality. Transformations are array contraction, transposition and transformation from Arrays of Structures (AoS) into Structures of Arrays (SoA). A SIMDization step is performed if possible, translating instructions into their SIMD counterparts. Finally, a transformed code is generated for each such strategy. Since these codes are generated with transformations relying on trace information, they may not be semantically equivalent to the initial code. They are called *mockups*. (4) Each transformed mockup is then run within the context of its host application. Its performance is measured to assess the relevance of the corresponding strategy.

In order to speed-up the process, the application is checkpointed during step 2 just before executing the hotspot region. Then, each transformed kernel test at step 4 restarts from the checkpointed state of the application.

4   Static/Dynamic Binary Code Analysis for SIMDization

A static and dynamic analysis of the binary code is performed. We assume a limited code fragment (a function for instance), identified with usual profiling tools, is the target of this analysis. This analysis finds loops, blocks and functions in the binary, instruments the code in order to produce traces of memory addresses and computes the dependence graph, essential for vectorization. For the instrumentation and generation of the binary code we use the MAQAO framework. We recall its main features thereafter. The following section explains how the array structures accessed by the code are detected through trace analysis.

4.1   Framework for Static/Dynamic Analysis of Binary Code

We use the MAQAO framework for performing both the static and dynamic analysis of binary code. MAQAO is a performance tuning tool [13] that analyzes the binary code of applications. It builds the control flow graph and the call graph of the code, and detects loop nests. It also proposes an API and a domain-specific language called MIL to instrument a binary code [14]. This instrumentation is able to capture any value in the code, and in particular can be used to trace memory accesses, count loop iterations, capture function parameters. Compared to PIN [15], a tool with similar functionalities, MAQAO performs static rewriting-based instrumentation from binary to binary and further analyzes the collected information in a post-mortem fashion. PIN, on the contrary, dynamically rewrites binary codes while they execute, and performs analysis on the fly. As most of MAQAO work is done offline, the overall cost for analyzing a binary with MAQAO is much smaller than with PIN. With MAQAO, it is possible to captures memory streams by instrumenting all instructions that access memory, on a specified code fragment (such as a function or loop). For each instruction instrumented, the flow of addresses captured is compressed on-the-fly using a lossless algorithm, NLR, designed by Ketterlin and Clauss [16]. This compressed trace represents the accessed regions with a union of polyhedra, captures access strides and multidimensional array indexing (when possible).

Beyond instrumentation probes, the MIL language makes it possible to add any kind of assembly instruction to the binary, thus to implement code transformation. Our framework does not yet attempt to manage register allocation. Consequently the code transformation must use identical registers, completely unused registers, or spill/fill. However, this current limitation may be lifted in the future. Moreover, MAQAO can perform an induction variable detection mechanism removing the need for dynamic pointer dependence checking through tracing, as part of the code transformation process.

4.2   Analysis of Data Structure Accesses

This analysis consists in determining the layout of data accessed by each assembly instruction. The data layout detection focuses on finding out: How many arrays are accessed, with how many dimensions, with which element structure (that is, how many fields per array element). This assumes that each load/store assembly instruction of the studied function accesses exactly one single array (no indirection, no pointer aliasing in particular).

Memory addresses accessed for each load/store of the code fragment are compacted as shown in Fig. 3. Traces are here represented by loops iterating over the successive address values taken during the execution. The first step of the analysis consists in identifying the load/store that access the same array. To this end, each region accessed by a load/store is converted to a simpler representation, using a strided interval (lower address, upper address, access stride). Out of clarity, in the trace the name of the array in Fig. 3 is shown in comments. Actually, the analyzer only knows the assembly instruction accessing this memory region. The goal is to find which traces share the same arrays.

Formally, let I denote the set of assembly instructions accessing memory. We define a relation $\equiv_{array}$ between instructions $i_1, i_2 \in I$ as: $i_1 \equiv_{array} i_2$ iff i_1 and i_2 access to the same array. $\equiv_{array}$ is an equivalence relation, the classes representing the different arrays. The idea is that two instructions with overlapping accessed memory region are equivalent. Algorithm 1 finds the different arrays by merging overlapping regions. Its complexity of is $O(N \log N)$, due to the sorts.

Lemma 1. *Algorithm 1 finds the sets of instructions that access to the same arrays. More formally, it computes $I / \equiv_{array}$.*

Proof. All instructions within a set CLASS are equivalent according to $\equiv_{array}$. This boils down to merging overlapping intervals. Consider an instruction added to CLASS, with index k in L. According to the algorithm, the lower address bound L_k of the region accessed by this instruction is such that $L_k \leq U_{k-1}$, with

U_{k-1} the upper bound of an other instruction in CLASS. There are k regions starting before L_k and only $k-1$ closed at U_{k-1}. Hence at least one region starting before L_k is ending after U_{k-1}, this shows that instruction k accesses the same interval as another instruction of the set CLASS. Reciprocally, we can show that if two instructions are not in the same set CLASS, they do not access the same array. Let p and q be their index in L, assuming $p < q$. Since they do not belong to the same set ARRAY, there exists k such that $L_k > U_{k-1}$ and $p < k \leq q$. It implies that there are $k-1$ regions that are ending before L_k, that is, all $k-1$ regions starting before L_k are also ending before L_k. The arrays

```
1   for ( nl = 0;  nl < ntimes;  nl++) {
2     for  ( i = 0;  i < N;  i+=2) {
3       a[i] = a[i−1] + b[i];
4     }
5   }
```

```
1   # Trace for access a[i−1]            Strided interval for a[i−1]
2   for i0 = 0 to 999
3     for i1 = 0 to 1535
4       val 0x1525d40 + 8*i1       => [ 0x1525d40 ; 0x1525d40 + 8*999; 8 ]
5     endfor
6   endfor
7   # Trace for access b[i]              Strided interval for b[i]
8   for i0 = 0 to 999
9     for i1 = 0 to 1535
10      val 0x1528d84 + 8*i1       => [ 0x1528d84 ; 0x1528d84 + 8*999; 8 ]
11    endfor
12  endfor
13  # Trace for access a[i]              Strided interval for a[i]
14  for i0 = 0 to 999
15    for i1 = 0 to 1535
16      val 0x1525d44 + 8*i1       => [ 0x1525d44 ; 0x1525d44 + 8*999; 8 ]
17    endfor
18  endfor
```

Fig. 3. Trace example on function s111 from TSVC. Each trace is compacted with NLR algorithm into loops in this simple example, iterating over successive addresses. A simplified representation with strided intervals is used.

Algorithm 1. Identifying distinct arrays from access traces.

Data: I = list of load/store triplets $[lower_i, upper_i, stride_i]$, $i = 1..N$
Result: OUT = I/R_{array}, the set of instructions grouped by array they access.

1 L = $\{lower_i, i = 1..N\}$;
2 U = $\{upper_i, i = 1..N\}$;
3 sort L by increasing address;
4 sort U by increasing address;
5 CLASS = $\{I_1\}$;
6 **for** $k = 2..N$ **do**
7   **if** $L_k > U_{k-1}$ **then**
8   OUT = OUT $\cup$ {CLASS};
9   CLASS = $\emptyset$;
10   CLASS = CLASS $\cup$ $\{I_k\}$;
11 OUT = OUT $\cup$ {CLASS};

of these regions are different from the array accessed by L_k. In particular, since $p < k$, the array accessed by instruction p is different from the array accessed by instruction q.

For example, the analysis of the three regions from Fig. 3 builds the sets $L = \{0\text{x}1525\text{d}40, 0\text{x}1525\text{d}44, 0\text{x}1528\text{d}84\}$ and $U = \{0\text{x}1525\text{d}40 + 8*999, 0\text{x}1525\text{d}44 + 8*999, 0\text{x}1528\text{d}84 + 8*999\}$. The two first regions are found as being accesses to the same array, while the third one is not since $0\text{x}1526\text{d}84 > 0\text{x}1525\text{d}44 + 8*999$.

Now, the second step of the analysis consists in finding load/store instructions accessing the same element field within an array of structures (e.g. t[0].x, t[1].x, .., t[n].x). Among the instructions accessing to the same array of structures, we define a relation $\equiv_{field}$ between each pair of instructions accessing the same field in the same array. Thus formally, for each two instructions i_1, i_2 accessing the same array ($i_1 \equiv_{array} i_2$), the relation $i_1 \equiv_{field} i_2$ is verified iff $i_1 \equiv_{array} i_2$ and:

$$lower_1 \equiv lower_2 \quad (\text{mod} \quad \underset{i \in [i_1]_{\equiv_{array}}}{\gcd} \quad (stride_i)).$$

The gcd of the strides of all accesses on the array corresponds to the size in bytes of the structure. The values of $lower_1$ and $lower_2$ modulo this size correspond to the offset of the field within a structure. Then, fields for each partition I/R_{array} can be sorted according to their $lower$ value modulo the gcd of the strides. Determining the field layout of an array of structures can be done with a $O(N \log N)$ complexity.

In the previous example, the two strided intervals $[0\text{x}1525\text{d}40; 0\text{x}1525\text{d}40 + 8*999; 8]$ and $[0\text{x}1525\text{d}44; 0\text{x}1525\text{d}44 + 8*999; 8]$ are not found equivalent, since $0\text{x}1525\text{d}40 \not\equiv 0\text{x}1525\text{d}44 \quad (\text{mod } 8)$. Therefore the two instructions access different fields in an array of structures. Note that in the initial C code, there is no structure. However, the stride 2 on the loop counter entails that all loads on a are on even indices while the stores are on odd indices, a behavior similar to an access to a 2 field structure. The following section explains how these structures are transformed.

Last, for all instructions accessing the same fields of the same array, strides of the NLR trace are considered in order to determine whether a transposition is required or not. In the NLR trace with its for loops, this boils down to determine whether the stride of the innermost loop is the smallest one. If a transposition is required for all instructions accessing the same field, then it is performed by the proposed transformation described in the following.

5   Fast Exploration and Assessment of Data Restructuration for SIMDization

Data layout together with access pattern knowledge provides precious clues about SIMDization issues and ways to address them. However the corrective steps to enable or improve SIMDization may have other, unwanted side-effects leading to an overall performance degradation instead of the expected gain. Therefore the second part of the transformation process we propose is to directly and quickly assess the potential of such a transformation on the binary code. For that, we adopt an *in vivo* approach, by running a "mock-up" of a transformed kernel within its host application. Thanks to the use of a checkpoint/restart mechanism, only the relevant part of the application is tested with the kernel mock-up. In this section we discuss technical aspects of our *in vivo* approach.

5.1   Checkpointing for Fast Exploration

One solution for assessing the potential of code transformations is to run the different versions generated and measure their execution times. This auto-tuning technique has proved its efficiency in particular for tuning performance of library functions. For application codes, this would mean to run the whole application multiple times, only for assessing an optimization on a limited code fragment, entailing large execution times.

We propose to resort instead to checkpoint/restart technique in order to be able to execute multiple versions of the same code, within the same context. The principle of this technique was first described by Lee and Hall [17]. The idea is to first run the application, instrumented so that there is a checkpoint at the entry of the function to optimize. The binary code of the function is then modified in order to change data structures and/or SIMDize one of its loops. This modified code is then restarted using the previous checkpoint. Note that the binary codes used for the checkpoint and for the restart are not the same. This technique works if binaries have the same size and if the only modified function is the function where the restart occurs. Binary sizes are kept the same by using code padding, and the instrumentation with MAQAO allows pinpointed code transformation (to functions or loops).

The advantages of this technique are numerous:

- By restarting different versions of the code, these codes can be evaluated within the same applicative context, at no cost.
- The method works with parallel, multithreaded codes.
- Array addresses, pointers keep the same value after a restart as at the time of checkpoint. It implies that the optimization can be dependent on the values collected by traces, in particular address traces. We use this approach to restructure data layouts. A first run after restart collects all memory accesses, and the analysis technique proposed in the previous section is applied. Then a new version of the code is generated (see next section) with restructured data layout and it is restarted in order to measure its performance.

The following section presents how the code is modified once the trace has been collected and arrays and structures are discovered. In our implementation, we use the Berkeley lab checkpoint/restart (BLCR) tool [18].

5.2 Array Contraction and AoS to SoA Transformation

From the addresses collected by the trace, the different arrays and structures are identified by the algorithm presented in Sect. 4.2. To transform Arrays of Structures into Structures of Arrays, new arrays are allocated. The restructuring corresponds to a mapping function, mapping indices of the initial array to indices in the new array. The mapping we propose has two objectives:

- Reduce the stride between elements accessed successively whenever possible
- Transform AoS into SoA. For this transformation, the size of the array is deduced from the trace.
- Transpose arrays if successive accesses are not performed along successive addresses, for multi-dimensional accesses detected through the NLR traces.

When the first instruction to access these data is a read, a copy performing this mapping is required. When the first instruction is a write, no copy is needed.

New arrays are allocated inside the function analyzed, before the loop to vectorize. Besides, if a copy from the initial array to the new array is required, it is also inserted right after the allocation of the new array. Allocation and copy are then placed after the last write to the initial array (if any). Several locations may be possible. We choose to place the copy at the earliest possible location in the code, so that the impact of the copy on performance may be reduced. The sizes of the new arrays allocated on the heap are determined by the trace and the type of transformation involved (whether applying contraction or not).

The array contraction consists in removing unnecessary strides separating elements of an array. Consider an array $[a; b; s]$, assuming each data is 4 bytes long, it is contracted into a new array $[a'; a' + (b - a) * 4/s; 4]$ with starting address a'. When multiple regions access the same array, as analyzed by the previous algorithm, the gcd of the strides for all regions is considered and the extreme addresses accessed define the boundaries of the initial array. The code allocating the contracted array is inserted for the mockup code.

Now consider an array of structures $[a; b; 4]$. The size of the structure, n, and the number of elements in the array, N are deduced from the trace analysis (see Sect. 4.2). A field of this structure is characterized by an offset k corresponding to the displacement in bytes from the beginning of a structure element. The ith element of field k in the array is positioned at $k + n * i$ bytes from the beginning of the array, for $0 \leq i < N$. To transform this AoS into SoA, the ith element of field k is mapped to the ith element of subarray k, at offset $k * N + 4 * i$. Therefore if the AoS $[a; b; 4]$ is remapped into the SoA $[a''; b''; 4]$ with $b'' - a'' = b - a$ (same size), each access region $[a_k; b_k; s_k]$ of the field k is remapped into $[a'' + k * N + 4 * (a_k - k - a)/n; a'' + k * N + 4 * (b_k - k - a)/n; 4 * s_k/n]$.

For the example of Fig. 3, considering the two regions accessing the same array but different fields, the size of the structure found is 8 byte long. The size of the new structure of arrays replacing the array of structure is $1000 * 8$ bytes. The two regions are mapped to a new array starting at index 0 for the first one and $1000 * 4$ for the second one. Their stride is now 4 instead of 8. The creation of this array and copy of the elements (only those that are read) is inserted in this case right before the loop.

In terms of code transformation, this implies that for any load and store instruction, its address is changed into addresses inside the new array. For a transformation of AoS into SoA, using the previous notation, an address $addr$ is changed into $a'' + k * N + 4 * (addr - k - a)/n$ with $a'' + k * N$ a constant corresponding to the address within the new array where the array for fields k starts. The assembly code for a load instruction load .., [address] for instance is changed into the following code (all constants are prefixed by #):

```
XOR   RDX, RDX
LEA   RAX, address
SUBQ  RAX, #a+k
MULQ  RAX, #4
DIVQ  #n
MOVQ  RAX, a'' // newly allocated array
ADDQ  RAX, #k*N
load .. , [RAX]
```

This code requires that registers %RDX and %RAX are available since the integer division makes an implicit use of them. This may requires to perform register reallocation on the modified code, or a spill/fill for these two registers. While this transformation is correct for any access, its impact on performance can be important due to the memory access of the spill/fill and the integer division. The later is replaced by a shift whenever n is a power of 2 (removing also the constraint on the use of $RDX : RAX$). A simpler transformation is possible whenever an induction variable detection computation on the initial code finds that the address accessed is of the form $a + n * i$ with i an induction variable (a register here). The transformation then consists in adding a new induction variable with stride 4 and modify the base register of the load. There is no integer division involved then. We use in our implementation this transformation whenever possible. The code modification is similar for the array contraction transformation. The code modification in case of a transposition is similar to the previous case.

5.3   SIMDization

Once the data layout has been transformed, the code is SIMDized. The transformation we propose here is simple and only vectorizes arrays of floats or doubles.

In order to trigger SIMDization, all arrays accessed have to fulfill two conditions: (i) Elements are either 4 or 8 byte long, and instructions are floating point operations; (ii) The strides used by all modified arrays is either 4 or 8 (depending on the data type). If one of the condition is not fulfilled, SIMDization is not performed and a warning is emitted.

Besides, the memory traces are used to compute a dependence graph, taking into account register and memory dependences, as presented in [19]. The conditions for a possible vectorization are deduced from such dependence graph and instruction schedule compatible with dependences is generated.

Arithmetic operations are vectorized using a simple correspondence between scalar/SIMD instructions. Load/store instructions are rewritten as aligned or unaligned accesses, depending on the address alignments. SSE registers are allocated. Finally, the iteration count is changed by adding a new loop counter. These transformations are eased by the fact that the trace provides the iteration count and array alignment information.

6 Experimental Results

We assess the accuracy of our mockup-driven predictions on a suite of benchmarks, TSVC. TSVC consists of 151 functions intended to explore the typical difficulties a compiler can meet in the context of vectorization. Out of these 151 benchmarks, 31 matches data layout access issues, our primary focus in this study. The others correspond to control issues, mostly already well handled by compilers. In Fig. 4, we report speedups obtained by *mockup* kernels and by manually restructured (*correct*) kernels over compiled basis kernel compiled with icc 13.0.1, on Intel Sandy Bridge E5-2650 @2 GHz. These kernels are a subset of the data layout issue category. More complex kernels of this category will be studied using future evolutions of our prototype infrastructure.

Non-contiguous stride accesses are an obstacle to vectorization, compilers may see the opportunity of vectorization but consider it not efficient enough to vectorize. This is the case for benchmarks *s111* and *s128*, performing accesses with strides 2. Their respective mockups show significant gain to expect from data restructuring.

When 2-dimensional arrays are accessed column-wise (in C) or row-wise (in Fortran), accesses with large strides are performed, and one may resort to data transposition prior to massive computations, in order to allow vectorization. Code mockup here predicts significant gains to expect from restructured kernel, which is effectively perfectly reached.

One big challenge for compiler autovectorization is brought by rescheduling issues, that is, codes where compilers see vector dependences it can not resolve, although such dependences could be fixed by permuting instructions or loop peeling. All *s241*, *s243*, *s211*, *s212*, *s1213*, *s244* and *s1244* benchmarks have rescheduling issues and are not vectorized by the compiler. Here, the dynamic dependence graph enables to find a correct schedule for SIMD code.

In some cases, a non-contiguous data pattern may not cause performance issues, as they are already well handled by the compiler and/or the architecture. Here, benchmarks showing no speedup over the basis kernel (*s1111*, *s131*, *s121*, *s151*) correspond to alignment issues, which can be solved by unaligned accesses or vector permutations. On this very architecture, unaligned accesses do not produce a significant performance overhead, therefore data restructuring will not bring better performance.

For all these measures, the time to restructure data (using a copy) is not included. Indeed, the benchmarks are small functions and a copy is, with a few exception, not amortized. Performance of the mockup is in most cases close to the

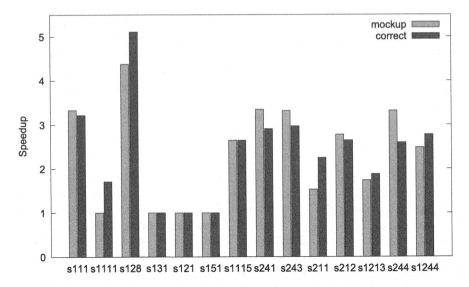

Fig. 4. TSVC mockup prediction on x86

real transformed code. When there are differences, this is explained by the fact that the mockup results from a binary transformation, while the correct hand-tuned code results from a source-to-source transformation. Hence, the binary code resulting from hand-tuning the source code may not be exactly the same as the mockup code due to compiler optimizations.

7 Vectorization Issues and Related Works

A lot of work has already been devoted to help programmers harness the power of SIMD instruction sets, once called "multimedia" extensions. Multiple approaches have been followed in this attempt to group isomorphic elementary computations together. Loop-level approaches have been explored for several decades. Back in 1992, Hanxleden and Kennedy [1] made proposals for balancing loop nest iterations over multiple lanes of a SIMD machine. MMX instruction sets and alike started to gather interest with works such as Krall's [2] proposing to apply vectorization techniques to generate code for SIMD extensions. Larsen introduced the concept of Superword-Level Parallelism (SLP) [3] which groups isomorphic statements together, when potentially packable and executable in parallel. More recently Nuzman et al. [4] explored SIMDization at the outer-loop level. Much work has also been devoted into employing polyhedral methods [5]. Several works have been conducted to allow compilers to accept more complex code and data structures, such as alignment mismatch [20], flow-control [21], non-contiguous data accesses [22] or minimizing in-register permutations [23], for examples. SIMDizing in the context of irregular data structures is also being studied [24]. All these works have in common that they accept unmodified source code as input and they attempt to generate the best SIMDized binary code for the target hardware. They do not involve the programmer in their attempt to produce good SIMD code and usually give little information back to the programmer when their attempt fails. Our proposal differs and complement these works in that it offers to diagnose and alter produced binary codes in order to help programmers improve they source code with respect to SIMDizability.

Some works have followed the path to act on the source code side. Frameworks such as the Scout [25] source-to-source compiler enable the programmer to annotate the source code with **pragma** directives that are subsequently translated to SIMDized code. A recent work of Evans *et al.* [26] presents a method to analyze vector potential, based on source annotated code and an on-the-fly dependence graph analysis using the PIN framework. Other works aim at specialized fields and will produce efficient code for a selected class of applications, e.g. stencil computations [6,27] for instance, or allow to auto-tune specific kernels [8]. Our solution differs in that it aims at helping the programmer to improve his/her *original* code in a generic manner instead of specializing it or augmenting it with annotations. It also again complements these works because it can analyse their output for quality assessment as well as to devise and experiment further optimizations.

Profiling tools such as Intel VTune or the suite Valgrind, for instance, can diagnose code efficiency and pinpoint issues such as memory access patterns with bad locality. Intel VTune may even suggest that the programmer resorts to SIMD intrinsics. However, such an action is not always desirable for code readability and maintainability.

Our approach is able to make higher-level transformation suggestions based on instruction flow dependence analysis of the binary code, and to quantify their expected performance gain over the code using *in vivo* code evaluation. Several previous works have proposed techniques to extract pieces of code for evaluation [17,28], and shown that such an operating mode is viable for performance measurements [29].

8   Conclusion

This paper presented a new technique for transforming and evaluating data layout transformations for SIMDization, directly from the binary code. This method changes Arrays of Structures for instance into Structures of Arrays, performs SIMDization if possible on the code and provides a quick assessment *"in-vivo"* of any performance gain/loss resulting from this transformation. Being trace-based, the transformation proposed is not to be integrated in a static compiler but provides the user with a good estimation of the real source-code transformation, before deciding to perform expensive source code modification. The transformation is achieved at the binary level, ensuring no interference with compiler optimizations. Moreover, we have proposed an original use of checkpoint/restart techniques in order to reduce the cost of our method. The preliminary results on TSVC benchmarks show that performance estimations are close to those actually obtained after a source code transformation.

For future work, we plan to extend the use of our technique to larger applications and to a wider range of data layout transformations. We are also working on addressing multithreaded applications. The trace collection stage already supports application with multiple threads, and most of the work will now concentrate on the strategy building stage.

Acknowledgement. This work has received funding from the European Union's Seventh Framework Programme for research, technological development and demonstration under grant agreements no 610402 Mont-Blanc 2.

References

1. von Hanxleden, R., Kennedy, K.: Relaxing SIMD control flow constraints using loop transformations. In: ACM SIGPLAN Conference on Programming Language Design and Implementation (1992)
2. Krall, A., Lelait, S.: Compilation techniques for multimedia processors. Int. J. Parallel Program. **28**(4), 347–361 (2000)
3. Larsen, S., Amarasinghe, S.: Exploiting superword level parallelism with multimedia instruction sets. In: ACM SIGPLAN Conference on Programming Language Design and Implementation (2000)
4. Nuzman, D., Zaks, A.: Outer-loop vectorization: revisited for short simd architectures. In: ACM/IEEE International Conference on Parallel Architectures and Compilation Techniques (PACT) (2008)
5. Bondhugula, U., Hartono, A., Ramanujam, J., Sadayappan, P.: A practical automatic polyhedral parallelizer and locality optimizer. In: ACM SIGPLAN Conference on Programming Language Design and Implementation (2008)
6. Henretty, T., Stock, K., Pouchet, L.-N., Franchetti, F., Ramanujam, J., Sadayappan, P.: Data layout transformation for stencil computations on short-vector SIMD architectures. In: Knoop, J. (ed.) CC 2011. LNCS, vol. 6601, pp. 225–245. Springer, Heidelberg (2011)
7. Intel: Vtune (2014). http://software.intel.com/en-us/intel-vtune-amplifier-xe
8. Videau, B., Marangozova-Martin, V., Genovese, L., Deutsch, T.: Optimizing 3D convolutions for wavelet transforms on CPUs with SSE units and GPUs. In: Wolf, F., Mohr, B., an Mey, D. (eds.) Euro-Par 2013. LNCS, vol. 8097, pp. 826–837. Springer, Heidelberg (2013)
9. Kong, M., Veras, R., Stock, K., Franchetti, F., Pouchet, L.N., Sadayappan, P.: When polyhedral transformations meet SIMD code generation. In: ACM SIGPLAN Conference on Programming Language Design and Implementation (2013)
10. Aumage, O., Barthou, D., Haine, C., Meunier, T.: Detecting SIMDization opportunities through static/dynamic dependence analysis. In: an Mey, D., Alexander, M., Bientinesi, P., Cannataro, M., Clauss, C., Costan, A., Kecskemeti, G., Morin, C., Ricci, L., Sahuquillo, J., Schulz, M., Scarano, V., Scott, S.L., Weidendorfer, J. (eds.) Euro-Par 2013. LNCS, vol. 8374, pp. 637–646. Springer, Heidelberg (2014)
11. Callahan, D., Dongarra, J., Levine, D.: Vectorizing compilers: a test suite and results. In: Conference on Supercomputing (1988)
12. Maleki, S., Gao, Y., Garzarn, M.J., Wong, T., Padua, D.A.: An evaluation of vectorization compilers. In: International Conference on Parallel Architectures and Compilation Techniques (PACT) (2011)

13. Barthou, D., Rubial, A.C., Jalby, W., Koliai, S., Valensi, C.: Performance tuning of x86 OpenMP codes with MAQAO. In: Müller, M.S., Resch, M.M., Schulz, A., Nagel, W.E. (eds.) Tools for High Performance Computing. Springer, Heidelberg (2010)
14. Charif-Rubial, A.S., Barthou, D., Valensi, C., Shende, S., Malony, A., Jalby, W.: Mil: A language to build program analysis tools through static binary instrumentation. In: IEEE International High Performance Computing Conference (HiPC), Hyberabad, India, December 2013, pp. 206–215 (2013)
15. Luk, C.K., Cohn, R., Muth, R., Patil, H., Klauser, A., Lowney, G., Wallace, S., Reddi, V.J., Hazelwood, K.: Pin: building customized program analysis tools with dynamic instrumentation. In: ACM SIGPLAN Conference on Programming Language Design and Implementation (2005)
16. Ketterlin, A., Clauss, P.: Prediction and trace compression of data access addresses through nested loop recognition. In: ACM/IEEE International Conference on Code Generation and Optimization, pp. 94–103. ACM, New York (2008)
17. Lee, Y.-J., Hall, M.: A code isolator: isolating code fragments from large programs. In: Eigenmann, R., Li, Z., Midkiff, S.P. (eds.) LCPC 2004. LNCS, vol. 3602, pp. 164–178. Springer, Heidelberg (2005)
18. Hargrove, P.H., Duell, J.C.: Berkeley lab checkpoint/restart (BLCR) for linux clusters. J. Phys.: Conf. Ser. 46(1), 494 (2006)
19. Aumage, O., Barthou, D., Haine, C., Meunier, T.: Detecting SIMDization opportunities through static/dynamic dependence analysis. In: Workshop on Productivity and Performance (PROPER), Aachen, Germany, September 2013
20. Eichenberger, A.E., Wu, P., O'Brien, K.: Vectorization for SIMD architectures with alignment constraints. In: ACM SIGPLAN Conference on Programming Language Design and Implementation (2004)
21. Shin, J., Hall, M., Chame, J.: Superword-level parallelism in the presence of control flow. In: ACM/IEEE International Conference on Code Generation and Optimization (2005)
22. Nuzman, D., Rosen, I., Zaks, A.: Auto-vectorization of interleaved data for SIMD. In: ACM SIGPLAN Conference on Programming Language Design and Implementation (2006)
23. Ren, G., Wu, P., Padua, D.: Optimizing data permutations for SIMD devices. In: ACM SIGPLAN Conference on Programming Language Design and Implementation (2006)
24. Ren, B., Agrawal, G., Larus, J.R., Mytkowicz, T., Poutanen, T., Schulte, W.: SIMD parallelization of applications that traverse irregular data structures. In: ACM/IEEE International Conference on Code Generation and Optimization (2013)
25. Krzikalla, O., Feldhoff, K., Müller-Pfefferkorn, R., Nagel, W.E.: Scout: a source-to-source transformator for SIMD-optimizations. In: Alexander, M., D'Ambra, P., Belloum, A., Bosilca, G., Cannataro, M., Danelutto, M., Di Martino, B., Gerndt, M., Jeannot, E., Namyst, R., Roman, J., Scott, S.L., Traff, J.L., Vallée, G., Weidendorfer, J. (eds.) Euro-Par 2011, Part II. LNCS, vol. 7156, pp. 137–145. Springer, Heidelberg (2012)
26. Evans, G.C., Abraham, S., Kuhn, B., Padua, D.A.: Vector seeker: a tool for finding vector potential. In: Workshop on Programming Models for SIMD/Vector Processing, pp. 41–48. ACM, New York (2014)
27. Jaeger, J., Barthou, D.: Automatic efficient data layout for multithreaded stencil codes on CPUs and GPUs. In: IEEE International High Performance Computing Conference, pp. 1–10. IEEE Computer Society, Pune, December 2012

28. Petit, E., Bodin, F., Papaure, G., Dru, F.: ASTEX: a hot path based thread extractor for distributed memory system on a chip. In: HiPEAC Industrial Workshop (2006)
29. Akel, C., Kashnikov, Y., de Oliveira Castro, P., Jalby, W.: Is source-code isolation viable for performance characterization? In: International Workshop on Parallel Software Tools and Tool Infrastructures (2013)

Unification of Static and Dynamic Analyses to Enable Vectorization

Ashay Rane[1]([✉]), Rakesh Krishnaiyer[2], Chris J. Newburn[2],
James Browne[1], Leonardo Fialho[1], and Zakhar Matveev[2]

[1] The University of Texas at Austin, Austin, USA
{ashay.rane,fialho}@utexas.edu, browne@cs.utexas.edu
[2] Intel Corporation, Santa Clara, USA
{rakesh.krishnaiyer,chris.newburn,zakhar.a.matveev}@intel.com

Abstract. Modern compilers execute sophisticated static analyses to enable optimization across a wide spectrum of code patterns. However, there are many cases where even the most sophisticated static analysis is insufficient or where the computation complexity makes complete static analysis impractical. It is often possible in these cases to discover further opportunities for optimization from dynamic profiling and provide this information to the compiler, either by adding directives or pragmas to the source, or by modifying the source algorithm or implementation. For current and emerging generations of chips, vectorization is one of the most important of these optimizations. This paper defines, implements, and applies a systematic process for combining the information acquired by static analysis by modern compilers with information acquired by a targeted, high-resolution, low-overhead dynamic profiling tool to enable additional and more effective vectorization. Opportunities for more effective vectorization are frequent and the performance gains obtained are substantial: we show a geometric mean across several benchmarks of over 1.5x in speedup on the Intel Xeon Phi coprocessor.

Keywords: Performance optimization · Dynamic profiling · Vectorization

1 Introduction

Modern compilers leverage sophisticated static analyses to enable aggressive optimizations for pursuing performance and power efficiency. There are, however, many circumstances where the information required to enable optimizations cannot be determined by static analysis alone. Additionally, compilers are bound by safety requirements to be conservative to avoid producing a different result. It is often possible in these cases to discover further opportunities for optimization from dynamic profiling and provide this information to the compiler, either by adding directives or pragmas to the source, or by modifying the algorithm or implementation. While many modern compilers have some capabilities

© Springer International Publishing Switzerland 2015
J. Brodman and P. Tu (Eds.): LCPC 2014, LNCS 8967, pp. 367–381, 2015.
DOI: 10.1007/978-3-319-17473-0_24

for dynamic profiling and can feed back dynamic profiling information into optimization algorithms, they are seldom used because of their high cost (runtime overhead) and low benefit (optimization potential). There are also separate tools for dynamic profiling and for performance optimization based on these dynamic profiles.

This paper defines, implements and applies a systematic process for combining the information acquired by static analysis by modern compilers with information acquired by a targeted, high-resolution, low-overhead dynamic profiling tool to enable additional and more effective vectorization. Vectorization was chosen as the target for this study because it is becoming one of the most important optimizations for modern multicore and manycore architectures.

Our end-to-end process of discovering and applying optimizations is based on: (a) an analysis of the minimal information that is needed for effective vectorization but is missing from static analysis which is critical to minimizing instrumentation overhead, (b) how this information can be used to define targeted, high-resolution, low-overhead dynamic profiling, (c) how dynamic profiling can collect the missing information and (d) insights from dynamic profiling. MACVEC suggests the exact location and text of the changes, but the user remains in control of whether to apply them. These steps enable MACVEC to exceed the performance that could ever be possible with static analysis alone.

The implementation of our dynamic profiling system for maximizing vectorization instruments only those loops which are not fully vectorized and which consume a significant program execution time. To minimize the overhead, instrumentation is specifically targeted to the additional information required for most effective vectorization. The compiler carries out all of the optimizations.

The key contributions of the paper include the following:

1. Development of the knowledge base required for unification of static analyses and dynamic profiling for enhancing vectorization (Sect. 2).
2. Implementation of the workflow using the Intel compiler and extending an existing dynamic profiling and performance optimization tool (Sects. 3 and 4).
3. Demonstration of the effectiveness of the unified process using small to moderate-sized applications and using a mix of benchmarks and a few real-word applications (Sect. 5).

2   Enhancing Vectorization Through Dynamic Profiling

Careful analysis of the vectorization reports generated by the Intel® Composer XE 2013 SP1 Update 3 (v14.0.3) compiler reveals information that the compiler needs for effective vectorization but which could not be derived using static analysis alone. Based on our studies, the commonly occuring reasons for not efficiently vectorizing a loop include the compiler not being able to determine: (a) the trip count, (b) the access strides for the arrays in the loop, (c) the alignment of arrays in the loop, (d) whether there were backward loop carried dependences among the arrays in the loop body, (e) failure to recognize non-temporal or streaming stores, and (f) the outcomes of branches.

The mapping from vectorization messages to the information gathered using dynamic profiling was done by comparing compiler messages and code patterns. The measurements which must be made by dynamic profiling to obtain this information are specified in the following paragraphs. MACVEC uses attribute, pragmas and directives that are in standard use by GCC wherever they are available, and those supported exclusively by the Intel® Composer XE 2013 SP1 Update 3 (v14.0.3) compiler where necessary. The association between the measurements and the specification of the information back to the compiler (in the form of pragmas or code modifications) required detailed knowledge of the large set of pragmas available with these compilers. The following paragraphs explain the metrics measured for each of these cases, the pragmas and directives required to optimize the code based on the observed measurements, and the applications or benchmarks that were used to validate the measurements.

All information in the recommendations made at the end pertain only to application code properties (ensuring portability across compilers where applicable). They are also mostly applicable for multiple target platforms with only a few exceptions. In most application codes for example, vectorization remains important on Intel Xeon processor and Intel Xeon Phi coprocessor.

Loop Trip Count: Loops tend to have poor vectorization efficiency unless the alignment- and remainder-handling costs are non-existent or are amortized away with a high trip count. Trip counts for each loop may also impact the choice of loops to vectorize or parallelize. Vectorization is normally thought of as being applicable to inner loops while outer loops are commonly parallelized. However, the compiler may choose (based on heuristics like the trip count and access patterns) to vectorize the outer loop rather than the inner loop. Loop trip counts (measured using simple counters in the loop body) that are smaller than a pre-decided threshold (1024) may be indicated using `#pragma loop_count`. The LCD benchmark was used to validate the loop trip count analysis.

Array Access Strides: Efficient vectorization of each statement in the loop body requires that all of the array accesses for each array in the loop have a unit stride with respect to the vectorized (inner or outer) loop. If the code does not exhibit unit strides, less efficient vectorization (requiring use of gather/scatter operations) may be possible. For each array referenced in the loop, the difference in the addresses for the references across consecutive iterations is recorded as the stride for that array. Based on the stride metrics, the compiler may be instructed to prefetch data (for example targeting indirect accesses that follow no regular strides) using `#pragma prefetch <indirect-array>`. The array access stride information may also be used to tell the compiler to generate an alternate gather sequence via the `-opt-gather-scatter-unroll` option. A synthetic array-of-struct microbenchmark was written to collect the measurements and to validate them.

Alignment of Arrays: Besides unit strides, an additional consideration for efficient vectorization is that the first loop iteration access to each array occur at cache-line aligned addresses or that all array references have the same relative alignment. Unless all vectorized references are cache line aligned, masking is required in a peeling loop, which reduces efficiency. Furthermore, unless all references are mutually aligned with respect to cache line boundaries, some shifting is likely to be required, also reducing efficiency. The address of the first referenced element for each array referenced in the loop is recorded. The measurements recorded are the addresses of the first referenceto each array in each statement in the loop body. Arrays can be aligned using `_mm_malloc()` for heap memory and using the `_attribute_((aligned(64)))` clause for global, static and stack memory. Vectorizable loops containing all aligned array references may be tagged using `#pragma vector aligned`[1]. A NBody application was used to validate array alignment measurements.

Overlapping Arrays: A loop is vectorizable only if arrays referenced in the loop do not have lexically backward dependences. Such dependencies may be introduced in the code if arrays overlap in memory. The span of addresses (derived from the first and last referenced addresses for each array) is used to identify if two differently-named arrays overlap in memory. Such a dynamic check provides a fast and accurate way of determining whether arrays overlap. The fact that pointers do not overlap can be conveyed to the compiler using the `restrict` keyword. The STREAM benchmark was used to validate measurements about overlapping arrays.

Non-Temporal or Streaming Stores: The non-temporal property for store instructions for arrays implies the array will not be referenced in the near future and this property can be derived on the basis of reuse distance. Using streaming stores for arrays requires that the sequence of stores write the entire cache line, the arrays is accessed with unit strides, without using a mask register and is aligned to cache-line boundary. Alignment, branch outcomes, strides and reuse distances are measured and a combination of these metrics with rudimentary static analysis (for identifying write-only arrays) is used to recommend the use of non-temporal stores or streaming stores. To indicate to the compiler to use streaming store instructions in vectorizable loops, `#pragma vector nontemporal` or the `-opt-streaming-stores= always` option may be used. The STREAM benchmark was used to validate the relevant measurements for this metric.

Branch Path Outcomes: Although branches are less suitable for vectorization, the compiler may still benefit if it knows that the direction taken by the branch is the same for most iterations of the loop. The data recorded is the count of true and false outcomes for each branch. Branches that always evaluate in one direction may be indicated so to the compiler using the `_builtin_expect()` attribute. Knowing that the control-flow will be coherent for all vector-lanes allows the compiler to often generate a more efficient code-path for the vector-loop. The LCD benchmark was used to validate branch-outcome metrics.

---

[1] http://software.intel.com/en-us/articles/data-alignment-to-assist-vectorization.

3 Workflow

This section describes the high-level workflow for integration of compiler static analysis with dynamic profiling and gives the tools used in our implementation of the workflow. The details of our implementation are given in Sect. 4.

The high-level workflow is generic and can be implemented with different compilers and instrumentation tools. This study uses the Intel® Composer XE 2013 SP1 Update 3 (v14.0.3) compiler and uses performance analysis results from the PerfExpert [7] open source profiling based optimization tool to implement a new tool called MACVEC. MACVEC is an instrumentation and analysis tool built by adding the measurements described in Sect. 2 to the instrumentation framework provided by MACPO [19]. PerfExpert, MACVEC and MACPO are open source tools readily available for download². Steps (b) through (g) are auomated in MACVEC.

(a) **Selecting Execution Environment:** We used production inputs to enable the application to spend significant time executing each phase of its workflow. Different representative input-sets may be needed to exercise different parts of the algorithm.

(b) **Determining Important Loops:** The PerfExpert performance optimization system was used to determine the loops which use more than a chosen fraction of the execution time of the application.

(c) **Identifying the Loops that are Not Fully Vectorized:** We used the vectorization reports generated by the Intel compiler (`-vec-report=6`) to identify loops that can benefit from better vectorization.

(d) **Building the Set of Loops to be Instrumented:** This is formed by the intersection of the loops identified in steps (b) and (c).

(e) **Instrumenting Selected Loops:** This is one of the key steps implemented in MACVEC. Section 4.1 explains the details of the instrumentation calls.

(f) **Generating Measurements:** By executing the user program, the instrumentation from the previous step records dynamic profiling measurements into in-memory data structures.

(g) **Identifying Recommendations for Additional Vectorization:** At the end of the user program execution, MACVEC runs various analyses over the collected measurements to generate recommendations for optimizing the program. Details of the analyses (and the steps used to convert the measurements into recommendations) are illustrated in Sect. 4.2.

(h) **Analyzing Validity of Optimizations:** In our setup, this process is currently performed manually.

(i) **Implementing Recommendations:** The program source code was manually changed to include the recommendations from MACVEC. Automation of this step using PerfExpert is in progress.

(j) **Evaluating Performance Gain:** Performance improvements resulting from the optimizations are described in Sect. 5.

---

² https://www.tacc.utexas.edu/perfexpert.

4   Implementation of Dynamic Profiling

MACVEC instruments the specified functions and loops using the Rose [18] (v0.9.5a) compiler's Abstract Syntax Tree (AST) of the user source code andRose compiler APIs. AST-level instrumentation (as opposed to IR-level instrumentation or binary instrumentation) helps MACVEC in producing metrics derived directly from the user code structure. Further, MACVEC's instrumentation-based analysis yields recommendations that are agnostic to the generated code.

The fact that MACVEC provides *source-level information* isolates MACVEC from the maturity and aggressiveness of the production compiler used to compile the user's code. For instance, a particularly aggressive vectorizing compiler may split a loop into a prolog *peel loop* to get references aligned to specific boundaries, a *main loop* to handle the steady state, and an epilog *remainder loop* to handle unaligned leftover iterations. The Rose compiler AST API operates at the source level, not at the level of loops in the generated code.

4.1   Compiler-Based Instrumentation

During the instrumentation phase, MACVEC adds function calls to the program source code to record the metrics identified in Sect. 2. MACVEC currently does not use alias-analysis information from the compiler. MACVEC inserts the function calls either before or after the loop body. As the function calls are placed outside of the loop body, the iteration count has only a small effect on the overhead. However, the number of nested loops and the trip count of outer loops influences the overhead substantially.

We compared the execution times with and without instrumentation using the Rose compiler. We instrumented all functions and loops in the codes from the Rodinia [4] benchmark suite that consumed at least 40 % of the total execution time. The mean of slowdowns (ratio of times from instrumented execution to non-instrumented execution) was 1.13x for array alignment checks, 1.08x for loop trip count measurements, 1.07x for branch-path analysis, 1.06x for array overlap checks and 1.05x for stride checks.

4.2   Generation of Recommendations

MACVEC analyses internally maintain a histogram of collected values, which are iterated over just before the program terminates. The nature of the generated recommendations naturally allow a few optimizations in the data collection process, which in turn helps to reduce the instrumentation overhead. For instance, analysis of loop trip count needs to check only whether the trip count is lower than a threshold. If the observed trip count is greater than the threshold, then the histogram update is skipped. Other similar optimizations (lazy initialization, fast-path and slow-path separation, among others) are useful in reducing the overhead of instrumentation.

MACVEC resolves measurements by thread. The data collection phase records each thread's information separately. MACVEC generates conservative recommendations from this per-thread information. For instance, MACVEC reports accesses to the arrays as aligned only if array references from all threads are aligned.

The steps to generate recommendations for each instrumentation case are explained below:

1. **Loop Trip Count:** The loop trip count is compared against a threshold (1024) to estimate whether vectorizing the loop will likely be inefficient. If so, MACVEC recommends inserting `#pragma loop_count` so that the compiler is aware of the low trip count before attempting to vectorize the loop.

2. **Stride Analysis:** If the measurements for array references indicate that the code exhibits strides that are not of length 1, MACVEC recommends converting array-of-structs references to struct-of-arrays references. If the stride values are more than 4 cache lines apart and if the code is being compiled for the Xeon Phi coprocessor, MACVEC recommends adding `#pragma prefetch <indirect-array>` and using the `-opt-gather-scatter-unroll`.

3. **Array Alignment Check:** The first-referenced address of the referenced array is used to understand the alignment of the data structure. If *all* arrays are aligned and if the loop is vectorizable, MACVEC recommends using the `#pragma vector aligned` directive. If arrays are not aligned or if they are mutually aligned to the same alignment value, MACVEC recommends aligning the arrays. Arrays can be requested to be aligned using `_mm_malloc()` for heap memory and using the `_attribute_((aligned(64)))` clause for global, static and stack memory.

4. **Non-temporal and Streaming Stores:** Arrays inside vectorizable loops that are written but never read within the loop, which are accessed using unit strides without a mask register and which exhibit high reuse distance (derived using reuse distance analysis) are good candidates for using streaming store instructions. In such cases, MACVEC recommends using the `-opt-streaming-stores=always` option. If an array simply exhibits low reuse and if the loop is vectorizable, MACVEC recommends adding the `#pragma vector nontemporal` directive for that array instead of recommending streaming stores.

5. **Array-Overlap Check:** MACVEC uses the difference between the lower and upper addresses of the referenced array as the span of the array. Using the calculated spans, MACVEC checks whether array references overlap. If the pointers do not overlap, MACVEC recommends adding the `restrict` keyword to the relevant pointer declarations.

6. **Branch Path Analysis:** Based on the branch outcomes, MACVEC determines whether the branch evaluates to mostly ($\geq 85\%$) true, mostly ($\geq 85\%$) false, always true or always false. If the branch was observed to evaluate to always true or always false, MACVEC recommends indicating the branch outcomes to the compiler using the `_builtin_expect()` attribute.

5   Case Studies

Four types of case studies are reported. The goal of the first case study was to get an upper bound on the performance improvement which could potentially be obtained by fully effective vectorization. The goal for the second set of case studies was to validate that MACVEC would arrive at the same recommendations for supplying additional information to the compiler as human experts. The third set of case studies applies the full workflow to small benchmark applications that had previously been hand-tuned by experts. This set of case studies includes codes from benchmark suites (including two from the Rodinia benchmarks) and one moderate-sized application. The goal for the fourth set of case studies was to check whether MACVEC could generate recommendations that improve the running time of the presumably well-tuned standard applications.

5.1   Execution Environment

All performance measurements and tests were carried out on the Stampede supercomputer at the Texas Advanced Computing Center. Each node on Stampede is comprised of two eight-core Intel® Xeon E5-2680 processors. Each of the eight cores on a chip has a 32 KB L1 instruction cache, a 32 KB L1 data cache and a 256 KB L2 cache. The L3 cache (20 MB) is shared by all eight cores on the chip. Each node also contains an Intel® Xeon Phi™ (Knights Corner)[3] coprocessor. Profiling runs both before and after optimization used the code generated by the Intel® Composer XE 2013 SP1 Update 3 (v14.0.3) compiler using the -O3 and -fopenmp flags. Applications compiled to run on the Xeon Phi used the -mmic flag as well. Thus, all applications were run with parallelization enabled using OpenMP. Although we have used OpenMP for parallelization, we believe the framework we describe in this paper will be applicable to codes using other parallelization techniques such as MPI, Intel® Cilk™ Plus[4], etc. All applications run on the Xeon processor were run with 16 threads while those on the Xeon Phi coprocessor were run with 244 threads. Applications were run on the Xeon Phi coprocessor using the native mode. Performance results are based on timing the computational kernel, as printed in the application output. Code instrumented by MACVEC was run on the Xeon processor only[5].

5.2   Upper Bound Case Studies

An upper bound on the potential performance enhancement obtainable through enhancing vectorization can be estimated by applying the first three steps of the workflow to an application and then determining the percentage of the execution

---

[3] http://software.intel.com/en-us/mic-developer.

[4] https://software.intel.com/en-us/intel-cilk-plus.

[5] The Rose compiler framework is not yet available on the Intel Xeon Phi coprocessors hence the code could be instrumented to run only on the Intel Xeon processor and not the Intel Xeon Phi coprocessor.

Table 1. Time spent in loops not fully-vectorized in the Rodinia suite.

Application	Execution time of non-fully-vectorized loops	Main reason(s) for not fully Vectorizable (as per compiler's static analysis)
backprop	32.52 %	Vector dependence.
euler	12.42 %	Non-standard loop, vector dependence.
euler_double	78.99 %	Non-standard loop.
pre_euler	75.94 %	Non-standard loop, vector dependence.
pre_euler_double	71.60 %	Non-standard loop, vector dependence.
heartwall	7.03 %	Vector dependence, statement cannot be vectorized.
lavaMD	37.42 %	Vector dependence.
kmeans	19.54 %	Vector dependence, non-standard loop.
leukocyte	35.01 %	Unsupported loop, vector dependence.
srad_v1	48.45 %	Vector dependence.
streamcluster	85.58 %	Unsupported loop, vector dependence

time consumed by the set of loops that are not fully vectorized. Table 1 shows the percentage of such exectution time for codes in the Rodinia [4] benchmark suite. Codes that finished executing in less than 10 seconds were not used in this study. The percentage of execution time in the loops which can, in the best-case scenario, potentially benefit from additional vectorization ranges from about 85 % for StreamCluster to about 7 % for Heartwall. Indeed, some of these loops may not be vectorizable because of backward dependencies or irregular strides. However the data does suggest that significant performance enhancements can be obtained if loops are fully vectorized.

Table 1 also shows the dominant reasons why loops were not vectorized. In many cases, the compiler assumed dependence among iterations of the (inner or outer) loop or the loop was not a counted loop with a single entry and a single exit. The dependence information can be verified using dynamic profiling.

5.3   Validation Case Studies

Satish et al. [21] and Krishnaiyer et al. [12] present a variety of codes where experts in compilers and performance analysis manually identified specific loops. These loops were characterized by required modifications in compiler directives or pragmas and relatively modest code changes that could enhance the degree and effectiveness of vectorization. Among these, the NBody and STREAM [16] (and a subset of the LCD benchmark codes) were chosen for determining the effectiveness of MACVEC's dynamic profiling. The NBody code implements a standard $O(N^2)$ algorithm to calculate force among a given set of bodies. The STREAM benchmark measures the memory bandwidth based on simple loops that copy values between arrays, possibly performing some arithmetic operations in the process. We use a variant of the STREAM benchmark that allocates memory dynamically. The LCD benchmarks are a collection of 100 Fortran loops that test the vectorization effectiveness. We use two loops from a C version of this benchmark for validation. The source-level pragmas, tuning modifications and compiler options were removed from the codes and the full workflow applied to each of these codes. The results from the runtime-measurement-based studies matched the output of the human experts.

5.4 Benchmark Case Studies

The LavaMD and SRAD codes from the Rodinia [4] benchmark suite and the Conjugate Gradient (CG) code from the NAS benchmarks [1] suite were used as test applications. The Rodinia codes were chosen because Rodinia focuses on benchmarking for accelerators. The LavaMD code calculates particle potential and relocation due to mutual forces between particles within a large 3D space. The SRAD code is a diffusion method for ultrasonic and radar imaging applications based on partial differential equations (PDEs). The NAS-CG code, with its unpredictable memory access patterns and considerable synchronization, provides a different execution pattern than the more regularly structured computations of applications in the Rodinia suite.

Table 2. Performance results on benchmark applications.

Category	Application	Sources of improvement	Improvement on Xeon	Improvement on Xeon Phi
Validation case studies	NBody	Array alignment.	0.93x	1.45x
	STREAM	Array alignment non-temporal stores, restrict keyword.	copy: 1.06x scale: 1.41x add: 1.30x triad: 1.29x	copy: 1.00x scale: 1.32x add: 1.29x triad: 1.30x
Benchmark case studies	NAS CG	Loop count, gather/scatter unroll, prefetch pragma.	1.06x	2.18x
	LavaMD	Restrict keyword.	2.19x	8.99x
	SRAD	Array alignment.	0.99x	1.09x
Application case studies	MILC	AOS to SOA transformation.	1.10x	1.60x
	LBM	Non-temporal stores, restrict keyword.	1.06x	1.20x
	LULESH	Restrict keyword.	1.03x	1.00x
-	Overall (geo. mean)	-	**1.18x**	**1.55x**

5.5   Application Case Studies

We chose MILC [22], LBM [20] and LULESH [10] for the application case studies because these codes are known to have complex loop structures and complex data structures and thus offer opportunities for potential benefit from dynamic profiling and analysis. The version of MILC used in these studies is used as a benchmark for system acceptance by the National Science Foundation (NSF). The LBM code[6] was provided to us by Carlos Rosales-Fernandez of the Texas Advanced Computing Center. We used the optimized version of LULESH [11] available from the Lawrence Livermore National Laboratory website[7].

5.6   Analysis of Case Studies

The validation case studies demonstrated that the automatic process for dynamic profiling and recommending code modifications matches the recommendations of human experts. These case studies indicated that the automated process for integration of dynamic profiling information into the compilation process can frequently yield substantial performance improvement with a small effort investment. Only minor changes in the application were required except for conversion of Arrays-of-Structures to Structures-of-Arrays.

The benchmark applications were tuned by changing at most ten lines of source code. Table 2 shows the applications, the sources of improvement and the resulting speedup on the Intel® Xeon processor and the Intel® Xeon Phi coprocessors. Three of the eight codes (LBM, LavaMD and Lulesh) were optimized using compiler flags alone. The speedup values are medians of five consecutive runs. The extent of the difference between the original and optimized running times varies from a 7 % regression to 8.9x speedup.

Data layout can have a significant impact on performance, as illustrated in the case of MILC. Using a structure-of-arrays layout to make consecutive references have a unit stride enables the use of vector-loads and vector-stores instead of gathers and scatters. Vector-loads and vector-stores have a shorter execution latency in the front-end of the processor and have a much better utilization of the memory system, as many requests now map to a single cache line.

5.7   Safety of Recommended Optimizations

The optimization process defined and applied in this paper has captured and structured the knowledge necessary to generate applicable recommendations for optimization. This step is particularly important for vectorization-related optimizations which require in-depth knowledge of compiler pragmas and runtime libraries (knowledge not generally known to application developers and users). The measurements from dynamic profiling, and thus the recommendations are, however, specific to the input chosen for dynamic profiling so that the recommendations may not be valid or at least as effective, across all possible input sets.

---

[6] http://code.google.com/p/mplabs.

[7] https://codesign.llnl.gov/lulesh.php.

The recommendations to inform the compiler of loop counts, array access strides, existence of streaming or non-temporal stores and branch path outcomes are "safe" in the sense that the correctness of the application will not be impacted if the information is not valid for different inputs although performance may be impacted. The recommendations informing the compiler of array alignments and array overlap (vector dependence) are not safe if alignments or array overlap depend on inputs or control flow path. It is, however, possible to generate source code checks to verify that the recommended optimization is valid for the current input and execution environment. These checks will cause invocation of the appropriate one of the vectorized- or the non-vectorized-version of the loop. Application developers will usually be able to readily verify safety of a recommended optimization due to their familiarity with the application code. These source code checks for safety can be automatically generated and presented to the user for use if needed.

To test the robustness of the vectorization optimizations, we ran MILC with 19 different inputs (formed by doubling each of 19 values accepted by the code as input, one by one). We chose to run this test on MILC (instead of any other benchmark) because the MILC application is relatively complex and also because the MILC input affects not just the operating problem size but also the control paths taken by the code – statements that are not applicable to the other codes. The MILC application includes some basic tests (that are roughly equivalent to assertion failures) which ensure that portions of the computation are valid. Apart from ensuring that our optimizations to MILC did not cause assertion failures, we also verified the 'residue' value printed by the application at the end of its output was the same for the naive and optimized versions of the application. The optimized code on the different inputs ran 4 % to 25 % faster on the Intel Xeon processor and about 36 % faster on the Intel Xeon Phi coprocessor. We omit the details of the experiment due to space constraints.

6   Related Research

There have been previous efforts to combine measurements from static and dynamic analyses. In recent years, most compilers have added profile guided optimization capabilities where a user-selected option causes the compiler to generate instrumentation to gather runtime information on specific execution behaviors of the program and have the compiler use this information in future compilations. There have been at least two such performance optimization systems [3,5]. Oancea and Rauchwerger [17] have combined static analysis and dynamic profiling to enhance parallelism in loop, resolving the independence of the loop's memory references using runtime analysis. Vector Seeker [6] optimistically measures the vector parallelism using dynamic profiling. Hornung and Keasler [9] argue that efficient vectorization is possible with current compiler technology and offer suggestions on how it can be accomplished. Multiple other works [14,23,24] analyze data dependencies in order to discover potential parallelism.

More recent research in this area done by Holewinski et al. [8] describes an approach to infer a program's SIMD parallelization potential by analyzing the dynamic data-dependence graph derived from a sequential execution trace. Maleki et al. [15] give a evaluation of how well modern compilers (as of 2011) vectorize. They conclude that there is a gap between modern compiler auto-vectorized loops and loops which could be successfully vectorized manually with additional information on the execution behavior. Their paper was a motivation for the research and tools of our work. Other works [12,13,21] show how human experts can combine knowledge of compilers and applications to enhance vectorization across multiple types of applications.

Similar to MACPO, Intel Advisor XE[8] [2] "Survey" and Advisor "Suitability" tools profile hotspots, and make recommendations on how source code and parallel runtime could be tweaked or modified to achieve greater (threading SMP) parallelism, and hence better performance. An analogous form of Advisor could be considered, that helps improve vector parallelism for targets with SIMD hardware. The results of this paper bolster the motivation for such an extension.

7   Summary and Future Work

A systematic and comprehensive process for integration of information from dynamic profiling into the compilation process was formulated, implemented, and applied. The steps requiring detailed knowledge of the compiler, analysis of the vectorization reports, and determining the relevant code modifications (i.e. steps (b) through (g) of the Workflow) have been automated. Our results on various workloads show a geomean of 1.5x improvement from supplementing static analysis with dynamically-profiled analysis of six conditions, and using commercially-de facto-standard pragmas and code modifications to communicate the results back to the compiler, under selective user control. This pilot study was found compelling enough to motivate possible inclusion of a MACVEC-like mechanism in the Intel Advisor tool, which uses various analyses to guide users to improved threading and vectorization.

One of the byproducts of this work will be a user guide to vectorization which will illustrate how applications should be structured to take maximum advantage of vector instructions present on today's computer architectures. Application of this process may be most beneficial for the emerging generations of many-core accelerator chips where performance is heavily dependent on both vectorization and parallelization.

There are three primary tasks to be completed in the future. The workflow will be integrated into the PerfExpert [7] framework enabling automated implementation of the recommended optimizations and safety checks. Second, instrumentation and the analysis will be extended from the currently-supported C and C++ languages to Fortran as well. Finally, this automated process will be extended to optimizations other than vectorization by replicating the automated process for the optimization reports generated by the compiler.

---

[8] http://software.intel.com/en-us/intel-advisor-xe.

Acknowledgments. This work is funded in part by Intel corporation and by the National Science Foundation under OCI award #0622780.

References

1. Bailey, D.H., Barszcz, E., Barton, J.T., Browning, D.S., Carter, R.L., Dagum, L., Fatoohi, R.A., Frederickson, P.O., Lasinski, T.A., Schreiber, R.S., Simon, H.D., Venkatakrishnan, V., Weeratunga, S.K.: The NAS parallel benchmarks - summary and preliminary results. In: Proceedings of the 1991 ACM/IEEE Conference on Supercomputing, Supercomputing 1991, pp. 158–165. ACM, New York (1991)
2. Brett, B., Kumar, P., Kim, M., Kim, H.: CHiP: a profiler to measure the effect of cache contention on scalability. In: Proceedings of the 2013 IEEE 27th International Symposium on Parallel and Distributed Processing Workshops, IPDPSW 2013, pp. 1565–1574. IEEE Computer Society, Washington, DC (2013)
3. Callahan, D., Dongarra, J., Levine, D.: Vectorizing compilers: a test suite and results. In: Proceedings of the 1988 ACM/IEEE Conference on Supercomputing, Supercomputing 1988, pp. 98–105. IEEE Computer Society Press, Los Alamitos (1988)
4. Che, S., Boyer, M., Meng, J., Tarjan, D., Sheaffer, J., Lee, S.H., Skadron, K.: Rodinia: a benchmark suite for heterogeneous computing. In: IEEE International Symposium on Workload Characterization, IISWC 2009, pp. 44–54, October 2009
5. Chung, I.H., Cong, G., Klepacki, D., Sbaraglia, S., Seelam, S., Wen, H.F.: A framework for automated performance bottleneck detection. In: IEEE International Symposium on Parallel and Distributed Processing, IPDPS 2008, pp. 1–7, April 2008
6. Evans, G.C., Abraham, S., Kuhn, B., Padua, D.A.: Vector seeker: a tool for finding vector potential. In: Proceedings of the 2014 Workshop on Programming Models for SIMD/Vector Processing, WPMVP 2014, pp. 41–48. ACM, New York (2014)
7. Fialho, L., Browne, J.: Framework and modular infrastructure for automation of architectural adaptation and performance optimization for HPC systems. In: Kunkel, J.M., Ludwig, T., Meuer, H.W. (eds.) ISC 2014. LNCS, vol. 8488, pp. 261–77. Springer, Heidelberg (2014)
8. Holewinski, J., Ramamurthi, R., Ravishankar, M., Fauzia, N., Pouchet, L.N., Rountev, A., Sadayappan, P.: Dynamic trace-based analysis of vectorization potential of applications. SIGPLAN Not. **47**(6), 371–82 (2012)
9. Hornung, R., Keasler, J.: A case for improved C++ compiler support to enable performance portability in large physics simulation codes. Technical report, Lawrence Livermore National Laboratory (LLNL), Livermore, CA (2013)
10. Karlin, I., Bhatele, A., Keasler, J., Chamberlain, B.L., Cohen, J., Devito, Z., Haque, R., Laney, D., Luke, E., Wang, F., Richards, D., Schulz, M., Still, C.H.: Exploring traditional and emerging parallel programming models using a proxy application. In: Parallel and Distributed Processing Symposium, International, pp. 919–932 (2013)
11. Karlin, I., Keasler, J., Neely, R.: Lulesh 2.0 updates and changes. Technical report LLNL-TR-641973, Lawrence Livermore National Laboratory (2013)
12. Krishnaiyer, R., Kultursay, E., Chawla, P., Preis, S., Zvezdin, A., Saito, H.: Compiler-based data prefetching and streaming non-temporal store generation for the intel(r) xeon phi(tm) coprocessor. In: 2013 IEEE 27th International Parallel and Distributed Processing Symposium Workshops Ph.D. Forum (IPDPSW), pp. 1575–1586, May 2013

13. Kristof, P., Yu, H., Li, Z., Tian, X.: Performance study of simd programming models on intel multicore processors. In: 2012 IEEE 26th International Parallel and Distributed Processing Symposium Workshops Ph.D. Forum (IPDPSW), pp. 2423–2432, May 2012
14. Larus, J.: Loop-level parallelism in numeric and symbolic programs. IEEE Trans. Parallel Distrib. Syst. **4**(7), 812–26 (1993)
15. Maleki, S., Gao, Y., Garzaran, M., Wong, T., Padua, D.: An evaluation of vectorizing compilers. In: 2011 International Conference on Parallel Architectures and Compilation Techniques (PACT), pp. 372–382, October 2011
16. McCalpin, J.D.: A survey of memory bandwidth and machine balance in current high performance computers. IEEE TCCA Newsl. 19–25 (1995)
17. Oancea, C.E., Rauchwerger, L.: Logical inference techniques for loop parallelization. In: Proceedings of the 33rd ACM SIGPLAN Conference on Programming Language Design and Implementation, PLDI 2012, pp. 509–520. ACM, New York (2012)
18. Quinlan, D.J.: ROSE: compiler support for object-oriented frameworks. Parallel Process. Lett. **10**(2/3), 215–26 (2000)
19. Rane, A., Browne, J.: Enhancing performance optimization of multicore/multichip nodes with data structure metrics. ACM Trans. Parallel Comput. **1**(1), 3:1–3:20 (2014)
20. Rosales, C., Whyte, D.S.: Dual grid lattice boltzmann method for multiphase flows. Int. J. Numer. Meth. Eng. **84**(9), 1068–84 (2010)
21. Satish, N., Kim, C., Chhugani, J., Saito, H., Krishnaiyer, R., Smelyanskiy, M., Girkar, M., Dubey, P.: Can traditional programming bridge the Ninja performance gap for parallel computing applications? In: Proceedings of the 39th Annual International Symposium on Computer Architecture, ISCA 2012, pp. 440–451. IEEE Computer Society, Washington, DC (2012)
22. Shi, G., Kindratenko, V., Gottlieb, S.: The bottom-up implementation of one MILC lattice QCD application on the cell blade. Int. J. Parallel Program. **37**(5), 488–507 (2009)
23. Zhong, H., Mehrara, M., Lieberman, S., Mahlke, S.: Uncovering hidden loop level parallelism in sequential applications. In: IEEE 14th International Symposium on High Performance Computer Architecture, HPCA 2008, pp. 290–301, February 2008
24. Zhuang, X., Eichenberger, A., Luo, Y., O'Brien, K., O'Brien, K.: Exploiting parallelism with dependence-aware scheduling. In: 18th International Conference on Parallel Architectures and Compilation Techniques, PACT 2009, pp. 193–202, September 2009

Efficient Exploitation of Hyper Loop Parallelism in Vectorization

Shixiong Xu[2]([✉]) and David Gregg[1,2]

[1] Lero, The Irish Software Engineering Research Centre,
Trinity College, University of Dublin, Dublin, Ireland
[2] Software Tools Group, Department of Computer Science,
Trinity College Dublin, the University of Dublin, Dublin, Ireland
{xush,dgregg}@scss.tcd.ie

Abstract. Modern processors can provide large amounts of processing power with vector SIMD units if the compiler or programmer can vectorize their code. With the advance of SIMD support in commodity processors, more and more advanced features are introduced, such as flexible SIMD lane-wise operations (e.g. blend instructions). However, existing vectorizing techniques fail to apply global SIMD lane-wise optimization due to the unawareness of the computation structure of the vectorizable loop. In this paper, we put forward an approach to automatic vectorization based on *hyper loop parallelism*, which is exposed by hyper loops. Hyper loops recover the loop structures of the vectorizable loop and help vectorization to apply global SIMD lane-wise optimization. We implemented our vectorizing technique in the Cetus source-to-source compiler to generate C code with SIMD intrinsics. The preliminary experimental results show that our vectorizing technique can achieve significant speedups up over the non-vectorized code in our test cases.

Keywords: Hyper loop parallelism · Automatic vectorization · Global SIMD lane-wise optimization · SIMD

1 Introduction

The introduction of Single Instruction Multiple Data (SIMD) units in processors increases the levels of parallelism in hardware, and results in a three-level hierarchy of parallelism, instruction level parallelism, SIMD parallelism, and thread-level parallelism. In order to take advantage of the SIMD parallelism, users usually resort to the automatic vectorization in compilers. So far, there are mainly two vectorizing approaches available in compilers, classic loop vectorization [1] and super-word level parallelism (SLP) vectorization [2]. These two methods usually supplement each other. Classic loop vectorization works on each statement in the vectorizable loop while SLP vectorization attempts to

This work was supported, in part, by Science Foundation Ireland grant 10/CE/I185 to Lero - the Irish Software Engineering Research Centre (www.lero.ie).

© Springer International Publishing Switzerland 2015
J. Brodman and P. Tu (Eds.): LCPC 2014, LNCS 8967, pp. 382–396, 2015.
DOI: 10.1007/978-3-319-17473-0_25

```
1  float y[128], x[128], C[128];
2  for (int i = 0; i < 64; i++) {
3     y[2*i]   += x[2*i] * C[2*i] -
4              x[2*i+1] * C[2*i+1];
5     y[2*i+1] += x[2*i] * C[2*i+1] +
6              x[2*i+1] * C[2*i];
7  }
```

Fig. 1. C-Saxpy

```
1  y[0:126:2] += x[0:126:2] * C[0:126:2] -
2            x[1:127:2] * C[1:127:2];
3
4  y[1:127:2] += x[0:126:2] * C[1:127:2]
5            + x[1:127:2] * C[0:126:2];
```

Fig. 2. C-Saxpy by classic loop vectorization.

```
1   // take full lanes
2   tmp0[0:127] = x[0:127:1] * C[0:127:1];
3   tmp1[0:127] = SwapEvenOddLanes (tmp0);
4   // actual computation on the even lanes
5   tmp1[0:127:1] = tmp0 - tmp1;
6   tmp2[0:127:1] = SwapEvenOddLanes
                (C[0:127:1]);
7   // take full lanes
8   tmp3[0:127:1] = x[0:127:1] *
                tmp2[0:127:1];
9   tmp4[0:127:1] = SwapEvenOddLanes (tmp3);
10  // actual computation on the odd lanes
11  tmp5[0:127:1] = tmp3 + tmp4;
12  // merge the results from both even and
                odd lanes
13  y[0:127:1] += MergeEvenOddLanes (tmp1,
                tmp5);
```

Fig. 3. C-Saxpy by hyper-loop parallelism vectorization

pack isomorphic operations in the basic blocks based on some heuristics (contiguous memory access [2] or data reuse [3]). What these two methods have in common is that they both ignore the overall computation structure exposed by the vectorizable loop.

With the advance of SIMD support in modern commodity processors with short vectors, more and more advanced features are introduced to programmers and compiler designers to exploit the performance of SIMD, such as the flexible lane-wise operations (e.g. masking load/store, blend instructions). When using these SIMD lane-wise operations, we have to consider how the SIMD lanes change between SIMD instructions. With the computation structure of the vectorizable loop, we can have a global view of how the SIMD lanes can be allocated in each SIMD instruction. This view of SIMD lanes helps us to achieve global SIMD lane-wise optimization, which may reduce unnecessary shuffling operations on SIMD lanes.

Take the C-Saxpy, which multiplies a complex vector by a constant complex vector and adds it to another complex vector, as an example, as shown in Fig. 1. When classic loop vectorization attempts to vectorize the loop, it tries to aggressively squeeze all the data needed by each memory operation into a SIMD vector regardless of how the data will be used throughout the loop body. As shown in Fig. 2, all memory operations are either interleaved loads (gather) or interleaved stores (scatter). The hardware support for native gather and scatter instructions is still not popular [4], thereby, most compilers use data permutation instructions to achieve gather and scatter operations.

If we carefully examine the computation structure of the loop body in Fig. 1, we can derive a vectorizing scheme with fewer data permutation instructions than the one by classic loop vectorization. As we can see from Fig. 3, all the memory operations are contiguous memory loads and stores, and only three data permutation instructions and one blend instruction are required to implement

SwapEvenOddLanes and MergeEvenOddLanes operations. This vectorizing scheme is obtained by putting in SIMD lane-wise operations to adjust the data needed by the computation across SIMD lanes according to the overall computation structure.

Two key components are required by the vectorizing scheme shown in Fig. 3. One is the computation structure recognition and the other is SIMD lane-wise mapping. Computation structures can be obtained by program slicing with suitable slicing criteria. On the other hand, SIMD lane-wise mapping requires detailed information on how to position data in SIMD lanes along the computation structure. For classic loop vectorization, as it strip-mines the vectorizable loop for vectorization, the numbering of the loop iterations of the resulting loop determines which SIMD lane a loop iteration will take. Inspired by this mapping between loop iterations and SIMD lanes, we put forward hyper loops based on program slices to recover the loop structure of the vectorizable loop. With hyper loops, we can apply global SIMD lane-wise optimization by taking advantage of the mapping between loop iterations and SIMD lanes.

We define the program slices that can be partitioned into groups with respect to certain relationships (i.e. contiguous memory stores) as hyper loop iterations. The computations in each hyper loop iteration of a group do not have to be isomorphic. As all the program slices are independent of each other, hyper loop iterations are all parallel. The parallelism exposed by the hyper loop iterations is hyper loop parallelism. In this paper, we put forward a vectorizing technique based on the hyper loop parallelism. Our vectorizing method addresses the problems of extracting hyper loop parallelism and efficiently mapping it onto the target processor. We implemented our vectorizing approach as a source-to-source compiler in the Cetus source-to-source compiler. The preliminary experimental results show that our vectorizing technique can achieve significant speedups over the non-vectorized code.

In this paper, we make the following contributions:

- We put forward a vectorizing technique based on the hyper loop parallelism revealed by hyper loops. Hyper loops build a mapping between hyper loop iterations and SIMD lanes, and this mapping helps vectorization to take advantage of the instructions that have flexible control on the SIMD lanes in modern commodity processors.
- We implemented our presented vectorizing technique as a source-to-source compiler based on the Cetus compiler infrastructure. The preliminary experimental results show that our vectorizing technique can achieve significant speedups over the non-vectorized code.

2   Hyper Loop Parallelism in Vectorization

2.1   Overview

Classic loop vectorization strip-mines vectorizable loops. The loop iterations of the resulting loops correspond to the SIMD lanes in the SIMD vectors. In order to take advantage of the instructions that have flexible control of the SIMD lanes in modern commodity processors, we put forward hyper loops to recover the implicit loop structures of the loop body.

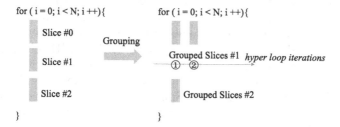

Fig. 4. Hyper loop parallelism for vectorization.

The loop body of a vectorizable loop generally can be partitioned into parts in terms of the downwards-exposed definitions. Program slicing is a widely used technique to compute a set of program statements, *a program slice*, which may affect the values at some point of interest (aka. *a slicing criterion*). Choosing the downwards-exposed definitions of the vectorizable loop as the set of slicing criteria, with the backward program slicing, we can derive a set of program slices, each of which represents a partition of statements of the loop. Without considering control dependence, a program slice within a loop body is essentially a sub-graph of the data dependence graph of the loop body. As each slice is collected within the loop body, a slice is a direct acyclic graph (DAG) $G(V, E)$, where V is the set of computations within the slice, and E are the define-use relationships between nodes in V.

There are three slices after program slicing in Fig. 4. Without considering the relationships between the slices, we can treat each slice as a loop with only one iteration. However, in real world applications, there usually exist relationships between the slices. The relationships between the slices often come from two aspects: (1) unrolled loops from the loops with no loop carried dependence; and (2) computations on the tuples of data organized in an array of structures. For the former case, each unrolled loop iteration is a slice and all the slices are isomorphic. In other words, the DAGs representing the unrolled loop iterations have the same structure and computations on each DAG are isomorphic correspondingly. On the other hand, for the computations on the tuples of data organized in an array of structures, the DAGs for the elements of the tuple may have different structures depending on the computation (e.g. C-Saxpy in Fig. 1). However, as each slice is for the computations regarding an element of the tuple, the relationships between elements (aka. contiguous memory access) build the relationships between the slices.

The relationships between slices (aka. contiguous downwards-exposed definitions) can be used to group slices into grouped slices, or grouped DAGs. We can deem a slice group as a hyper loop where the number of hyper loop iterations is the same as the number of slices in the group. As each slice is an independent partition of the loop body, hyper loops are all parallel and eligible to vectorization. Grouped slices help vectorization to achieve flexible control on SIMD lanes. For instance, as shown in Fig. 4, according to the iteration number of the hyper loop, when mapping the grouped slices to the SIMD vector, the two slices in the grouped slices #1 prefer to take the even and odd lanes, respectively. With this precise information on SIMD lanes, vectorization can apply global SIMD lane-wise optimization when mapping the slices to the SIMD vector in order to reduce the number of shuffling operations on SIMD lanes.

In this paper, we propose a vectorizing technique by exploiting the hyper loop parallelism exposed by the hyper loop. Similar to other vectorization frameworks, our vectorizing technique consists of two stages, vectorization analysis and vectorization transformation.

2.2   Vectorization Analysis

Before collecting program slices for hyper loop parallelism, we use existing data dependence analysis to analyze whether a loop is vectorizable or not. Moreover, we apply data-flow analysis to find the downwards exposed definitions in the vectorizable loop and identify the types of the definitions, *reduction definition* or *ordinary definition*.

Collect Slices. All the downwards-exposed definitions in the loop are used as the slicing criteria for program slicing. As the data dependence graph is already built in the vectorization analysis, backward program slicing can be easily applied. As shown in Fig. 5, there are two ordinary definitions, y[2*i] and y[2*i+1]. We can get two slices from program slicing. Note that, the dash lines depict the define-use relationships among statements and connect a node to its parent in the DAGs representing the slices.

Group Slices. Grouping slices is a key stage for discovering hyper loop parallelism. In this stage, slices collected are first partitioned into two sets according to the types of downward exposed definitions.

Grouping slices works similar to the super-word level parallelism (SLP) vectorization that tries to pack isomorphic instructions into groups for vectorization [2]. In contrast to the SLP vectorization, the grouping of slices starts from

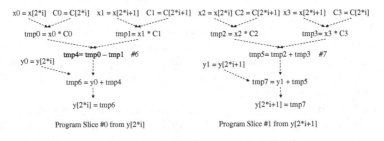

Fig. 5. Collect program slices.

contiguous memory stores which are the downwards exposed definitions for program slicing, and packs isomorphic operations from different slices. As stated in Sect. 2.1, two slices in the same group do not necessarily have the same computation structure. Thus, it is possible that some computations are not isomorphic. We define two types of grouping, *fully grouped* and *partially grouped*. If all the computations from two slices are isomorphic correspondingly, we call it *fully grouped*, otherwise *partially grouped*.

For partially grouped slices, in order to find more opportunities for vectorization, we apply grouping to the parts which are not grouped when grouping different slices. For example, when grouping the node #6 and node #7 in Fig. 5, as the computations from both nodes are not isomorphic. Hence, the grouping on both slice #0 and slice #1 terminates. In order to find more grouping opportunities, the grouping continues on each slice separately, and groups nodes with isomorphic operations within each slice.

Moreover, when dealing with partially grouping, we attach actions on the edges between two nodes in the grouped DAGs. We put forward two actions, *extract* and *merge*, to depict how the data flows. The extract(*number*) deals with data-flow from a grouped node to a non-grouped node while the merge(*number*) handles the data-flow from a non-grouped node to a grouped node. The parameter *number* in both actions specifies the position of definition in the source node or the position of use in the destination node.

For the slices collected from the C-Saxpy, as shown in Fig. 5, Fig. 6 illustrates the results of grouping slices. Because the computations for the definitions of the two slices are different in some parts, the two slices are not fully grouped. Three grouped nodes (node #0 - node #2) are created by the grouping on the two slices while six grouped nodes (node #3 - node #8) are created by the grouping on the parts of slices which cannot be grouped.

Calculate Computation Attributes. Slices for grouping may overlap with each other depending on the computations. For fully grouped slices, the overlapping may lead to a grouped DAG that is not efficient for directly vectorization

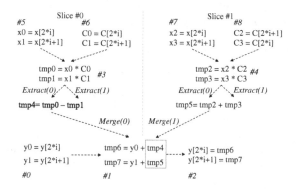

Fig. 6. Group program slices.

transformation. For example, the grouped DAG of vector normalization is shown in Fig. 7. All the nodes in the dashed boxes are from the overlapped parts of the three slices. If this grouped DAG is directly used for vectorization transformation, there would be a lot of redundant computation within SIMD lanes that may not be optimized out by compilers.

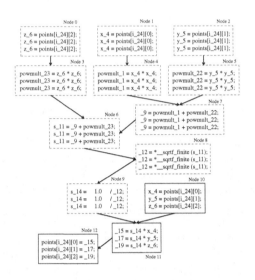

Fig. 7. Overlapping of fully grouped slices.

In order to achieve better vectorization transformation on the fully grouped slices, we calculate the computation attributes from the data access of each node in the grouped DAGs. As memory loads are in the *leaf* nodes of the DAGs, calculation starts with *leaf* nodes, and propagates the computation attributes to the root nodes. Each node by default has an *implicit* computation attribute decided by the data accesses pattens (e.g. consecutive, gathering). Two more *explicit* computation attributes are calculated for vectorization transformation, *reducible* and *scatterable*, as shown in Fig. 8.

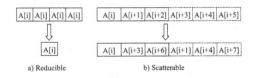

a) Reducible   b) Scatterable

Fig. 8. Reducible and scatterable computation attributes.

2.3   Vectorization Transformation

Expand Grouped Slices. After all the grouped DAGs have been collected and computation attributes for each node in the fully grouped DAGs are calculated, the vectorization transformation transforms each grouped DAG into a vectorized DAG with virtual vector operations on virtual registers. We use the idea of virtual vector registers and vector operations similar to [5]. The loop unrolling factor for vectorization transformation is calculated by first finding the least common multiple (L.C.M.) value of the width of the physical vector register and the size of the grouped node with the minimum number of isomorphic operations, then dividing the value by the size of the smallest grouped node. The width of the virtual register of each node is decided by the multiplication of the loop unrolling factor and the size of the node.

For the fully grouped DAGs, since each node is already annotated with computation attributes, the vectorization transformation makes decisions on how to schedule data operations and computation along with generating virtual vector operations. In other words, the vectorization transformation decides when, where, and which kind of data operation is needed, such as consecutive load/store, gathered load.

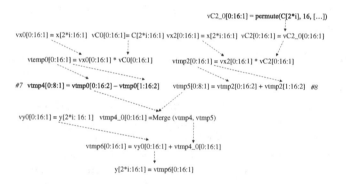

Fig. 9. Expand program slices.

The data and computation scheduling is made by the simple heuristics as follows: **(1)** All the reducible *leaf* nodes of the DAGs are always reduced into nodes with a single operation; the data accesses in the reduced leaf nodes can be gatherable, consecutive (or replicable for constants) depending on the data access pattern; **(2)** According to the cost of data permutation, consecutive loads have higher priority than gathered loads; consecutive stores have higher priority than scattered stores. **(3)** If the child nodes of a node are all reduced, the node is also reduced; **(4)** If one of the child nodes of a node is reduced and expanded as gathered and the other child nodes are not reduced and but scatterable, all these non-reduced child nodes will be scattered and the corresponding computation sequence in the parent node will be scattered as well.

For the fully grouped DAG in Fig. 7, according to the heuristics mentioned above, the reducible leaf nodes 0–2 are first reduced. As the data accesses in the nodes 0–2 are interleaved with stride 3, data gathering operations are introduced when these reduced nodes are expanded. According to the rule 3, the reducible nodes 3–9 are reduced and expanded with gathered data thanks to the reduced child nodes. For the join node 11, according to the rule 4, although node 10 has consecutive data accesses, it is transformed into a node with scattered loads. As a result, the computation sequence in node 11 is skewed correspondingly. Because node 12 requires a consecutive store, data permutation is needed to transform the data from the skewed computation in node 11 back to consecutive data for the store operation. As we can see, rule 4 helps defer the data permutation operations needed to the final store operation, which may cut the number of vector registers required by data reorganization optimization and reduce the register pressure in the generated code.

When expanding the grouped DAGs into the vectorized DAGs, we use *SIMD lane descriptors* to describe the patterns of SIMD lanes for each node. SIMD lane descriptors have the format of id[start_position: size: stride], where id is the name of an array, a pointer or a virtual vector, size is the number of lanes, stride is the lane pattern. In this paper, we consider strided SIMD lane pattens. The support for arbitrary SIMD lane patterns is beyond the scope of this paper. For the grouped DAGs in Fig. 6, the vectorized DAG after expanding is shown in Fig. 9.

Global SIMD Lane-Wise Optimization. If all the nodes in the expanded grouped DAGs have valid SIMD lane descriptors, the vectorization transformation applies global SIMD lane-wise optimization on the expanded grouped DAGs. The global SIMD lane-wise optimization tries to optimize the allocation of SIMD lanes according to the changes of SIMD lanes between nodes in the DAGs by inserting new nodes for four SIMD lanes operations - pack, unpack, merge and permute. pack and unpack deal with the changes of the vector size. merge performs blending of two vectors with the given SIMD lane information. permute handles the changes of ordering of SIMD lanes between two vectors in the same size. The operations SwapEvenOddLanes and MergeEvenOddLanes in Fig. 10 are concrete instances of the operations permute and merge, respectively.

The global SIMD lane optimization consists of two passes, a top-down pass and a bottom-up pass on the expanded DAGs. The top-down pass tries to adjust the widths of virtual vectors and SIMD lane patterns according the memory loads in the leaf nodes in the grouped DAGs. For example, the node #8 in the expanded grouped DAG shown in Fig. 9 has a destination vector vtmp5 with the SIMD lane pattern of [0:8:1]. The top-down pass changes the SIMD lane pattern into [0:16:2] according to the operand vtmp2[0:16:2] because both operands have strided SIMD lane patterns. Note that, since there is no other information to guide the choosing of SIMD lane patterns, the top-down pass always picks the SIMD lane pattern of the first operand as the pattern of the destination vector.

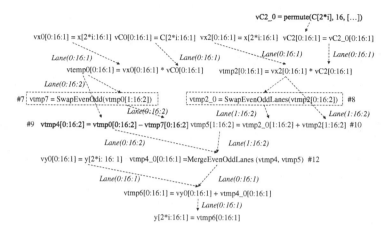

Fig. 10. Global SIMD lane-wise optimization.

On the other hand, the bottom-up pass propagates the SIMD lane information of the root nodes to the leaf nodes and inserts the four SIMD lane operations accordingly. The bottom-up pass, in particular, takes care of the join nodes represented by `Merge`. For instance, after the top-down pass, the destination vectors **vtmp4** and **vtmp5** have the same SIMD lane pattern of [0:16:2]. When comes to the merge node #12 in Fig. 10, according to the relationships between hyper loop iterations and SIMD lanes, the optimization will assign the even lanes to the **vtmp4** while giving odd lanes to the **vtmp5**. Thus, the desirable SIMD lane pattern [0:16:2] and [1:16:2] are propagated to the node #9 and node #10, respectively. Guided by the desirable SIMD lane patterns, a `SwapEvenOddLanes` operation is introduced to transform the SIMD lane pattern of **vtmp2** from [0:16:2] to [1:16:2] as the node #8.

3 Implementation

We implemented our proposed vectorization approach as a source-to-source compiler based on the Cetus compiler infrastructure [6]. The compilation flow for our vectorization approach is shown in Fig. 11. The Cetus compiler uses a single level internal representation (IR) which contains all the information needed for high-level loop optimization. Although the IR closely conforms to the source code, expressions in this IR may have multiple levels which hinders compilers from detecting whether the expressions in two statements are isomorphic or not. To tackle this problem, we introduce a *Statement Simplification* pass to lower each statement into short statements with only one unary, binary or ternary expression and add temporary variables to hold the immediate values of these resulting expressions. In addition, we introduce a simple *If-conversion* pass to eliminate part of control dependence by replacing *if* statements with conditional statements.

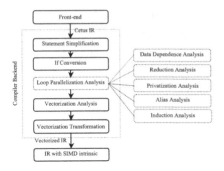

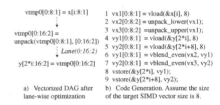

Fig. 11. Compilation flow of hyper loop parallelism vectorization.

Fig. 12. An example of code generation.

The vectorization analysis and transformation are applied as described in Sect. 2. After vectorization transformation, we lower the virtual vector operations to Intel AVX2 SIMD intrinsics. As the code generator is independent of the target architecture, our vectorizer can be easily extended to support other architectures (e.g., Intel AVX-512). When lowering the SIMD lane-wise operations to the SIMD intrinsics, our compiler uses data permutation and blend instructions to implement these operations. As shown in Fig. 12, when dealing with strided stores, the code generator emits contiguous vector loads (line 4–5), blends the results to be stored with the load vectors according to the stride (line 6–7), and stores the blended results with contiguous vector stores (line 8–9).

In the code generation, data permutation optimization is applied to the interleaved data access as well. Instead of general optimization on data permutation [7,8], such as the one specific to strides of power-of-two [7], we treat each specific case of interleaved data access separately. For example, when dealing with interleaved data accesses with stride 3, we adopt the data permutation scheme considered optimal for this case [9].

4   Preliminary Experimental Results

4.1   Experimental Setup

As our compiler generates C code with SIMD intrinsics for Intel AVX2, all the experiments are conducted on an Intel Haswell platform, Intel(R) Core(TM) i7-4770, with Intel AVX2 running Ubuntu Linux 13.10. We use the Intel C compiler (ICC) 14.02 for automatic vectorization with compiler options `-march=core-avx2 -O3 -fno-alias` for performance comparison. The non-vectorized execution time is collected by ICC with compiler options `-march=core-avx2 -O3 -no-vec-fno-alias`.

4.2   Benchmarks

We choose two groups of benchmarks to evaluate the effectiveness of our proposed vectorizing technique based on the hyper-loop parallelism. The Group I benchmarks are all suitable for fully grouping and some of them require the data and computation scheduling guided by the computation attributes (Sect. 2.3). The Group II benchmarks contain some vectorizable loops that can only be partially grouped, and most of the vectorizable loops can benefit from the global SIMD lane-wise optimization.

- **Group I:** Five basic operations on 3D-vectors, **multiplication, dot production, normalization, rotation and cross production**, are often encapsulated as library functions in widely used libraries, such as Open Source Computer Vision Library (OpenCV). **YUVtoRGB** and **RGBtoYUV** are important applications in image processing. The 3D-vectors used in these benchmarks is organized in an array of structures.
- **Group II: C-Saxpy,** which multiplies a complex vector by a constant complex vector and adds it to another complex vector. Two benchmarks from the NAS Parallel Benchmarks, FT and MG. **FT** contains the computational kernel of a 3-D Fast Fourier Transform (FFT). **MG** uses a V-cycle Multi Grid method to compute the solution of the 3-D scalar Poisson equation.

4.3   Performance

The overall performance of the Group-I benchmarks is given in Fig. 13. As we can see, the performance of vectorized vector multiplication, dot production, rotation and cross production, YUVtoRGB, RGBtoYUV by ICC is all worse than the non-vectorized code. The reasons for the performance degradation are (1) ICC by default chooses gather instructions (aka. *vgather*) to deal with interleaved data accesses with stride 3, and these instructions are not efficiently supported

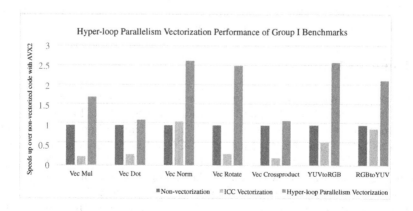

Fig. 13. Performance of Group I benchmarks.

by the hardware [10]; (2) ICC has no support of optimization on data scattering with stride 3, thereby it generates a sequence of scalar instructions to extract data out of vector registers. The vectorized vector normalization by our method outperforms ICC because of the data permutation optimization specific to interleaved access with stride 3.

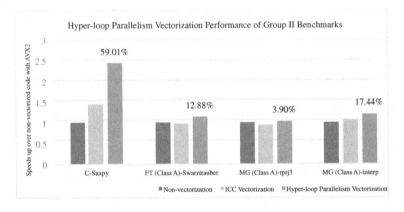

Fig. 14. Performance of Group II benchmarks.

Figure 14 presents the overall performance of the Group-II benchmarks. This group of benchmarks mainly test the effectiveness of the global SIMD-lane wise optimization. For the C-Saxpy, as we can see from Fig. 3, fewer data permutation instructions are required by the SIMD lane-wise optimization than the loop vectorization in Fig. 2. The reduction of data permutation instructions leads to a great speedup. Similar to the C-Saxpy, our vectorizing technique achieves up to 17.44 % performance improvement over the non-vectorized execution for the functions from FT and MG while the vectorization by ICC degrades the performance of FT-Swarztrauber and MG-rprj3. The performance gains of the Group-II benchmarks by our vectorizing technique demonstrate the effectiveness of the global SIMD-lane wise optimization.

5   Related Work

Most prior work on automatic vectorization is performed on the loop level [1,11–13], the basic block level [2,3], and the whole function level [14]. Some of these vectorizing techniques are adopted in both commercial and open-source compilers such as Intel Compiler, Open64 [15], GCC, LLVM. There is also extensive work on automatic vectorization with polyhedral model [16]. Our hyper loop parallelism (HLP) vectorization resembles the classic loop vectorization by taking advantage of the mapping between loop iterations and SIMD lanes.

Super-word level parallelism (SLP) [2] vectorization is the closest related work but it cannot handle complex computation patterns, such as intra-loop reduction. Although the variant of SLP in GCC handles intra-loop reduction, it may incur redundant computations similar to the one in Fig. 7. Besides, the implementation of SLP in GCC [7] is limited to only the cases where the number of operations for packing is power-of-two. Our work is inspired by Wu et al. [17], which introduces sub-graph level parallelism (SGLP), a coarser level of vectorization within basic blocks. Our proposed HLP is similar to the SGLP, but we consider HLP as a complement to classic loop parallelism. Besides, SGLP tries to identify opportunities for vectorization within the already vectorized basic blocks, while our work focuses on vectorization of non-vectorized code. The most significant difference between HLP and SGLP is that when mapping the SIMD parallelism to the target architecture, our method takes into account the instructions that flexibly control the SIMD lanes.

An integrated SIMDization framework [18] is put forward to address several orthogonal aspects of SIMDization, including SIMD parallelism extraction from different program scopes (from basic blocks to inner loops), etc. Our HLP vectorization achieves the same goal of the basic block aggregation in this work. Furthermore, our vectorization transformation and code generation is similar to the length de-virtualization in [18] which also works on virtual vector registers.

General code generation for interleaved data accesses with strides of power-of-two is presented in [7] and implemented in GCC. This approach achieves portability but not always gives the optimal code for a specific target architecture. Ren et al. [8] work on optimizing data permutations on vectorized code. Instead of general data permutation optimization, our approach directly generates well-known optimal code for a specific case of interleaved data access in order to achieve high performance.

6 Conclusion and Future Work

In this paper, we put forward a vectorizing technique based on the hyper loop parallelism, which is revealed by the hyper loops. The hyper loops recover the loop structures of the vectorizable loop and help vectorization to employ global SIMD lane-wise optimization. We implemented our vectorizing technique in the Cetus source-to-source compiler to generate C code with SIMD intrinsics. The preliminary experimental results show that our vectorizing technique can achieve significant speedups over the non-vectorized code in our test cases. One possible direction for future work is to extend the usage of hyper loop parallelism from innermost loop vectorization to outer-loop vectorization [11].

References

1. Kennedy, K., Allen, J.R.: Optimizing Compilers for Modern Architectures: A Dependence-Based Approach. Morgan Kaufmann Publishers Inc., San Francisco (2002)
2. Larsen, S., Amarasinghe, S.: Exploiting superword level parallelism with multimedia instruction sets. In: The 2000 Conference on Programming Language Design and Implementation, PLDI 2000 (2000)

3. Liu, J., Zhang, Y., Jang, O., Ding, W., Kandemir, M.: A compiler framework for extracting superword level parallelism. In: Proceedings of the 33rd ACM SIGPLAN Conference on Programming Language Design and Implementation, PLDI 2012, pp. 347–358. ACM, New York (2012)

4. Ramachandran, A., Vienne, J., Van Der Wijngaart, R., Koesterke, L., Sharapov, I.: Performance evaluation of NAS parallel benchmarks on Intel Xeon Phi. In: 2013 42nd International Conference on Parallel Processing (ICPP), pp. 736–743, October 2013

5. Bocchino, Jr., R.L., Adve, V.S.: Vector LLVA: a virtual vector instruction set for media processing. In: The 2006 International Conference on Virtual Execution Environments (2006)

6. Bae, H., et al.: The cetus source-to-source compiler infrastructure: overview and evaluation. Int. J. Parallel Program. **41**(6), 753–767 (2013)

7. Nuzman, D., et al.: Auto-vectorization of Interleaved Data for SIMD. In: The 2006 Conference on Programming Language Design and Implementation, PLDI 2006 (2006)

8. Ren, G., et al.: Optimizing data permutations for SIMD devices. In: The 2006 Conference on Programming Language Design and Implementation (2006)

9. Melax, S.: 3D Vector Normalization Using 256-Bit Intel® Advanced Vector Extensions. Intel Developer Zone (2012)

10. Pennycook, S.J., et al.: Exploring SIMD for molecular dynamics, using Intel Xeon processors and Inte Xeon Phi coprocessors. In: The 27th International Symposium on Parallel and Distributed Processing, IPDPS 2013 (2013)

11. Nuzman, D., Zaks, A.: Outer-loop vectorization: revisited for short SIMD architectures. In: The 2008 Conference on Parallel Architectures and Compilation Techniques (2008)

12. Nuzman, D., et al.: Vapor SIMD: auto-vectorize once, run everywhere. In: The 2011 International Symposium on Code Generation and Optimization (2011)

13. Kim, S., Han, H.: Efficient SIMD code generation for irregular kernels. In: The 2012 Symposium on Principles and Practice of Parallel Programming, PPoPP 2012 (2012)

14. Karrenberg, R., Hack, S.: Whole-function vectorization. In: The 9th International Symposium on Code Generation and Optimization (2011)

15. Das, D., Chakraborty, S.S., Lai, M.: Experience with partial SIMDization in Open64 compiler using dynamic programming. In: Open64 Workshop (2012)

16. Trifunovic, K., et al.: Polyhedral-model guided loop-nest auto-vectorization. In: The 2009 International Conference on Parallel Architectures and Compilation Techniques (2009)

17. Park, Y., et al.: SIMD defragmenter: efficient ILP realization on data-parallel architectures. In: Proceedings of the Seventeenth International Conference on Architectural Support for Programming Languages and Operating Systems, ASPLOS XVII (2012)

18. Wu, P., et al.: An integrated simdization framework using virtual vectors. In: The 2005 Annual International Conference on Supercomputing, SC 2005 (2005)

Author Index

Printed in the United States
By Bookmasters